RESPONSIBILITY

RESPONSIBILITY

Edited by

**Ellen Frankel Paul, Fred D. Miller, Jr.,
and Jeffrey Paul**

CAMBRIDGE UNIVERSITY PRESS
Cambridge, New York, Melbourne, Madrid, Cape Town, Singapore, São Paulo

Cambridge University Press
The Edinburgh Building, Cambridge CB2 2RU, UK

www.cambridge.org
Information on this title: www.cambridge.org/9780521654500

First published 1999

A catalogue record for this publication is available from the British Library

Library of Congress Cataloguing-in-Publication Data

Responsibility / edited by Ellen Frankel Paul,
Fred D. Miller, Jr., and Jeffrey Paul.   p.   cm.
Includes bibliographical references and index.
ISBN 0-521-65450-5
1. Responsibility.   I. Paul, Ellen Frankel.   II. Miller,
Fred Dycus, 1944-   III. Paul, Jeffrey.
BJ1451.R46   1999
170-dc21   99-24050
CIP

ISBN-13 978-0-521-65450-0 paperback
ISBN-10 0-521-65450-5 paperback

Transferred to digital printing 2005

The essays in this book have also been published,
without introduction and index, in the semiannual journal
Social Philosophy & Policy, Volume 16, Number 2,
which is available by subscription.

CONTENTS

INTRODUCTION

The concept of responsibility lies at the heart of a number of central questions in moral philosophy and legal theory. Under what conditions is it appropriate to praise or blame agents for their actions (or their omissions)? When is it legitimate for a legal system to hold an agent accountable for the consequences of his behavior? Are people's decisions and actions in some sense causally determined, and, if they are, is this determinism compatible with our moral and legal practices of assigning responsibility?

The essays in this volume address these questions and confront related issues. Some analyze different theories of causality, asking which theory offers the best account of human agency and the most satisfactory resolution of troubling controversies about free will and determinism. Some essays look at responsibility in the legal realm, seeking to determine how the law should assign liability for negligence, or whether the courts should allow defendants to offer excuses for their wrongdoing or to claim some form of "diminished responsibility." Other essays explore libertarian views about political freedom and accountability, asking whether libertarian positions on consent, contract law, and responsibility are consistent, or whether restitution is superior to retribution or deterrence as a basis for a theory of corrective justice. Still others examine the notion of partial or divided responsibility, or the relationship between responsibility and the emotions.

The first six essays deal with various issues relating to legal responsibility. Michael S. Moore's "Causation and Responsibility" explores the concept of causation which is presupposed by the liability doctrines of Anglo-American tort and criminal law. Moore begins by isolating a number of characteristics of the law's view of the causation of harms. On this view, causation is not mere correlation; nor is every necessary condition of some harm a cause of that harm. Causation is a scalar property: something can be more or less of a cause. What's more, causation can diminish over the number of events through which it is transmitted; and causal chains can be broken by intervening causes. Omissions or failures to act, on this view, are not themselves causes, though one may be liable for them on noncausal grounds. Once Moore has established this set of common-sense presuppositions about causation, he attempts to discover whether any of the commonly held metaphysical theories of causation can endow it with the characteristics that the law requires. He examines the four leading types of theories of causation—Humean regularity theories, neo-Humean theories, probability theories, and counterfactual theories—and finds that none of them are able to accommodate the law's demands on the concept. He concludes that rather than abandoning the law's common-sense views about causation, we should continue our search for a metaphysical theory of causation that can support these views.

In "Negligence," Kenneth W. Simons examines the moral underpinnings of our practice of holding people legally responsible for negligence — that is, the creation of an unjustified and low-probability risk of causing harm. Simons contends that the common-sense moral precept that one should not be negligent reflects neither a coldly calculating economic or utilitarian conception of morality, nor an absolutist deontological conception that ignores all costs or disadvantages of taking precautions against risk. Rather, ordinary moral judgments, informed by plausible nonutilitarian and deontological moral principles, can make sense of the duty not to act negligently. Simons argues that a pluralistic balancing approach to negligence can recognize the breadth of values expressed in these judgments and principles. He goes on to discuss the institutional implications of his view, touching on a range of subjects, including collective responsibility, the "reasonable person" standard, and the relationship between moral duties and legal rules. He concludes with a discussion of the foundations of tort law, suggesting that principles of fault, rather than of corrective justice, offer the better interpretation of Anglo-American tort doctrine.

The libertarian view of contract law is the subject of Leo Katz's contribution to this volume, "Responsibility and Consent: The Libertarian's Problems with Freedom of Contract." Katz begins by observing that libertarians support freedom of contract, provided that there is no force or fraud involved and that the agreement imposes no adverse effects on third parties. Yet libertarians also believe in certain ideas regarding responsibility: for example, the idea that one is not responsible for failing to rescue someone in peril, but that one is responsible if one actively does him some harm. The central argument of Katz's essay is that libertarians' beliefs about consent and freedom of contract are in conflict with their beliefs about responsibility. In order to show that this is so, Katz describes three types of contracts in which the libertarian's intuitions about consent would incline him to approve of the contract, while his intuitions about responsibility would lead him to condemn it. Drawing on real-life cases and invented examples to illustrate his points, Katz argues that the tension between responsibility and freedom of contract is real, and that it has important implications even for those who disagree with libertarian legal and political theory. He shows how this tension helps to illuminate the nature of consent, the distinction between responsibility for acts and for omissions, and the significance of promises exacted under duress.

Like Katz, Roderick T. Long is concerned with libertarian views on legal responsibility. In "The Irrelevance of Responsibility," Long argues that judgments about whether a wrongdoer is responsible or nonresponsible should not determine how he should be treated by the legal system. Libertarians generally believe, Long observes, that the life appropriate to human beings—as rational, political animals—is one that involves renouncing the use of force except in response to the aggressive force of others. Hence, the presence or absence of responsibility on the part of a wrongdoer makes no difference to the degree of force that may legitimately be used in response to his actions. No more force may be used against a responsible aggressor than against a nonresponsible one, since only aggression licenses retaliatory force, and the responsible aggressor commits no greater amount of aggression than the nonresponsible one. If this view is correct, Long maintains, then all legal practices imposing greater costs on responsible wrongdoers than on nonresponsible ones must be considered unjust. In the course of his discussion, Long defends a theory of corrective justice based primarily on restitution rather than on retribution or deterrence.

The notion of "diminished responsibility" is the focus of John Staddon's contribution to this volume, "On Responsibility in Science and Law." Staddon begins by noting that responsibility is an intrinsically behavioristic concept, since responsibilities are discharged by action, not thought; and he goes on to challenge the idea that if behavior is causally determined, a person cannot be held responsible for his actions. Responsibility, he suggests, depends on a degree of determinism, namely, predictable response to reward and punishment. Scientifically defined, responsibility has two components: normal sensitivity to reward and punishment, and the ability to learn from instruction and example. Together, these components determine an agent's deterrability. While normal adults possess both components (to varying degrees), children, animals, and the mentally ill lack one or both. The problem of diminished responsibility, Staddon argues, is fundamentally a question of how we should deal with individual differences in deterrability. He concludes that moral and political considerations must determine whether diminished responsibility is treated as mitigation (as when a defendant is held to be suffering from a "mental defect") or leads to increased penalties (for those who are considered "repeat offenders").

Michael Stocker's "Responsibility and the Abuse Excuse" deals with a particularly prominent basis for claims of diminished responsibility: the idea that being a victim of past abuse can in some sense lessen one's culpability for a crime committed against one's abuser (or against someone else). Stocker asks whether we should accept abuse excuses in criminal trials, arguing that the answer to the question is far from simple and straightforward. Within a single category of excuses (for example, the "battered woman" defense), there are a wide range of particular cases, each with its own distinguishing elements; thus, an excuse that may be valid in one case may not be valid in another. Stocker challenges opponents of abuse excuses who would seek to disallow them in every case.

He focuses on the work of James Q. Wilson and other critics, who claim that allowing abuse excuses threatens our sense of responsibility and encourages jurors not to judge the behavior of defendants but to try to explain it—a practice that plays on jurors' sympathies and leads to excessive leniency. Many of these critics contend that the acceptance of abuse excuses would cause potential wrongdoers to exert less effort in resisting the temptation to break the law, and would lead them to be less deterred by legal penalties. Stocker argues that the critics have not made a convincing case, and that a background of abuse may well be acceptable as a mitigating factor, particularly in situations where the magnitude of the punishment does not fit well with the circumstances of the crime.

While Stocker and others discuss responsibility in the legal realm, Alvin I. Goldman explores responsibility in the political realm—specifically, in the context of elections. In his essay "Why Citizens Should Vote: A Causal Responsibility Approach," Goldman observes that responses to the question of whether citizens should vote usually center on the fact that it is highly unlikely, in large elections, that a single voter's ballot will be decisive. In setting out a new approach to this problem, Goldman focuses on the fact that an individual's vote can be a partial cause of an electoral outcome even if it is merely an overdetermining cause of that outcome. He sketches a model of "vectorial causal systems" in which states of affairs result from the interplay of different forces (in this case, votes) that can be treated as vectors. This analysis of causation implies that a person will be more causally responsible for a good candidate's victory if he votes for the candidate than he would be if he abstained. Moreover, even if the candidate loses, a voter will avoid causal responsibility for the loss if he votes for the candidate rather than abstaining. Goldman concludes that these considerations often provide citizens with good reasons to vote.

Goldman's essay suggests that responsibility for the outcome of an election can be shared among a group of individuals, and the theme of shared or distributed responsibility is taken up by Henry S. Richardson in his essay "Institutionally Divided Moral Responsibility." Richardson addresses the issue of forward-looking responsibility—the kind of responsibility people sometimes take, prospectively, to look out for a certain range of concerns. He proposes that what differentiates taking on such a responsibility from merely having a duty is that the former involves some authorization—probably strictly delimited—to revise any preexisting moral rules. Utilizing this notion of forward-looking moral responsibility, Richardson then asks how it is distributed across people. Does everyone have the same authorization (if any) to revise moral rules? Or does prospective moral responsibility vary systematically according to individuals' roles? Richardson argues for a version of the latter possibility, according to which prospective moral responsibilities, including their component authorizations to revise moral rules, vary in a socially institutionalized way. He suggests that this division of moral responsibility, in the context of deliberative democracy, provides us with a way of evaluating and (if necessary) altering existing moral practices and social institutions.

Susan Sauvé Meyer offers a historical perspective on responsibility and causation in her contribution to this volume, "Fate, Fatalism, and Agency in Stoicism." Meyer examines the doctrine of determinism—the view that everything that happens is determined by antecedent causes—and asks whether it is compatible with the practice of holding agents responsible for their actions. She argues that the thesis of fate put forward by the ancient Greek Stoics is a determinist theory which can nevertheless support attributions of responsibility. The Stoic thesis, she maintains, is a brand of determinism that is very different from modern varieties, since it is articulated using causal notions that are very different from modern ones. The "chain of causes" that the Stoics identify with fate is not a sequence of events, but rather a system of mutual causal influence among the constituents of the universe. Drawing on the doctrines of Chrysippus, Alexander, Cicero, and other major Stoic thinkers, Meyer elaborates the Stoic view and contrasts it with the thesis of fatalism—the view that nothing is up to us, since everything is predetermined. A proper understanding of the thesis of fate, she contends, allows us to explain away the apparent evidence for attributing fatalism to the Stoics, and to see how some characteristic elements of the Stoics' ethics are rooted in their physical theory. In the end, she suggests, Stoic notions of causation may prove superior to modern notions in offering us a better way of assessing the implications of determinism for human responsibility.

The compatibility of determinism and responsibility is also the subject of Alfred R. Mele's essay "Ultimate Responsibility and Dumb Luck." The idea of ultimate responsibility, Mele notes, requires the falsity of causal determinism: agents are possessed of such responsibility only if they are causally undetermined sources of at least some of their decisions or choices. Yet at the same time, if determinism is false, then agents are subject to a kind of luck that may seem to preclude ultimate responsibility. If one's decisions and actions are simply matters of luck, then it is difficult to see how one could be held morally responsible for them. In developing his view of ultimate responsibility, Mele provides a detailed discussion of the notion of "ultimacy" and its relationship to the "principle of alternate possibilities"—the idea that someone is morally responsible for what he has done only if he could have done otherwise. Mele defends the thesis that ultimate responsibility is consistent with indeterministic luck, that it is a possible attribute of human beings, and that it may reasonably be valued more highly by some people than any kind of responsibility that is consistent with determinism. He offers an account of what is desirable about ultimate responsibility from the perspective of someone who values a certain kind of freedom that is incompatible with a deterministic worldview.

In the collection's final essay, "Taking Responsibility for Our Emotions," Nancy Sherman explores ways in which people might be held to have some responsibility for their emotional states. Sherman notes that we often praise people for their compassion, think less of them for their ingratitude or hatred, or reproach them for their self-righteousness or unjust anger. In the cases that she considers, the ascriptions of responsibility are not simply for the offensive behaviors or actions which may accompany the emotions, but for the emotions themselves as motives or states of mind. Sherman argues for a limited claim of moral responsibility for emotions based on the notion of emotional agency. In doing so, she develops a broadly Aristotelian position, according to which character (including emotional states as well as dispositions toward action) develops through direct and indirect actions. There are intentional actions we take to mediate our emotional experiences; we are not merely passive sufferers of our emotions. Sherman supports this view by drawing on developmental and clinical research on emotions and their growth: observational research on children suggests that, from earliest infancy, children mediate and regulate their emotions. Moreover, she argues, the role of agency in a person's emotional life can be seen in the therapeutic context of psychoanalysis, where patients take responsibility for their emotions by loosening some of the defensive structures that stand in the way of more mature character development. Thus, in these cases, we can see that agents are able to assume some measure of responsibility for their emotional lives.

The notion of responsibility occupies a crucial position in ethical and legal theory. The eleven essays in this volume present the views of leading scholars on the nature of responsibility and its relationship to questions about human agency, free will, causation, and corrective justice.

ACKNOWLEDGMENTS

The editors wish to acknowledge several individuals at the Social Philosophy and Policy Center, Bowling Green State University, who provided invaluable assistance in the preparation of this volume. They include Mary Dilsaver, Terrie Weaver, and Carrie-Ann Biondi.

We wish to thank Executive Manager Kory Swanson, for his tireless administrative support; Publication Specialist Tamara Sharp, for her patient attention to detail; and Managing Editor Harry Dolan, for editorial assistance above and beyond the call of duty.

CONTRIBUTORS

Michael S. Moore is Leon Meltzer Professor of Law, Professor of Philosophy, and Co-Director of the Institute of Law and Philosophy, at the University of Pennsylvania. He has previously taught at Stanford University, the University of Virginia, Harvard University, the University of California at Berkeley, and the University of California at Irvine. His books include *Placing Blame: A General Theory of the Criminal Law* (1998), *Act and Crime: The Implications of the Philosophy of Action for Criminal Law* (1993), *Law and Psychiatry: Rethinking the Relationship* (1984), *Foundations of Criminal Law* (1998, with Leo Katz and Stephen Morse), and *Metaphysical Foundations of Jurisprudence* (forthcoming in 1999).

Kenneth W. Simons is Professor of Law at Boston University. He holds a baccalaureate degree in philosophy from Yale University and a law degree from the University of Michigan. A former law clerk to Justice Thurgood Marshall of the United States Supreme Court, he has written in the fields of tort law, criminal law, constitutional law, and law and philosophy. His publications examine a variety of law and philosophy topics, including consent, assumption of risk, and contributory negligence; corrective justice; mental states in criminal, tort, and constitutional law; mistake and impossibility in criminal law; and the logic of egalitarian norms.

Leo Katz is Professor of Law at the University of Pennsylvania. He writes about moral issues having to do with criminal and corporate law, and is the author of *Bad Acts and Guilty Minds: Conundrums of the Criminal Law* (1987) and *Ill-Gotten Gains: Evasion, Blackmail, Fraud, and Kindred Puzzles of the Law* (1996).

Roderick T. Long is Instructor in Philosophy at Auburn University, as well as Foundation Scholar of the Free Nation Foundation. He received his B.A. from Harvard University in 1985, and his Ph.D. from Cornell University in 1992. He has served as Assistant Professor of Philosophy at the University of North Carolina at Chapel Hill, Visiting Assistant Professor at the University of Michigan, and Visiting Scholar at the Social Philosophy and Policy Center at Bowling Green State University. He has published in the areas of moral and political philosophy, ancient philosophy, and philosophy of action, and is the author of a book manuscript entitled *Aristotle on Fate and Freedom*. He is currently at work on a book tentatively titled *Duty and Advantage: Toward a Reconciliation*.

John Staddon is James B. Duke Professor of Psychology, and Professor of Zoology and Neurobiology, at Duke University, where he has taught since

1967. His research is on the evolution and mechanisms of learning in humans and animals, and he edits the journals *Behavioural Processes* and *Behavior & Philosophy*. He is the author of a number of experimental and theoretical papers and of three books: *Adaptive Behavior and Learning* (1983), *Learning: An Introduction to the Principles of Adaptive Behavior* (with R. Ettinger, 1989), and *Behaviorism: Mind, Mechanism, and Society* (1993). He is also the editor of *Handbook of Operant Behavior* (with W. K. Honig, 1977), *Limits to Action: The Allocation of Individual Behavior* (1980), and *Models for Action: Mechanisms for Adaptive Behavior* (with C. D. L. Wynne, 1998).

Michael Stocker is Guttag Professor of Ethics and Political Philosophy at Syracuse University. He has written numerous articles on topics in ethics and moral psychology, dealing with emotions, affectivity, pleasure, friendship, and love. His book *Plural and Conflicting Values* (1990) develops a moral theory that takes seriously our concrete experience of the demands of morality, including our experience of moral conflict; and his most recent book, *Valuing Emotions* (1996), is a study of emotions from the perspective of ethics, moral psychology, and psychoanalysis.

Alvin I. Goldman is Regents Professor of Philosophy at the University of Arizona. He is best known for his work on action theory, epistemology, and philosophy of cognitive science, including such books as *A Theory of Human Action* (1970), *Epistemology and Cognition* (1986), and *Philosophical Applications of Cognitive Science* (1993). In the area of social theory, he has written on the nature of social power, on legal procedure, and on democracy. The latter two topics are treated in his recent book *Knowledge in a Social World* (1999).

Henry S. Richardson is Associate Professor of Philosophy at Georgetown University. He is the author of *Practical Reasoning about Final Ends* (1994) and of essays on moral reasoning and its history, on liberal political theory, and on democratic deliberation. His current area of interest is the nature of a democracy's reasoning about ends.

Susan Sauvé Meyer is Associate Professor of Philosophy and Director of the Graduate Program in Philosophy at the University of Pennsylvania. She received a B.A. in Philosophy and Greek from the University of Toronto in 1982, and a Ph.D. from the Classical Philosophy program at Cornell University in 1987. She was Assistant and Associate Professor of Philosophy and of the Classics at Harvard University from 1987 to 1994. She is the author of *Aristotle on Moral Responsibility: Character and Cause* (1994), and of articles on moral and natural philosophy in the ancient world.

Alfred R. Mele is Vail Professor of Philosophy at Davidson College. He is the author of *Irrationality* (1987), *Springs of Action* (1992), and *Autono-*

mous Agents (1995), and his edited books include *The Philosophy of Action* (1997) and *Mental Causation* (1993).

Nancy Sherman is Professor of Philosophy at Georgetown University and Visiting Distinguished Chair in Ethics at the United States Naval Academy (1997–1999). She is the author of *The Fabric of Character: Aristotle's Theory of Virtue* (1989) and *Making a Necessity of Virtue: Aristotle and Kant on Virtue* (1997), and the editor of *Critical Essays: Aristotle's Ethics* (1999). Her publications include numerous articles in ancient philosophy and Kantian ethics, as well as essays in moral psychology and psychoanalysis. She has taught previously at Yale University, and has held visiting posts at Johns Hopkins University and the University of Maryland. She received her Ph.D. from Harvard University.

CAUSATION AND RESPONSIBILITY*

By Michael S. Moore

I. Introduction: Liability, Responsibility, and Metaphysics

In various areas of Anglo-American law, legal liability turns on causation. In torts and contracts, we are each liable only for those harms we have *caused* by the actions that breach our legal duties. Such doctrines explicitly make causation an element of liability. In criminal law, sometimes the causal element for liability is equally explicit, as when a statute makes punishable any act that has *"caused . . . abuse to the child. . . ."*[1] More often, the causal element in criminal liability is more implicit, as when criminal statutes prohibit *killings, maimings, rapings, burnings,* etc. Such causally complex action verbs are correctly applied only to defendants who have caused death, caused disfigurement, caused penetration, caused fire damage, etc.[2]

One might think that the simple fact that these causation-drenched legal texts exist is enough to justify judges and legal theorists in taking an immediate leap into the scientific and philosophical theories of causation. Such a leap would be based on the supposition that when a legal text uses a word from science and everyday life like "cause," it must then mean for the word to be interpreted in its ordinary or scientific sense. Such a supposition is belied by the practice of most lawyers and legal theorists. Since at least the 1920s in America, the standard educated view has been that "cause" as used in the law is mostly or entirely a legal construct, serving the law's distinctive purposes and not corresponding to the concept that may be employed by other enterprises or disciplines. Specifically, the idea has been that "cause" as used in scientific explanations has little to do with "cause" as used to attribute moral and legal responsibil-

* I wish to thank Ken Abraham, Richard Epstein, Ellen Frankel Paul, Alvin Goldman, Sandy Kadish, Leo Katz, Alfred Mele, and Stephen Perry for their comments on an earlier draft of this essay. On the theory of causation developed in this essay, they did not cause the essay to be better, nor did they cause any mistaken statements that there might be (given my own free, informed, deliberate, intervening choices). Still, they aided my making the essay better, and they might have prevented such mistakes as there may be in the essay, and I cheerfully hold them responsible on those noncausal bases. These nice distinctions do not apply to my lifetime collaborator on this project, Heidi Hurd. She and I have discussed these issues so many times that I am unsure which thoughts are mine and which are hers. Hers is thus a causal responsibility, for good or for ill.
[1] Annotated Code of Maryland, Art. 27, Section 35A(2).
[2] Argued for in Michael S. Moore, *Act and Crime: The Implications of the Philosophy of Action for the Criminal Law* (Oxford: Clarendon Press, 1993), ch. 8.

ity. The oft-quoted words of Sir Frederick Pollock give one influential expression of this conclusion: "The lawyer cannot afford to adventure himself with philosophers in the logical and metaphysical controversies that beset the idea of cause."[3]

Part of the lawyerly distaste for metaphysical adventures about causation stems from a deep and abiding skepticism about metaphysics in general, whether it be a metaphysics of morals, minds, events, or causal relations. There are several strands to such skepticism. One strand is purely metaphysical: the doubt is that there is any reality to answer questions like, "What is a moral quality?," "What is an intention?," "How do we individuate events?" Another strand is epistemic: even if there are such things as causal relations, moral qualities, mental states, and natural events, and even if such things do possess unitary natures, we less-than-omniscient persons cannot know such things with any certainty. Yet another strand is political: even if there are such things and even if they can be known with certainty by someone, knowledge of such technical matters cannot be very widely shared or easily communicated; as a result, such truths ought to be avoided in designing workable legal institutions, because such truths will be controversial and thus productive of needless conflict.[4]

These kinds of doubts cannot be allayed in the abstract. The only way to allay such doubts is to seek to produce a plausible, understandable, communicable, metaphysical notion of causation. Searching for such a notion is also the only way such doubts can be justified. This basis for lawyerly disdain for the metaphysics of causation, thus, can hardly demotivate my present enquiry.

There does exist, however, a nonskeptical basis for denying the relevance of the metaphysics of causation to the interpretation of legal usages of "cause," and, if correct, this view would demotivate any enquiry such as this. Such a basis begins with the quite correct insight that legal texts are to be interpreted in light of the purposes (values, functions, "spirit," "mischief," etc.) such texts serve.[5] Often such purposes will justify an interpreter in holding the legal meaning of a term to be quite different from the ordinary meaning of the term in nonlegal English. "Malice," for example, means roughly "recklessness" in Anglo-American criminal law, whereas it means spiteful or otherwise bad motive in ordinary English.[6]

---

[3] Sir Frederick Pollock, *Torts*, 6th ed. (New York: Banks Law Publishing Co., 1901), 36.

[4] Such politics-based skepticism about metaphysics surfaced recently with regard to my use of the metaphysics of events to answer certain questions of criminal law. Compare Samuel Freeman, "Criminal Liability and the Duty to Aid the Distressed," *University of Pennsylvania Law Review* 142 (1994): 1455–56, with Michael S. Moore, "More on Act and Crime," *University of Pennsylvania Law Review* 142 (1994): 1750–59.

[5] On purposive interpretation of legal texts, see Michael S. Moore, "The Semantics of Judging," *Southern California Law Review* 54 (1981): 279–81; and Moore, "A Natural Law Theory of Interpretation," *Southern California Law Review* 58 (1985): 383–88.

[6] On the criminal-law meaning of "malice" in the law of homicide, see Moore, "Natural Law Theory," 332–36.

It is certainly possible that "cause" is like "malice" in this regard. Whether this is so depends on what one takes to be the purpose of those legal texts that use "cause." Consider American tort law by way of example. Following the welfare economics of A. C. Pigou, it became fashionable to think that the purpose of liability rules in tort law was to force each enterprise or activity within an economy to pay its "true costs."[7] Those costs included damage caused to others by the activity as much as they included traditional items of cost like labor, raw materials, capital, etc. The thought was that only if each enterprise paid its true costs would the goods or services produced by that enterprise be correctly priced, and only if such correct pricing occurred would markets achieve an efficient allocation of resources. This came to be known as "enterprise liability" in the tort law of 1950s America.

If the point of tort law were to achieve an efficient allocation of resources, and if such efficiency could be achieved only by discovering the "true costs" of each activity in terms of that activity's harmful effects, then "cause" as used in tort liability rules should mean whatever the metaphysics of causation tells us the word means. For on this theory it is the harmful effects that an activity really causes that are the true costs for that activity; and this rationale thus demands a robust use of some metaphysical view about causation.

Contrast this Pigouvian view of tort law with the post-1960 view of Ronald Coase: tort law indeed exists in order to achieve an efficient allocation of resources, yet such efficiency will be achieved whether tort liability tracks causal responsibility or not.[8] Coase's essential insight was that opportunity costs are real costs too, so that a forgone opportunity to accept a payment in lieu of causing another person some harm already forces the harm-causer to "internalize" all costs of his activities. Such harm-causer need not be liable for such harms in order to have him pay for the "true costs" of his activity; he already "pays" by forgoing the opportunity to be bought off by the sufferer of the harm. As each harm-causer and harm-sufferer decides on the desired level of his activity, he will thus take into account all effects of his interaction without tort liability forcing him to do so.[9]

On this Coasean analysis of tort law, there is simply no need for liability to turn on causation. Rather, either tort liability is irrelevant to efficient resource allocation (in a world of low transaction costs), or tort liability should be placed on the cheapest cost-avoider (in a world where trans-

---

[7] A late expression of this view of tort law is to be found in Guido Calabresi, "Some Thoughts on Risk Distribution and the Law of Torts," *Yale Law Journal* 70 (1961): 499–553.

[8] Ronald Coase, "The Problem of Social Cost," *Journal of Law and Economics* 3 (1960): 1–44.

[9] I thus put aside those who interpret Coase to be a causal skeptic. (See, e.g., Richard Epstein, "A Theory of Strict Liability," *Journal of Legal Studies* 2 [1973]: 164–65, for an interpretation of Coase according to which the Coasean insight was that we cannot say what is the cause of what.) Coase made a much better point than this "interactive effects" interpretation gives him credit for: it is that causation does not matter for the efficient allocation of resources.

action costs are high) in order to induce that person to take the cost-effective precautions. In either case, legal liability should not track causal responsibility, for even when there are high transaction costs the causer need not be the cheapest cost-avoider.

The irrelevance of causation to efficiency has left economists struggling to make sense of "cause" as used in American tort liability rules. Since no metaphysical reading of "cause" is appropriate to the goal of efficiency, some policy calculus is given as the legal meaning of "cause." Such policy calculus typically generates a probabilistic interpretation of "cause" in tort law, so that any activity that raises the conditional probability of some harm that has occurred is said to have "caused" that harm.[10] For any theory seeking to use tort law to give incentives to efficient behavior in a world of high transaction costs, this probabilistic interpretation is seemingly just what is required. To criticize such probabilistic interpretation of legal cause on the ground that probability is a poor metaphysical account of what causation is, would thus be beside the point . . . if efficiency is the point of tort law.[11]

My own view, undefended here, is that it is not. On my view, the best goal for tort law to serve is that of corrective justice. Such a corrective-justice view of tort law asserts that we all have primary moral duties not to hurt others; when we culpably violate such primary moral duties, we then have a secondary moral duty to correct the injustice we have caused. Tort liability rules are no more than the enforcement of these antecedently existing moral duties of corrective justice.

This corrective-justice view of tort law demands a robustly metaphysical interpretation of legal cause. For legal liability tracks moral responsibility on this view, and moral responsibility is for those harms we *cause*. "Cause" has to mean what we mean when we assign moral responsibility *for* some harm, and what we mean in morality is to name a causal relation that is natural and *not* of the law's creation.

This is even more clearly true of criminal law. If the point of criminal law were the utilitarian point of deterring crime, then a constructed idea of legal cause perhaps could be justified; such a functional definition would take into account the incentive effects of various liability rules. But the function of criminal law is not utilitarian; it is retributive. Criminal law serves the exclusive function of achieving retributive justice.[12] This

---

[10] See, e.g., Guido Calabresi, "Concerning Cause and the Law of Torts: An Essay for Harry Kalven, Jr.," *University of Chicago Law Review* 43 (1975): 69–108; Steven Shavell, "An Analysis of Causation and the Scope of Liability in the Law of Torts," *Journal of Legal Studies* 9 (1980): 463–503; and William Landes and Richard Posner, "Causation in Tort Law: An Economic Approach," *Journal of Legal Studies* 12 (1983): 109–34.
[11] For a good discussion of the economists' misuse of "cause" to name an increase in conditional probability, see Richard Wright, "Actual Causation versus Probabilistic Linkage: The Bane of Economic Analysis," *Journal of Legal Studies* 14 (1985): 435–56; and Wright, "The Efficiency Theory of Causation and Responsibility: Unscientific Formalism and False Semantics," *Chicago-Kent Law Review* 63 (1987): 553–78.
[12] Or so I argue in Michael S. Moore, *Placing Blame: A General Theory of the Criminal Law* (Oxford: Clarendon Press, 1997), chs. 2–4.

requires that its liability rules track closely the moral criteria for blame-worthiness. One of those criteria is causation of morally prohibited states of affairs.[13] Thus, again, "cause" as used in criminal law must mean what it means in morality, and what it means in morality is to name a relation that is natural and *not* of the law's creation.

Putting aside any policy-based approach to defining "cause" for legal purposes allows us to ignore at least half of the legal literature on causation. For much of that literature is explicit in its eschewal of any attempt to plug in a correct metaphysical account of causation as the legal meaning of "cause." This is certainly true of economists like Guido Calabresi,[14] Steven Shavell,[15] William Landes, and Richard Posner,[16] whose analysis of legal cause (as probabilistic) is not based on the metaphysical view that the causal relation is in fact a probabilistic relation.[17] This is also true of those other descendants of the American Legal Realists, the Critical Legal Studies scholars like Mark Kelman.[18] Such "crits" join the older Legal Realists like Wex Malone,[19] Henry Edgarton,[20] and Leon Green[21] in relegating "legal cause" to the role of a mere label that decorates policy judgments made on strictly noncausal grounds. Such legal tests for causation as the "one house rule" in torts,[22] the "year and a day" rule in homicide,[23] the "harm within the risk" test of both torts[24] and criminal law,[25] the foreseeability test of proximate causa-

[13] See ibid., ch. 5, where I take issue with the Kantian view that our deserts are determined by our culpability ("inner wickedness") and not by the effects of our actions in the real world.

[14] Calabresi, "Concerning Cause" (*supra* note 10).

[15] Shavell, "Analysis of Causation" (*supra* note 10).

[16] Landes and Posner, "Causation in Tort Law" (*supra* note 10).

[17] Contrast the simple, conditional probability analysis used by economists (*supra* note 10) with the more complicated probability analysis of causation by philosophers. See, e.g., Wesley Salmon, "Probabilistic Causality," *Pacific Philosophical Quarterly* 61 (1980): 50–74. No philosopher would propose a simple increase in the conditional probability of an event E by the existence of an event C as an analysis of causation, for that completely fails to distinguish epiphenomena, accidental correlations, and preempted conditions, on the one hand, from true causal relations, on the other. Yet from the point of view of an incentive-based system that eschews any attempt to analyze a pre-legal notion of causation, such an increase in conditional probability may be an appropriate trigger for legal liability.

[18] Mark Kelman, "The Necessary Myth of Objective Causation Judgments in Liberal Political Theory," *Chicago-Kent Law Review* 63 (1987): 579–637.

[19] Wex Malone, "Ruminations on Cause-in-Fact," *Stanford Law Review* 9 (1956): 60–99.

[20] Henry Edgarton, "Legal Cause," *University of Pennsylvania Law Review* 72 (1924): 211–44, 343–75.

[21] Leon Green, *Rationale of Proximate Cause* (Kansas City, MO: Vernon Law Book Co., 1927).

[22] *Ryan v. New York Central R.R.*, 35 N.Y. 210, 91 Am. Dec. 49 (1866). (Railroad liable only for the first house that its negligently emitted sparks ignite, not for each subsequent house that first house, in turn, ignites.)

[23] See Joshua Dressler, *Understanding Criminal Law*, 2d ed. (New York: Matthew-Bender, 1995): 466–67. (A death occurring more than a year and a day from the act of a defendant conclusively presumed not to be the effect of that act.)

[24] See Green, *Rationale* (*supra* note 21). On this test, one asks whether the harm that happened was an instance of the type of harm whose risk made the defendant's action negligent to perform; this is not a causal inquiry, but rather a culpability inquiry.

[25] American Law Institute, Model Penal Code, section 2.03.

tion,[26] and the explicitly ad hoc policy balancing advocated by Edgarton and others,[27] all make no claims to reflecting any underlying reality about causation. They are policy-justified tests that divorce causation in the law from any understanding of causation outside the law. In what follows, I shall thus ignore this part of the legal literature on causation.

What I shall focus on are those cases, doctrines, and legal theories whose authors were at least attempting to get the metaphysics right in their analysis of causation in the law. What I wish to examine in the body of this essay is whether the law that has developed as a result of such attempts in fact contains within it a coherent conception of causation. I do not ask in what follows whether the concept of causation presupposed by the law is true; I ask only whether there is any concept that is sufficiently coherent that it *could be* true.

II. The Seeming Demands of the Law on the Concept of Causation

During the heyday of ordinary-language philosophy, Peter Strawson urged a task he termed "descriptive metaphysics."[28] The idea was that instead of asking how things are, we could ask how a given body of discourse presupposed things are. In other words, we can tease out the metaphysical presuppositions of a body of practices without ourselves committing to the metaphysics of such practices.

This is the task I set for myself in this essay. Without (here) taking a position on what metaphysics of causation is correct, I attempt to describe what the liability doctrines we have in the law presuppose causation to be like. I save for another day the question of whether this metaphysical view of causation is true.

I shall approach the law's presuppositions about causation in two steps. In this section of the essay, I shall take at face value the usages of "cause" by various legal doctrines, here assuming that all such doctrines are what they purport to be, doctrines of cause-based liability. In the next section of the essay, I shall be more critical, throwing out some doctrines on the grounds that they cannot be doctrines of cause-based liability, despite their self-labeling in these terms. This second step allows us to narrow the concept of cause employed by the law to a point where there might be

---

[26] On foreseeability, see Moore, *Placing Blame* (*supra* note 12), ch. 8. The test purports to ask a single question: Was the harm that happened foreseeable to the defendant as he acted?

[27] Edgarton, "Legal Cause" (*supra* note 20). ("Proximate cause" is the label put on the conclusion of balancing social and individual interests on a case-by-case basis.)

[28] P. F. Strawson, *Individuals* (London: Methuen, 1959). Ordinary-language philosophy (e.g., at Oxford University from 1945 to 1965) went further than I go in the text. Such ordinary-language philosophers as Gilbert Ryle, Ludwig Wittgenstein, and J. L. Austin thought that the *only* metaphysics one can do is the descriptive metaphysics described in the text. For a critique, see Michael Moore, "The Interpretive Turn: A Turn for the Worse?" *Stanford Law Review* 41 (1989): 927–34.

some chance of discovering an answering concept of cause in some plausible metaphysics.

A. *Distinguishing causation from mere correlation*

Juries are routinely instructed that they must not confuse mere temporal succession between the defendant's act and some harm, with causation between the two. For example, the defendant's negligently maintained transom hit the plaintiff at a certain place on his head; the plaintiff subsequently developed cancer at that spot. Not only is such temporal succession not identical to causation, but such succession is not even very good evidence of causation. Evidence of such succession, without something more, is not enough evidence of causation to get to a jury.[29]

What if the plaintiff introduces evidence that such trauma on heads is *always* followed by such cancers? This may well be enough evidence of causation to get to the jury, but it is still not to be identified as causation. Juries are still instructed that even invariant succession does not inevitably betoken causation.[30] After all, it might be true that there have been and will be only five such head traumas ever, that all five are followed by cancers, and yet, that there is no causal connection between any of these head traumas and cancer. It is universally true that all clumps of gold that ever have existed and that ever will exist are less than a cubic mile in size; yet there is no causal relationship between the fact that some clump is gold and the fact that such clump is less than a cubic mile in size.

Seemingly missing in examples such as the last is any *necessitation* of the second fact by the first. Missing is the kind of necessity seemingly present between the fact that a clump is uranium and the fact that a clump is less than a cubic mile in size. A clump of uranium *cannot* be a cubic mile in size (because it would exceed critical mass); that necessity backs up and explains why, in fact, there never has been a cubic mile of uranium. No such necessity backs up and explains why there never has been a cubic mile of gold.[31]

Thus, universal correlation cannot be identified as causation (even if the former is good evidence of the latter). Needed is some kind of necessity explaining why there is a universal correlation between two types of events such as head traumas and cancers.

Surprisingly, perhaps, such universal correlation backed up by some kind of necessity is still not to be identified as causation. For yet to be

---

[29] See, e.g., *Kramer Service, Inc. v. Wilkins*, 184 Miss. 483, 186 So. 625 (1939).

[30] Although *invariant* succession is admissable as good evidence of causation.

[31] The example is David Armstrong's in his argument that accidentally true generalizations must be distinguished from true causal laws. See Armstrong, *What Is a Law of Nature?* (Cambridge: Cambridge University Press, 1983).

ruled out is the problem of epiphenomenal correlations.[32] In the case of
the head trauma and the cancer, suppose it were true that the kind of
cancer involved is caused by, and can only be caused by, the kind of blow
the defendant inflicted. Suppose further that the contusion on the victim's
skin is not only caused by such a blow, but also it can only be caused by
such a blow. Since the cancer takes longer to develop than the contusion,
the cancer of necessity always succeeds the contusion, and thus one might
think that the contusion caused the cancer. Yet we know this is false: the
blow caused the cancer (it's my hypothetical) as well as the contusion, but
the contusion is merely epiphenomenal to the cancer—in which case a
universally true correlation, and one which is backed by a kind of necessity, is still not to be equated with causation.

All of this is, of course, quite commonsensical and not peculiar to the
law's use of "cause."[33] Yet in its requirements that a jury be attuned to the
possibility that a temporal sequence (no matter how universal and necessary) may not be a causal sequence, the law adopts common sense
without change.

B. Distinguishing between equally indispensable conditions: The cause/condition distinction

The law, like common sense, assumes that causes necessitate their effects, as we have seen. They, in that sense, "make" such effects happen.
The law also joins common sense in thinking that usually causes make a
difference. This is expressed by the law in its widely used *sine qua non*
doctrine, a doctrine which requires a jury to ask, "But for the defendant's
acts, would the harm have happened?"[34]

An immediately obvious problem (for the idea that a cause is that
which makes the difference for the happening of some effect) is that there
are so many such conditions.[35] Sir Francis Drake could not have defeated
the Spanish Armada without ships, without the lumber with which to
build such ships, without oxygen in the air in England, without a Queen
with some backbone, etc., etc. If all such conditions necessary to the happening of some event x are causes of x, then every case of causation is a
case of *multiple* causation. (Such garden-variety multiple cause cases are

---

[32] For discussions of the epiphenomena problem, see Salmon, "Probabilistic Causality"
(*supra* note 17); David Lewis, "Causation," *Journal of Philosophy* 70 (1973): 556–67; and
Jaegwon Kim, "Epiphenomenal and Supervenient Causation," in *Midwest Studies in Philosophy IX: Causation and Causal Theories*, ed. Peter French, Theodore Vehling, and Howard
Wettstein (Minneapolis: University of Minnesota Press, 1984).

[33] For a discussion of how law, morals, common sense, and science all converge to distinguish correlation from causation, see Moritz Schlick, "Causality in Everyday Life and in
Recent Science," *University of California Publications in Philosophy* 15 (1932): 99–125.

[34] This is the dominant test for cause-in-fact in both torts and criminal law in America.
See, e.g., *New York Central R.R. v. Grimstad*, 264 F.2d 334 (2d Cir. 1920); and American Law
Institute, Model Penal Code, section 2.03(1).

[35] See Moore, *Act and Crime* (*supra* note 2), 267–76.

to be distinguished from the overdetermination kind of cases discussed in the next subsection.)

John Stuart Mill, with whom this problem is most famously associated, took exactly this view.[36] Each temporally present necessary condition had equal claim with every other such condition to be called the cause of some happening, in any suitably scientific sense of "cause." Mill relegated the discrimination we do make in ordinary speech, between "the cause" and "a mere background condition," to pragmatic features of the contexts in which such things were said. If we are doctors, we pick out the factors that we can treat; if we are moralists, those that are blamable; if we are historians, those that have appeal to normal human interest, as "the cause."[37] In reality, Mill held, all such conditions together constituted the cause.

It is often said that the law is much more discriminating than science in its usages of "cause."[38] This is easy to show with regard to temporally successive chains of conditions; as I shall explore later, the law's concept of cause presupposes that causation both tapers off over time and breaks off suddenly at certain points in time.

It is rare, however, that the law actually discriminates between *temporally co-present*, equally necessary conditions—what I am calling the ordinary, garden-variety multiple cause situations. It is only with its occasional "sole cause" doctrines that the law discriminates between equally necessary conditions, honoring one but not others as "the cause." Thus, one version of the irresistible-impulse test of insanity asks whether "the alleged crime was so connected with such mental disease, in the relation of cause and effect, as to have been the product of it *solely*."[39] Similarly, one version of the abuse-of-process tort imposes liability only if the improper ("abusing") motive was the *sole* reason motivating the defendant's use of court process. Since there are always other co-temporal conditions necessary for the actions at issue in these cases, and yet liability is imposed despite this multiplicity, the law presupposes some criterion for distinguishing causes from merely necessary conditions.

C. Preserving the possibility of overdetermining causes

A well-known conundrum in the law concerns what are often called the overdetermination cases.[40] These are what might be called the exotic

---

[36] John Stuart Mill, *A System of Logic*, Book III, ch. V, section 3.

[37] For a discussion of these pragmatic features in various contexts, see Joel Feinberg, *Doing and Deserving* (Princeton: Princeton University Press, 1970).

[38] Jeremiah Smith, "Legal Cause in Actions of Tort," *Harvard Law Review* 25 (1911–12): 104.

[39] *Parsons v. State*, 81 Ala. 577, 597, 5 So. 854, 866–67 (1887).

[40] The best contemporary legal discussion of these cases is to be found in Richard Wright, "Causation in Tort Law," *California Law Review* 73 (1985): 1775–98. Overdetermination cases are to be distinguished from garden-variety multiple cause cases. In the latter, no one event or state is sufficient to produce the harm, because more than one event is individually necessary to produce the harm. Such sets of individually necessary, only jointly sufficient conditions, are very frequent and may well be the most frequent kind of case. Wright

variety of multiple cause cases, in contrast to the garden-variety multiple cause cases discussed in the previous subsection. These are cases where there is more than one set of conditions sufficient to bring about the harm, in which case neither set is necessary to the occurrence of the harm. The law rather crisply assumes: (a) that we can distinguish concurrent over-determination cases from preemptive overdetermination cases; (b) that for the concurrent type cases, each set of sufficient conditions is regarded as the cause of the entire harm; (c) that for the preemptive type cases, we can distinguish preempting causes from preempted factors; and (d) that preempted sets of sufficient conditions are not causes of the harm and that preempting conditions are causes of the harm.[41]

Thus, in the much-discussed "two fire" cases, where each fire is suffi-cient to destroy the building that has burned to the ground: (a) we should distinguish concurrent cases where the two fires join, and the larger fire resulting from this then burns down the structure,[42] from preemptive cases where one fire arrives first and burns down the structure, leaving nothing to be burnt by the second fire when it arrives; (b) when the fires join (the concurrent case), each fire is the cause of the destruction of the building; (c) where the fires do not join (the preemptive case), the first fire preempts the ability of the second fire to cause the building's destruction; and (d) therefore, in the latter case, only the first fire is the cause of the harm, and the second fire is not a cause of the harm.

With regard to (a) above, there is some ambiguity as to how we are to classify what I shall call *asymmetrical* overdetermination cases. That is, suppose the fire set by the defendant is much smaller than the second fire; the two join as before and the resultant fire destroys the structure. The second fire would have been sufficient by itself to have destroyed the structure, but the defendant's smaller fire would not have been, since it would have been extinguished by the available equipment before it could have destroyed the structure. There is some authority for the proposition that the larger fire is a preemptive cause, not a concurrent cause, and that therefore the defendant's fire is preempted as a cause of the harm.[43] Preferable, I think, is Richard Wright's view: these are concurrent causa-tion cases, making both fire-starters liable for the whole damage.[44] Each

---

mentions (in ibid., 1793) a kind of case intermediate between regular multiple cause cases and the overdetermination variety. If there are three fires, no one of which is sufficient, but any two of which are sufficient, to burn the plaintiff's structure, then no fire is individually necessary to produce the harm. Although I do not separately treat these, we should consider these too to be overdetermination cases.

[41] See ibid.

[42] These are the facts of *Anderson v. Minneapolis St. Paul & S. St. Marie R.R. Co.*, 146 Minn. 430, 179 NW 45 (1920); and *Kingston v. Chicago and N.W. Ry.*, 191 Wis. 610, 211 N.W. 913 (1927).

[43] Cf. *City of Piqua v. Morris*, 98 Ohio St. 42, 120 N.E. 300 (1918) (negligent maintenance of drainage wickets held not a cause of plaintiff's injury from overflowing reservoir, because the flood would have overflowed the reservoir even if the wickets were not clogged).

[44] Wright, "Causation in Tort Law" (*supra* note 40), 1794, 1800.

fire was still doing its burning (unless of course it could be shown that the large fire literally extinguished the defendant's fire by taking its oxygen or fuel), and each was a cause of the building's destruction.

With regard to (b) above, there is some authority for the proposition that it matters to the causal question exactly how each fire was started. Where (i) each fire is the result of culpable action by an individual, each individual's culpable act in starting his fire is the cause of the harm. But where only one fire is the result of the defendant's culpable action, and the other fire is the result of (ii) another person's innocent action, (iii) a natural event, or (iv) the victim's own culpable action, then the defendant's fire is not a cause of the building's destruction.[45]

This pattern of liability repeats itself for all kinds of physically caused injuries. Thus, where two defendants independently stab or shoot the victim, who dies of loss of blood, each is the cause of the victim's death.[46] However, where the first defendant inflicts a stab wound on the victim that would prove fatal given enough time, but the second defendant kills the victim instantly by shooting him, the shooting preempts the stabbing as the exclusive cause of death (so long as the shooting is "independent" of the stabbing in the sense that the latter in no way causes the former, as where a stabbing motivates the shooter to put the victim out of his misery).[47] Likewise, where two defendants shoot the victim through the head, but one of the bullets kills the victim before the second arrives, only the first shooter is said to have caused the death of the victim.[48] Where at the same time two defendants each ride their motorcycles by the victim's horse, which is startled and injures the victim, each caused the injury despite the sufficiency of the noise from each motorcycle to have done the job;[49] but it is otherwise if one motorcycle arrives first, scaring the horse before the second arrives.

This pattern of liability is also extended beyond physically caused injuries to overdetermined omissions, reasons, and dangerous conditions cases. With regard to omissions, suppose that each of two individuals has the legal duty to input his part of a code in order to prevent a rocket launch, and that it takes both parts of the code being separately inputted to prevent the launch. If each omits to input his part, each is the cause of the rocket launch. By contrast, where one person has a legal duty to fix a car's brakes, and another has the duty to use the brakes when the occasion demands it, and both omit to do their duty, the second omission is

[45] *Cook v. Minneapolis, St. Paul and S. St. Marie Ry.*, 98 Wis. 624, 74 N.W. 561 (1898).
[46] Agatha Christie, *Murder on the Orient Express* (New York: Pocket Books, 1960). See also *People v. Lewis*, 124 Cal. 551, 57 P. 470 (1899) (initial gunshot and later knife wound both caused victim's death, because "drop by drop his life current welled out from both wounds and at the very instant of death the gunshot wound was contributing to the event").
[47] See generally H. L. A. Hart and Tony Honoré, *Causation in the Law*, 2d ed. (Oxford: Clarendon Press, 1985), 124, 239.
[48] *People v. Dlugash*, 41 N.Y. 2d 725, 363 N.E.2d 1155, 395 N.Y.S.2d 419 (1977).
[49] *Corey v. Havener*, 182 Mass. 250, 65 N. E. 69 (1902).

said to preempt the operation of the first, making the accident the responsibility of only the second omitter.[50]

Occasionally the law concerns itself with the reasons for which an action was done. The reason sometimes, for example, is defined in such a way that one must act "with the intent to help the enemy."[51] If one acts for "mixed motives"—where a sufficient reason motivating the action was to help the enemy, but where another, also sufficient reason motivating the action was to help a friend—this suffices for conviction. Concurrent, overdetermined reasons are each causally operative. By contrast, if one wanted to help the enemy, stood ready to do so, but was then threatened with death if one did not do the act in question, this second sufficient reason preempts the first and is the exclusive cause of one's action.[52]

With regard to dangerous conditions, I shall below discuss how the removal of opportunities to prevent harm presents special problems meriting separate consideration. When I let the water out of your swimming pool, pull out the chair behind you, or take the only food available to you, I have created a dangerous condition by depriving you of an opportunity that you otherwise could have used to your own advantage. When nature takes its course, so that you injure yourself by diving into an empty pool, by hitting a hard floor, or by partially starving, I am said to have caused your injuries.

Suppose that a very large man is drowning in the ocean, that it takes two lifeguards to save him, and that the two lifeguards are about to do that from their respective lifeguard stands when each is prevented from doing so by an enemy of the drowning man. When the man drowns, I am confident that each lifeguard-preventer would be held to have caused the victim's death. A different case, it is thought, is J. A. McLaughlin's famous hypothetical:[53] A and B each independently intend to kill V, who is headed into the desert. A drains V's water keg, replacing the water with salt; B steals the keg; V dies of thirst in the desert. This is commonly said to be a case of preemptive overdetermination, not concurrent overdetermination, yet there is no agreement on who is doing the preempting, A or B. Some legal commentators hold A to be the preemptive cause of V's death;[54] others hold B;[55] and some even think that neither caused V's death because each preempted the other.[56]

---

[50] Wright, "Causation in Tort Law" (*supra* note 40), 1787.

[51] The less seriously punished treason statute in force in England during the Second World War. See *Rex. v. Stean*, [1947] K.B. 997, 32 Crim. App. Rep. 61, 1947-1 All Eng. L. Rep. 813.

[52] *Rex. v. Stean.*

[53] J. A. McLaughlin, "Proximate Cause," *Harvard Law Review* 39 (1925): 155 n. 25.

[54] This is Richard Wright's conclusion. See Wright, "Causation in Tort Law" (*supra* note 40), 1802.

[55] This is Wright's conclusion on a slightly varied version of the hypothetical, in ibid. See also J. L. Mackie, *The Cement of the Universe* (Oxford: Oxford University Press, 1980), 45–46.

[56] This is Hart and Honoré's conclusion in *Causation in the Law*, 239–40.

The overdetermination cases present a complex set of distinctions drawn by the law. We must simplify this pattern if we are to extract any coherent conception of causation presupposed by the law. In particular, we need to examine whether omissions can be causes, whether acts which create dangerous conditions by removing safety features can be causes, and whether culpability can affect causation. I shall thus defer commenting on what conclusions we should infer from the overdetermination cases until we have done some pruning in these directions.

D. The scalar nature of legal causation

Some qualities and relations are two-valued, all or nothing, like being the natural parent of someone else, or being dead. Others are matters of continuous variation, like color or age. In various places, the law assumes that the causal relation is in the latter category, so that there can be more or less of a causal relation, not just its total presence or total absence.

The clearest doctrinal home for this presupposition is in the idea of causal apportionment.[57] Causal apportionment would apportion liability in tort by degrees of causal contribution. This is in marked contrast to comparative fault, which at least formally apportions liability based on comparisons of culpability, not of causal contribution.[58] Comparative fault schemes make use of causal notions, but the use they make is only to require the fault to be causally relevant; "causal fault" thus refers to fault that is causally relevant, and the phrase is not an invitation to apportion damage based on degrees of fault *and* on degrees of causal contribution.

True causal apportionment is a doctrinal rarity, however much jurors may smuggle in such considerations to their calculation of comparative fault. Only in the product-misuse area of strict liability has explicit comparative causation gained much of a foothold.[59] Still, scholarly proposals often make use of the notion.[60] To the extent that such proposals are or become law, a scalar nature to causation is clearly presupposed.

[57] On the idea of causal apportionment, see Mario Rizzo and Frank Arnold, "Causal Apportionment in the Law of Torts: An Economic Approach," *Columbia Law Review* 80 (1980): 1399–1429; Kaye and Aickn, "A Comment on Causal Apportionment," *Journal of Legal Studies* 13 (1984): 191–208; and Mario Rizzo and Frank Arnold, "Causal Apportionment: Reply to the Critics," *Journal of Legal Studies* 20 (1986): 219–26. In his essay in this volume, Alvin Goldman nicely sets out how our obligations to vote—even when our individual vote is not a necessary condition for the election's outcome—can be explained on like grounds (of causal contribution to the outcome for which one's vote was not a necessary condition). See Goldman, "Why Citizens Should Vote: A Causal Responsibility Approach."
[58] In its original opinion creating comparative fault in California (*Li v. Yellow Cab Co. of California*, 532 P. 2d, 1226 [Cal. Sup. Ct. 1975]), the California Supreme Court held that one should apportion tort liability "in direct proportion to the extent of the parties' causal responsibility" (119 Cal. Rptr. 858 footnote 6a. [1975] [advance sheets only]). Prior to final publication, the court recognized its error, proportioning liability to degrees of fault, not to degrees of causation.
[59] See the citations in Rizzo and Arnold, "Causal Apportionment" (*supra* note 57), 1402.
[60] See ibid.

The second set of legal doctrines laying bare this presupposition is the "substantial factor" test first proposed by Jeremiah Smith[61] and adopted by both the *Restatement of Torts* and the *Restatement (Second) of Torts*.[62] Smith's idea was that we can judge whether a mere necessary condition to some injury was a legal cause of that injury, by asking whether it was a "substantial" cause (or factor) of the injury. Clearly a quantitative measure is intended here, presupposing that causation can be a matter of degree.

Two other doctrinal homes for this scalar idea about causation are to be found in certain excuses and justifications in criminal law and in torts. Consider first the legal excuse of duress in homicide cases. According to the common law, acting under the threat of another can never be a defense to murder—murder is so awful that one is supposed to "just say no" to the threatener.[63] For a time, however, English law distinguished the accomplice who only drove the car from the trigger man who did the killing, in that the former could avail himself of the defense of duress even though the latter could not.[64] This I take to be a causal discrimination: even though the accomplice contributes to the victim's death in the sense that he makes it possible, his causal contribution is nowhere near that of the actual killer. On the view that a lesser causal responsibility is necessarily a lesser moral responsibility, the lesser wrong done by the accomplice could thus be eligible to be excused by the existence of a sufficiently serious threat.

The English courts eventually abandoned the distinction,[65] but why they did so is also instructive: as they saw, there can be a great deal of difference between the causal contributions of accomplices. Consider the facts of *Abbott*:[66] the defendant held the victim while she was being skewered by a sabre, it taking several thrusts because the sword kept hitting bone. In such a case, the court properly concluded that the causal contribution of the accomplice (the holder) was not so much less than that of the principal (the skewerer) and refused the defense of duress to either.

Consider next the general justification defense ("balance-of-evils," or "necessity") in criminal law and in torts.[67] Despite the broad language of these doctrines, it is generally agreed that one is not justified in doing a normally criminal or tortious act—that is, an act causing bad consequences—simply because the act will also cause more good consequences.[68] Rather,

[61] See Smith, "Legal Cause" (*supra* note 38).
[62] *Restatement of Torts*, sections 431–35 (1934); *Restatement (Second) of Torts*, sections 431–33 (1965).
[63] *Regina v. Howe*, [1987-1] All Eng. L. Rep. 771.
[64] *Director of Public Prosecutions for Northern Ireland v. Lynch*, [1975] A.C. 653.
[65] *Regina v. Howe*.
[66] *Abbott v. The Queen*, [1976-3] All Eng. L. Rep. 140.
[67] See Michael Moore, "Torture and the Balance of Evils," *Israel Law Review* 23 (1989): 280–344; revised and reprinted as chapter 17 of Moore, *Placing Blame* (*supra* note 12).
[68] Moore, *Placing Blame*, ch. 17, 680–84.

the act must cause its bad consequences in the right way in order to be eligible for justification by its good consequences. Thus, we may not kill one person in order to harvest his organs, which are needed by five other, near-death patients. Yet we may (a) pick one person to be sacrificed for the survival of the others, if that one is going to die anyway with all the others if no one is sacrificed;[69] (b) pick one for someone else to kill, as where we send out one of our own in exchange for four hostages held by another when we know that the one will be killed in lieu of the four hostages who are released;[70] (c) redirect an already moving force (such as a flood, an avalanche, or a runaway trolley) so that instead of killing five people it only kills one;[71] and (d) omit to save one person in order to save five others equally in peril.[72]

All of these I take to be causal discriminations.[73] Put crudely, when we are not much of a cause of the evil the law normally prohibits, we may act so as to prevent greater evils; but when we are substantially the cause of the first evil, we may not act even though such action would prevent greater evils. Put this way, one sees the presupposition of causal scalarity clearly in these licenses for consequentialist justification.

E. The limited transitivity of the causal relation

A relation (R) is transitive when, if x Ry and y Rz, then x Rz. The causal relation would be transitive if one could trace causal chains through time in this way. If my lighting a match causes rum to ignite, and the ignition of the rum causes the entire ship to burn,[74] and the burning of the ship causes a large loss at Lloyd's of London, and the large loss at Lloyd's causes a certain insurance executive to take his own life—and if the causal relationship were transitive—then my lighting a match caused the death of the insurance executive (together with yet further consequences like the loss of support for his widow, etc.).

Although sometimes legal theoreticians have thought that the only truly causal notion used in the law is fully transitive in this way,[75] in fact no area of law traces causal responsibility indefinitely. One of the long recognized deficiencies with the necessary-condition test of factual causation is that, used alone, it would generate an unlimited liability into the

---

[69] Ibid., 692–94.
[70] Ibid., 696–98.
[71] Ibid., 694–96.
[72] Ibid., 689–90.
[73] Ibid., 698–703.
[74] These are the facts of *Regina v. Faulkner*, 13 Cox C.C. 550 (Ireland, Court of Crown Cases Reserved, 1877).
[75] See the *Restatement (Second) of Torts*, section 431, comment a (1965), which proclaims that in law, "cause" is used "in the popular sense, in which there always lurks the idea of responsibility, rather than in the so-called 'philosophic sense' which includes every one of the great number of events without which any happening would not have occurred."

future.[76] Our liability doctrines thus presuppose that causation is the kind of relation that can "peter out." The metaphorical picture is of the ripples emanating from a stone dropped into a quiet pond: gradually they diminish to nothing the further the ripples travel from their source. This attribute of legal causation presupposes that the relation is scalar, because only a more-or-less sort of relation can gradually peter out. Yet this attribute is a specific use of such scalarity, for it asserts a proportionality between proximity and more causation, between distance and less causation.

Early writers from Sir Francis Bacon[77] (who coined the Latin, *causa proxima*) on, held that spatiotemporal proximity of cause to effect, was that on which such strength of causation depended. Plausibility is lent to this Baconian view by the "spatiotemporal coincidence" cases. Consider the case of the streetcar motorman who recklessly speeds early on his route in one part of the city.[78] No one is injured while he is speeding, and when he catches up to his schedule he resumes his normal, non-reckless speed. Nonetheless, because he sped early on his route, he arrives at the last part of his route just in time to have a tree fall on his car, injuring a passenger. One may think that it is the simple fact of spatiotemporal distance (between the motorman's negligent act and the harm) that accounts for nonliability here.[79]

Yet simple spatial or temporal distance does not seem to be what diminishes or "tires" causation. Poisoned candy sent from California to Delaware, or from the moon, is still the cause of the victim's death if she eats it and is poisoned;[80] poisoned candy left in a place and in a state where it will be found and eaten a generation later, still causes death at that much-later time. Spatiotemporal proximity thus seems a proxy for something else.

One possibility is to look for those free, informed, voluntary human choices, or those abnormal conjunctions of natural events amounting to a coincidence, intervening between the defendant's act and the harm. Spatiotemporal distance might be a proxy for these kinds of "intervening causes." Yet intervening causes are not what is wanted here (although they may account for the streetcar coincidence case above). Such causes are abrupt (see the next subsection) in the way they break causal chains,

[76] See, e.g., Smith, "Legal Cause" (*supra* note 38), 109. The *sine qua non* test, or necessary-condition test, is discussed in the text accompanying note 34 *supra*.

[77] Sir Francis Bacon, "Maxims of the Law," in Bacon, *The Elements of the Common Law of England* (London: Assigns of I. Moore, 1630), 1.

[78] *Berry v. Borough of Sugar Notch*, 191 Pa. 345, 43 Atl. 240 (1899). For another coincidence case, see *Denny v. N.Y. Central R.R.*, 13 Gray (Mass.) 481 (1859) (railroad's negligence in delaying at one section of track, and its subsequent arrival at a flood plain just when a flood sweeps down and destroys goods on the train, held not to be a cause of the damage to the goods).

[79] Cf. *Bird v. St. Paul F. and Minneapolis Ins. Co.*, 224 N.Y. 47, 120 N.E. 86 (1918) ("There is no use in arguing that distance ought not to count, if life and experience tell us that it does"); and Edgarton, "Legal Cause" (*supra* note 20), 369–70.

[80] *People v. Botkin*, 132 Cal. 231, 64 Pac. 286 (1901).

whereas what is wanted is something that allows causation to diminish gradually in its strength. My own suggestion is that what the law uses here is simply sheer numbers of events that intervene between the defendant's act and the harm. None of these events need itself be an intervening cause as the law defines that phrase; rather, when there are too many event-"links" in the causal chain, it becomes too attenuated to support judgments of transitivity.[81]

The particular scalarity the law presupposes causation to have is thus a diminishment in the strength of causation in proportion to the number of events through which it is transmitted. Where all causal relata are events, if t causes w, w causes x, x causes y, and y causes z, t may well cause y but not z. That is what I mean by the limited transitivity of the causal relation as it is presupposed by our proximate-cause doctrines.

F. The sudden breaking of causal chains by (apparently) fresh causal starts

In addition to the gradual petering out of causation over sheer numbers of intervening events, the law assumes that the causal relation can be ended suddenly by the intervention of one of those special kinds of intervening events which the law designates an intervening (or superseding) cause. Such intervening causes may interrupt the causal contribution of an otherwise potent cause (in which case we have an instance of preemptive overdetermination); or such intervening causes may build on the causal contribution of the defendant's action.[82] In either case the intervention of such causes between the defendant's act and the harm relieves the defendant of any causal responsibility for that harm.

In *Causation in the Law*, H. L. A. Hart and Tony Honoré nicely detailed how the law recognizes two sorts of intervening causes.[83] One involves the free, informed, voluntary act of a third party that intervenes between

---

[81] A refinement may be necessary here. If the causal relation is transmitted over many events that are of the same *type*, then the diminishment of causation often seems to be less. See, e.g., *Scott v. Shepherd*, 96 All Eng. L. Rep. 525 (K.B. 1773) (liability for causing injury to plaintiff by explosion of a lighted squib that was thrown into a crowded marketplace by defendant, and then rethrown by each subsequent possessor of it so as to rid himself of the danger). The analogy here is to a long row of dominos; the falling of each is plausibly individuated as one event, but their ability to transmit causal force seems unrelated to the number of such events. A colorful example offered by Alfred Mele is a variation of *People v. Botkin* (*supra* note 80): Would it matter if the poisoned candy was sent from California to Delaware by Pony Express (with numerous handoffs) rather than by train?

[82] This line is much more difficult to draw than is recognized in any of the legal literature, yet it is a necessary line to draw in that preemption intervening causes do not have to meet the criteria below articulated for an intervening cause.

[83] Hart and Honoré, *Causation in the Law* (*supra* note 47). Although the clarity and the nonlegal analogues of the idea of an intervening cause were new with Hart and Honoré, they built on a solid body of case law. This case law is detailed in Charles Carpenter, "Workable Rules for Determining Proximate Cause," *California Law Review* 20 (1932): 229–59, 396–419, 471–539. Hart and Honoré's detailing of the case law is in *Causation in the Law*, 133–85, 325–62.

the defendant's act and the victim's injury. Thus, a defendant company negligently spills gasoline from its railroad tanker car into a city street, yet what ignites the gasoline and burns down the town is the intentional lighting of the gasoline by a cigar-throwing arsonist.[84] Even though the defendant's negligent spilling of the gasoline was quite necessary to the town's destruction, the arsonist's choice to use the results of the railroad's negligence to his own ends relieves the railroad of causal responsibility for the town's destruction. The choice by the arsonist operates as a fresh causal intervention breaking any causal chain that might otherwise have existed between the spilling of the gasoline and the destruction of the town.

Only free, informed, voluntary actions by a third-party intervenor will break causal chains in this way. As Hart and Honoré describe the cases, if

   (i)   the bodily movement of the arsonist was *involuntary*, in the sense that the cigar slipped from the hand and was not dropped or thrown;
   (ii) the act of throwing the cigar *was not intentional* with respect to the burning of the gasoline, because the cigar-thrower was ignorant of the presence of the gasoline in the street;
   (iii) the act of throwing the cigar was done under the duress of dire threats, and so was in that sense *involuntary*;
   (iv) the act of throwing the cigar was done under the limited opportunities for choice created by natural necessity, as where the cigar would otherwise painfully burn its holder;
   (v)   the cigar-thrower was so young, so crazy, or so intoxicated as to be adjudged irresponsible;

then the cigar-throwing act does not break the causal chain and the defendant's initial act of spilling the gasoline causes the destruction of the town.[85]

The second kind of intervening cause involves natural events, not deliberate human intervenors. Suppose that the defendant is negligent in its installation and maintenance of the roof bolts holding a multi-ton warehouse roof in place. If the roof bolts fail so that the roof falls on and injures workmen below, the defendant's negligent actions will be said to have caused the injuries to the workmen. This will be true even if a stiff (but not unusual) breeze contributed to the injuries, in the sense that without the pressures on the roof created by the breeze the roof would not have fallen when it did. If, however, the breeze is that kind of extraordinary event we call "an act of God," so that the roof does not simply fall but flies

---

[84] *Watson v. Kentucky and Indiana Bridge and Ry. Co.*, 137 Ky. 619, 126 S.W. 146 (1910).
[85] Hart and Honoré, *Causation in the Law*, 74–77.

over one hundred feet before it injures its victims, then such a gale will be an intervening cause relieving the defendant of causal responsibility for the injury.[86]

Hart and Honoré call such cases acts of "coincidence."[87] They analyze such intervening causes as satisfying five requirements. First, there must be an *abnormal conjunction* of natural events. Only winds extraordinary for this time and place qualify as abnormal; breezes normal for this time and place do not qualify. Second, the event in question must have *causal significance*. Merely co-present abnormalities do not qualify. Third, the wind must be *causally independent* of the defendant's actions. If the defendant's design for the building so focused the winds' strength as to make them abnormally high, the winds are not intervening causes. Fourth, the coincidence must be *uncontrived* by the defendant. If the defendant sent out the workmen to work where he hoped the forthcoming storm would blow off the roof, then he has used the storm for his own ends and it is not an intervening cause. Fifth, the intervening natural event must be *subsequent* to the defendant's action. Preexisting conditions, no matter how abnormal or coincidental they may be, do not eliminate the causal connection between the defendant's act and the harm.

There is an odd lacuna in both the case law and academic discussions of causation raised by the fourth criterion for a coincidence. One would have thought that the purposeful exploitation of a natural-event coincidence would give rise to a kind of noncausal liability, strictly analogous to the kind of "aiding of human intervenors" liability shortly to be discussed. Yet Hart and Honoré are correct that the cases treat contrived coincidences on strictly causal grounds. Thus, in the case of the extraordinary winds carrying the heavy roof to where it injured a workman, if the defendant had foreseen such a wind and the possibility of such resultant roof movement and had sent the workman to the spot in order to injure him, such "contrived coincidence" is treated as no coincidence at all. The wind then does not operate as an intervening cause; rather, the defendant is held liable for causing the injury.[88]

The law could have developed differently. It might have eschewed causal talk in such cases, just as it has in the analogous human intervenor cases. It might have said that all that need be shown in either case is that the defendant made it somewhat easier for either natural circumstances or human intervenors to do their causal work, in order to place a noncausal "aiding" liability on defendants. We shall pursue this neglected possibility when we seek to economize the law's metaphysical presuppositions in Section III.

---

[86] These are roughly the facts of *Kimble v. Mackintosh Hemphill Co.*, 359 Pa. 461, 59 A.2d 68 (1948).

[87] Hart and Honoré, *Causation in the Law*, 77–81.

[88] See cases cited, and discussion, in ibid., 170–71.

The law's notion of intervening cause is actually somewhat broader than the two criteria described by Hart and Honoré. Particularly with nondeliberate human intervenors, there are many cases in which, if the intervention is freakish or dramatic enough, the intervention is held to break the causal connection between the defendant's act and the harm. The more freakish of these cases can no doubt be explained by applying the Hart and Honoré criteria for natural coincidence, to human interventions.[89] That is, suppose that in the spilled-gasoline scenario a good Samaritan sees the gasoline, decides to drain it off the street, slips and falls in it, rushes to a house to dry off, instead ignites himself by running into a cigar-smoker, seeks to put out the fire on his body by jumping into a pool, which has unbeknownst to him become filled with the same gasoline, and sets off the entire town. Even though this case involves a human intervention, if we apply the criteria for a coincidence we may well find this to be one.

Also accounting for some of these merely negligent human intervenor cases are the factors at work in our judgment of preemptive overdetermination cases. If one defendant has intentionally poisoned the victim, who is gradually dying of the poison, but another defendant inadvertently (innocently or negligently) shoots the victim dead instantly, the second defendant's shooting is a preemptive cause.[90] It is a kind of intervening cause, no matter how unintentional or how lacking in culpability in any way it may have been. The shooting's status as an intervening cause also does not depend on any freakishness of the kind that makes one think of coincidence. We simply know that the victim died of the gunshot, not of the poison.

With these qualifications for some merely negligent intervenors breaking causal chains, Hart and Honoré accurately describe the law as regarding a free, informed, voluntary act of a human intervenor as breaking causal chains. Despite this, Hart and Honoré rather inelegantly excepted the giving of reasons and the provision of opportunity from their thesis.[91] That is, if the defendant suggested, offered, encouraged, threatened, or otherwise induced another into causing a harm, then such reason-giving behavior was a cause of that harm despite the intervening choice of the person to whom the defendant gave such reasons. Analogously, if the defendant's culpability consisted in providing an opportunity to another

---

[89] This is something which Hart and Honoré suggest in ibid., 136, 182–85.

[90] E.g., *State v. Scates*, 50 N.C. 409 (1858) (defendant who burned child not liable for the child's death if an intervening blow on the head by a third party killed the dying child).

[91] In the original edition of their book, Hart and Honoré simply except such situations from the normal rule about intentional intervening agents. See H. L. A. Hart and A. M. Honoré, *Causation in the Law* (Oxford: Clarendon Press, 1959). As Joel Feinberg noted, these were ad hoc, unexplained, and seemingly unlimited as exceptions. See Feinberg, "Causing Voluntary Actions," in Feinberg, *Doing and Deserving* (*supra* note 37). In the second edition of *Causation in the Law* (*supra* note 47), chapters VII and XIII now deal extensively with the provision of opportunities and the giving of reasons as "non-central" kinds of causings.

to cause harm—say by leaving the keys in the ignition of a bulldozer that some vandals then run down a hill into a house[92]—then such opportunity-providing acts are the cause of the harm despite the intentional acts of those who seize the opportunity.

The legal fact that Hart and Honoré were trying to accommodate is the fact that there is liability for such actions in both torts and criminal law. Oddly overlooked, however, was the fact that the law largely deals with the reason-giving half of this phenomenon in noncausal terms. That is, the liability of one who solicits, offers, suggests, or procures another to cause a harm is not for causing the harm; rather, the former is liable for the harm on the criminal-law theory of accomplice liability[93] and on the tort-law theory of a joint tort feasor by virtue of acting in concert. The principal in such a theory must cause the harm in question to be held liable, but it is well established that the procurer need not cause the harm; his soliciting, offering, suggesting, or procuring is enough for accomplice liability (or joint-and-several tort liability) without need of any causal relationship to the harm itself.[94]

The only catch here is that the procurer who induces the principal to cause the harm must do his inducing with the purpose (or "specific intent") that he induce the principal to cause the harm. If one gives reasons to another to cause a harm, but does so innocently, negligently, recklessly, or merely knowingly, this lesser culpability is insufficient for liability. In such cases the reason-giving procurer must be liable on causal grounds if he is to be liable at all; but the intervening choice of the one who causes the harm eliminates any causal responsibility here. The up-shot is that a less-than-purposeful inducer is not liable for either aiding or causing.

The procurer who threatens another and in that way induces another to cause harm is distinguished from other types of procurers. The threatening procurer places the harm-causer under duress, making his choice to cause the harm not sufficiently voluntary to be an intervening cause. Thus, the threatener is liable for causing the harm he induces another to cause by his threats, and this causal liability does not require the high level of culpability (purpose) with which other types of procurers must do their procuring in order to be liable on an accomplice theory.

The existence of these two different bases for holding someone liable in both criminal law and tort law has generated considerable confusion. Suppose that a more-culpable procurer or other aider induces or other-

---

[92] *Richardson v. Ham*, 44 Cal.2d 772, 285 P.2d 269 (1955).

[93] Particularly clear and systematic about this is Sanford Kadish, "A Theory of Complicity," in R. Gavison, ed., *Issues in Contemporary Legal Philosophy: The Influence of H. L. A. Hart* (Oxford: Oxford University Press, 1987); and Kadish, "Causation and Complicity: A Study in the Interpretation of Doctrine," *California Law Review* 73 (1985): 323–410; reprinted in Kadish, *Blame and Punishment* (New York: MacMillan, 1987).

[94] See the two essays by Kadish cited in note 93 *supra*.

wise aids a less-culpable principal to cause some harm. For example, A tells B, falsely, that B's wife is having an affair with C. A tells B this with the intent that B (who is very jealous, has a nasty temper, and is prone to violence) will kill C. B does so in a fit of jealous rage, making B guilty in many jurisdictions of voluntary manslaughter. A, the theory goes, is guilty of aiding B in the voluntary-manslaughter killing of C, but A is not a voluntary-manslaughter killer of C himself because A did not cause C's death. But A is also guilty of causing C's death by his use of a partly innocent agent, B; since A was not provoked, his causing of C's death is murder. A both is and is not the cause of C's death, because B's act both is not and is an intervening cause of C's death![95]

Things are somewhat different where liability is predicated on the provision of opportunities to another to cause harm. There is a form of accomplice liability here in criminal law, as there is a form of joint tort feasor liability here for one not acting in concert. One can be liable in tort law or criminal law for aiding another to cause harm, when the aid is not of the reason-giving kind but is, rather, of a kind that makes it easier for the principal to cause the harm even when he does not know of the aid he has been given. I may intercept a warning telegram that otherwise would have warned the victim that a murderer is looking for him; I have no agreement with the murderer, we are not "acting in concert," and he does not know that I exist or that he has been aided. Yet such aid is sufficient for liability here, and the liability is noncausal.[96] I am held liable for making it easier for the harm to be caused; I am not liable for causing the harm, because intervening between my act of aiding and the harm is the free choice of the murderer.

So far, this is very much the same as it was for the reason-giving kind of aiding. And what was true of the latter is also true here: such not-in-concert aiders must act with the highly culpable mental state of *purpose* to be liable as accomplices. Merely negligent, reckless, or even knowing aid is insufficient for accomplice liability. Unlike the reason-giving situation, however, when an actor provides opportunities to another to cause harm, and the first actor is negligent precisely because of the risk of such causing of harm by another, there is a causal liability placed on the first actor, at least in tort law. Thus, where a defendant railroad negligently carries a passenger beyond her destination and then leaves the passenger on a dark and dangerous stretch of track, and the risk that makes this negligent is realized—the passenger is raped by a third party—the railroad is liable in torts for the rape.[97] Similarly, when a construction company leaves keys in a bulldozer after the close of work, and the risk that makes this negligent is realized—vandals start up the bulldozer and run it down-

---

[95] See Glanville Williams, *Criminal Law—The General Part*, 2d ed. (London: B. Henworths, 1961), 391.

[96] *State ex. rel. Att'y Gen'l v. Tally*, 102 Ala. 25, 15 So. 722 (1894).

[97] *Hines v. Garrett*, 131 Va. 125, 108 S.E. 690 (1921).

hill from the construction site into the plaintiff's house—the construction company is liable in torts for the damage.[98] In such a case, the free, informed, voluntary choice of the primary wrongdoer is *not* considered to be an intervening cause.

Putting aside, for now, this last exception (about tort liability for negligently providing opportunities to wrongdoers), the existence of a noncausal, accomplice basis for liability allows one to alleviate the apparent tension between saying *both* that free, informed, voluntary acts break causal chains *and* that the provision of reasons or of opportunities that a third party then freely chooses to exploit nonetheless causes the harm such a third party brings about. Rather, one can more consistently maintain that such third-party choices always break causal chains and yet maintain that sometimes noncausal liability is placed upon the original actor anyway.

This accommodating strategy works as well as it does because accomplice liability is designed to pick up behind the intervening-cause doctrine (of the free, informed, voluntary actor).[99] That is, if the would-be principal does not have the kind of free, informed, voluntary choice that breaks causal chains, then the would-be accomplice is liable for the harm on causal grounds, not on accomplice grounds. Suppose A threatens P with serious injury unless P causes a certain harm. If P causes the harm, P has an excuse of duress, and P's choice is not an intervening cause, so that A is liable for causing the harm. Similarly, if A knows that P is ignorant, crazy, intoxicated, under the duress of another or of natural circumstance, and A exploits this weakness by getting P to cause some harm, A again is liable on causal, not accomplice, grounds. It is only when P meets the conditions for being an intervening cause, so that A cannot be held on causal grounds, that the law makes use of accomplice liability.

G. The limited liability for omissions

The law has always had difficulty in dealing with omissions. It helps to be clear at the start about what omissions are: they are literally no things at all.[100] Suppose A stands on the dock and watches V drown, when A could have saved V with little risk or even inconvenience to himself. A has omitted to save V. What this means is that A did nothing to save V. More technically: there was no act-token of A's that had the causal properties needed for it to be an instance of the type of action, saving V. The omission to save V is literally the absence of any action of saving V by A.

For most omissions, the Anglo-American law of torts and crimes provides no liability. For some omitters, however, there is liability: (1) where

[98] *Richardson v. Ham* (*supra* note 92).
[99] See the two essays by Kadish cited in note 93 *supra*.
[100] Michael Moore, *Act and Crime* (*supra* note 2), 28–29; Moore, "More on Act and Crime," *University of Pennsylvania Law Review* 142 (1994): 1788.

A is the parent or other close relation of V, A is liable; (2) where A culpably causes V's condition of peril, A is liable; (3) where A innocently causes V's condition of peril, A is liable; (4) where A undertakes to rescue, but either abandons his undertaking, or performs it culpably, A is liable.[101]

There are two standard routes that attempt to account for these legal facts on causal grounds. The first rests on the premise that all omissions are causes, so that A's omission to save V is a kind of *killing* of V.[102] What distinguishes the usual case (where there is no liability) from the exceptional cases (where there is liability) is a noncausal notion of legal duty. Strangers owe no legal duty not to kill by omission (although they do have a duty not to kill by commission); close relatives, causers-of-the-condition of peril, and rescue-undertakers do have a legal duty not to kill by omission as well as by commission.

The second route begins with the opposite premise: almost all omissions are not causes of the harms they omit to prevent. In the exceptional cases, however, such omissions are causes. One might think this (rather crazily, to be sure) on the ground that the bare fact of legal duty can give causal potency to omissions that are otherwise without it.[103] More plausibly, this route looks behind the legal conclusion about duty to the facts that give rise to the various legal duties not to omit. Each of these facts, so goes the argument, represents a kind of causal involvement in the victim's situation.[104] By causing the condition of peril, by undertaking to rescue, or by entering into an intimate relation with the victim, A would have so entered into the genesis of the victim's harm as to be its cause.

H. Preserving the extensionality of causal statements while accommodating the distinction between "an act that is negligent causing" and "the negligence causing"

Imagine a case where unlabeled rat poison is placed with food near a stove in a kitchen.[105] A person in the kitchen is injured when the rat poison explodes because of the heat of the stove. A court focusing on the danger that such unlabeled rat poison might mistakenly be consumed might well say both (1) that the act of placing the rat poison in the kitchen caused the injury; and (2) that the act of placing *unlabeled* rat poison in the

[101] Joshua Dressler, *Understanding Criminal Law* (New York: Mathew Bender, 1987), 83.

[102] See, e.g., George Fletcher, "On the Moral Irrelevance of Bodily Movements," *University of Pennsylvania Law Review* 142 (1994): 1443–53.

[103] This is Joseph Beale's apparent view, in Beale, "The Proximate Consequences of an Act," *Harvard Law Review* 33 (1920): 637.

[104] See Epstein, "A Theory of Strict Liability" (*supra* note 9), 192; and Eric Mack, "Bad Samaritanism and the Causation of Harm," *Philosophy and Public Affairs* 9 (1980): 240–41, 242–43.

[105] This is the famous hypothetical used by Robert Keeton, *Legal Cause in the Law of Torts* (Columbus, OH: Ohio State University Press, 1963), 3. The hypothetical is based on the facts of *Larrimore v. American National Insurance Co.*, 184 Okla. 614, 89 P.2d 340 (1939).

kitchen did not cause the injury. Since the second is the description of the act that describes it in the way which reveals the act to be negligent, the second description is the basis for the causal judgment, relieving the defendant of liability.

It is not clear how the law can make both of these statements, at least on the most plausible view of event individuation. There was only one act of placing rat poison, even though there are many descriptions of that act differing from one another by their mentioning of differing properties possessed by that act.[106] It was "the first act the defendant did that morning"; it was "the stupidest act he did that day"; it was "the placing of unlabeled rat poison with the food in the kitchen"; and it was "the placing of combustible items near the stove."

Yet if this is but one act with many different descriptions, then it seems the law is guilty of violating Leibniz's principle that identicals are indiscernible in all of their properties.[107] That is, if "x" is one description of the act, and "y" is another, and x = y because there is but one numerically distinct act, then anything that can be truthfully said of x can also be truthfully said of y, and vice versa. Formalized, the principle is: $(x)(y)[(x = y) \supset (Fx \equiv Fy)]$. This is sometimes called the principle of substitutability *salva veritate*, because if x and y are one and the same thing, we can everywhere substitute one description for the other without changing the truth value of the overall expression in which they appear.

The legal example given seems to violate this principle. If "placing the rat poison" and "placing the unlabeled rat poison" are just two different descriptions of the same act, then any property of one must also be a property of the other. Yet the relational property, being the cause of the injury, is said to be true of the act described as "placing the rat poison," and false of the act described as "placing the unlabeled rat poison."

If one is a radical skeptic about law, one might celebrate this lack of extensionality to statements of legal causation.[108] For such statements' dependence upon description for a truth value is just what is wanted by the skeptic in order to deny sense to these statements. Anything can be the legal cause of anything else, or not, depending on which descriptions of the events are arbitrarily selected.

Such skepticism gives up on there being any relation in the world named by "cause." If we want to look for a concept of cause that the law uses and that makes sense, then we have to see what can be done to alleviate this problem, not celebrate its existence. The most obvious way

---

[106] For a defense of the view that there is only one act here, although there are many different descriptions of it, see Moore, *Act and Crime* (*supra* note 2), ch. 11.

[107] For a discussion of Leibniz's principle in a legal context, see Michael Moore, "Foreseeing Harm Opaquely," in John Gardner, Jeremy Horder, and Stephen Shute, eds., *Action and Value in Criminal Law* (Oxford: Oxford University Press, 1993).

[108] This is what Mark Kelman does, albeit with an imperfect grasp of just what extensionality is. See Kelman, "Necessary Myth" (*supra* note 18), 604–6.

to accommodate the pair of legal statements with which we began is to change what, quite literally, the statements are about.[109] Specifically, the idea is that the second statement is not about the *act* of placing the rat poison in the kitchen; rather, the statement's subject is really the *fact* that that act had a certain property, being the placement of a poison that was both near food and unlabeled.[110] So translated, the second statement really says that the fact that the act was one of placing *unlabeled* rat poison in the kitchen had no causal relevance to the fact that the injury took place.

Now there is no incompatibility between the two statements with which we began. It can be true that the *act* of placing the rat poison caused the injury, and yet also true that the *fact* that the injury occurred was not caused by the *fact* that the rat poison placed in the kitchen was unlabeled. The event that is the action is not the same as the fact that that event had a certain property, so both of these statements can be true without violating Leibniz's principle.

The law thus presupposes that there are such things as facts about events, as well as the events themselves. Such facts about events are often called tropes, or abstract particulars, or concrete universals.[111] The general idea is that the possession of a property by an event is a thing in its own right, in addition to both the particular thing (the event) and the universal thing (the property). Such having-of-a-property things can then be both causes and effects, as both the law and common sense recognize in their discourses.

The law could be committed to such a trope metaphysics in one of two ways.[112] In the moderate form, the law could assert that both events, and facts about events, can be causes and effects. The law would then have to spell out when events are to be used as causal relata, and when facts are to be used instead, because, as we have seen, events and facts give quite different answers to causal questions. The law would also have to make sense of two such different things standing in the causal relation. Alternatively, the law could be more extreme in its tropist metaphysical commitments: it could hold that the only true causal relata are tropes, that its usage of events is not to be taken seriously, and that the latter event-talk can be paraphrased away when it becomes troublesome.[113] In either the

[109] For a discussion of this reference-shifting strategy, see Moore, "Foreseeing Harm" (*supra* note 107).

[110] For an excellent discussion of the difference between facts and events, see Jonathan Bennett, *Events and Their Names* (Indianapolis: Bobbs-Merrill, 1988).

[111] See Keith Campbell, *Abstract Particulars* (Cambridge, MA: Blackwell, 1990). It is not uncontroversial whether facts are tropes, or whether they consist instead of a complex of substance-particulars and universals. See "Introduction," in P. H. Mellor and Alex Oliver, eds., *Properties* (Oxford: Oxford University Press, 1997), 18–20.

[112] These two kinds of commitments to tropes are distinguished in Chris Daly, "Tropes," *Proceedings of the Aristotelian Society* 94 (1994): 253–61; rewritten and reprinted in Mellor and Oliver, eds., *Properties* (*supra* note 111).

[113] See J. L. Mackie's position on facts versus events as causal relata, in *The Cement of the Universe* (*supra* note 55).

moderate or the extreme form, the law must make sense of there being such tropes and of tropes' being the kinds of things that can stand in the causal relation.

I. The causal relation must be temporally asymmetrical

The law joins common sense in presupposing that the causal relation is asymmetrical: if x causes y, then it is not the case that y causes x. Further, the law assumes that this asymmetry exists in only one direction in time: if x causes y, then y cannot precede x in time. Apparent counterexamples— such as when we attribute the solid hit on a golf ball to a golfer's follow-through on his swing[114]—are to be paraphrased away. A more accurate rendering is that the golfer's focus on his follow-through at or just before contact with the ball is what causes a square hit with the ball; since the mental focus precedes the hit, no violation of the temporal asymmetry of the causal relation is to be found in such examples.

The law's presupposition that causality is temporally asymmetrical is to be found in the law's liability doctrines. If A sets off his dynamite and scares B's minks into killing their young,[115] A may be liable for B's loss of minks; B is not liable for A's loss of his dynamite, because in no sense did the killing of their young by B's minks cause A's dynamite to be destroyed.

J. The greater the culpability with which an act is done, the greater the causal power of that act

There is a tendency, noted by many of the earlier commentators on causation in the law,[116] for courts to find a highly culpable actor to have caused a harm when a less culpable actor would not have been said to have caused such a harm. Culpability might increase because of the grossness of the negligence of the defendant; because his act was not only tortious but criminal; because his act was not merely negligent, but reckless or intentional; or because his motives were particularly bad.[117] In any case, such increased culpability has been treated as a kind of aphrodisiac to causation, enhancing the latter's reach and power.

Such a relationship between culpability and causation is distinct from the relationship discussed in connection with "contrived coincidences." In the latter cases, the defendant not only intends the type of harm that actually occurs—he also utilizes the quirks of nature as his intended means to bring about the harm. The cases presently considered make a cruder judgment: just because the defendant has greater culpability in

---

[114] Jennifer Hornsby, *Actions* (London: Routledge, 1980), 76 n. 1.

[115] These are the facts of *Foster v. Preston Mill Co.*, 44 Wash.2d 440, 268 P.2d 645 (1954).

[116] See, e.g., Smith, "Legal Cause in Actions of Tort" (*supra* note 38), 230–32.

[117] All of these cases are detailed in Edgarton, "Legal Cause" (*supra* note 20), 356–60.

virtually any dimension, he can be held liable for causing the harm even
when the causal relationship between his act and the harm is quite
attenuated.

III. Pruning the Law's Demands on a Concept of Causation

The single greatest common fault of the legal literature on causation
has been its credulity with regard to the law's demands on the concept of
causation. Typically, legal theorists have taken legal usages of "cause" at
face value in the sense that, without questioning such usages, they have
thought that their theory of legal causation had to fit all of them. For
theorists with ambitions to account for legal causation in terms of a metaphysics of causation, this credulity and conservatism has made their task
impossible. The law has mixed too many extraneous elements into what
it calls "causation" for there to be much hope for any metaphysical translation. In this section, I shall, accordingly, seek to prune back these legal
usages of causation so that the demands made on the concept are not
obviously impossible ones for any metaphysics to meet.

A. Eliminating any supposed aphrodisiac effect
of culpability on causal potency

I shall begin with the last demand just discussed, that causation be a
relation affected by the degree of culpability with which the act (that is
the putative cause) was done. As skeptics about causation in the law have
often pointed out,[118] there is no metaphysical account of causation that
could meet this demand. For to meet this demand would require the
(metaphysically) strange view that the mental state of the actor itself had
a causal influence on the injury, independent of its influence through the
act that executes such mental state. If the defendant intends some harm
H, and he acts in a way such that H comes about, albeit in a rather
freakish way, then on this view the intent literally adds causal power to
the act of the defendant's that executed his intention. The only way the
intention could do this is by itself causing H, in addition to the causing of
H done by the intention through the defendant's action. Absent some
stronger evidence than we have about the telekinetic powers of our minds,
this is surely impossible. Intending H by itself does not make H occur,
and even clicking your heels three times won't help.

Now consider the role of gross negligence as a causal extender (as
compared to ordinary negligence). To be grossly negligent, one need
have no attitudinal difference vis-à-vis the person who is only ordinarily negligent; to be grossly negligent, it is enough that one does an

---

[118] Ibid.

objectively stupid act, namely, one where the harms risked far exceed any possible gains. (In the colorful language of the late Judge MacGruder, the difference between negligence and gross negligence is the difference between being a fool and being a damned fool.) In such cases of gross negligence, we do not even have a mental state of the actor to do the magically extra causal work. Rather, the moral quality of culpability (in the form of gross negligence) would have to pull the extra load here. Even to those moral realists like myself who are sympathetic to the causal power of moral qualities,[119] this seems a strange causal power to attribute to such qualities. The normal sorts of things moral qualities are said to cause are behaviors and beliefs of persons; this view would require us to think that moral qualities like culpability can also causally contribute—again, directly and without mediation by the acts of the individual who is culpable—to earthquakes and train wrecks.

If one finds the needed metaphysics to be too implausible to be even seriously considered, then one should reject those cases (and the doctrines they announce) that would impose this demand on legal causation. Such cases should be considered to be a kind of understandable mistake—understandable because often we cloud our judgment on one issue by our fervor on another, but a mistake because we have no need to double-count our culpability judgments. We should adjust our overall judgments of moral responsibility and legal liability by giving culpability its proper due, no more, no less; having done this, we have no reason to gerrymander other components of responsibility, such as causation, so as to give even more weight to culpability. If we are clear-headed about this, we will simply get rid of such doctrines, not try to accommodate them in our construction of the law's presupposed concept of causation.

The doctrines that we need to prune back here are four in number. First and foremost, we should eliminate the entire family of doctrines that allow the comparatively greater culpability of a defendant to extend the causal power of his actions through space and time. I refer to the proximate-cause doctrines alluded to earlier,[120] doctrines holding that "no harm is too remote if it is intended," etc.

The second place in which culpability is given magical causal powers is in the overdetermination cases of the concurrent type. Our earlier example was the two fires, independently set and each sufficient to burn the structure, that join to burn the structure. The doctrinal suggestion was that it matters to a culpable defendant's status as a cause of the destruction whether the other fire was also culpably set, or whether it was either innocently set or was a fire of natural origin. For reasons similar to those

---

[119] Michael Moore, "Moral Reality," *Wisconsin Law Review* 1982, 1061–1156; Moore, "Moral Reality Revisited," *Michigan Law Review* 90 (1992): 2424–2533.
[120] See the text accompanying note 117 *supra*.

just discussed, there is no metaphysics that can make sense of this distinction.[121] If the only difference between the second fires in the range of cases we are considering is the culpable intention, culpable negligence, or moral agency of the second fires' sources, that can make no difference in the defendant's causal responsibility. The suggestion that it does should be rejected, and the law should be treated (as it mostly is anyway) as finding the defendant causally responsible for the destruction in all variations of these concurrent overdetermination cases. This does not necessarily mean that the defendant will be liable in all of these cases, for there may be some noncausal doctrines that save certain causally responsible defendants from liability. Where the concurrent, overdetermining cause is the *victim's* own culpable fire-starting (in the two-fires-that-join sort of example), then the noncausal doctrines of "contributory negligence" and "assumption of the risk" will relieve the culpable fire-starting defendant of liability in tort (although not in criminal law).

The third doctrine to be eliminated here is the doctrine of contrived coincidences. As we have seen, contrived coincidences are not said to break causal chains. The factory owner who hopes that his workers will get hit by the roof being carried by an extraordinary wind, and sends them out for that reason, cannot escape a cause-based liability for their deaths despite the intervening act of God.

Here again, we have to alter doctrine if we are to have any hope of finding a coherent conception of cause presupposed by the law. For it cannot be the case that the very same storm is an intervening cause, or is not, depending on the state of mind of the defendant; it cannot be the case that the very same acts and omissions of the defendant are the cause of the workmen's deaths, or not, depending on the state of mind of that defendant. Again, our minds do not have these kinds of telekinetic powers.

We ought to say that the criteria for an intervening cause do not include contrivance by the defendant. This means that irrespective of whether the defendant intended the storm to kill the workmen, the defendant did not cause their deaths.

As I have suggested in Section II, this negative conclusion about cause-based liability does not end the possibility of a noncausal liability. Perhaps liability in such cases should be predicated on a kind of accomplice liability. Just as one who purposely aids an intervening human agent to cause a harm is liable as an accomplice for that harm, so one who purposely aids an intervening act of God to cause a harm should be liable as

[121] Skeptics about causation have perceived this, leading them to invoke these cases regularly. See Edgarton, "Legal Cause" (*supra* note 20), 346–47 ("D's act stands in the same *logical* relation to the result, whether the other actor is a wrongdoer, an innocent person, or a thunderstorm"); Shavell, "An Analysis of Causation and the Scope of Liability in the Law of Torts" (*supra* note 10), 495; and Landes and Posner, "Causation in Tort Law: An Economic Approach" (*supra* note 10), 110.

an accomplice for that harm. One has made it easier, and perhaps one has even made it possible, for the storm to cause its harm, and one has done so with the specific intent that this happen. That should be enough for liability, just as it is in the human-intervenor situation. And in both situations, no resort need be had to any cause-based liability. One has only aided, not caused, the bringing about of the harm.

Here, as in the case of human intervenors, one might well worry that such a noncausal basis of liability could be extended to the lesser forms of culpability of negligence, recklessness, and knowledge. If such extensions were made, then the intervening-cause doctrine would, again, not be rendered senseless, but it would be rendered pointless. However, here as well as in the provision-of-opportunity cases, such extensions cut against the central idea that animates accomplice liability: we can relax our normal causation requirement (from causing to mere aiding) only because of the high level of culpability with which the aider acts. Accomplice liability is like attempt liability in this regard. In both cases, one substitutes a lesser causal requirement[122] (respectively, of aid, or of proximity to success) because the actor is motivated by the wrong to be done to another. Such alternative, noncausal liabilities are less justifiable if one also relaxes culpability below this highest level.

The fourth doctrine requiring modification (on the ground that culpability judgments must be separated from causal judgments) deals with what I earlier called the negligent-provision-of-opportunity cases. In such cases, as we have seen, the foreseeability (to the defendant) of the intervention by a third party changes the causal status of both that intervention and the act of the defendant. Such alteration is inconsistent with a metaphysical reading of causation, on the same grounds as we have just seen. Nonetheless, I shall defer discussion of this fourth doctrine until we have examined omission liability (for reasons that will become apparent later).

B. Eliminating the demand that omissions be treated as causes

We should abandon both of the previously described strategies which seek to account on causal grounds for the limited liability for omissions in tort and criminal law. The first regards all omissions as causes, distinguishing the few for which liability is imposed from the many where it is not on noncausal grounds of legal duty.

There are metaphysical theories of causation that seemingly have the ability to explain how omissions can be causes. Counterfactual theories of causation (discussed briefly in Section IV), in particular, look promising

---

[122] I explore the lesser (but not nonexistent) causal requirement for attempt liability in Moore, *Act and Crime* (*supra* note 2), ch. 8.

in this regard. The problem with the first strategy, then, is not its meta-physical impossibility; rather, the problem is moral. In the first place, if we literally can kill, rob, rape, maim, etc., by omission as well as by commission, then how can we explain the usual absence of legal or moral duties not to kill, etc., by omission? Our obligations apply to causally complex act-types like killing, and if omissions cause deaths and are thus killings, why are these kinds of killings permissible for us? If we have a legal duty not to kill, and if omissions to prevent deaths are killings, then why do we not have a general legal duty not to omit to save? Secondly, where we do have a moral and a legal duty not to omit to prevent harm, why are our failures to do so regarded as so much less blameworthy than are our failures to refrain from killing, etc., by commission? Our negative duties not to kill by commission are so much stronger than are our pos-itive duties not to kill by omission (that is, not to omit to save). Yet if these omissions truly are a breach of our obligation not to cause death—that is, not to kill—why should this distinction be drawn at all, and with such force?

We have a moral distinction we want to draw here. It is the distinction between our responsibility for making the world worse and our respon-sibility for making it better. The easiest, most intuitive way to draw this distinction is by using causation to mark the difference. We violate our negative duties when we cause harm, but not when we fail to prevent such harm; when there are less stringent positive duties, we breach them by failing to prevent harm, not by causing that harm.

Regarding omissions as causes is thus a mistake. Avoiding that mistake does not require us to change our doctrines of liability. Rather, it allows us to make better moral sense of the doctrines we have. Not making this mistake also has the added benefit of relieving us from causal perplexities about the overdetermination omission cases. We need not puzzle over cases like the omission to repair the brakes followed by the omission to use the brakes (which would not work if they were used). We lack intu-itions about whether these cases are concurrent or preemptive kinds of cases, and, if they are preemptive, which omission preempts which. We lack any such intuitions because these are not causal issues at all, so we *should* be at a loss as to how to apply these causal distinctions.

The second strategy for explaining omission liability avoids the mis-take of thinking of all omissions as causes. Yet this strategy reintroduces the mistake in its attempt to explain liability in the exceptional cases where we do owe positive duties to others. The crudest form of the mistake here is to think that the bare fact of legal duty can turn an omission from a noncause into a cause:

> [W]hereas an actor may always rightly be held to answer for the consequences of his act, since he has taken it upon himself to change the course of events, it is otherwise with a non-actor; he should be

held responsible only if his failure to act was in itself a legal wrong, that is, if he had a duty to act. The non-action of one who has no legal duty to act is nothing. It does not alter the course of human events, and therefore it has no consequences. It is true that an omission of a legal duty also does not alter the course of events; but the non-actor, having been obliged by law to change events, is rightly held responsible for the consequences of not doing so.[123]

Surely the bare fact of legal duty cannot transform an omission from a nothing that can cause nothing, to a nothing that can cause something!

A more plausible approach is to take the existence of a legal duty not to omit to be a proxy for some other, more plausible causal discrimination. Thus, as Eric Mack[124] and Richard Epstein[125] argue, if we examine the four bases for a duty not to omit (described in Section IIG), we will discover a plausible causal responsibility in each case. The grain of truth in this argument lies in there being some kind of causal involvement by the defendant with the victim in the exceptional cases of duties not to omit. Yet what is crucial to see is that the liability of the defendants in these cases is not for any such causal involvement. When we hold an omitter liable because he had a duty not to omit to rescue one whose rescue he has undertaken, we are not holding him liable on the ground that his acts of undertaking the rescue caused the victim's death. Rather, our liability doctrines explicitly and correctly hold the failed rescuer liable for his omission to rescue, even though his duty not to omit rescue arose from those acts of undertaking rescue. Those acts needn't have worsened the victim's peril, nor need they have been done with a culpable *mens rea*, in order to give rise to the duty not to omit; by contrast, if such acts were an independent basis of liability on causal grounds, both these things would have to be proven about the acts of undertaking rescue.[126]

The upshot is that in the four situations earlier described, we hold omitters responsible for their omissions, not for any earlier acts of theirs that gave rise to their duty not to omit. This means that in these cases we are imposing a noncausal liability, and we should be up front about it. We are liable in such cases because we failed to prevent harm, not because we caused harm. Accordingly, no theory of causation in the law need accommodate such liability.

Of course, shelving omission liability under "noncausal" will not relieve us from all problems about omissions. In particular, we may still worry about the kinds of capacities (to have prevented a given harm) defendants must have had in order to be fairly held liable for failing to

[123] Beale, "Proximate Consequences" (*supra* note 103), 637.
[124] Mack, "Bad Samaritanism" (*supra* note 104).
[125] Epstein, "A Theory of Strict Liability" (*supra* note 9).
[126] This latter point is argued more extensively in Moore, *Act and Crime* (*supra* note 2), 31–34.

prevent that harm. And those capacity judgments may get quite tricky, as when we deal with what I earlier called the "overdetermination omission" cases; for in such cases each person's failure in his positive obligations seems to take away the other's capacity not to fail in his own obligations. Still, these problems are not problems that a theory of legal causation need resolve, for they make no demands on the concept of causation needed by the law.

C. Cleaning up the doctrines of intervening causation

One of the most troublesome areas of legal doctrine about causation is that having to do with the sudden breaking of causal chains by fresh causal starts. As we have seen, such fresh (or "intervening," or "superseding") causal starts are of three kinds: deliberate third-party intervention; extraordinary natural events amounting to a coincidence (or an "act of God"); and subsequent but preempting causes.

I have pruned all I intend to prune with respect to the second of these three kinds of intervening causes. Eliminating the defendant's intention as a criterion for when an extraordinary natural event should amount to a coincidence (and, thus, an intervening cause) is the major reform needed here. Yet notice that accomplice liability can and should be extended to place liability on just those defendants on whom the doctrine of contrived coincidence placed it. One who purposefully utilizes extraordinary natural events to produce harm to others should be liable, albeit not on causal grounds.

Such will be my general strategy in pruning the doctrines about the other two kinds of intervening causes. Often I shall urge that a noncausal basis for liability should be established to preserve the liability of one who is presently but erroneously held liable on causal grounds. In light of the just concluded discussion of omissions, we can now add omission liability to accomplice liability as a second, noncausal means for preserving existing legal results while economizing on the law's demands on causation.

I shall begin with the intervening human agent doctrines. Here there are two categories of troublesome cases, one having to do with supposedly cause-based liability for negligently providing another person with the opportunity to do some harm, and the other having to do with supposedly cause-based liability for giving another person reasons to cause some harm. I begin with the provision-of-opportunity cases.

1. The negligent-provision-of-opportunity cases: Noncausal but omissive liability. As we have seen, in cases like that of the railroad that drops its passenger off into a dangerous situation and the construction company that leaves its bulldozer (with the keys in it) perched above a house, the negligent provision of opportunity makes the defendant liable despite the intervening use of the opportunity by a free, informed, voluntary wrongdoer. Such liability is a puzzle. Negligence is insufficient *mens rea* for accomplice liability, which requires purposeful aiding of the wrongdoer. Yet this seemingly forces us to concede an ad hoc exception to the intervening human agency doctrine.

Hart and Honoré's original reaction to these cases was simply to carve out an ad hoc exception and leave it at that.[127] In the second edition of their *Causation in the Law*, however, they sought to explain such liability in terms of a newly discovered, second kind of causal relation. On this new view, such cases represent a weaker form of causation called "occasioning," "enabling," or "inclining" causation. Such a special kind of causal relation is peripheral or penumbral to the "central case" of causation, where intervening intentional actors break causal chains; for such a weaker relation, its weakness paradoxically proves to be a kind of strength, for intervening intentional actors do not break these "weaker-linked" causal chains.[128]

This is pretty obviously hopeless as a reconciliation of the intervening human agency doctrine with the negligent-provision-of-opportunity cases. The original ad hoc solution is no solution at all, because it makes causation depend on whether the harm that happened was one within the risk that made it negligent to act—and this, on Hart and Honoré's own showing,[129] is a noncausal notion. Causation cannot be a real relationship in the world and be influenced by this kind of culpability ("harm within the risk") analysis. Likewise, the invention of noncentral notions of causation is of no help. Not only are such postulated special senses of concepts always suspicious, postulated as they are to save a theory that is otherwise in trouble; but left unexplained is why this second kind of causal relationship is not generally sufficient for liability if it is sufficient in the negligent-provision-of-opportunity cases. Why, for example, is the railroad which negligently spilled its gasoline throughout a town not liable when an intentional arsonist torches it off? Because, you say, the risk of the arsonist is not the risk that made it negligent to spill the gasoline? Yet that is, again, to resort to the noncausal criterion of "harm within the risk." The relation between the *action* of the railroad and the burning of the town seems in all relevant respects similar to the relation between the *action* of the railroad and the rape of its bounced passenger: each such action made possible (provided the "opportunity" for) the

---

[127] See note 91 and the accompanying text.

[128] Hart and Honoré, *Causation in the Law* (*supra* note 47), 186:

> The main feature that unifies "inducing wrongful acts" and "occasioning harm" is that these two types of "causal connection" (to use the expression in the wide sense commonly found in legal writings) are not negatived by the factors that negative the simpler type of causal connection . . . for both . . . may be traced through an intervening voluntary action and the second form may also be traced through an intervening coincidence.

[129] Ibid., lxii–lxv, 286–90.

causing of harm by a third party. It is only a culpability discrimination ("harm within the risk") that distinguishes these cases, and this kind of discrimination should be irrelevant to causation.

We could invent a negligence kind of accomplice liability for the provision-of-opportunity cases. Yet if we did this, we would face a problem analogous to that faced by Hart and Honoré: why isn't anyone who negligently acts in a way that makes possible the intervening intentional wrong of another liable on this ground? Such extensive accomplice liability does not make a hash out of our causal notions, as do Hart and Honoré's solutions; but such liability would render pointless the law's insistence that intervening intentional actors break causal chains.

Preferable to any of these solutions would be to decide that the provision-of-opportunity cases in torts are wrongly decided. Criminal law does not hold railroads or construction companies liable for negligently allowing others to rape, or to destroy buildings. (At most, criminal law creates separable crimes of leaving keys in the ignition, leaving vehicles unlocked, serving too much liquor to known drivers, etc.) One could preferably urge that tort-law doctrine is simply mistaken in imposing liabilities for harms when only an opportunity was negligently provided to another to cause such harms.

My own sense is that tort law is not mistaken here, however. Liability is proper in the negligent-provision-of-opportunity cases. However, the liability is not cause-based liability (nor is it liability for purposefully aiding another to cause). Rather, these are cases of true omission liability. When the railroad is held liable for the rape of its passenger, it is not liable because it caused the rape by a third party; rather, it failed to prevent the rape when it could so easily have done so by carrying the passenger to a place of safety. Likewise, a construction company is not liable because it caused the destruction of the house by leaving the keys in the ignition of its bulldozer; it is liable because it failed to prevent such damage when it could so easily have done so by removing the keys.

The duty not to omit in these cases arises because of the "culpable causing of the condition of peril" exception discussed above. The defendants in these cases have caused the victim to be placed in peril, and have culpably caused this because the peril presented by intervening third-party actors was so foreseeable. Their omission to correct a situation they have caused is the true basis for their liability here.

Such a noncausal, omission rationale explains why mere negligent provision of opportunity, which opportunity is utilized by a third-party wrongdoer, is not enough for liability. Rather, the opportunity must be provided to a wrongdoer the risk of whose intervention made the original actor negligent to start with. It is only prevention of the realization of *this* peril that is the first actor's duty; that other actors may come along and utilize the opportunity provided is not enough. Thus, when the railroad's negligence consists in the spilling of gasoline, that negligence does not consist specifically in the foreseeable intervention of an arsonist.[130] Such arson is not the peril for whose creation the railroad was responsible, and thus for whose correction it has a duty. Likewise, when a railroad's negligence consists in carrying a passenger too far, but it does not drop her off in a place of danger but in a reputable hotel, where she is raped, the railroad has no liability because that was not the peril that made it negligent to carry her beyond her destination.[131]

One way to test whether we hold defendants liable in these cases for their omissions (when the duty not to omit arises from their having caused the peril), or whether we hold them liable for the culpable action causing the harm, is to eliminate culpability at the earlier time. Suppose the railroad is not at all negligent in carrying a passenger beyond her destination to some end-of-the-line, deserted freight yards; she was also not at fault, let us suppose, but overslept due to involuntary intoxication. If the railroad which has innocently caused her condition of peril—being at an isolated, dark, and dangerous location—were to fail to carry her further (when it could do so easily because another train is heading there anyway), and she is raped, then I take the railroad to be liable. It is liable because it omitted to prevent her rape when it could have done so at little cost or inconvenience to itself. It is not liable for having caused her rape by its action of carrying her to the end of the line, because that action was not culpable in any way.

Another way to test whether the proper basis for liability here is causal or omissive, is to imagine a scenario where there is no fair opportunity of the railroad to prevent the injury. Suppose, as in the actual case, the railroad negligently carries her beyond her destination to a dangerous place. However, this time the railroad arranges transportation back for her as soon as it can, and places her in the safest position possible in the interim. If she is still raped in that interim period, I take it that there would be no liability. Yet if the basis of liability in the actual case was the negligent action of carrying the passenger beyond her destination, there should be liability here. The reason there is not is because without any capacity to have prevented the rape, the railroad cannot be held liable for any omission to prevent it. Thus, it is omission that is the true basis for liability here.

It may seem that criminal law is remiss in not imposing punishment in these provision-of-opportunity cases. For criminal law, like tort law, provides that there is a duty not to omit when one has innocently or culpably caused the victim's condition of peril, and thus it might seem that there should be criminal omission liability wherever there is omission liability in tort law. Yet most of these provision-of-opportunity cases are negli-

---

[130] *Watson* (*supra* note 84).
[131] This is a variation of the facts in *Central of Georgia Ry. Co. v. Price*, 106 Ga. 176, 32 S.E. 77 (1898).

gence cases, and by-and-large criminal law does not punish negligence. Where criminal law does punish negligence, as in negligent homicide, there should be criminal liability in this class of cases—not for causing death, but for negligently failing to prevent someone else from causing death. And in those cases where the defendant is more than negligent—he knows to a practical certainty that vandals will use his bulldozer to ram another's house if he leaves the keys in the ignition—he should be convictable of any crime of property destruction requiring a *mens rea* of knowingly or recklessly failing to prevent someone else from causing such destruction. Criminal law thus does parallel tort law here, if one looks closely.

The upshot is that we do not need to modify the notion of an intervening cause to accommodate liability in the provision-of-opportunity cases. There is liability in such cases, but such liability is noncausal: one can be liable for purposefully aiding, or for knowing, reckless, or negligent omitting. This allows us to say clearly that a free, informed, voluntary third party's intervention between the defendant's act and the victim's harm breaks the causal chain between that act and that harm.

2. The giving-of-reasons cases revisited: The playoff of causal versus accomplice liability. If we now turn from the provision-of-opportunity to the giving-of-reasons cases, we also can sharpen the law's commitment to the status of a free, informed, voluntary act constituting an intervening cause. Such clarification is desperately needed, because the law otherwise seems committed to a flat contradiction here.

The contradiction is to be found in the partly innocent agent cases. As stated earlier, the official rationale for punishing the reason-giving procurer for a more serious crime, and the one procured (who committed the crime) for a less serious crime, is that the procurer is an accomplice as to the less serious crime but a principal as to the more serious crime. Take my earlier example of the intentional use of a provokable individual to have another person killed; the procurer tells the hot-tempered and jealous man that his wife is having an affair with the intended victim of the homicide. The procurer is said to have aided and abetted the voluntary manslaughter (provoked intentional killing) committed by the hot-tempered, jealous man; the procurer is also said to have caused the death of the victim himself through the use of a comparatively innocent agent, and therefore is guilty of murder as a principal. The contradiction lies in saying *both* that the choice to kill by the hot-tempered husband is, and that it is not, an intervening cause—and, thus, that the procurer's telling of the falsehood both did not, and did, cause the death of the victim.

This contradiction is easily eliminated if we but seize one horn of the dilemma or the other in any given case. That is, sometimes the one who is induced to commit a crime is so distressed, ignorant, or compelled as not to be an intervening cause on the ordinary criteria for that concept. If the killer is misled about whether he is killing, or misled about facts that would justify the killing, then his choice to act is not intentional with respect to material facts. If the killer is threatened, or placed in a hard choice situation, or rendered not in control of his faculties, his choice also does not constitute an intervening cause on the ordinary criteria of that concept. In these cases, the one who induces the killer to kill, himself causes death. If the inducer's culpability is greater (or lesser, for that matter) than that of the one he uses, it is his own culpability that is used to measure the degree of his crime.

The only reservation one might have about this conclusion lies in the linguistic oddity one may experience in saying that the inducer *kills*. Indeed, this sense of linguistic oddity will increase for other verbs, like "rape," "hit," "maim," and "take." Surely, one might think, it is the person who is induced to do these things who does them; the inducer of rape does not rape, the inducer of a hitting does not himself hit, etc.[132]

Yet this linguistic discomfort should be momentary. If one looks at the acts prohibited by the criminal law, all of them are described by causally loaded verbs. Just as one kills by causing death, so one rapes by causing penetration, one hits by causing contact, one maims by causing disfigurement, and one takes by causing movement of the object taken. It is true that we often have a stereotype of how these causings are done—we picture the actor using his own body as the means. Yet these stereotypes do not give the meaning of these verbs. Those who induce others to use their bodies to cause the states of affairs which the law prohibits violate our pragmatic (in the linguists' sense) expectations of the typical way these states of affairs are brought about; such unusual routes no more relieve one from being considered a cause of such a state of affairs than would the use of any other unusual means. Inducers quite literally rape, hit, maim, and take, and are properly held liable for doing so.[133]

Furthermore, if one is uncomfortable with this linguistic conclusion, then one should urge adoption of language similar to that of the American Law Institute's Model Penal Code, section 2.06(2)(a). My rewording of that subsection would make one liable for the conduct of another person when, acting with the culpability sufficient for commission of the offense, he causes an agent who lacks the voluntariness, intention, or capacities sufficient for the status of an intervening cause, to engage in such conduct. If there is a linguistic problem here, one can simply stip-

---

[132] The argument is pressed by Kadish in the essays cited in note 93 *supra*; Bennett, *Events and Their Names* (*supra* note 110); Donald Davidson, *Actions and Events* (Oxford: Oxford University Press, 1980); and Judith Jarvis Thomson, *Acts and Other Events* (Ithaca, NY: Cornell University Press, 1977). Such a view is adopted in *Dusenberry v. Commonwealth*, 220 Va. 770, 263 S.E.2d 392 (1980) (no rape by a defendant who inserted the penis of another into the victim).

[133] I have argued this at some length in Moore, *Act and Crime* (*supra* note 2), ch. 8.

ulate it away. Where there is a causal relation between the inducer's
reason-giving action and the harm, there should be liability as a principal,
whatever the etymological accidents of language are construed to require.

Alternatively, sometimes the one who wields the knife meets the ordinary criterion for an intervening cause. The hot-tempered, jealous husband is, to my mind, such a person. He intentionally killed; his only
ignorance was immaterial, since believing your wife to have had an affair
is not a justification for homicide, not even in Texas anymore. His only
"involuntariness" is due to his own emotional impulses, which, despite
the partial defense of provocation, do not compel one to kill.[134] Easier
cases are those where the inducer tells another where his intended victim
may be found; when the victim is found and shot, the shooter's action is
an intervening cause, making the teller's liability only that of an accomplice.

The conundrum in the law of accomplice liability, with which we began
this subsection, is also present in certain of these cases. If the provider of
false information in my main example can only be guilty as an accomplice
and not as a principal, then under standard doctrine he may be held liable
for no greater degree of homicide than can be proved of his principal.
Since this is the hot-tempered man who may only be convicted of heat-
of-passion manslaughter, this would limit the inducer to liability for aiding and abetting manslaughter. Yet the inducer's culpability is greater,
since he intended to kill and was not provoked. If one finds this reasoning
to be compelling, then the standardly stated rule should be discarded: an
accomplice may be held liable for a higher degree of crime than the
principal of whom he is the accomplice. One should make this reform
directly, and not attempt to warp causal doctrines to accommodate it.

As it happens, such a reform is undesirable for the reasons Sandy
Kadish has argued in detail.[135] The inducer's comparatively greater culpability is irrelevant to his proportional punishment. In cases where the
actor who is induced does constitute an intervening cause, there can be no
greater punishment for the inducer on causal grounds: for, by hypothesis,
the inducer did not cause the legally prohibited state of affairs. Likewise,
there should be no greater punishment for the inducer on accomplice
grounds: for, by hypothesis, the more serious crime was not perpetrated
by the induced actor, and thus there was no such crime whose perpetra-
tion the inducer could have aided. If one must punish the inducer more
than the induced actor, it should be on the basis of attempt, not causation
or complicity: perhaps one wants to say that the provider of false infor-

[134] See Moore, *Placing Blame* (*supra* note 12), ch. 13.
[135] See the essays by Kadish cited in note 93 *supra*. Kadish persuasively argues that the
accomplice who does not cause the legally prohibited state of affairs (because the acts of
the principal constitute intervening causes) is like the lucky attemptor who does not cause
the harm he attempts; both are quite culpable, yet neither can be held responsible for a harm
he did not cause.

mation attempted to *murder* the victim (who was only killed by a manslaughterer). Attempt liability is our usual pigeonhole for increased punishment for culpability alone, if that seems desirable in such cases.

3. *The subsequent, preempting cause cases: Eliminating any causal basis for whatever residual liability there may be for a preempted, overdetermined cause.* As we saw at the end of the discussion of intervening causes in Section II, a human act or natural event can be an intervening cause even if it does not meet the Hart and Honoré criteria. Preempting causes, if they occur subsequent to the "cause" they preempt, are a kind of intervening cause too. If a victim is falling to his death but is shot—either intentionally, negligently, or innocently, it doesn't matter—then the cause of his fall is not the cause of his death. Similarly, if a skydiver, whose parachute fails to open, is falling to his death and is electrocuted as he passes through the usual afternoon electrical storm, the negligent preparation of his parachute by another did not cause his death; rather, the storm killed him.[136]

Previously I used this preemption rationale to explain why there are cases where merely negligent (as opposed to intentional) human intervention sometimes breaks causal chains. Now, however, we need to examine the cases where there is liability on the part of the original actor despite the intervention of a seemingly preemptive cause. Consider, first, the case where the original actor purposely takes advantage of the preemptive cause in that, foreseeing such preemptive cause, he does what he needs to do to ensure that such preemptive cause can do its work to harm the victim. For example, the defendant knows that the victim is going swimming in the ocean, that the undertow is strong, and that the victim is a sufficiently poor swimmer that he will not likely survive the experience. Desiring exactly this result, he ties up the lifeguard in his stand. The victim enters the water and, because of the undertow, drowns.

The defendant undoubtedly is liable, in both criminal law and tort law; he is liable, most courts would say, because he *caused* the death. Yet notice exactly what the defendant caused: he caused the lifeguard to omit to rescue the victim from the undertow. If I am right that omissions do no causal work, then how can causing another to omit to save someone become a causing of death? If the omission does not have the requisite causal property, how can that which causes the omission have that property? If omissions are not causes, how can they transmit causal force?

Rather than trying to reconcile the idea that omissions cannot be causes with the idea that the omitter who is caused to omit by someone else nonetheless can transmit causal power, we would do better to recognize a noncausal liability here. The defendant in cases like these has again aided nature, in this case, the undertow. What the defendant did was to remove one of the victim's protections and then let nature take its course.

---

[136] *Dillon v. Twin State Gas and Electric Co.*, 85 N.H. 449, 163 A. 111 (1932).

This is again a purposeful aiding, even if what is aided is not another person but a natural event, and even though that natural event is not some extraordinary act of God (as in the contrived coincidence cases).

Now return to the overdetermination variant of this case: the victim is a large man whom it will take two lifeguards to save; fortunately, two are available for the job; unfortunately, two defendants, each acting independently of (not in concert with) the other, tie up each of the lifeguards, and the victim drowns in the undertow. As I said before, I am confident that each defendant is liable for the death, and that this result obtains no matter which defendant tied up his respective lifeguard first. Each made it easier for nature to cause the death, and each is liable for thus aiding the causing of death by nature, but not for causing death himself.

Utilizing this noncausal, accomplice-to-nature basis of liability also allows us to sort through the troublesome McLaughlin hypothetical.[137] When A replaces the water in V's keg with salt, and B steals the keg, and V dies of thirst in the desert, neither has caused V's death. A combination of natural processes we can lump together and call "nature" killed V. However, A aided nature in its killing by removing V's protection against these natural processes, and A is liable for the death on that basis. B attempted to aid nature, but there was no aiding to be done when he stole the keg. B is no more liable for aiding here than he would be if he had stolen V's watch, his camera, or anything else (like a keg of salt) totally unhelpful to V's survival.

In the Hart and Honoré variation of the McLaughlin example,[138] also discussed by J. L. Mackie[139] and Richard Wright,[140] A poisons V's water and B drains the poisoned water out of the keg before V dies of thirst in the desert. Again, neither A nor B caused V's death. Had V drunk the poisoned water and died of poisoning, then A would have caused V's death; but V did not die of poisoning. Nor did A aid nature or even try to; A tried to kill V by his own causal mechanism, and is liable for attempted murder. B, by contrast, did two things by draining the water: first, he prevented A from causing V's death; and second, he aided nature in killing V. Nature's only means of killing V was thirst, and thirst was the mechanism aided by B. He is liable for V's death as an aider of nature.

Now let us turn from purpose to lesser states of culpability, such as negligence or recklessness. For example, the defendant either knows or has reason to know that the victim is going swimming in the ocean, that the undertow is strong, and that the victim is a sufficiently poor swimmer that he will not likely survive the experience unaided. Despite this, the

---

[137] See McLaughlin, "Proximate Cause" (*supra* note 53).
[138] Hart and Honoré, *Causation in the Law* (*supra* note 47), 239–40.
[139] Mackie, *Cement of the Universe* (*supra* note 55), 45–46.
[140] Wright, "Causation in Tort Law" (*supra* note 40), 1802.

defendant negligently drives his car on the beach, hitting the lifeguard and incapacitating him from rescuing the victim.

Such a scenario may sound like the product of a law professor's overactive imagination, but in reality such cases are common as dirt. If I negligently: drain water from your pool, and you dive in; or bump the chair on which you are about to sit, and you fall to the floor; or destroy the lighting on a dangerous stair, and you fall because you cannot see; or destroy the brakes on your car, so that you cannot stop; or run my car into a flood barrier, weakening it such that the next flood breaks through; then I am liable, at least in torts, for your injuries.

These are the "dangerous conditions" cases on which many a causal theory in law has foundered.[141] For to the extent that the undertow, the diving, the sitting, the descending, the driving, and the flood are subsequent, preempting causes, there cannot be cause-based liability here. Yet absent any purposive exploitation of these natural forces by the original actor, there should not be an "aiding of nature" basis for liability either. Liability in such cases is thus a puzzle.

My suggestion is that these, too, are cases of omission liability. It is our failure to prevent the harm that our own actions have made likely, that is the true basis for liability in these cases. The positive legal duty (to eliminate the perils described) is based on our having caused the condition of peril, but the liability is still omission liability, not causal.

IV. CONCLUSION: THE PROSPECTS FOR A METAPHYSICS OF LEGAL CAUSATION

My "pruned" concept of causation presupposed by the law will have the following characteristics:

(1) Mere correlation is not causation. Some particular event x is not a cause of another particular event y just because x is an instance of some type of event X, y is an instance of some type of event Y, and Y regularly follows X. Something more is required. When the correlation is a weak, probabilistic one, so that an event of type X raises the conditional probability of an event of type Y, one has to "screen off" spurious causes from real ones by asking more complicated probability questions.[142] Something more is required even when the correlation is a stronger, universal one, where events of type Y always follow events of type X. Such correlations are modes of proving that a causal relation exists

[141] Notably Beale, "Proximate Consequences" (*supra* note 103); and Epstein, "A Theory of Strict Liability" (*supra* note 9).
[142] See the discussion in Salmon, "Probabilistic Causality" (*supra* note 17).

between x and y; they are not themselves constitutive of such a causal relation. As a special case of this last point, the correlation that exists between epiphenomena is not a causal relation. If x causes y and z, and y always occurs prior to z, y does not cause z. My jogging in the morning both scares my dog and makes me tired; my dog's fright does not make me tired.

(2) Not every condition necessary for the happening of some harm y is a cause of y. When the law enquires after the "sole cause" of some event, the existence of many such necessary conditions does not rule out some other event x being designated the sole cause.

(3) The causal relation may exist between an act x and a harm y even if x is not a necessary condition for the occurrence of y because some other condition z is sufficient for the occurrence of y; such causal relation will exist where x and z are concurrent overdeterminers, and it will also exist when x preempts z as a cause of y. In short, for x to cause y, it is not necessary that x be a necessary condition for y.

(4) The causal relation may sometimes not exist between an act x and a harm y even though x is a sufficient condition for the happening of y. This will be true in the preemptive overdetermination cases where another condition z sufficient for y preempts x from causing y. In short, for x to cause y, it is not sufficient that x be a sufficient condition for y.

(5) Causation is a scalar property. An act x may be *more* of a cause of a harm y than some other event z, even though z too is a cause of y.

(6) Causation diminishes over the number of events through which it is transmitted. This makes the causal relation one of only limited transitivity.

(7) Causal chains may be sharply broken and not merely gradually diminished. The intervening causes responsible for such breaks may be of three kinds: deliberate human interventions, freakishly abnormal natural events, and subsequent preemptive causes. Although there may be liability for failing to prevent certain such interventions, or for aiding such interventions in doing their causal work, there is no causal relationship across such intervening events at the basis of such liability.

(8) Omissions, being no things at all, do no causal work. While there is a counterfactual question to ask about omissions when they are the basis for liability—namely, the "capacity" question of whether the omitter could have prevented the harm—this is not a causal question.

(9) The causal relationship is asymmetrical, so that if x causes y, then y does not cause x. Moreover, the asymmetry is tempo-

ral, in that if x causes y, then x must not be preceded temporally by y.

(10) Both whole events and aspects of whole events ("tropes") are
the relata of the causal relation. Causal contexts are exten-
sional, and this extensionality can be preserved only by allowing both whole events and their aspects to be causal relata.

The question is whether there is any metaphysical theory of causation
that can endow causation with these ten characteristics. None of the four
major theories of causation look very promising in this direction. These
four theories are all generalist theories stemming from the enormously
influential views of David Hume.

Of these four theories, the best known is the view usually attributed to
Hume himself, the regularity theory of causation.[143] Such a theory is
strongly reductionist because of two—numbers (2) and (4) below—of its
four essential tenets:

(1) The principle of uniformity in nature: There are regular conjunctions of classes of events in nature.

(2) The analytic reductionist principle about causal laws: A causal
law is no more than a description of these regular conjunctions of
classes of events.

(3) The universal presupposition about causal laws: Every singular
causal statement, such as, "Event-token x caused event-token y,"
presupposes some causal law between types of events X and Y,
where x is an instance of X and y is an instance of Y.

(4) The analytic reductionist principle about singular causal statements: The singular causal statement, x caused y, means no more
than:
(a) x existed, y existed;
(b) y did not precede x temporally; and
(c) x is an instance of some type X, and y is an instance of some
type Y, such that there is an X/Y causal law.

Given the long-recognized and much-discussed difficulty of the Humean regularity theory in generating the first of the ten characteristics of
causation, many philosophers otherwise sympathetic to Hume's theory
disavow the second of these four tenets. Rather, on this modified theory,
causal laws describe primitive causal relations between universals, rela-

[143] I am unconcerned with whether the regularity theory sketched below was really
believed by Hume. On this, see, e.g., Barry Stroud, *Hume* (London: Routledge and Kegan
Paul, 1977), chs. 3 and 4; and Galen Strawson, *The Secret Connexion* (Oxford: Clarendon
Press, 1989). The Humean theory is an interesting and an influential one even if it turns out
that Hume never held it.

tions that cannot be reduced to Humean regularities.[144] Such a theory is usually termed "neo-Humean," despite this putting of "causal glue" back in precisely where Hume eliminated it; the label is nonetheless appropriate because the theory reaffirms the rest of Hume's principles. The essence of causation on this neo-Humean theory is nomic (or lawful) sufficiency.

Both the Humean and the neo-Humean theories face deep and well-charted problems in accommodating the ten characteristics of causation presupposed by the law. One of these, number (1), poses special problems only for the standard Humean theory. The neo-Humean theory is formulated specifically to get around the "mere correlation" and "mere epiphenomena" problems.[145] Still, plenty of difficulties remain.

Both Humean and neo-Humean theories have a difficult time in accounting for the noncausal status of preempted sufficient conditions in the preemptive overdetermination cases. After all, in the "two fires" cases where the fires do not join, why isn't the second fire as sufficient for the damage as the first? Indeed, isn't the second fire connected to the damage by the very *same* causal law that connects the first fire to that damage? If so, how can it be that the second fire is *not* a cause while the first fire is a cause? Neo-Humeans like Mackie and Wright try to distinguish the preempted fire from the preempting fire on the grounds that it is only "actual" or "present" sets of sufficient conditions that can be causes.[146] They use this requirement to say that the second fire was not present or actual where and when the house burned down. Yet their supposed spatiotemporal criteria turn out to be causal: when a victim is poisoned by A's tea, and then is shot dead by B,[147] the poison can be described as not "actual" or "present" only in the sense that it did not *cause* the death. "Causation" is not analyzed by "actual sufficient conditions"; it is presupposed by this second notion.

Both Humean and neo-Humean theories have a difficult time accommodating the scalarity and limited transitivity of legal causation—characteristics (5) and (6) above. Universal regularities and nomic sufficiency are all-or-nothing matters; they do not admit of the quantitative conceptions needed by the law.

On Humean or neo-Humean theories of causation, it is also a puzzle how causal chains can be broken by intervening third-party actions or by abnormal natural events—characteristic (7) above. Regularities and causal laws seem able to cross such interventions easily. Hart and Honoré's account of why causal chains are broken by these two kinds of occurrences does little to alleviate this puzzle. They argue that our central or paradigm case of causation is captured by transitive verbs of action, such

---

[144] See Armstrong, *What Is a Law of Nature?* (*supra* note 31).

[145] Ibid.

[146] Mackie, *Cement of the Universe* (*supra* note 55); Wright, "Causation in Tort Law" (*supra* note 40), 1795.

[147] This is Wright's example; see Wright, "Causation in Tort Law," 1795.

as "he did it." When deliberate acts of a third party or abnormal natural events intervene between the defendant's act and the harm, any analogy to these central cases is broken.[148] This is a particularly unconvincing use of the old paradigm-case semantics, which was itself never very convincing at the best of times.[149] We should be explaining the usage of causally complex verbs of action by causation, not the other way around.

A more promising explanation of why these two kinds of events break causal chains might run as follows. Abnormal conjunctions of natural events amounting to a coincidence are, in common parlance, inexplicable events. One might think that there are no causal laws that explain such events, nor any *regular* conjunction of such events, else we would not call them coincidences. Such coincidences are popularly regarded as "acts of God" precisely because it is pure chance, not scientific law, that explains their genesis. Likewise, one might think that there are no covering laws that explain intentional human behavior; such behavior is always, thus, on this view, a kind of coincidence. One might think this on (metaphysically) libertarian grounds: deliberate human choices are free in the sense that they are uncaused. They are thus like *literal* acts of God, being *first* causes of each chain they initiate. They too, then, would act as barriers through which the causal contribution of earlier factors could not penetrate.[150] Alternatively, one might regard deliberate human choices as one would the *metaphorical* acts of God to which natural coincidences are likened; while there are singular causes of such choices, there are no psycho-physical laws that make causal explanations of such choices possible.[151] Thus, such explanatorily anomalous items might again prevent the kind of regular or law-like connection needed by the Humean or neo-Humean theories.

Both of these construals are obviously rather tenuous. They illustrate the kind of metaphysics that would have to be true if, on the Humean or neo-Humean theories of causation, causal relations are broken by natural coincidences or deliberate human interventions. If such claims of inexplicability are too tenuous to be sustained, some other metaphysical theory of causation must be found to match the law's needs in this regard.

There is nothing in the ideas of a universal regularity or of a universal causal law (or in their associated idea of a sufficient condition) that precludes an omission from being a part of a set of conditions sufficient to guarantee some harm. The absence of an event can seemingly complete a set of conditions as well as the presence of an event can. Accordingly, the

[148] Hart and Honoré, *Causation in the Law* (*supra* note 47), 28–32, lxxvii–lxxxi.

[149] I discuss the paradigm-case argument in Moore, "The Semantics of Judging" (*supra* note 5), 281–92.

[150] This is an interpretation of Hart and Honoré offered in the essays by Kadish cited in note 93 *supra*. Hart himself questioned this libertarian interpretation of intervening causation when one of Kadish's papers was initially presented in Jerusalem in 1984.

[151] This is a rendering of Donald Davidson's "anomalous monism." See Davidson, *Actions and Events* (*supra* note 132).

Humean and neo-Humean theories fail to account for the legal idea that omissions are not causes.

The asymmetrical nature of causation, and the fixed direction of causation through time, are well-known problems for Humean and neo-Humean theories. Laws and regularities seem perfectly symmetrical in their linkages of events, so that an X/Y law or regularity is equally a Y/X law or regularity. Ad hoc stipulations are possible—as in Humean tenet (4)(b) above—but they fail to satisfy because the asymmetrical direction of causation is not linked in any way to the essential nature of causation (regularities or laws, on these theories).

Lastly, regularities or laws connecting (sufficient sets of) types of events to some other type of event are democratic between each type of event making up the sufficient sets. As Mill famously observed,[152] each type of event or other condition making up a sufficient set is equally entitled to be called a cause; only pragmatic features of speech license the honoring of one such type of event as "the cause." Such undiscriminating theories of causation cannot account for the more discriminating notion of causation presupposed by the law.

All of these same objections resurface if we reject both classic Humean theory and the neo-Humean theory but accept the probability theorists' own version of Hume. On this third major theory of causation, one again accepts most of Hume's four principles, except that one substitutes probabilistic laws for either universal laws or universal regularities.[153] The comparatively minor nature of this emendation of Humean and neo-Humean theories is what accounts for a sharing of the above-mentioned problems with those other two theories. The striking exception to this is the ability of a probabilistic theory of causation to make sense of both scalarity and limited transitivity. Probability is a more-or-less affair, making a quantitative assessment of causation seemingly easy. Probability also diminishes through successive links: if x makes y 40 percent likely, and y makes z 40 percent likely, x makes z only 16 percent likely. Causation can "peter out" on a probabilistic theory of causation.

The fourth and last major theory is the counterfactual theory of causation.[154] The nature of such a theory is easily missed because most usages of counterfactuals with relation to causation have nothing to do with this theory. Neo-Humeans, in particular, often state that causal laws are to be distinguished from accidental generalizations by the ability of the former but not the latter to support counterfactual judgments. In such a way, counterfactuals become intertwined with the idea of causal laws.

As a truly independent theory of causation, the counterfactual theory makes no essential use of the idea of causal laws.[155] When one asks the

[152] Mill, A System of Logic (supra note 36).

[153] See generally Patrick Suppes, A Probabilistic Theory of Causality (Oxford: Oxford University Press, 1970).

[154] The defining article on this theory is David Lewis's "Causation" (supra note 32).

[155] As Lewis makes clear in ibid.

counterfactual question, "But for x would y have occurred?," one is not asking whether there is an X/Y law. Rather, one is asking: In the possible world that is closest to the actual world but where x does *not* occur, does y then occur? Such a "closest possible world" will inevitably not be one where all causal laws of the actual world will hold true, and this may include the X/Y law, if there is one.

There are, of course, severe problems here in making sense of the modal notion of a possible world without holding constant the causal laws of the actual world. There are even worse problems in making sense of there being "closer" and "closest" possible worlds. But these problems go to the truth of the counterfactual theory. My enquiry here is one of fit, not of truth: how well does the counterfactual theory fit the law's demands on a concept of causation?

It is widely recognized that the counterfactual theory has a difficult time accommodating the law's firm notions that in the concurrent over-determination cases, both sets of sufficient conditions are causes, and that in the preemptive overdetermination cases, the preempting fire is the cause despite the existence of another sufficient condition (the preempted fire). For in both situations, the existence of a second fire that was inde-pendently sufficient to have caused the harm seems to imply that the first fire was not necessary.

The standard moves for getting around this objection are unsatisfactory. In the concurrent overdetermination situation, the usual idea is that we can individuate the harm finely enough so that *this* harm (in all its fine detail) would not have happened but for both fires joining and then burning the building as they did.[156] Such a response is both unsuccessful and unmo-tivated. It is unsuccessful because each fire that independently would have burned the house could be as qualitatively identical (to the joint fire that did burn the house) as you please, in which case no amount of fine-grained event-individuation will get rid of the troublesome conclusion that neither fire was necessary to producing that harm. It is unmotivated because there is nothing in the counterfactual idea of causation that suggests such ex-tremely fine-grained event-individuation, nor is there any principled way to say how far we should go down this road in any individual case. "As far as it takes to get the intuitively right causal conclusion" is about the only principle that comes to mind, and this "principle" relies on some non-counterfactual idea of causation for its content.

In the preemptive overdetermination cases, the response is that the factor(s) that interferes with the ability of the second fire to do its work would still have been present even if the first fire had been absent.[157] The fuel around the house, or the oxygen, for example, would have been consumed even if there was no first fire to have consumed them; the second fire then would not have consumed the house, making the first

[156] See the discussion in Wright, "Causation in Tort Law" (*supra* note 40), 1777–80.
[157] Lewis, "Causation" (*supra* note 32), 204.

fire necessary after all. David Lewis urges that the possible world in which such interfering factors remain present (despite the absence of the first fire, which in the actual world caused them to be present) is "closer" to the actual world than is the possible world where such factors are absent.[158] This strikes me as an ad hoc stipulation of what is closest, giving a meaning to "closest possible world" that seems dependent on some non-counterfactual idea of causation.[159]

The counterfactual theory also does not fare well in meeting other of the law's demands on the concept of causation. Necessity, like sufficiency, is an all-or-nothing property that does not admit of degrees; it is difficult to see how the counterfactual theory can accommodate the scalarity and the limited transitivity of legal causation. The counterfactual analysis also seems completely indifferent to supposed intervening causes; if the defendant's action made possible such intervention, then the defendant caused whatever harms that intervention caused on the counterfactual analysis. Omissions can be as necessary to any harm's occurrence as any actions; the counterfactual analysis of causation must thus resort to some noncausal basis to explain the absence of any general omission liability.

With regard to asymmetry, it is not true that just because x is necessary for y, then y must also be necessary for x. Therefore, as a first cut, the counterfactual relation is asymmetrical, as is the causal relation being analyzed. Yet in the overdetermination cases, each fire is sufficient for the harm; this means that the harm is necessary for each fire's occurrence. Without some analysis of causation that includes more than counterfactual dependence, the burning of the house at t_2 on this theory caused the occurrence of each fire at t_1. One can, of course, simply stipulate that causes must not succeed their effects, so as to bar this unwanted conclusion. Yet what in the supposed counterfactual nature of causation motivates this otherwise ad hoc stipulation?

Lastly, the necessary condition (or counterfactual) analysis of causation is highly promiscuous in its nonselectivity of causes.[160] Every necessary condition is equally a cause of some harm, in marked contrast to the law's assumption that most necessary conditions may simply make up the background field in which causes operate without themselves being causes.

None of the four major theories bequeathed to us by David Hume thus holds much promise in delineating a concept of cause to match that presupposed by the law. In principle, one of these theories could still be true, in which event one might say, "so much the worse for the law." Yet, in fact, the ten characteristics sketched above are not presuppositions about causation that are peculiar to the law. Here, as in so many other places, what the law has done is to reflect some very common-sense ideas about causation. Any theory that gives up on accommodating these ten

[158] Ibid.
[159] See Moore, *Placing Blame* (*supra* note 12), 351.
[160] See Moore, *Act and Crime* (*supra* note 2), 268–69.

demands also gives up on fitting the concept of cause we all use in daily life as we explain and evaluate various goings-on in the world. It is, in fact, a damning failure for a theory of causation not to accommodate most of these ten characteristics, as the rich discussions of these issues in the philosophy of science attest.[161]

Assuming that such accommodation is not forthcoming for any of these four theories, one is left to look elsewhere for a plausible metaphysics of causation. It has recently been suggested that we look to singularist, not generalist, theories of causation.[162] A singularist theory rejects Hume's reductionist fourth tenet sketched above. A singularist, that is, refuses to analyze the singular causal statement, "x caused y," in terms of causal laws. Such a theory will thus be committed to the existence of singular causal relations (and not, as are generalist theories, only committed to the existence of universal or probabilistic uniformities, or of universal or probabilistic relations between universals).

Whether such a singularist theory can meet the ten demands of the law depends entirely on what the nature of the singular causal relation is taken to be. If that relation is taken to be a kind of epistemic primitive, unanalyzable in terms of any other properties,[163] then the causal relation seemingly can possess these ten characteristics without difficulty—for, lacking any essential nature to constrain the analysis, why not? Yet such plasticity is not a virtue of a theory of causation, but a deficit. Alternatively, if the singular causal relation is taken to be one of physical force, as some singularists propose,[164] then some analysis which is a whole lot better than what we have will need to be found; it will have to detail how such forces "come to rest," peter out, or are cut off by some other force.[165] That, however, is a topic for another day.

Law and Philosophy, University of Pennsylvania

---

[161] Thus, it is standard to use the overdetermination cases, the asymmetry of the causal relation, the problems of epiphenomena and other mere correlations, and the selectivity of "the cause," as arguments testing the *truth* of various theories of causation, and not just the legal adequacy of such theories. See, e.g., Douglas Ehring, *Causation and Persistence: A Theory of Causation* (Oxford: Oxford University Press, 1997).

[162] This is Michael Tooley's suggestion, in his "Causation: Reductionism versus Realism," *Philosophy and Phenomenological Research* 50 (Supp. 1990): 215–36; and in Tooley, *Causation: A Realist Approach* (Oxford: Oxford University Press, 1987).

[163] As it is in Elizabeth Anscombe, *Causality and Determination* (Cambridge: Cambridge University Press, 1971); and C. J. Ducasse, "On the Nature and the Observability of the Causal Relation," *Journal of Philosophy* 23 (1926): 57–68.

[164] See, for example, David Fair, "Causation and the Flow of Energy," *Erkenntnis* 14 (1979): 219–50.

[165] These are the metaphors employed by the cause-as-force theorists in law, Joseph Beale (*supra* note 103), and Richard Epstein (*supra* note 9).

NEGLIGENCE*

By Kenneth W. Simons

I. Introduction

Faced with the choice between creating a risk of harm and taking a precaution against that risk, should I take the precaution? Does the proper analysis of this trade-off require a maximizing, utilitarian approach? If not, how does one properly analyze the trade-off?

These questions are important, for we often are uncertain about the effects of our actions. Accordingly, we often must consider whether our actions create an unreasonable risk of injury—that is, whether our actions are negligent.

Consider two examples:

(1) *The (mythical) Ford Pinto:*[1] The manufacturer of an automobile discovers that strengthening the fuel tank on 12.5 million existing vehicles would cost $11 per vehicle and would prevent 180 burn deaths, 180 serious burn injuries, and 2,100 burned vehicles. Calculating a unit cost of $200,000 per death, $67,000 per injury, and $700 per burned vehicle, the manufacturer concludes that the total cost of preventing the injuries is $137.5 million, while the accident losses that the precaution would prevent amount to $49.5 million. Accordingly, the manufacturer chooses not to take the precaution.

*I thank participants at the Boston University School of Law faculty workshop, as well as the other contributors to this volume, and its editors, for their helpful questions and comments. David Schur provided valuable research and editing assistance. I am especially indebted to Hugh Baxter, David Lyons, and Larry Solum for their advice.
[1] See Gary T. Schwartz, "The Myth of the Ford Pinto Case," *Rutgers Law Review* 43, no. 4 (Summer 1991): 1013–68, for a full account. See also Richard A. Posner, *Tort Law: Cases and Economic Analysis* (Boston: Little, Brown & Co., 1982), 225–26.
The account in the text reflects the popular mythical account of the Ford Pinto controversy, but it is misleading in critical respects. On the one hand, it ignores the question of Ford's responsibility and liability for an original negligent design in locating the fuel tank in an unusually vulnerable position. Of course, if the original design was defective, Ford should be liable for any resulting injuries, even if the post-manufacture precaution of strengthening the fuel tank was too costly. On the other hand, the dollar values were computed in 1973; Ford did not, in fact, rely on these figures in deciding against strengthening the fuel tank; the controversially low "value of life" figures were supplied by a federal government agency, not by Ford; the vehicles included all cars sold in the United States in a typical year, not just the Ford Pinto; and the study in question focused on rollover accidents, not rear-end collisions. See Schwartz, "Myth," 1020–28.

(2) *Two speeding drivers*: Amy drives at high speed to the hospital to obtain medical care for her child, whom she reasonably believes to be in need of emergency medical care. Beatrice drives at high speed to a critical business meeting; she reasonably believes that if she misses the meeting, there will be a significant delay in implementing a health delivery system, a delay that might cost several lives.

For many, the mythical Ford Pinto example epitomizes the defects of a utilitarian approach to negligence, especially the cost-benefit variant of that approach. And the comparison of Amy with Beatrice creates similar worries. Amy, but not Beatrice, seems justified in speeding; but this suggests that whether speeding is justified does not depend merely on the level of benefits that speeding would foreseeably produce.

This essay examines the question of responsibility for negligence mainly from the perspective of private morality, though it also analyzes legal norms embodying prohibitions against negligence. I hope to illuminate the complexity and richness of a problem that is often treated in reductionist fashion, not only by maximizing, utilitarian approaches, but also by some leading deontological approaches.[2] I also will suggest that negligence is better understood as an aspect of fault than as an aspect of corrective justice, contrary to the prevailing deontological views.

In Section II, I more carefully define the problem of negligence. First, I differentiate three senses of negligence (unjustifiable risk, conduct that violates a "reasonable person" criterion, and culpable inadvertence). This essay focuses on the first sense. Second, I emphasize that negligence presupposes an *ex ante* perspective. A negligent actor is one who either realizes, or should realize, that she has (unjustifiably) created a "low-probability" risk of harm (in a sense that will be explained). Third, I ask what is special about negligence. Do distinctive moral principles apply, or is negligence simply an instance of moral principles that would normally apply *ex post*, or *ex ante*, if we knew to a certainty the results of our actions? For the most part, I conclude, negligence is not a qualitatively distinct subject of moral inquiry.

In Section III, I explore negligence as an aspect of private morality, of personal responsibility: What should a person do when faced with a choice between risk and precaution? The common-sense moral precept that one should not be negligent, I conclude, reflects neither the coldly calculating utilitarian conception suggested by some forms of economic analysis of law, nor an absolutist deontological conception that blithely ignores the consequences, costs, or disadvantages of taking precautions

---

[2] Broadly speaking, utilitarian approaches judge the morality of an act by the aggregate utility of the consequences of that act, while deontological approaches instead (or also) consider whether the act is right or wrong in itself.

against risk. Beginning with a utilitarian account, I progressively modify the analysis to encompass a variety of nonutilitarian concerns. In the end, a pluralistic balancing approach is the most suitable for recognizing the breadth of values expressed in ordinary moral judgments about risk and in relevant nonutilitarian principles.

In Section IV, I briefly examine some distinctive features of law and analyze more carefully how legal norms of negligence should be defined and enforced, with particular attention to their relation to private moral norms.

Finally, in Section V, I suggest that principles of fault (or unjustified conduct), rather than of corrective justice (or the correction of harms), are the better interpretation and more convincing deontological justification of Anglo-American tort doctrine. The *ex ante* fault perspective supports a primary duty not to *act* negligently; the duty to compensate for harms one has negligently caused is distinctly secondary. Although compensation is ordinarily the only feasible remedy for isolated acts of negligence, this is a contingent fact, not a necessary implication of the deontological view of negligence.

II. The Scope of the Problem

A. What is negligence?

The topic of this essay is "negligence," by which I mean the failure to take a reasonable precaution against risks of harm. A "negligent" actor is one who acts as he should not have acted (or omits to act when he should have acted), and thereby creates an unreasonable risk of injury to others. This meaning of negligence has great importance in both morality and law, as I will try to show.

Negligence has other meanings. Negligence can characterize *beliefs*, rather than conduct. Thus, a person's beliefs might be negligent, meaning that her subjective conviction (that X is the case) is not based on reasonable grounds. Or she might be negligent in *not* believing Y (meaning that she should believe Y, or that a reasonable person would believe Y).[3] Moreover, a person might express a negligent *attitude* toward her conduct or the results of her conduct—meaning, perhaps, that she failed to show a reasonable degree of concern. Further, negligence can refer only to some aspect or aspects of a person's conduct, beliefs, or attitude, not to a global judgment about how she should have acted. We might conclude that a driver was negligent in not noticing a pedestrian, without necessarily

---

[3] However, the question of whether an actor's beliefs are reasonable is, in a limited way, relevant to whether the actor's conduct is reasonable. For we cannot make sense of the concept of an *ex ante* probability of a risk of harm without an epistemic account of risk. See Section IIB below.

implying that he must have been negligent and should have taken a precaution against causing an accident, *all things considered*.[4]

Three conceptions of negligence are especially important in morality and law. One conception emphasizes *unjustifiable risk*. A negligent act is one that creates an unreasonable or unjustifiable risk of future harm. A second emphasizes evaluation according to a *"reasonable person"* criterion. A negligent act, belief, or attitude is an act that a reasonable person would not perform, or a belief or attitude that a reasonable person would not harbor. A third conception emphasizes culpable or unreasonable *inadvertence*: the actor, although not consciously aware of a risk, should have been aware.[5] This conception is often employed to distinguish the negligent actor from the "reckless" actor who recognizes an unreasonable risk before taking it.

The three conceptions often overlap in fact, but they are distinct in principle. One might call an act negligent because it creates unjustifiable risks, apart from whether a "reasonable person" would act differently. (Under a so-called "subjective" test of negligence, you are not negligent if you do the best that you can given your personal capacities, but you still might create unjustifiable risks.) Conversely, one might employ a reasonable person test for evaluating choices that have virtually certain consequences. (In self-defense, for example, the predominant legal test essentially asks whether a reasonable person in the shoes of the defendant would

---

[4] Suppose no precaution would have avoided the accident, even if the driver *had* been paying proper attention.

In law, negligence is sometimes a culpability requirement of only one element of a crime, tort, or other legal norm, in which case it might have subsidiary importance. In the crime of assaulting a police officer, for example, liability might depend on the actor being at least "negligent" as to the risk that the person he is assaulting is a police officer; but the more serious culpability obviously is that entailed by the act and intention of assaulting a person.

[5] As a matter of ordinary language, "negligence" might indeed presuppose inadvertence:

> "Carelessness" and, consequently, "negligence" signify neither a "state of mind," such as indifference, nor merely a "type of conduct," such as a failure to take precautions against harm. "Carelessness" or "negligence" is a failure to give active measure-taking attention to the risks inherent in the successful prosecution of some activity.

Alan R. White, *Grounds of Liability* (Oxford: Clarendon Press, 1985), 102.

However, I use the term in the broader sense that White calls a "type of conduct." The ordinary language usage is, I believe, beginning to expand toward this broader usage. In any event, the sense of negligence as unreasonably risky conduct has more general importance in morality and law.

Of course, inadvertence is not always culpable. Moreover, when inadvertence is culpable, this might be because one should have adopted a different action-guiding strategy that would have avoided risk, not simply because one "should have been aware" of the risk. See Joel Feinberg, "Sua Culpa," in Feinberg, *Doing and Deserving: Essays in the Theory of Responsibility* (Princeton: Princeton University Press, 1970), 194 ("Overly attentive drivers with the strongest scruples and the best intentions can drive as negligently as inattentive drivers and, indeed, a good deal more negligently than experienced drivers of strong and reliable habits who rely on those habits while daydreaming. . . ."); see also Kenneth W. Simons, "Rethinking Mental States," *Boston University Law Review* 72, no. 3 (May 1992): 550–51.

employ the intentional force that the defendant employed.)[6] Similarly, one might call a belief negligent because a reasonable person would believe otherwise; but this explanation need not presuppose that the actor has unjustifiably *risked* anything.

The first conception, the unreasonable creation of (and failure to take a precaution against) a future risk of harm, is probably the most important sense of negligence. The second, "reasonable person" conception is essentially a legal conception, reflecting certain pragmatic and institutional features distinctive of law, as I suggest below. The third, "inadvertence" conception is not without importance, but the problems that it presents are beyond this essay's scope.

An additional point about scope concerns the interests that a norm against negligent conduct protects. In both law and morality, negligent creation of a risk of *physical injury* has special importance. Accordingly, I restrict my analysis here to the interest in avoiding physical injury.[7]

A final point about the negligence concept is this: Lack of justification is part of the ordinary meaning of negligence. This feature creates an interesting asymmetry between negligence and the other forms of wrongdoing with which negligence is usually compared. Negligence is a composite concept: a negligent actor both creates a risk (that he could have avoided) and is unjustified in doing so. By contrast, an intentional killer intends to bring about a death, and a knowing killer (as conventionally defined) is one who believes that death is a virtually certain result of his acts; but in either case, it is possible that the actor *is* justified (for example, because he is defending himself against a culpable aggressor). Lack of justification is built into the very concept of negligence, but it is not built into the concept of intentionally or knowingly bringing about a harm.[8]

This asymmetry could be eliminated either by building lack of justification into the definition of intentional and knowing harms, or by isolating lack of justification as a separate element of negligence. On the latter approach, negligence could be divided into two parts: the creation of

---

[6] This is an oversimplification. The law typically predefines certain categories of force as conclusively reasonable, and adds an explicit "reasonable person" criterion only for certain questions, including the actor's belief that force was being threatened or that defensive force was immediately necessary.

[7] To be sure, sometimes "negligence" is used in a wider sense. One can negligently forget a spouse's birthday, or make a negligent accounting mistake that causes only economic harm. And the epistemic sense of "negligence" is very wide: with respect to any subject whatsoever, a belief can be formed negligently (i.e., without sufficient grounds), or one can be negligent in failing to form a true belief (based on the grounds available). In law, however, the most important sense of negligence is with respect to risks of physical injury, for those are the dominant uses of negligence in tort and criminal law, which in turn are the dominant legal fields in which the negligence concept is used. In morality, as well, negligent creation of physical harms has special importance.

[8] However, certain descriptions of intentional harms do presuppose that the harms are unjustifiable. To "murder" another is not merely to cause his death intentionally, but also to do so without justification. I thank Larry Solum for this point.

(say) a "significant" risk to others, and the lack of justification for creating "significant" risks to others. In the end, however, we would need to create a range of norms governing risk-creation—a norm governing "trivial" risk-creation (under which we inquire whether the actor had a justification for creating a "trivial" risk), a similar norm governing "modest" risks that do not reach the level of "significant," and so forth. But it is simpler to state the requirement this way: The justification for imposing a risk must, in general, be stronger as the probability and seriousness of the risk increase.[9]

Still, building lack of justification into the very concept of negligence has this important implication: a judgment that an actor is negligent is an "all things considered" judgment that the actor was unjustified and should not have acted as he did. By contrast, a judgment that the actor intentionally or knowingly caused a harm has no such implication.

In sum, this essay considers what one should do, when faced with a choice between risk and precaution. It examines negligence as an aspect of action-guiding morality, and as a legal norm expressing that moral norm. Of course, distinct and important questions remain with respect to the kind of person one should be, how one should express appropriate concern about the negative consequences one justifiably brings about (including feeling regret, apologizing, or compensating the victim), and similar difficult topics.

B. The ex ante perspective

Implicit in negligence analysis is a crucial assumption: that personal responsibility is judged *ex ante*, not (merely) *ex post*. Suppose we are trying to decide whether someone has acted negligently—for example, by driving 40 miles per hour around a particular curve under particular road conditions, or by performing an operation using one medical technique rather than another. Then we should imagine ourselves "stopping the videotape" (so to speak) at the moment when the decision to act was made, and determining then and there whether the actor should have acted differently, in light of the comparative risks and other reasonably expected advantages and disadvantages of the alternative action. A negligent agent is one who acts as she should not have acted, judged from this *ex ante* perspective.

---

[9] In criminal law, when the probability and seriousness of the risk are sufficiently great (e.g., when one knowingly or intentionally kills), the burden of persuading the fact-finder of lack of justification sometimes shifts to the defendant, and the grounds of justification are also limited to certain narrow categories such as self-defense, defense of others, or necessity. These legal features reflect the fact that such risks are more often morally unjustifiable. But it would, in principle, be possible to have a "sliding scale" test encompassing all wrongs, and requiring stronger justification as the perceived probability of the risk approaches 100 percent.

If, instead, personal responsibility were judged *ex post*, negligence would not be a distinct topic of moral and legal inquiry. After the fact, we would simply ask whether, for example, the harm actually caused was justified in light of the benefits achieved by not taking a precaution. For example, even if you justifiably believed *ex ante* that driving your very sick child to the emergency room at a high speed was a *reasonable* risk to take, the *ex post* view asserts that if you caused property damage along the way, and if it turns out that speeding was not actually necessary to protect your child's health, then your conduct was simply *unjustified*. Conversely, even if it should have appeared to you *ex ante* that speeding to a business meeting in order to facilitate a valuable deal was an *unreasonable* risk to take, the *ex post* view asserts that if your speeding did not, as it turns out, cause anyone harm, then the speeding was *justified*.

The concept of *ex post* justification is certainly intelligible.[10] But if negligence is to be understood as an instance of personal fault, of unjustifiable risk-creation, it must be judged *ex ante*. A person's manner of driving, or a doctor's choice of medical technique, can be morally negligent whether or not it causes harm.[11] Of course, other forms of culpable behavior are also judged *ex ante*. It is culpable to attempt to kill someone, whether or not one succeeds. Negligent driving, attempted murder, and other forms of culpable conduct are culpable at least in part because of the bad consequences that the agent expects, or (if he does not expect them) that he should expect—or because of the bad consequences that he desires, or (if he does not desire them) that he should have a stronger desire to avoid.[12]

The *ex ante* analysis is not without controversy. It raises two significant problems, one normative, the other empirical. The normative problem is the question of moral luck. If I act in a particular culpable manner and a bad result follows, while you act in the same manner but a bad result does not follow, am I more to blame, because of my "bad luck"? Arguably, I am not, insofar as the difference in result might be due to factors not within my control, or factors for which I am not morally responsible: a sudden gust of wind, a third party's intervention, or the like. Those who believe

---

[10] A fully consequentialist account does have difficulty making sense of *ex post* justification, insofar as we cannot be certain, until the end of time, whether an act will turn out for the best. (I thank David Lyons for this point.) On the other hand, if we relativize the *ex post* judgment to the information known at the time of judgment, a qualified consequentialist assessment is possible. The idea of an *ex post* judgment of an act normally does presuppose such a relative judgment, occurring at some time subsequent to the act being judged.

[11] In law, negligence sometimes refers to unreasonable conduct, and sometimes to unreasonable conduct that incurs legal liability (usually, but not always, in the form of *ex post* compensation).

[12] The unjustifiable bringing about of a harm or death is often conceptualized as "wrongdoing" (the badness of an act), as compared to "culpability" (the blameworthiness of an actor). The latter category concerns the offender's degree of blame for bringing about a wrong, and thus includes the actor's mental states and excuses. For some doubts about this conceptualization, see Kenneth W. Simons, "Deontology, Negligence, Tort, and Crime," *Boston University Law Review* 76, nos. 1 and 2 (February/April 1996): 285–89.

to the contrary, who accept "moral luck," partially endorse the *ex post* perspective. They believe that whether the harm occurs, even if this is partly a question of luck, affects the seriousness of the wrong.

Thoughtful commentators disagree about moral luck.[13] For purposes of this essay, however, a resolution is unnecessary. For even if we do not completely reject the principle of moral luck, we should at least insist on some minimum *ex ante* responsibility as a predicate for any personal responsibility, even if we permit moral luck to *increase* blame or responsibility beyond that minimum.[14]

The empirical problem with *ex ante* analysis is the problem of hindsight bias. Cognitive scientists point out that ordinary people, and even professionals such as doctors, are "biased" in their assessment of *ex ante* probabilities in the following way: if a risky decision (such as the choice of a medical technique) is described as actually causing a harmful result, people give a much higher estimate of the *ex ante* risk than if the decision is described without reference to the result.[15] Insofar as this phenomenon is deep-seated, an unbiased, *ex ante* perspective will be very difficult to achieve. (For example, juries in tort cases would be unable to assess *ex ante* negligence fairly unless they were kept in the dark about whether the plaintiff had been harmed—a highly unrealistic option!)

A further question about the *ex ante* perspective concerns the proper understanding of *ex ante* "risk." If risk is to be an *ex ante* concept, it requires some sort of estimate of the probability of future harm (and benefit),[16] and that estimate will be based on evidence as of a certain point

---

[13] For endorsements of moral luck, see Thomas Nagel, "Moral Luck," in Nagel, *Mortal Questions* (Cambridge: Cambridge University Press, 1979); Bernard Williams, "Moral Luck," in Williams, *Moral Luck: Philosophical Papers, 1973–1980* (Cambridge: Cambridge University Press, 1981); and Tony Honoré, "Responsibility and Luck," *Law Quarterly Review* 104 (October 1988): 530–53. For criticism, see Feinberg, *Doing and Deserving*, 31–33; and Steven Sverdlik, "Crime and Moral Luck," *American Philosophical Quarterly* 25, no. 1 (January 1988): 79–86.

[14] See Michael S. Moore, "The Independent Moral Significance of Wrongdoing," *Journal of Contemporary Legal Issues* 5 (Spring 1994): 281; and Kenneth W. Simons, "When Is Strict Criminal Liability Just?" *Journal of Criminal Law and Criminology* 87, no. 4 (Summer 1997): 1111–12.

[15] Baruch Fischhoff, "For Those Condemned to Study the Past: Heuristics and Biases in Hindsight," in D. Kahneman, P. Slovic, and A. Tversky, eds., *Judgment under Uncertainty: Heuristics and Biases* (New York: Cambridge University Press, 1982), 341; Baruch Fischhoff, "Debiasing," in ibid., 427–31. For an experimental study finding hindsight bias in judgments of negligence, see Susan J. LaBine and Gary LaBine, "Determinations of Negligence and the Hindsight Bias," *Law and Human Behavior* 20, no. 5 (1996): 501–16.

[16] The risk that negligence analysis presupposes is typically risk about future harm, not about future benefit. Is this a necessary feature of the negligence concept? Is an actor negligent if the risk pertains only to the future *benefit* that might justify imposing the risk of harm, and not to the future harm itself? Suppose I speed my car through your rose bushes, with a high probability of causing property damage, because I believe I must bring my child to the hospital. If I am unreasonable in thinking that there is any significant health risk to my child, am I negligent in causing that damage? In a sense, I am; but the more typical sense of negligence confines the concept to low-probability risks of *harm*. This issue also arises with the use of defensive force, insofar as one might be justified even if there is only a modest probability that the use of such force will be socially beneficial (in preventing harm to the victim).

in time.[17] But should we evaluate future risk subjectively, from the perspective of the actual agent's knowledge base and capacity for inference, or instead objectively, that is, from a more ideal perspective? If we are to capture the broadest sense of negligence, the more ideal perspective is appropriate. (Otherwise, we could not describe as negligent an actor who inaccurately perceives his surroundings, or who reasons irrationally, even if his defects are due to his own culpable neglect, such as intoxication.)

Under the *ex ante* perspective, then, the concept of a negligent actor includes a person whose estimates of the risk of future harm are unreasonable or unjustifiable. And, to contrast negligence with the more serious form of culpability of *knowingly* creating a harm, I will draw a rough distinction between "low-probability" and "high-probability" estimates. The negligent actor is one who either realizes, or should realize, that she has (unjustifiably) created a "low-probability" risk of harm; while the "knowing" actor is one who either realizes, or should realize, that she has (either justifiably or unjustifiably) created a "high-probability" risk of harm.[18] As a shorthand, I will often refer to negligence as the unreasonable creation of a "risk" of harm, meaning a "low-probability" risk.

A final point about the *ex ante* perspective is as follows. The *ex ante* probability of harm distinguishes the actor who negligently creates a risk from the "knowing" actor who believes that the risk of harm is certain or almost certain. But how does the negligent actor compare with an *intentional* actor? Here we must distinguish two cases. One who intends to

[17] Probabilities can be either "objective" or "epistemic." That a coin toss will come up heads half the time is an "objective" probability; that a particular medical technique, even when carefully performed, creates a 2 percent risk of death is an "epistemic" probability. Epistemic probability is the form that is relevant to negligence. For a helpful explanation, see Stephen R. Perry, "Risk, Harm, and Responsibility," in David G. Owen, ed., *Philosophical Foundations of Tort Law* (New York: Oxford University Press, 1995), ch. 14.

One can also distinguish "risk" (probabilities that can be precisely measured) from "uncertainty" (all other probabilities). See W. Kip Viscusi, *Fatal Tradeoffs* (New York: Oxford University Press, 1992), 153–54; Nicholas Rescher, *Risk: A Philosophical Introduction to the Theory of Risk Evaluation and Management* (Washington, DC: University Press of America, 1983), ch. 8; and Clayton P. Gillette and James E. Krier, "Risk, Courts, and Agencies," *University of Pennsylvania Law Review* 138, no. 4 (April 1990): 1028 n. 1. But for purposes of understanding the general concept of negligence, this distinction is not critical.

[18] In this essay, I place quotation marks around the term "knowing" when I use the term in the special sense just noted in the text. This sense is unconventional in an important respect: we do not normally say that an agent has "knowingly" created a harm when the actor *should* have known that the harm was highly likely to occur. Rather, we reserve the term "knowingly" for one who *subjectively believes* that the harm was highly likely. I sometimes use the less conventional form in order to focus on negligence as a form of unreasonable risk-creation, and to contrast it with more risky behavior. If I were instead focusing on negligence as a form of inadvertent risk-creation, then I would contrast such inadvertence with knowledge as conventionally understood (subjective awareness of a high-probability risk of harm) and with one meaning of recklessness (subjective awareness of a low-probability risk of harm).

Negligent and "knowing" actors differ in their estimates of the *probability* of harm. A separate question is the *severity or extent* of the relevant harm. A *ceteris paribus* condition is implicit in my comparison of negligent and "knowing" actors. Negligently creating a risk of a nuclear disaster is obviously more culpable than "knowingly" stepping on someone's foot.

bring about a *harm* should not be considered merely "negligent," even if he believes that he has only a small chance of success in bringing about the harm. (The attempted or successful murderer who actually and reasonably believes that the *ex ante* chance of success is 20 percent is not merely "negligent.") On the other hand, if an agent does not intend to bring about a harm, but does intend to create a *risk* of harm, she should probably be considered merely negligent, so long as the *ex ante* probability of harm is low. (A teenager who drives near a pedestrian for the thrill of endangering him would thus be deemed negligent, but not an intentional wrongdoer.)[19]

How we should classify the intentional and the conscious creation of varying degrees of risk is inevitably arbitrary. But one point of recognizing a distinct moral and legal "negligence" category is to identify a type of culpability that is less serious, and easier to justify, than the culpability of (unjustified) knowing and intentional actors. Those who intend to cause *harm* most clearly fall within a more serious category. Those who intend neither harm nor the risk of harm clearly fall within a less serious category. The categorization of those who intend only to create a *risk* of harm is less certain; it depends on the specific account of culpability one endorses.[20]

C. What is special about negligence?

Negligence, in the sense of the (unjustifiable) creation of a future risk of harm, is generally understood to pose distinct problems and to deserve separate analysis in morality and law. But this raises a puzzle. What is so special about posing a *risk* of future harm? Does the circumstance that the actor posed a lower rather than a very high risk of harm really create a distinct moral (and legal) category, governed by distinctive principles? For the most part, I will conclude, it does not.

If negligence is not a distinctive problem, then we should not look for distinctive principles to judge whether or not a risky act is justifiable. Once we have determined the proper moral and legal analysis of harms that will occur with certainty (or of harms that have already occurred), we

[19] Of course, if she intends to cause the pedestrian fear, then she indeed intends a "harm," insofar as fear is an actual (though intangible) harm. Still, one who intends a more serious form of harm (such as physical harm) is more culpable.

It is much easier to justify intentionally creating a *risk* of a given type of harm than to justify intentionally causing that harm. As an instance of the former, consider the promoter of a trapeze act who chooses not to use a safety net, in order to make the act more exciting.

[20] On a deontological account, whether an actor intends to create a risk, as opposed to creating it as a knowing side-effect, is indeed relevant to whether, all things considered, the actor's risk-creation is justified, as I will argue below.

There is much more to say about the relevance of intention and of other conative states such as "culpable indifference" to risk or to harm. For a thorough account of the moral and legal differences between cognitive and conative mental states, see Simons, "Rethinking Mental States."

would simply apply the same analysis when the probability of harm is less. Moreover, if the widest sense of negligence is used, encompassing not only risks of *physical harm* but also the endangering of any morally relevant interest or value through human action, then negligence seems to describe nothing less than the whole of action-guiding morality.[21]

Consider, for example, the doctrine of double effect. That doctrine, supported by many deontologists, asserts that there is an important moral distinction between intending to cause a harm and knowingly bringing about a harm as a certain side-effect or further effect of what one intends: intending to harm (and thereby causing harm) is absolutely forbidden, or is subject to a heavy burden of justification, while knowingly causing harm is easier to justify. (Contrast intending to kill civilians in wartime, in order to terrorize the population, with knowingly killing the same number of civilians as a regrettable side-effect of attacking a military target.) This doctrine could also apply, however, where the probability of the harm occurring is less than a virtual certainty. Intending to create a serious *risk* of harm (and thereby causing the harm) would then be absolutely or prima facie wrong, while knowingly creating a serious *risk* of harm would be easier to justify. (Contrast Alice driving near a pedestrian for the thrill of endangering him, with Betty driving just as close to a pedestrian as an unavoidable incident of bringing her sick child to the hospital.)

The same puzzle arises with moral norms other than the doctrine of double effect. Consider the famous "trolley problem."[22] A trolley's brakes fail. If I do not turn the trolley, it will kill five workmen; if I turn the trolley onto a spur of the track, it will kill one. Should I turn the trolley, thereby causing one death; or decline to turn the trolley, with the result that five will die? It is difficult to see why the problem should change if one discounted the expected harm from each choice by an equivalent amount. Thus, suppose I know that the brakes have a 10 percent (rather than 100

---

[21] Ronald Milo adopts a wider version that he calls "moral negligence" to encompass "any kind of morally wrong act due to a particular kind of shortcoming on the part of the agent—namely, a culpable failure to take those precautions necessary to assure oneself, before acting, that what one proposes to do is not in violation of one's moral principles." Ronald D. Milo, *Immorality* (Princeton: Princeton University Press, 1984), 84. This is an *epistemic* duty, to ascertain whether one's act would violate moral principles; Milo points out that an additional question is whether (and in what way) we are culpable for nevertheless taking the risk of violating our principles. See ibid., 85.

[22] See Philippa Foot, "The Problem of Abortion and the Doctrine of the Double Effect," in Foot, *Virtues and Vices* (Berkeley: University of California Press, 1978), 23–24; and Judith Jarvis Thomson, "The Trolley Problem," in Thomson, *The Realm of Rights* (Cambridge: Harvard University Press, 1990), ch. 7. The trolley problem is often posed in contrast with the following "transplant" problem: a surgeon is considering whether to carve up an unwilling patient and transplant his organs as the only means available to save five other lives. See Thomson, *Realm of Rights*, 137. Some explain the impermissibility of the trade-off in the transplant case, and its permissibility in the trolley case, by reference to the doctrine of double effect (insofar as the deaths of the workmen supposedly are foreseen but not intended, while the death of the patient supposedly is intended). But I agree with Thomson and others that this explanation does not suffice.

percent) chance of failing, whichever direction the trolley takes. The expected value of the harm from turning the trolley is now 0.1 deaths (rather than one), and the expected value of the harm from *not* turning the trolley is now 0.5 deaths (rather than five). Under this variation, the same considerations still inform the moral question of whether one must, may, or may not turn the trolley. If diverting a threat under these circumstances is morally permissible when the alternative expected harms are one versus five deaths, it appears to be permissible when the alternative expected harms are a 10 percent probability of death versus a 50 percent probability (or 1 percent versus 5 percent).

Moreover, if probabilities were a critical and independent determinant of moral permissibility, then what we are permitted to do would rest on the nature of the risk description, which is sometimes arbitrary. For example, when actors engage in repetitive or far-reaching activities, it is somewhat arbitrary whether one describes the risks in temporally or spatially limited terms, or instead in more capacious terms; yet the first description will yield a lower probability than the second. The chance that I will injure someone through moderate speeding over my lifetime might be 15 percent; while the chance that my moderate speeding will injure someone in a single trip to the beach is vanishingly small.[23]

Further, even when one creates an intentional or knowing harm, one can be justified in so acting even when the reasonably foreseeable probability that the justifying facts exist is considerably *less* than one. One might, for example, be morally entitled to use defensive force so long as one reasonably believes that there is a *significant risk* that one would otherwise suffer substantial, unavoidable harm.

A number of reasons might be offered to explain why negligence is a distinctive subject of moral and legal analysis. A first reason can safely be

---

[23] Or, to return to the Ford Pinto example, the risk that any *individual* Ford Pinto vehicle would catch fire and cause a burn death (that reasonable precaution would have avoided) was .0000144, over a fleet of 12.5 million vehicles; but the expected number of burn deaths over the entire fleet of Ford Pintos was a probability greater than one—namely, 180 expected deaths. See Simons, "Rethinking Mental States," 292 n. 69.

To be sure, a more careful identification of the relevant frame of reference for assessing probabilities might eliminate this arbitrariness. (Compare the question of whether an individual owner must take a precaution, with the question of whether Ford must do so for all cars with the problem.) Under this approach, however, it becomes difficult to identify risks, acontextually, as "low" rather than "high" probability, i.e., as negligent rather than "knowing."

In the end, a completely acontextual identification of risks as "low" rather than "high" seems impossible. The distinction between negligence and "knowledge" appears to be a relative judgment. Consider a question that has troubled legal scholars: whether a manufacturer of a product who knows that a small number of users (out of a much larger class) are virtually certain to suffer physical harm should be treated as "knowingly" inflicting that harm. If the issue is whether his conduct demands as strong a justification as a manufacturer who knows that every user will suffer the same degree of physical harm, the answer is clearly no. And if the issue is whether the conduct of either manufacturer would demand as strong a justification if the risks of harm were substantially lower, again the answer is clearly no. But there might be no nonarbitrary way to characterize any of these four cases as "negligent" or "knowing" in an absolute sense.

put to one side. This is the point that many negligent acts involve a risk that will not eventuate in physical harm for a considerable period of time. Thus, such acts might, in the interim, cause significant emotional harm to potential victims. (Consider the fear that the presence of toxic chemicals induces in exposed populations.) But this point does not distinguish negligent from higher-probability harms; for it depends on latency, not on the fact that the risk is less than certain.[24]

A second, and more persuasive, reason why negligence is considered a distinctive moral and legal concept flows from the following fact: people often react to *lower*-probability risks of future harm in a distinctive way. For example, people often overestimate the magnitude of very small probabilities.[25] Moreover, when probabilities are lower, people might be more likely to differ among themselves, and more likely to differ with "expert" assessments, about the magnitude of risk. These differences could be due to such cognitive heuristics as framing (whether an option is characterized as suffering a loss, or instead as failing to obtain a possible benefit), the availability heuristic (whether similar instances easily come to mind), anchoring (where people have difficulty altering their initial estimates), and representativeness (whether others report high or low risks of the same phenomenon).[26] But these variations in perspectives are likely to be much less when the expected probabilities are high (for example, if a new food product is almost certain to cause slight indigestion in all users). One plausible response to these variations in perspectives is the effort to develop a unifying methodology; and a utilitarian calculus based on subjective preferences is an obvious candidate. In short, the permissibility of imposing lower-probability risks might be thought to demand a distinctive *type* of moral justification.[27]

A third reason for distinctive treatment only warrants a quantitative, not a qualitative, distinction between negligence, on the one hand, and higher-probability or "knowing" harms, on the other. This is the point that, often, the smaller the risk of harm, the easier it is to justify creating that risk. Thus, intentionally causing the death of another human being

---

[24] Thus, one might know to a certainty that one will suffer a harm either in the immediate *or* in the distant future; the distant harm might cause a different type or degree of emotional stress than the immediate harm. To be sure, the contemporary emotional harm produced by long-latency risks that are virtually *certain* to result in ultimate harm will often be disproportionately greater than the harm produced by less certain risks. (It will often be more than five times as painful to worry about a virtually certain future death than to worry about a 20 percent risk of death.) But these emotional harm cases do not justify distinct treatment of negligence in general. Not all cases of risk generate significant emotional harm. (In many cases, the risk is unknown or underappreciated.) At most, the considerations just discussed would justify special treatment of certain emotional harm cases.

[25] See Viscusi, *Fatal Tradeoffs*, 150.

[26] See Gillette and Krier, "Risk, Courts, and Agencies," 1091–93; and Richard H. Pildes and Cass R. Sunstein, "Reinventing the Regulatory State," *University of Chicago Law Review* 62, no. 1 (Winter 1995): 55–64.

[27] In the end, however, I will reject this argument.

when one believes that that result is a certainty is almost always (or, on some views, always) unjustifiable; but intentionally creating what one believes to be a modest *risk* of death is more often justifiable. Deliberately running someone over with your car is obviously more difficult to justify than deliberately creating a risk that you will run someone over.

A fourth reason, related to the previous one, is the possibility that the deontological constraint against knowingly or intentionally causing a person serious harm is *much* more stringent than the constraint against negligently causing such a harm. The difference might be qualitative, not merely quantitative. Consider the following two examples (for which I thank Leo Katz). Suppose Alfa speeds in the vicinity of a pedestrian, knowing that she is almost certain to kill him, because this is the only way to save the lives of five passengers whom she must bring to the hospital. Benna speeds in the vicinity of a pedestrian, aware that she is running a 20 percent risk of killing him, because that is the only way to save the life of *one* passenger whom she must bring to the hospital. Many would conclude that Alfa acted impermissibly while Benna acted permissibly. Most would at least conclude that justifying Alfa's conduct is more difficult than justifying Benna's. And yet the justifying benefits in each case are five times the expected harm. (Put another way, if 20 Alfa-situations and 100 Benna-situations arise each year, then the Alfa-situations and Benna-situations will each result in 20 deaths and the saving of 100 lives annually.)

These examples suggest a special moral concern, and a constraint of special stringency, when an actor creates a very high risk of killing another. The concern is not just an extension of the principles of justification that apply when one creates a much lower risk of death. For the constraint requires *more* than a simple proportional increase in the justifying benefit to correspond to a similar increase in the level of risk.[28]

With this important caveat, I conclude that negligence is not as distinctive a topic of moral and legal inquiry as it is often believed to be. Negligence often does not demand special analysis, except as a matter of degree. For example, the basic point of the doctrine of double effect, that knowingly causing X is much easier to justify than intending to cause X, is no less valid when X is a small risk of harm than when it is a virtual certainty of harm. (Consider a variation of the terror-bombing example: intentionally exposing a group of noncombatants even to a small *risk* of future harm is more difficult to justify than exposing them to such a risk

---

[28] To some extent, the law recognizes this distinction, for it sometimes shifts the burden of persuasion, and narrows the grounds of justification, when the conduct moves from negligent to knowing or intentional. See note 9 *supra*.

I have suggested that a constraint of special stringency applies when a person knowingly or intentionally creates a high risk of *death*. Whether an unusually stringent constraint also applies to a person who knowingly or intentionally creates a high risk of a *lesser* harm than death is less certain, but I cannot explore the matter here.

as a known but regrettable side-effect of a purely military action.) Thus, normative principles that apply to risks one reasonably believes are certain to occur should ordinarily also apply to lower-probability risks, *mutatis mutandis*. (On the other hand, as a *factual* matter, the creation of lower-probability risks will more often be justifiable.)

III. Private Morality

This section examines negligence, not as a question of law, but as an issue of personal responsibility. How should we choose between risk and precaution?

Although most moral theorists have given far more attention to intentional and knowing harms, we should consider how different moral perspectives would affect the analysis of negligence. In this section, my approach is to examine common-sense moral judgments and convictions about risk, and also to relate these to more general consequentialist and deontological frameworks.

Utilitarianism is often offered as the best account, or even the only plausible account, of when risky conduct is justifiable.[29] I thus begin with this perspective, before examining others.

A. Utilitarianism

Some would analyze negligence as a straightforward question of rational choice, as follows. If an agent would incur all the costs and reap all the benefits of risky action, she would rationally maximize the benefits and minimize the costs. Then we could extrapolate from this intrapersonal case to the interpersonal case. This approach has some initial plausibility.

Suppose you are a hermit living in the woods, and you are trying to decide how sturdy a deck to build as an addition to your house. Simplifying, you might consider three options—a flimsy deck, a sturdy deck, and a super-sturdy deck. What would be relevant to your decision? The sturdier the deck, the more costly it will be, in terms of labor and materials. But a stronger deck will last longer, and it will also be safer. It might also offer other advantages, including the ability to hold grills and lawn furniture, or firewood, or your private sculpture collection.

Most people would consider factors such as these in deciding what type of deck to build. Many of the factors require at least rough estimates of probability. How long will a "sturdy" deck last? We know that the probability of its lasting one year is very high; ten years is fairly high; one hundred years, perhaps low. Similarly, how likely is an injury? How do you expect to use the deck—for eating? Reading? Training your pet lion? Moreover, most of us would (if only implicitly) normally consider the *marginal* costs

[29] See Heidi M. Hurd, "The Deontology of Negligence," *Boston University Law Review* 76, nos. 1 and 2 (February/April 1996): 249–72.

and benefits. Is it worth the extra money to build a super-sturdy deck, as opposed to a sturdy deck, relative to the extra durability, safety, and functionality benefits (discounted according to their probabilities)?

This intrapersonal example provides intuitive support for a norm of rational egoism. It seems plainly irrational not to consider all the costs and benefits of alternatives. The prudent course, it appears, is to maximize benefits and minimize costs. It is then tempting to extend the intrapersonal analysis to the interpersonal context.

Suppose you, the hermit, decide to rejoin society. You expect to invite others to your house. Now the expected benefits of building a deck include the benefits to others, the sociability benefits to you, and the collective benefits of friendship and community. And the expected costs might include greater expenditures of labor and material, and new risks of personal injury to others.

Most of these new costs and benefits are similar in kind to the costs and benefits in the intrapersonal case. Why not conclude, then, that the maximizing approach appropriate in the intrapersonal case is also appropriate in the interpersonal case?

Some have so concluded. For example, in his influential book *Economic Analysis of Law*, Richard Posner employs precisely this argument.[30] An individual will balance the marginal cost or burden (B) of taking a precaution against the marginal probability (P) and magnitude (L) of the loss to that individual if the precaution is not taken. If B is less than P times L, the individual will rationally take the precaution.[31] But if the losses are to others, we need a legal liability rule to ensure that the individual takes the correct precaution. (The idea that courts should balance B, P, and L to determine whether an actor is negligent was espoused by Judge Learned Hand in the now-famous "Learned Hand formula.")[32]

This is the informal, intuitive case for a maximizing, aggregative conception of negligence. Reasonable care in the choice of risky activities

---

[30] Richard A. Posner, *Economic Analysis of Law*, 5th ed. (New York: Aspen Law and Business, 1998), 179–83.

[31] Actually, this test (known as the "BPL" test) contemplates that the rational actor would aggregate the different risks that would be prevented by a precaution, e.g., risks of minor physical injury (discounted by their probability), of major physical injury (also discounted), of death, of major property damage, of minor property damage, and so forth.

[32] The landmark case is *United States v. Carroll Towing Co.*, 159 F.2d 169, 173 (2d Cir. 1947). Whether Judge Learned Hand actually intended his "BPL" test to be the sort of cost-benefit economic test that Posner defends is a controversial question.

In his early writing, Richard Epstein analyzes the contrast differently, concluding that extrapolation from the intrapersonal to the interpersonal case justifies a general rule of *strict* liability. However, his focus is not on which decision among risky alternatives is best, but rather on who should bear the costs of the decision. In the intrapersonal case, he points out, all the costs and benefits accrue to the actor. In the interpersonal case, however, the actor might derive the benefits while the victim might bear the costs. Epstein suggests that the actor has no right to dump the costs of his action on another. Richard A. Epstein, "A Theory of Strict Liability," *Journal of Legal Studies* 2, no. 1 (January 1973): 159. For a critique of this argument, see Ernest J. Weinrib, *The Idea of Private Law* (Cambridge: Harvard University Press, 1995), 171–75.

consists of maximizing the net differential between benefits and costs. What is wrong with this conception?

The problems are many. First, even in the intrapersonal case, it is not true that an actor ought always to maximize the net benefit. A maximizing strategy, because of the *way* in which it values, would undermine some kinds of morally important relationships and interests.[33] For example, it is not wrong to weigh financial gains against the value of friendship in some circumstances (as when one is deciding whether to move to a new city in order to obtain a more lucrative job). But it does not follow that friendship always has a price attached to it; one should not break a date with a friend because a third person offers payment to do so. The latter practice would undermine the value of friendship in a way that the former would not.[34] More pertinent to a discussion of negligence, one should not create what would otherwise be reasonable risks to oneself in order to promote a personal value that would be inconsistent with one's own objective self-worth. For example, one should not drive at very high speed on a deserted street simply to experience the thrill of a near-death experience; but one may, and perhaps should, drive at an equivalent speed in order to reach a hospital in time to save one's own life.

Second, the intrapersonal case normally raises no problem about *consent*. By contrast, in the interpersonal case, others endangered by your risky conduct might not consent at all; or if, in some sense, they do accept the risk, they often do not consent in as full a sense as you do in the intrapersonal case.

Third, the extrapolation to the interpersonal case implicitly characterizes society as a kind of interest-maximizing "super-person." Yet, as many critics of utilitarianism have argued, this characterization ignores the point that society is composed of individuals, each with his or her own life to lead.[35] A principle that aggregates the welfare or utility of all persons (and then requires maximization of that utility) thus needs a distinctive justification.[36]

Fourth, the extrapolation is indeterminate and potentially both too weak and too strong. The constraints on risky action are too *weak* if the original actor (in the intrapersonal case) is one who took very little interest in his own safety; for the result of the interpersonal extrapolation is that he will be justified in imposing enormous risks of harm on others relative to small benefits to himself. (At the same time, however, he will be willing

---

[33] See, generally, Elizabeth Anderson, *Value in Ethics and Economics* (Cambridge: Harvard University Press, 1993), 66–73.

[34] See ibid., 70, discussing Joseph Raz, *The Morality of Freedom* (Oxford: Clarendon Press, 1986), 349.

[35] See John Rawls, *A Theory of Justice* (Cambridge: Harvard University Press, 1971), 27–29; see also Bernard Williams, in J. J. C. Smart and Bernard Williams, *Utilitarianism: For and Against* (Cambridge: Cambridge University Press, 1973), 116–17; and Raz, *Morality of Freedom*, 271–87.

[36] At the same time, simple extrapolation will *fail* to capture the collective benefits that can be achieved only through social interaction. When and only when the hermit rejoins society, the collective benefits of friendship and community are possible.

to *accept* enormous risks to himself relative to small benefits to others.) On the other hand, the constraints on risky action might be considered too *strong* if the original actor is one who placed extraordinary value on his own safety. For then the interpersonal result is that he will only be justified in imposing slight risks to others, even when the benefits to himself are great. (At the same time, he will be willing to accept only small risks to himself even when the benefits to others are great.)

Can these problems be overcome by a less catholic view of what it is reasonable to do in the intrapersonal case? Perhaps a reasonable regard for your own safety does require that you give it at least weight X (or precisely weight Y). Then we could extrapolate that you should give the safety of others at least weight X (or precisely weight Y) in the interpersonal case.

Still, this extrapolation is problematic. In the intrapersonal case, it is highly implausible that all persons must give any precise weight (Y) to any of their ethically relevant interests, including their safety. At most, you might be ethically obliged to give your safety at least a certain weight (X), while you would be permitted but not required to give it more weight. But even if this is so, there is still no reason to assume that you must give weight X, but need not give more than weight X, to the safety interests of others when your actions affect them. It is quite plausible that you are entitled to show very little regard for your own safety or health relative to your other interests (such as love of excitement, desire not to burden others, and the like). It is not plausible that you can extrapolate this entitlement to the situation in which the safety or health risks are imposed on others while the corresponding benefits belong to you.[37]

Another way to see the problem with extrapolation is to compare a case in which a third party is in a position where she must make a decision for

[37] In his attempt to explain American tort law, Stephen Gilles employs the extrapolation approach (which he terms the "single-owner" heuristic) in an especially interesting way. He asks what value the average injurer would assign to precaution costs. But, recognizing that the average injurer might assign too low a value to the expected accident costs to others, Gilles also asks what value the average *victim* would assign to those costs. "Because the average injurer and the average victim, taken together, constitute the average *person*, the inquiry reduces to whether the average person would take the precaution if he or she bore both the costs and benefits in full." Stephen G. Gilles, "The Invisible Hand Formula," *Virginia Law Review* 80, no. 5 (August 1994): 1035.

In American tort law, however, the negligence test employs a "reasonable" or "ideal" valuation, not an "average" valuation. Gilles tries to handle this objection by referring to the accident valuation of victims, not of injurers. Still, it seems that he should refer to the "reasonable" precaution valuation of injurers. For the average injurer might place undue weight on the cost of certain precautions (e.g., the average Boston driver is probably unduly worried about his pride when he refuses to allow other drivers to share the road).

Gilles ultimately settles on an "altruistic reasonable person standard," asking what care an "average reasonable person takes of his or her own person and property" (ibid., 1037, 1038). The problem remains, however, that "average" and "reasonable" (or ideal) standards can deviate.

If one moves from an "average" to a "reasonable" valuation, one has moved from a factual, descriptive account of utilities to a normative, social valuation. (See the discussion below of a modified utilitarian calculus.)

the benefit of one person with a case in which she must make a decision for the benefit of two or more persons. Consider the following argument from Judith Jarvis Thomson (with her example slightly altered): If D is in a position where she must decide what is best for Y, she is permitted to make some relatively close marginal trade-offs (for example, cutting out unconscious Y's kidney to save Y's life) which we would not countenance if D were in a position where she must decide what is best for both X *and* Y (cutting out unconscious X's kidney to save Y). To be permissible, the trade-off in the latter case must tilt much more strongly in Y's favor than the trade-off in the former case.[38]

In the end, extrapolation is unpersuasive. People differ greatly in their concern about their own safety, not to mention the type and strength of their other interests, purposes, and values that would (intrapersonally) justify risking their own safety. (Some place enormous value on their own health, others on the pleasures of risk-taking, or on saving time or expense; and so forth.) People have a moral prerogative or permission, within a rather wide range, to balance these interests in many different ways. Yet it is doubtful that moral principles for *interpersonal* risk-imposition should be so variable or that the acceptable range should be so wide. The interpersonal variations are complex and often unknown to the risk-imposer (or victim). Just as important, accommodating these differences within an interpersonal moral norm governing risk-imposition seems wrong in principle, not just difficult in practice. I should not feel free to ride my bicycle more quickly and recklessly in the vicinity of a depressed or masochistic person than in the vicinity of a person who attaches extraordinary value to his personal appearance and thus is extraordinarily averse to personal injury.

On the other hand, the utilitarian approach does have some attractive features. It demands that we consider carefully all the consequences of our actions. In the particular context of negligence, this demand seems especially apt, since even the immediate consequences are variable and, by definition, not highly probable. Choosing a particular risky course of action A as opposed to course of action B (or no action C) might have numerous possible consequences, differing in their probability and their magnitude if they occur. Utilitarianism offers a method for combining these disparate consequences via a single formula.

B. Modified utilitarianism

Utilitarians are not without responses to some of the above problems. In several ways, they might tinker with the utility calculus to bring it

---

[38] See Thomson, *Realm of Rights*, 197–99. It might be permissible to take *blood* from unconscious X in order to save Y.

closer to ordinary judgments about risk and closer to common-sense morality.

First, consider ordinary attitudes toward risk. Clayton Gillette and James Krier point out that lay opinions about risk, although they systematically differ from expert opinions in various ways, are not necessarily inferior. Experts tend to focus only on overall mortality or morbidity in comparing risks: "a death is a death." Lay opinions tend to be much richer and more nuanced. This richness might reveal, not irrationality, but different values— for example, justifiable concerns about whether a risk has been voluntarily incurred, or will result in a catastrophic harm, or will have delayed effects, or is irreversible in its effects, or is man-made as opposed to natural.[39] Still, Gillette and Krier seem to assume that these values can be accommodated within a broadly utilitarian, "cost-minimization" framework.[40] Extending their analysis, one might add a "premium" to those risks that are involuntarily as opposed to voluntarily incurred. And one might similarly modify the utilitarian calculus to accommodate the cognitive heuristics (such as framing and anchoring, mentioned above) that laypersons often use.

Second, utilitarianism is often criticized for its indifference to how benefits and burdens are distributed. But a broader form of consequentialism can accommodate concerns about the fairness of distribution.[41] For example, the best action might be that which maximizes benefits, subject to a distributive condition. The condition might be ensuring a minimum level of benefits for all affected persons, or not producing certain extremes of inequality (especially with respect to imposing losses rather than failing to confer benefits), or not concentrating large harms (or the risk of large harms) on certain individuals.

We must be careful, however, to distinguish two questions: (1) whether the fairness of distribution is relevant to the action a person may or should take, and (2) how the costs and benefits of a (concededly) permissible action should be distributed. Negligence as a form of culpability or wrongdoing addresses only the first problem. (In tort law, strict liability,

[39] Gillette and Krier, "Risk, Courts, and Agencies," 1071-79.
[40] Ibid., 1028 n. 2. They do, however, acknowledge a possible role for distributive principles.
[41] See, e.g., Derek Parfit, "Equality or Priority?" The Lindley Lecture (University of Kansas, November 21, 1991); and David O. Brink, Moral Realism and the Foundations of Ethics (New York: Cambridge University Press, 1989), 270-73 (where Brink argues that an objective form of utilitarianism can endorse a distribution-sensitive theory of value).
Concern about distributive effects is a powerful reason not to adopt Richard Posner's suggested wealth-maximization version of utilitarianism. This version evaluates choices by the criteria of willingness and ability to pay, rather than utility. But these criteria create an additional problem of distributive justice, beyond that entailed by utilitarianism. For example, under the wealth-maximization approach, it is better to endanger the safety of a poor person than the safety of a wealthy person: "a person should feel free to drive faster in a poor than in a wealthy neighborhood because expected accident costs are on average lower in the former," as Posner candidly concedes. Richard A. Posner, "Wealth Maximization and Tort Law: A Philosophical Inquiry," in Owen, ed., Philosophical Foundations, 110.

or liability without fault, addresses the second problem: even though the strictly liable actor might have acted permissibly, fairness or some other principle requires him to pay the costs of his action.)[42]

Often, in deciding what action a person is permitted or required to take, we properly do *not* consider how the costs and benefits ultimately should be distributed. The classic examples are necessity cases: a starving backpacker is permitted to break into an unoccupied cabin and steal some food, and a ship owner is permitted to damage another's dock to save his crew or even his ship, even though each should ultimately pay for the goods that he consumes or damages.[43]

Sometimes, however, distribution is relevant to what an agent may or should do in the first instance. Suppose a thief issues this demand: "I'll take $500 from X, or instead I'll take $10 from each of seventy people. You choose." A proper concern for fair distribution of losses supports your choosing the second option. Or, more relevant to the negligence debate, suppose a company is deciding how to dispose of toxic waste, either by imposing a modest risk of future harm on a community that is poor, or that has already been the dumping ground for waste; or by imposing a slightly higher risk of harm on a more wealthy or more pristine community. The latter choice is certainly defensible. One's choice of location should be sensitive to the distribution of the risk of harm, as well as to its aggregate amount; and in some cases, it would be better to distribute a larger amount of risk if that is the only way to distribute the risk more fairly.[44]

---

[42] Criminal law does not redistribute costs. Therefore, if strict criminal liability is justifiable, the justification must be different. See Jules Coleman, *Risks and Wrongs* (New York: Cambridge University Press, 1992), 222–23; and Simons, "When Is Strict Criminal Liability Just?"

[43] However, it is also proper to consider not only the actor's primary conduct, but also his ability to insure against the risks of his conduct. The permissibility of engaging in some activity might itself depend on ability to absorb certain risks of one's conduct. We forbid people from driving without insurance, in part because we want them to be financially responsible even for the non-negligent accidents they cause. See Kenneth W. Simons, "Jules Coleman and Corrective Justice in Tort Law: A Critique and Reformulation," *Harvard Journal of Law and Public Policy* 15, no. 3 (Summer 1992): 880. See also Thomson, *Realm of Rights*, 159.

[44] What counts as a fair distribution is beyond the scope of this essay. In environmental law, government regulators have increasingly attended to the distribution of risk as well as its aggregate level. See Pildes and Sunstein, "Reinventing the Regulatory State," 44.

The special concern that many feel about "catastrophic" loss is partly based on a distributive concern:

> Imagine . . . a decision maker who is forced to choose between two actions. The first action poses a 1 in 1,000 chance of causing 100,000 deaths spread randomly across the country; the second has a 1 in 1,200 chance of causing the near obliteration of a city of 100,000. A rational decision maker could obviously select the first alternative, notwithstanding its larger expected loss.

Gillette and Krier, "Risk, Courts, and Agencies," 1078.

Moreover, imposing a large harm (or the risk of a large harm) on a single person is often impermissible when it is offset only by small benefits to each of a large number of persons,[45] and even when it is offset only by the avoidance of small *losses* to each of a large number of persons. As an instance of the latter, consider an example from Ronald Dworkin: "Suppose ... that my child's life depends on a noisy ambulance that annoys a large number of people who would collectively pay more not to be annoyed than all the funds I have."[46]

A third way in which utilitarianism can be modified to accommodate some of the above criticisms is that preferences can be filtered or "laundered."[47] A more objective form of utilitarianism can replace private preferences, pleasure, happiness, or utility, with "social" utility.[48] On this view, for example, the utility calculus would give no weight to the pleasure that a reckless driver obtains from the thrill of endangering others, or to the pleasure that racists obtain from the knowledge that they have created an environmental hazard that disproportionately endangers blacks.

Of course, this qualification of utility is itself problematical in several ways. The qualification undermines some of the advantages of the utilitarian approach, including its neutrality among preferences or forms of utility. It is also indeterminate. How does one distinguish items with no (or even negative) social utility from those with positive social utility? If we give no weight to a person's thrill from endangering others, should we similarly give no weight to a person's thrill from driving at high speed, where the thrill does not actually depend on the risk to others' safety?

Moreover, the laundering approach can be ad hoc; sometimes it appears to reflect *non*utilitarian moral judgments, not a neutral criterion of "socially acceptable" utility. And, most importantly, the approach sometimes misdescribes the *way* in which the relevant moral principle operates. For example, many utilitarians would grant that racist or sadistic preferences should not be even part of the justification of actions. But do we best reflect this moral principle by modifying the general utilitarian calculus to ignore such preferences? Consider a case in which the actual motive of the actor was racist or sadistic, but other legitimate justifications were available to him. (Suppose an employer fires a minority employee for racist reasons, but, unknown to the employer, the employee

[45] See Thomson, *Realm of Rights*, 166–68; and Raz, *Morality of Freedom*, 276. For example, the conclusion that it is wrong to humiliate another for fun is unaffected by the number of persons who would derive pleasure from such an act. Anderson, *Value in Ethics and Economics*, 69.

[46] Ronald Dworkin, *Law's Empire* (Cambridge: Harvard University Press, 1986), 307.

[47] See Robert E. Goodin, *Utilitarianism as a Public Philosophy* (Cambridge: Cambridge University Press, 1995), ch. 9 ("Laundering Preferences").

[48] See Brink, *Moral Realism*.

was embezzling funds.) A properly "laundered" utilitarian calculus might still consider the action justifiable, while a nonutilitarian approach might condemn the action, notwithstanding its utilitarian net benefits.[49]

This concern that "laundering" mischaracterizes the underlying moral principles applies as well to the first modification of utilitarianism discussed above—namely, translating the special characterization of certain risks (as "involuntary" rather than "voluntary," or man-made rather than natural) into a quantitative "premium" in the utilitarian calculus. Again, we might not correctly capture the reason why we are concerned about "involuntary" risk impositions if we were simply to apply a risk premium (for example, if we first computed the appropriate value of a "voluntary" risk, and then, in the case of an "involuntary" risk, multiplied the first value by two). Rather, fully voluntary acceptance of certain risks (such as the risks of experimental medical treatment) might mean that the creation of those risks is not wrongful at all. And, for risks that vary in their "involuntariness," the best analysis might have a different structure than a utilitarian calculus. (It might, for example, forbid the imposition of any high-level involuntary risks, and permit the imposition of low-level involuntary risks only if the risks either are widely shared in the community or are absorbed only for a limited period of time.)

C. Nonutilitarian approaches

1. *Rejecting the utilitarian rationale itself.* A more basic critique rejects the utilitarian notion that maximizing the aggregate good consequences for all persons is the correct moral principle for problems of risky action. First, it appears that the utilitarian approach cannot definitively characterize negligent acts as instances of wrongdoing. Second, the utilitarian approach can appear heartless and cold-blooded. The first critique, I will suggest, is more potent than the second.

A comprehensive utilitarian approach considers all consequences that affect utility. The consequences include the long-term as well as the short-term, and the best decision procedure as well as the best decision (considered in the abstract). On such an approach, the right thing to do in balancing risks of harm against benefits does not merely depend on which choice has the greater expected utility as measured by *immediate* consequences (such as anticipated risks of injury to others, and anticipated benefits to the actor).

For example, in deciding how fast to ride my bicycle, I should not consider only whether the immediate risks of injury to others outweigh

---

[49] In Goodin's terminology, the prohibition on racially motivated actions might reflect a violation of rights and thus might be better understood as an "output filter," not the "input filter" accomplished by laundering preferences. Goodin, *Utilitarianism*, 133–37.

the immediate benefits to myself and others (in terms of pleasure, speedily arriving at my destination, and so forth). In principle, I should also consider whether my decision will cause others (such as pedestrians) to adjust their behavior in specific ways, and, more subtly, whether my decision will reinforce or undermine social norms governing risky behavior.

Moreover, we should also consider, as a second-order question, which individual decision procedures should be employed. Should agents, in the process of deciding what to do, explicitly try to maximize benefits and minimize costs? Should they instead defer to certain rules of thumb or norms about safe behavior (such as conforming to social custom)? Should they be entirely benevolent, ignoring all of their own interests? Should they be entirely egoistic, considering only their own interests? Should they delegate decision making, where feasible, to a parent, or a trusted friend? In principle, any of these approaches might turn out to be optimal (considering both the immediate costs and benefits of the action and the costs and benefits of varying decision-making procedures for producing the optimal action). More likely, different approaches will be optimal in different circumstances (such as consumption of goods in a market, or health decisions when one is incompetent).

A utilitarian approach can indeed address these complications, but in doing so, it will lose much of its supposed simplicity. More fundamentally, however, utilitarianism encounters great difficulty in accounting for the judgment that negligent acts are a species of wrongdoing or culpability. For utilitarianism (and consequentialism generally) cannot fully explain the retrospective orientation of important categories of moral judgment. Suppose Emily rides her bicycle too fast, in light of the expected risks and benefits, and thereby endangers you. She is negligent if, from the *ex ante* perspective, her balancing of the risks and benefits was unreasonable (whether or not her conduct results in harm). Having done wrong, she deserves censure, and she might incur other duties: perhaps she ought to apologize, or take affirmative steps to give you medical or other aid, or pay for the resulting harm. Why is she subject to blame or to these other duties? On the utilitarian account, it is because holding her to be under these duties will produce the best overall consequences. That means we must wait, as it were, to see how things turn out, before we can confidently blame her (or before we can justify any other duty). Will blaming her have desirable consequences overall? It might, but it might not. Blaming her might be misunderstood by her devoted friends and family, blinded by love, as an *ad hominem*, undeserved attack; at the same time, blaming her might only have the most trivial effect in strengthening the social norm against negligent bicycling, or in discouraging her own negligent bicycling.

One of the most important nonconsequentialist features of retributive-justice accounts of criminal law, and of corrective-justice accounts of tort law, is their retrospective orientation.[50] In deciding whether to punish a negligent act, or to enjoin it, or to assess damages for the harm that results from it, we need not wait to see how many future acts of negligence these responses would deter. And the same is true of our simple decision whether to blame the actor as wrong or culpable. (Nor is it the case that we must at least be able to predict that such future deterrent benefits are reasonably likely.)

Of course, this retrospective orientation does, in the case of negligence, coexist with a prospective and consequentialist feature—the feature that the action is culpable or wrong because it unreasonably risks a *future* harm, a harm that would be a consequence of the action. But this consequentialist feature is limited, and does not undermine the essentially nonconsequentialist quality of blaming, of retributive justice, or of corrective justice.[51]

Another problem with utilitarianism is that, in some versions, it turns subtle and important questions of personal or social choice into problems of calculation. Permitting these difficult trade-offs to depend on the result of a computation seems to devalue the interests at stake. It can even seem cold-blooded.

This concern is part of the reason why the Ford Pinto example troubles so many observers. A consequentialist has some powerful replies, however. First, he might say that the objection ignores reality. Our choices do have consequences, which we should not ignore. Indeed, whatever choice we make might have unfortunate consequences for human welfare: the choice against precaution increases risks of personal injury, but the choice to take a precaution might interfere with the function of a product, or price it out of reach of a significant number of consumers. One who claims that we should never trade off life or bodily injury against other interests is asserting a moral position that is unrealistic or simply fanatical.

Second, one of the reasons that the Ford Pinto example provokes outrage is a sense that the actor, having made a justifiable choice, might feel free to ignore the negative consequences of his decision. But, the consequentialist could point out, this conclusion need not follow. One might defend an actor's making a calculated trade-off, but at the same time insist that he has secondary duties with respect to the harm that he

---

[50] Strictly speaking, the orientation is "non-prospective" rather than retrospective. Our judgment that a negligent act deserves retributive blame could be contemporaneous with (or even prior to) the act. What I want to distinguish (as "prospective") is a judgment that depends on whether the *further* consequences of the act are optimal.

[51] Indeed, the *ex ante* and action-guiding features of the negligence perspective mean that negligence is *necessarily* a consequentialist doctrine. But this is so only in the very limited sense that the harmful consequences immediately risked by the negligent act are critical to the actor's culpability. In precisely the same sense, the wrongfulness of attempted murder, too, depends on the expected or intended consequences of the attempted murderer's acts. Only in this limited sense is our reason for blaming negligent actors or attempted murderers necessarily "consequentialist."

justifiably causes—including a duty to inform the potential victims, to apologize, and sometimes even to compensate for some or all of the harm that they will suffer.[52]

2. Nonutilitarian balancing. How can one endorse the careful evaluation of (at least some) consequences without turning the problem of choice into a problem of calculation? First, one should concede that there is normally no single metric—such as money, or wealth, or utility (in any nontrivial sense)—into which all relevant values can be translated. Commensurability in this strong sense is normally unattainable.[53] Second, at a minimum the moral agent could explicitly consider a list of relevant factors, ignoring some factors as irrelevant, and identifying the direction in which the relevant factors point.[54] The Learned Hand test (discussed earlier) could itself be so understood. It instructs that the following factor militates against taking the risk and *in favor* of taking a precaution: namely, the expected accident costs if no precaution is taken. And it might instruct us to count the following factors as militating *against* taking a precaution: the additional risks that taking a precaution would create, and the *socially reasonable* costs to the agent.[55] (This last qualification excludes such "costs" as loss of pleasure from indulging sadistic and racist preferences, as discussed above.)

This approach does not yet provide much guidance or much predictability. But can we really do any better? On one view, moral judgment consists only in an intuitionistic (that is, pluralistic and essentially unstructured) balancing of reasons.[56]

A nonutilitarian account *can* give a more principled explanation than this of how we should balance or trade off values. If we balance, even at the margin, the analysis need not collapse into a maximizing, utilitarian framework.

Balancing need not be utilitarian, or even consequentialist. For example, in deciding whether to turn a trolley and divert a threat from five people onto one, or in deciding whether to stop the trolley by throwing

[52] We might also ask producers of dangerous products to contribute to a social insurance fund for the victims.

On the general idea that tragic choices require a morally sensitive actor to show regret, see Martha Nussbaum, *The Fragility of Goodness: Luck and Ethics in Greek Tragedy and Philosophy* (Cambridge: Cambridge University Press, 1986). See, generally, Jeremy Waldron, "Rights in Conflict," in Waldron, *Liberal Rights* (Cambridge: Cambridge University Press, 1993), 214–15.

[53] See, generally, Cass Sunstein, "Incommensurability and Valuation in Law," *Michigan Law Review* 92, no. 4 (February 1994): 779–861.

[54] For an application of this approach to social regulation of risk, see Pildes and Sunstein, "Reinventing the Regulatory State," 64–66, 127 (where they endorse the "disaggregation" of costs and benefits so that citizens and decision makers make value choices more openly).

[55] In American tort law, the *Restatement (Second) of Torts* catalogues relevant *social* interests to be balanced. And the commentary to the *Restatement* does not emphasize the incentive effects of the balancing test that the *Restatement* endorses, as one would expect if the test were thoroughly consequentialist. See *Restatement (Second) of Torts*, sections 291–93 (1965).

[56] See Rawls, *A Theory of Justice*, 34–40 (where Rawls criticizes such intuitionism, and also distinguishes it from metaethical and epistemological intuitionism).

a passenger off the trolley onto the tracks, I do need to make comparisons: but I might be attending only to the stringency or relative weight of the possible victims' claims against me, or of my duties not to kill them, and not to the long-term *consequences* of permitting this type of action.[57] In the context of risky action, it is just not plausible that one has an absolute, exceptionless duty not to create any risks greater than some specified level;[58] nor is it the case that if my duty is not absolute, the limits to the duty must be consequentialist.[59] Or, to take a more prosaic example, my duty to tell the truth can conflict with my duty of loyalty to a friend. In deciding whether to tell a benevolent lie to protect my friend's feelings, I might weigh the stringency of each duty, and the extent to which alternative actions would undermine the value of friendship and the values underlying a duty to tell the truth. But such a balance is consistent with many deontological accounts, and is quite different from a consequentialist summing up of the net future benefits and harms flowing from my action.

On the other hand, consequentialism, and in particular utilitarianism, appears to offer a relatively simple, and therefore attractive, method of balancing. It is thus understandable that balancing and trade-offs (especially at the margin) are closely identified with utilitarian analysis.[60]

Is it possible to develop a clear, nonconsequentialist formula for negligence, one that accommodates competing values but avoids the problems of a pure (or even a distribution-sensitive) maximizing approach? Consider two efforts—a "disproportion" test, and a "freedom versus security" balancing test. I will conclude that these efforts, while promising, are inadequate. The first is too ill-defined, while the second is too reductionist to capture the full array of values that should be balanced.

a. Disproportion test. One possibility is a disproportion test. On this approach, if an injurer's risky conduct would expose potential victims to expected risks of $P \times L$ (probability of loss times magnitude of loss) and could be avoided only at marginal cost B, then, in order for the injurer to

---

[57] See Thomson, *Realm of Rights*, chs. 6 (on trade-offs) and 7 (on the trolley problem). Moreover, even within the narrower frame of the alternative actions available, the agent's permission to divert the trolley onto an innocent victim does not imply a permission to throw an innocent passenger onto the tracks to stop the trolley (as Thomson observes). Thus, even the immediate consequences (in terms of net lives saved) are not dispositive of permissibility.

[58] For one endorsement of such a threshold test, see Weinrib, *The Idea of Private Law*, 148–50. For a response, see Kenneth W. Simons, "Justification in Private Law" (book review of Weinrib), *Cornell Law Review* 81, no. 3 (March 1996): 711–12. Some proponents of threshold tests mean to endorse strict liability rather than negligence; my disagreement does not extend to them.

[59] But see Hurd, "Deontology of Negligence." For a critique, see Simons, "Deontology" (*supra* note 12), 290–95.

[60] Accordingly, many tort commentators view the "BPL" test and even the vaguer balancing test of the *Restatement (Second) of Torts* as necessarily utilitarian. See Richard Wright, "The Standards of Care in Negligence Law," in Owen, ed., *Philosophical Foundations*, 250 (listing sources).

be permitted to impose the risk, P × L must not only be greater than B, it must be *much* (or disproportionately) greater.[61] This could also be called a "thumb on the scale" test: in weighing the potential victim's interest in personal security against the potential injurer's interest in freedom of activity to impose risks, we should place a (heavy) thumb on the scale, giving special weight to the interest in personal security.[62]

These tests sound plausible and appealing, but, unless substantially recast, they provide a useless criterion. If we have identified the appropriate factors to balance, and if the method of balancing is also justifiable, then these tests say the following: One should not take a risk (as opposed to taking a precaution against the risk) simply because the advantages of taking the risk are greater than the disadvantages. Rather, one should take such a risk only if the advantages of doing so are *much* greater than the disadvantages (normally, only if the benefits to the injurer are much greater than the expected injuries to victims, discounted according to their probability).

This approach is either indeterminate or irrational. For unless one has a common metric or other justifiable method for measuring the competing interests or values, how does one know whether the interest in physical security and safety is "just" weightier than the interest in freedom of activity, as opposed to "much" weightier, so as to apply the "disproportion" or "much weightier" criterion? On the other hand, if one *does* have a common metric for measuring the competing interests, or if one does have some other justifiable method of balancing, why shouldn't the actor simply choose the alternative that furthers the "weightier" value, even if that value is only weightier by a peppercorn?

Let me be more specific. Is the interest in avoiding the risk of having one's arm broken "usually" greater than the interest in driving ten miles per hour faster, or "usually" greater than the interest in avoiding the expense of a more effective bumper?[63] These questions are meaningless unless we specify more clearly both the degree of risk of a broken arm, and the disadvantages of taking a precaution. Yet once we specify these factors, and adopt a justifiable method of balancing, shouldn't we indeed balance "at the margin"? That is, shouldn't we examine whether the

---

[61] Some have asserted that British courts employ the disproportion test, rather than a supposed simple cost-benefit American test, to gauge negligence in tort law. See Gilles, "Invisible Hand Formula," 1026 n. 8; and Gregory C. Keating, "Reasonableness and Rationality in Negligence Theory," *Stanford Law Review* 48, no. 2 (January 1996): 352–53. It is possible, however, that the British test merely shifts the burden of persuasion, and therefore does not create the problems noted in the text. See Gilles, "Invisible Hand Formula."

Ernest Weinrib appears to endorse some combination of the disproportion test and the "threshold of risk" test. See Simons, "Justification in Private Law," 702–4.

[62] See Keating, "Reasonableness," 354: "The *magnitude* of the harm that death, serious physical injury, and property damage threaten to persons' capacity to pursue their conceptions of the good is *usually* much greater than the *magnitude* of the harm threatened by increased precaution costs."

[63] See ibid.

advantages of any particular action (even a narrowly defined action) exceed the disadvantages?

I suspect that the worry about weighing "at the margin" is a legitimate concern about turning moral analysis into a bloodless form of calculation. What one should do should not depend on plugging numbers into a formula. And we should often be suspicious of methodologies that purport to balance along a "razor's edge,"[64] such that trivial factual differences in the weight of a given factor render an otherwise permissible action impermissible (or vice versa).

These concerns are well-founded if the most justifiable method of balancing requires a strong form of commensurability, that is, translation of all values into a single metric such as money or wealth. But weaker forms of commensurability are more plausible for most moral decisions, including decisions about risky alternatives.[65] For example, consider the question of whether a doctor should disclose to a patient all adverse risks of medical treatment of which the doctor is aware. There is a range of possible rules, from a rule of no disclosure (if the doctor believes that nondisclosure of a particular risk is in the best interest of the patient), to a rule of relatively full disclosure (of all risks that most patients would consider material), to a rule of disclosure tailored to the second-order preference of patients (that is, disclosure of whatever scope of risks the patient herself prefers to be disclosed).[66] These different rules embody different conceptions of the proper scope of patient autonomy and physician discretion in decision making about medical risks. Whether a given risk should be disclosed in a given case is much more likely to depend on these subtle value judgments than on the precise magnitude of the risk or on the precise financial or temporal burden to the doctor.

At the same time, however, even this more qualitative form of balancing will be sensitive to facts. Accordingly, close questions will sometimes arise about whether, for example, a particular risk is one that most patients would consider material. If we conclude that a doctor should disclose a 1 percent risk that hernia surgery will result in permanent numbness at the location of the surgery, but we find this a very close question, then

---

[64] See ibid., 353.

[65] Incommensurability between values A and B occurs in the strongest sense when adding to or subtracting from value A does not affect the choice between A and B. See Raz, *Morality of Freedom*, 322–26. (An example might be the question of whether Bach or Darwin was "more brilliant"; if either had been a little more or less brilliant than he in fact was, it would still be the case that neither was more brilliant than the other. Anderson, *Value in Ethics and Economics*, 55–56.)

Such incommensurability is rare. For example, if the choice between patient autonomy and burdens to a doctor of disclosing a risk were strongly incommensurable in this sense, then no increase or decrease in the burden to the doctor, or in the value of autonomy, would affect the choice. But that seems highly doubtful. In cases of risky activity, I believe, the competing values are, at most, incommensurable in this strong sense only within a limited range or "margin." See Raz, *Morality of Freedom*, 327–28.

[66] The British adopt a form of the first rule; most American jurisdictions adopt a form of the second; and some American jurisdictions permit the patient to waive disclosure, thus recognizing a version of the third.

the doctor might have no duty to disclose a 0.5 percent risk. In this sense, "marginal" decisions will still occur.

The "thumb on the scale" approach might also be designed to express special concern for one value in the balance, *relative* to some other, deficient way of valuing it. But this concern can be accommodated in a balancing test without suggesting the implausible conclusion that there will never be marginal cases. For example, one might conclude that the social value to be given to patient autonomy is greater than the value that most patients actually express in the marketplace (either because of marketplace distortions in capturing the private valuations of patients, or because recognizing patient autonomy is a collective social good, the value of which transcends the sum of individual valuations). Thus, even if patient surveys reveal that most patients only strongly care about risk information that has at least a 20 percent probability of changing their mind about treatment, the "thumb" might justify a rule that doctors disclose risk information with at least a 10 percent probability of changing a patient's mind.[67] Notice, however, that this use of a "thumb on the scale" is much more limited than the general use described earlier.

b. Balancing "freedom" against "security." Another proposal to systematize the nonconsequentialist balancing of values is the suggestion that the morality (and legality) of actions risking physical injury depends on a balance of "freedom" against "security"—the freedom of the injurer to engage in activity, compared to the interest of the victim in security against physical harm. A number of academics have supported some version of this balance,[68] and the theories of Immanuel Kant and John Rawls have been offered as justifications for such a balance.[69]

---

[67] For another example of a "relative valuation" approach, see Thomson, *Realm of Rights*, 197–99, where she argues that, to save A's life, a guardian can authorize a fairly serious nonfatal operation on A (such as cutting off A's leg), while a guardian of both X and Y cannot balance so close to the margin in authorizing an operation on X in order to save Y's life. More generally, insofar as extrapolating from an intrapersonal to an interpersonal case is feasible and defensible, we should at least apply a significant "premium" and should require a much greater total benefit in the interpersonal case than in the intrapersonal, in order to justify nonconsensual imposition of risks on others who do not receive any direct benefit from imposing those risks.

[68] See Keating, "Reasonableness," 319–27 (where he discusses balancing the injurer's freedom of action against the victim's interest in physical security); and Weinrib, *The Idea of Private Law*, 84–113 (where he discusses deriving tort principles from a paradigm of "doing and suffering"). Professor Richard Wright, in "Rights, Justice, and Tort Law," and "The Standards of Care in Negligence Law," in Owen, ed., *Philosophical Foundations*, describes corrective justice in tort law as expressing the Kantian notion that adversely affecting another's person or stock of resources is objectively inconsistent with the other's equal negative freedom. I agree with many of Wright's conclusions, including the inadequacy of the utilitarian account and its failure to explain the relevance of the actor's motive, the victim's consent, and other important factors. However, I am not persuaded that Wright's own reductionist framework can explain all the features of tort doctrine that he purports to explain. Rather, I believe that those features are more readily justified by a pluralistic analysis.

[69] See Keating, "Reasonableness"; Weinrib, *The Idea of Private Law*; and Wright, "Rights, Justice, and Tort Law."

This contrast is indeed helpful, but it is only part of the story. A number of values relevant to the permissibility of action do not fit easily into the categories of "freedom" and "security." One example is that just mentioned—patient autonomy in making decisions about medical treatment. If we reduce this value to "security," we ask only whether the patient's interest in decision making will in fact promote her physical safety. This approach ignores the possibility that some sacrifice in physical security is warranted in the interest of the patient's freedom to decide. If our only concern was the patient's physical well-being, we might support a significant degree of medical paternalism; but many would reject paternalism in favor of protecting a patient's ability to make decisions about her own bodily integrity.

    c. Balancing: A pluralist approach. In the end, a pluralist form of balancing is the most attractive approach. What does a pluralist approach look like? Let me note some important features.

    First, the actor will often be promoting social as well as personal purposes in his risky activity. Rather than broadly classifying all these purposes as aspects of an undifferentiated interest in "freedom of activity," we should attend to, and differentially value, the particular goods being sought. More virtuous motives, such as an altruistic concern for one's children, or for the welfare of a person in need of rescue, can be valued more highly than personal pleasure from the thrill of athletic effort. Serving a community's medical needs might have more weight than responding to people's consumption desires.[70]

    Second, qualitative features of the risk and of the harm can be important. For example, is the risk fully understood by those in danger? Is it voluntarily incurred?[71] Are its benefits and burdens widely and equally shared? Does it conform to general expectations of the level of risk typical of the activity? With respect to harms, are they easily compensable (in money damages or otherwise)? Do they seriously interfere with the victim's long-term life plans?[72]

    Third, rather than attending only to the advantages and disadvantages that the actor's risky activities foreseeably produce, we should attend also to the *reasons* why the actor was willing to take the risk, and to other features of the context in which the risk of harm was brought about. Insofar as the activity produced a risk of physical harm, was this risk or this harm intended, or merely an unfortunate side-effect? (Recall the "doc-

---

[70] See Anderson, *Value in Ethics and Economics,* 158–63.

[71] Whether explicit consent is a morally necessary precondition of imposing risk on others depends, in part, on the gravity of the risk. Below a certain threshold of risk, perhaps, no explicit consent is required. But the requirement of obtaining consent turns on the kind, as well as the level, of risk. Direct physical invasions of bodily integrity, such as through medical treatment, are far more likely to require explicit consent than are other risky acts with no greater, or even a lesser, risk of causing physical harm.

[72] See Keating, "Reasonableness," 344. However, I find problematic Keating's explicit reliance on a Rawlsian social-justice framework to justify private tort doctrine.

trine of double effect" examples, above.)[73] Did the actor at least make genuine efforts, even if inadequate, to reduce the risks? Was the risk part of a beneficial package that the actor offered to the victim? (Compare the risks to a product's consumer with the risks to a bystander injured by a product.)

One important aspect of how the risk is created is whether the actor has a special responsibility not to bring about wrongs, that is, an agent-relative duty not to act in certain ways, rather than an agent-neutral duty to minimize bad states of affairs. Consider here Robert Nozick's concern about a "utilitarianism of rights."[74] Nonconsequentialist norms sometimes forbid an actor from wronging a person, or violating his rights, even when the actor would thereby prevent others from committing more wrongs (or committing more rights-violations). For example, such norms forbid lying to prevent more lies, or convicting one innocent person in order to prevent more innocent people from being convicted.[75] The following example is more relevant to the topic of negligence: "A doctor may not neglect the health of her patient, a corporate executive whose demise will cause his firm to cease neglecting its workers' health."[76]

Fourth, the permissibility of a risky act sometimes depends on the social role of the actor. Professionals are properly held to special standards of skill and integrity; parents have special duties to their children; friends have special obligations to one another. Once again, it is doubtful that these special responsibilities can be reduced to concerns about "freedom" and "security."

Fifth, permissibility might also reflect basic distinctions between acting and omitting to act, or between harming and failing to confer a benefit. Thus, we might permit D to expose P to X amount of harm in order to avoid exposing P to Y amount of harm, so long as X is less than Y.[77] And yet we might not permit D to expose P to X amount of harm merely in order to provide a larger quantity Y of social *benefits*. (*A fortiori*, D may not expose P to X amount of harm merely to provide a larger quantity Y of *personal* benefit to D.)

[73] The actor's purpose or intention to bring about a harm has enormous significance. Even if such a purposeful actor reasonably believes that he is unlikely to succeed (and thus would otherwise be considered no more than negligent), he will usually be considered more culpable than an actor who believes he is likely to bring about the harm but does not intend it. See Simons, "Rethinking Mental States," 478–82.

[74] Robert Nozick, *Anarchy, State, and Utopia* (New York: Basic Books, 1974), 28. See also Raz, *Morality of Freedom*, 278.

[75] See, e.g., Thomas Nagel, "Personal Rights and Public Space," *Philosophy and Public Affairs* 24, no. 2 (Spring 1995): 89–90 (where Nagel relates this prohibition to the idea of an agent's "inviolability"). See also F. M. Kamm, "Non-consequentialism, the Person as an End-in-Itself, and the Significance of Status," *Philosophy and Public Affairs* 21, no. 4 (Fall 1992): 381–89.

[76] Anderson, *Value in Ethics and Economics*, 73.

[77] We might permit this even where Q rather than P is exposed to Y amount of harm, if P and Q are sufficiently similar in their vulnerability to an original threat of harm, as in a variation of the trolley problem.

In sum, when we evaluate the moral permissibility of risky action, we should draw qualitative as well as quantitative distinctions between the goods or values at stake. Just how those qualitative distinctions should be captured is a difficult question. Perhaps some values have an absolute "lexical priority" over others;[78] perhaps they "trump" other values;[79] perhaps they operate only as "side-constraints,"[80] or as claims with varying degrees of stringency,[81] or with "prima facie" weight.[82] But on any of these views, the consideration of competing values requires more subtle analysis than the simple maximization of aggregate value.

D. Hybrid (consequentialist and nonconsequentialist) views

Any plausible moral view will consider consequences. But there are several ways in which a moral view might include both consequentialist and nonconsequentialist concerns. First, as noted above, a modified utilitarian view might, for *nonconsequentialist* reasons, exclude certain preferences, pleasures, or values (such as the benefits a racist receives from indulging his preferences).

Second, nonconsequentialist concerns might serve as limits or side-constraints on achieving consequentialist goals. Thus, a general utilitarian approach to balancing the advantages and disadvantages of taking risks, and a utilitarian focus on preventing future acts of negligence, could be combined with moral side-constraints—for example, restricting blame to individuals who possess minimal general capacities to foresee risks and to avoid creating them.

Third, an apparently consequentialist balancing of the advantages and disadvantages of taking risks might reflect only a local rather than a global maximizing strategy. Suppose that the only reason for insisting that a moral agent maximize the expected costs and benefits of his action in choosing whether to take a risk is a retrospective, not a prospective, reason: creating unnecessary social costs is blameworthy. (As Richard Posner once put it, "we are indignant at a negligent injury because our moral natures are offended by economic waste, illustrated by an accident avoidable at a lower cost than the expected accident cost.")[83] But suppose the agent is not being blamed for failing to contribute to a broader, or global, maximizing strategy: in deciding whether to blame the agent, we

---

[78] See Rawls, *A Theory of Justice*, 42–45. Rawls describes a "lexical" ordering as one which "requires us to satisfy the first principle in the ordering before we can move on to the second, the second before we can consider the third, and so on."

[79] See Ronald Dworkin, *Taking Rights Seriously* (Cambridge: Harvard University Press, 1978), xi (where Dworkin argues that individual rights are political "trumps" held by individuals over collective goals [including utilitarianism]).

[80] See Nozick, *Anarchy, State, and Utopia*, ch. 3.

[81] See Thomson, *Realm of Rights*, chs. 6, 7.

[82] See W. D. Ross, *The Right and the Good* (Oxford: Clarendon Press, 1930).

[83] Posner, *Tort Law*, 8.

pay no heed to the possible further beneficial consequences of blaming him (including deterrence of similar acts by him or by others). Then consequentialist considerations do not yet justify blaming the actor. For we have not followed those considerations to their reasoned limit. Instead, we have truncated the consequentialist strategy—either arbitrarily, or, more likely, because we have a nonconsequentialist reason for the limit. (For example, we might believe that actors should impartially consider the interests of victims and injurers, apart from the future benefits of employing such an attitude.)

Fourth, the *converse* type of hybrid is also defensible. Instead of adopting a (truncated) utilitarian criterion of negligence while ignoring potential deterrence, we might adopt a nonutilitarian criterion of negligence yet care about deterrence. Suppose, to take an extreme view, that the criterion of wrongdoing is this: it is impermissible to impose any risks on persons who do not fully consent in advance. This criterion is compatible with deterrence, if the main point of our blaming practice is to minimize future instances of nonconsensual risk-imposition.[84]

Which approach to combining consequentialist and nonconsequentialist concerns is most persuasive and normatively attractive? I will not attempt to resolve that question here, at the level of principle. But I do wish to emphasize that a number of different hybrids are normatively defensible, and that common-sense morality does reflect both consequentialist and nonconsequentialist concerns. Moreover, in a significant range of cases involving risks of physical injury, maximizing the value of good expected consequences is morally defensible, and indeed justifies the same decisions about risk that a nonmaximizing, nonconsequentialist balancing approach justifies. The question of how fast a person should drive, for example, normally does not present serious problems about the fair distribution of risk, about the types of human interest (such as sadistic preferences) that are morally valuable, about some interests having lexical priority over others, or about distinctive responsibilities attaching to special roles. Rather, the principal issues are the relative magnitude of the risks of injury, and the relative social benefits, of driving at differing speeds.

Now reconsider the (mythical) Ford Pinto case. The following hybrid approach is plausible. It is permissible for a product manufacturer to balance costs and benefits, so long as consumers are aware of the risks and are able to consent to them (through market decisions), and so long as the distributional effects are just. (Thus, we might consider the extent to which cost savings from not taking precautions will be passed on to vehicle users and potential victims.) A value must indeed be placed on

---

[84] For a similar analysis in the context of tort doctrine, see Gary Schwartz, "Mixed Theories of Tort Law: Affirming Both Deterrence and Corrective Justice," *Texas Law Review* 75, no. 7 (June 1977): 1828–33.

human life, for purposes of deciding what level of precaution the manufacturer should take;[85] but the "value" need not be a fixed figure, invariant in different contexts.[86] Also, the values to be balanced should
include such qualitative ones as whether the risk of death by fire or
explosion is especially dreaded. It is therefore highly unlikely that a mathematical calculation will be dispositive.

On the other hand, balancing risks of injury against social benefits is
not always permissible. Consider the second example from the introduction, the example of Amy and Beatrice. Although Amy's creation of risks
of physical injury as a byproduct of obtaining a possible health benefit for
her own child is permissible, Beatrice's creation of similar risks as a
byproduct of indirectly producing a diffuse future social good is impermissible. It matters how one brings about a benefit, not just how large the
benefit is.[87]

Finally, the analysis to this point confirms the earlier suggestion that
the differences between the negligent and "knowing" (or intentional)
creation of harm are largely a question of degree. Although similar principles apply, the creation of lower-probability risks will, as a *factual* matter, more often be justifiable. For lower-probability risks more often require
balancing of competing alternatives, more often trigger concern about
consequences, and are less often subject to absolute or strong prima facie
duties.

IV. Law

The relation of nonlegal standards of moral responsibility for negligence to legal negligence standards is a complex subject. Here I will only
touch on a few points.

1. One function of legal standards is to reinforce moral standards. Criminal law and tort negligence standards do reflect and reinforce the moral
standards discussed above. The moral duty not to act negligently is an
important source of a variety of legal rules, including tort-law injunctive
remedies for nuisance, tort-law damages for the harms brought about by
negligence, criminal-law sanctions for risky behavior and for the harms
brought about by such risky behavior, and governmental regulation of
risk. Indeed, when legal responses to risk seem directly to *contradict* conventional moral standards, popular opposition is sometimes remarkably
intense. An example is the difficulty that many states have encountered
replacing tort fault liability for certain automobile accidents with a no-

---

[85] On a deontological view, this value need not be equal to the amount provided as
compensation after the fact.
[86] See Pildes and Sunstein, "Reinventing the Regulatory State," 43–86.
[87] For an illuminating discussion of this feature of deontological reasoning, see Leo Katz,
Ill-Gotten Gains (Chicago: University of Chicago Press, 1997).

fault standard, notwithstanding the enormous financial costs of the former system.[88]

2. Legal institutions obviously have enormous advantages over private moral standards in addressing a host of problems, including collective action, inadequate information, the difficulty of coordinating one's actions with those of others, and insufficient incentives to comply with moral norms. Coercive legal institutions permit risks to be reduced in widely varying ways (from police protection, to traffic rules, to facilitating economic markets), and to a degree that would otherwise be unachievable.

3. The moral duty of reasonable care itself depends in part on legal rules. For example, if we focus only on isolated individual responsibility for risk-creation, we ignore the point that the risks that I may fairly impose on others depend on what others will do, or are entitled to do. Yet what others will or may do is often significantly determined by legal rules—including property and contract law, and laws that coordinate activities (such as traffic rules).

4. The distinctive features of legal institutions help explain some distinctive features of legal conceptions of negligence. Consider the legal construct of the "reasonable person." Moral theory has no need for such a construct; we could, in principle, directly articulate the relevant principles for permissible and impermissible action, and for culpable and nonculpable behavior, without such an ideal. But the constructive legal approach can be very different from the direct approach.

At first glance, the distinction between (a) demanding a good or morally sufficient justification for imposing a particular risk, and (b) asking whether a reasonable person would impose that risk, might seem trivial. It is not. Depending on how one constructs a "reasonable person," this evaluation could be quite different from the direct evaluation of justifications. For example, the analysis of the justifiable use of defensive force could directly specify the relevant factors (one may not use more force than the amount of force one is defending against; one may defend only where necessary to prevent a future harm). Or the analysis could instead employ a "reasonable person" criterion, specifying merely that acceptable force should be judged by the standard of when, and to what extent, force would be used by a "reasonably prudent person, cautious about his own and others' safety, and not overwhelmed by emotion," or something of the like. The latter standard is likely to produce a less determinate set of results than the former standard, and could produce either a narrower or a broader self-defense privilege.

---

[88] Despite much academic support for automobile no-fault insurance as a replacement for tort negligence liability, and despite evidence that no-fault schemes save considerably on the enforcement costs of negligence liability, many people are offended by the idea that someone can negligently damage their car or their body without paying directly for that harm. (Of course, the opposition of trial lawyers is also an important part of this story.)

A "reasonable person" test often serves an important institutional function: one institution lays down some general constraints or permissions,
while another specifies the details via a "reasonable person" test. This
institutional division of labor permits a trier of fact to develop normative
standards case by case, instead of having a legislature define them *ex ante*.
(Thus, a legislature might define criminal or tort negligence simply as
"lack of reasonable care," leaving a jury or other fact-finder with the
considerable task of spelling out the meaning of that standard.) Absent
this institutional differentiation, a "reasonable person" test would have
little use.[89]

Sometimes, to be sure, the "reasonable person" construct is merely a
convenient shorthand for moral considerations that could be spelled out
if one had the time or inclination to do so. Thus, it is not surprising that
reasonableness standards are often used in describing *epistemic* duties,
that is, duties to form reasonably accurate beliefs. What a "reasonable
person" would believe or foresee could be specifically articulated in terms
of types and strength of evidence, relevant purposes, and the like; but the
inquiry is sufficiently complex, and there is sufficient consensus about
what people "should" believe, that the shorthand is acceptable. The same
might be true when the question is whether an actor conducted an activity with adequate skill. Thus, it is convenient to refer to the skill that a
reasonable driver would exercise in braking, or making a turn; but, in
principle, we might be able to spell out the factors relevant to a "reasonable" exercise of skill.[90]

5. Legal institutions are capable of doing much more about risks of
harm than simply reinforcing private norms against unjustifiable risk-
taking. Government can (and should) address risks that are no individual
person's responsibility. Consider, for example, risks of harm created by
nature, not by persons. Government might have a duty to forecast bad
weather and other natural disasters, and to conduct medical or safety
research.

[89] This division of labor also allows the formal legal standard to remain constant through
time, while flexible in its application. (I thank Hugh Baxter for this point.)

Whether a virtue-theory approach can give content to a "reasonable person" standard is
an interesting question, but one that I do not have the space to explore here. On virtue
theory generally, see Daniel Statman, ed., *Virtue Ethics* (Washington, DC: Georgetown University Press, 1997).

[90] Insofar as a "reasonable person" test is meant to establish a standard that people can
fairly be blamed for not satisfying, the test should be at least partially subjective—i.e., it
should assess the individual capacities of the agent. See Perry, "Risk, Harm, and Responsibility," 344. Legal standards are sometimes more "objective" than this, both for practical
reasons (avoiding problems of proof and of fraud) and also, perhaps, in order to express a
(strict liability) principle of fairness (e.g., the principle that others in the community are
entitled to a relatively high standard of conduct, even if this requires blaming or holding
liable some who cannot reasonably be expected to meet the standard). Thus, courts typically
ignore intellectual deficiencies, and also religious convictions that prompt actors to impose
higher than usual risks on others (or on themselves).

On the other hand, the collective and coercive features of law clearly make it an inappropriate instrument for enforcing all private moral norms. The range of human actions that are negligent and deserve modest moral blame far exceeds the range of actions that properly deserve legal redress through tort or regulatory sanction; and the range of actions that properly deserve criminal condemnation is much narrower still. The law should not be concerned with trivial risks of harm, or with forms of neglect and errors of judgment that are common and understandable. An automobile owner's failure to abide by the manufacturer's maintenance schedule is not on a par with drunk driving. Citizens should have the liberty to be modestly negligent, especially insofar as the law seeks to prevent or enjoin the act of negligence, as opposed to compensating for its ill effects.

6. If law simply enforced the moral norms that were customary in a community, or that were supported by most respected philosophers (even if such consensus were possible!), law would obviously risk losing its legitimacy. The content of legal norms should have a democratic pedigree. Private moral norms obviously differ in this respect: they are not "enacted" through a democratic process. To this extent, the model of law reinforcing ordinary moral judgments is problematic. For example, if a common-law court in a tort case saw its function as enforcing private moral norms (and if legislatures could not overrule that choice), tort doctrine would have only an attenuated grounding in democratic choice.

The legitimacy problem is profound. Some would invoke this difficulty to support a utilitarian approach, relying on utilitarianism's apparent neutrality between different preferences, its indifference to the sources and relative value of preferences, and its associated anti-perfectionism. But utilitarianism itself is clearly a controversial moral perspective. Although some versions of utilitarianism might succeed in not taking sides at the ground level of individual conceptions of the good, utilitarianism most certainly takes sides on the "higher-level" questions of how to resolve conflicts among such conceptions and how to define the social, rather than individual, good.

To resolve these difficulties, one needs a defensible political theory that explains which norms can justifiably be legally enforced in light of the variety of moral views people hold in a pluralist society. Developing such a theory is not easy, and I certainly will not attempt it here.[91]

V. Tort Law, Fault, and Corrective Justice

Tort law is a useful context in which to test some of the above analysis. The tort law construct of a "reasonable person" illustrates some distinc-

---

[91] The difficulty that John Rawls has encountered in convincing skeptics of the value of his own attempted solution underscores the seriousness of this problem. See John Rawls, *Political Liberalism* (New York: Columbia University Press, 1996); and Rawls, "The Idea of Public Reason Revisited," *University of Chicago Law Review* 64, no. 3 (Summer 1997): 765–807.

tive features of law, while the *ex ante* concept of negligence helps illuminate the debate between "corrective justice" and "fault" interpretations of tort doctrine.

1. In Anglo-American tort law, the typical jury instruction explaining the meaning of negligence refers only to the conduct exercised by a largely undefined "reasonable person" or "reasonably prudent person in the circumstances."[92] Such an instruction invites juries to identify and articulate the moral norms of the community.[93] At the same time, courts have developed distinct doctrines for such problems as causation and the scope of duty (for example, duties of landowners, special relationships, no general duty to rescue). Often these more specific doctrines reinforce community moral judgments, but sometimes they reflect the distinctive role and limits of legal institutions. For example, ordinary morality surely imposes at least some minimal duty to rescue a stranger in need, but tort law refuses to impose a general duty to rescue. An important justification for that refusal is a concern to protect personal liberty from state regulation, even the rather incidental form of state regulation that tort liability imposes.

Moreover, although the general "reasonably prudent person" test might seem to be without substantive content, courts do give greater definition to the concept of negligence in appellate rulings, and in some particular doctrinal areas, especially product liability. Their definitions vary, but they do support some of the nonutilitarian moral conceptions of negligence explained above.[94]

2. An important question for the interpretation and justification of negligence doctrine is whether we treat *fault* or *corrective justice* as a more fundamental concept. By "fault," I mean unjustified conduct, including negligence and unjustified intentional harms. By "corrective justice," I mean the Aristotelian idea that an agent has a duty to rectify a harm that he has caused, when it would be unjust to leave the harm unredressed.[95]

---

[92] See Gilles, "Invisible Hand Formula," 1017.

[93] See Michael Wells, "Scientific Policymaking and the Torts Revolution," *Georgia Law Review* 26, no. 3 (Spring 1992): 731; and Catherine Pierce Wells, "Tort Law as Corrective Justice: A Pragmatic Justification for Jury Adjudication," *Michigan Law Review* 88, no. 8 (August 1990): 2348–2413.

[94] Sometimes, jury instructions explaining negligence reflect a duty of impartiality, of considering interests of others as you would consider your own. See *Restatement (Second) of Torts*, section 283 cmt. e (1965); Keating, "Reasonableness," 337–38; and Gilles, "Invisible Hand Formula," 1038. For further discussion of the moral content of negligence doctrine, see Simons, "Deontology," 277–85.

[95] The criticism that follows might not apply to much broader interpretations of corrective justice, such as Margaret Radin's understanding of corrective justice as any principles governing our response to the wrongful or unjust unsettling of entitlements. See Margaret Jane Radin, "Compensation and Commensurability," *Duke Law Journal* 43, no. 1 (October 1993): 60. On the other hand, insofar as Radin's view refers only to *ex post* "correction" of a wrong, it might not fully encompass the *ex ante* perspective of negligence.

Most recent academic writings that defend a nonutilitarian account of tort law treat corrective justice as more basic than fault. I believe that this is a mistake. (It is also a mistake that I have committed in the past.)

As an interpretation of existing tort doctrine, the corrective-justice view understates the significance of fault, and overstates the significance of strict liability principles. Anglo-American tort law does not begin with the presumption that a loss should be shifted to the injurer. Rather, it normally does not shift a loss unless the loss was caused by faulty conduct. The categories in which strict liability is recognizea are limited;[96] even product liability, which according to much judicial rhetoric is strict, is predominantly fault-based.[97]

To be sure, nominally fault-based tort doctrines might contain elements of strict liability that are better explained by corrective justice. The objective test of negligence, for example, sometimes sets a standard that the defendant cannot fairly be expected to meet. This severity might reflect utilitarian concerns about fraud and difficulty of proof. But it might also reflect a particular corrective-justice rationale: that one who is victimized by another's excusable failure to live up to the normal standard of care in the community is entitled to compensation (even if she cannot fairly complain that the other was at fault and should have acted differently).

Also, as a practical matter, insofar as hindsight bias is pervasive, triers of fact in tort cases will often greatly overestimate the *ex ante* probability of harm, once they know (as they always do) that the harm has actually occurred. Accordingly, the actual application of a purported *ex ante* negligence test probably results in a substantially stricter form of liability than negligence doctrine can justify. (A conscientious judge therefore should advise a jury to avoid such hindsight bias.)

Still, in the end, fault principles explain Anglo-American tort doctrine better than corrective-justice principles do. Moreover, fault principles also offer a better *justification* than corrective justice for most of tort law. A principal reason is the *ex ante* perspective of fault. An actor's primary duty is not to create unreasonable, unjustifiable risks of injury. The duty to compensate or to provide another form of redress, in case the actor actually causes harm, is distinctly secondary. If it were possible to *enjoin* negligent acts, before they could result in harm, we would often do so. It is simply a fortuity of the natural world that most individual acts of negligence are too isolated, random, and unpredictable to be prevented *ex ante*; but the logic of fault suggests that they should often be prevented,

---

[96] These include: abnormally dangerous activities (such as the use of explosives), wild animals, product liability to some extent, and vicarious liability. (The latter imposes strict liability for the tort of another; but that other tort is usually fault-based.)

[97] Liability for defective design and defective warnings is largely fault-based. Liability for manufacturing defects is strict, however.

if that were feasible.[98] By contrast, nonfault principles of strict liability do indeed suppose that harm is actually done; they impose a *primary* duty to compensate for such harm.[99]

Concededly, the corrective-justice interpretation seems to be supported by the following feature of tort law: normally the same damages (full compensation) are available regardless of the degree of the actor's culpability. Even a strictly liable defendant, who might not be culpable at all, pays full compensation. (Compare this to criminal law, in which the penalty varies with the culpability or dangerousness of the actor, not just with the harm done.) This might suggest that negligence reflects a corrective-justice orientation toward redressing the harm done to the victim, not an orientation toward imposing duties on those who have acted with fault. Still, the occasional availability of punitive damages shows a clear concern with fault, transcending the concern to redress a loss. And in any event, the prevailing practice of normally awarding only damages for harm done reflects pragmatics, not a principled preference for damages over injunctions or other forms of prevention when (as is rarely the case) the latter responses are feasible.[100]

A corrective-justice theorist might further reply by pointing out an especially attractive feature of his approach: the fact that it distinguishes corrective justice from distributive justice. Corrective justice is not concerned with whether the victim was entitled to the property that the injurer harmed, or to the bodily integrity that the injurer intentionally or accidentally invaded. Rather, it presupposes an initial set of entitlements, and asks when the injurer should compensate the victim or provide some

[98] Indeed, in nuisance law, if a person's use of his property is unreasonable, and if certain other criteria are satisfied, injunctive relief is presumed to be the proper remedy.

The qualification "often" leaves room for a liberty constraint on state power when the moral fault of the defendant is modest. If an actor drives drunk, it is permissible for the state to prevent or enjoin his conduct. If a driver fails to follow the automobile manufacturer's maintenance schedule, enjoining him to do so would be an excessive use of state power. In either case, however, requiring compensation for harms caused by the actor's neglect might be a legitimate use of state power. (See the discussion in the prior section.)

A corrective-justice theorist might reply that compensatory liability in such a case exemplifies strict liability rather than fault. But (as I have argued elsewhere) a genuine fault approach could justify imposing an *ex ante* tort "fine" to approximate the expected costs of the neglect (in either of the cases mentioned in the previous paragraph). Kenneth W. Simons, "Corrective Justice and Liability for Risk-Creation: A Comment," *U.C.L.A. Law Review* 38, no. 1 (October 1990): 113–42. If this is correct, then *ex post* compensation can also be viewed as fault-based.

[99] I do not address here "strict liability" principles of *conditional* fault, e.g., a requirement that a business provide insurance or some other *ex ante* assurance that it will be able to pay for harms that it might cause. See Simons, "Jules Coleman and Corrective Justice," 880.

[100] Indeed, it would be justifiable to employ a different measure of damages in strict liability cases than in negligence cases—for example, routinely adding a "kicker" to negligence damages (beyond those damages that would leave the victim indifferent between damages and harm) to reflect the special wrong of creating unreasonable risks to others. For similar suggestions, see Keating, "Reasonableness," 349 n. 125, and sources cited there.

other appropriate remedy for unjustly disturbing those entitlements. What entitlements people should have is the subject of a distinct mode of justice, distributive justice.

But a fault analysis can, and indeed should, draw the same distinction, and should not attempt to resolve the distinct issue of the initial justice of entitlements. At the same time, a fault analysis has this advantage over corrective justice: it can more easily condemn behavior that risks, but has not yet caused, harm to entitlements.

VI. CONCLUSION

Several important themes emerge from this essay. First, "negligence" is both an important concept and an ambiguous one. Of its many meanings, I have concentrated upon the sense of creating an unjustifiable, low-probability risk of future harm. Second, I have attempted to dispel the prevalent view that only a maximizing, utilitarian approach can render intelligible certain features of negligence analysis—its focus on the *marginal* advantages and disadvantages of the actor's taking a specific precaution, its consideration and balancing of the short-term effects of different actions, and its sensitivity to a multiplicity of factors. Perhaps certain absolutist deontological perspectives are inconsistent with these features; but other deontological perspectives (not to mention other nonutilitarian and partially nonconsequentialist perspectives) can easily accommodate them. Third, I have tried to show how these moral perspectives are reflected in legal rules, and particularly in tort doctrine. Careful examination of the concept of negligence helps resolve an important debate about the nature of tort law, supporting the view that fault, rather than corrective justice, is the better interpretation and justification of Anglo-American tort doctrine.

In some ways, the ambitions of this essay have been modest. I have not attempted to conclusively justify a definitive set of negligence principles that should govern us as a matter of private morality or as a matter of legal enforcement. But I hope that I have succeeded in showing that conventional moral understandings, and plausible moral principles, contradict the reigning utilitarian account of negligence.

Law, Boston University

RESPONSIBILITY AND CONSENT: THE LIBERTARIAN'S PROBLEMS WITH FREEDOM OF CONTRACT*

By Leo Katz

I. Introduction

Libertarians believe certain things about rights and responsibilities, about when one person is to be held responsible for invading the rights of another. Libertarians also believe certain things about consent, about when someone should be held to a contract he has entered into. What they don't realize is that the first set of beliefs doesn't mix well with the second set of beliefs—that their intuitions about rights and responsibilities quite simply don't square with their intuitions about consent. Or so I shall be trying to show in this essay.

What I have to say is not exclusively a matter of concern to libertarians. Even people who would not consider themselves libertarians usually share a fair number of libertarian beliefs. They are especially likely to share some of the libertarian's core beliefs. That is because the libertarian's core beliefs—as I will be describing them below—are really a pretty deeply entrenched part of our everyday morality. It is hard to conceive how one would do without them. To be sure, nonlibertarians hold many *further* beliefs—beliefs that would make libertarians recoil. But the fact of overlap means that the problems and tensions I will be uncovering in the libertarian's creed plague many if not most nonlibertarians as well.

Nor is what I have to say exclusively a matter of concern to moral theorists. Lawyers and judges, too, should care about it. Many profoundly puzzling legal questions, it will turn out, arise out of the libertarian tensions I am about to describe. Many issues courts have found most troubling, many cases in which they have been accused of falling prey to confusion and incoherence, are but manifestations of the difficulties delineated in this essay. Thus, one of the things this essay sets out to do is to show how the ethereal-looking philosophical tensions I identify translate into very concrete legal quandaries.

Before identifying the problems with what libertarians believe, we will have to get clear on what it is that they believe. Simplest to describe are the libertarian's ideas about consent and freedom of contract. Put most crudely, the libertarian thinks that contracts between competent parties

---

* This essay has greatly benefited from the comments of the other contributors to this volume, but most especially from the extended comments of Ellen Frankel Paul and Claire Finkelstein.

ought to be enforceable, provided there was no force, no fraud, and the contract has no adverse effect on third parties. This, however, is quite a bit too crude for our purposes; so let me clarify it straightaway.

Let us begin with the "no force" requirement, which to some libertarians will be more familiar under various synonymous formulations: each contracting party's consent must be voluntary, free of duress, free of coercion, free of compulsion, or just plain free. One might construe this to mean that there is an unacceptable amount of duress whenever a contracting party's options are severely narrowed by unfortunate circumstances. But that is not how the libertarian understands things—at least not if we take Robert Nozick's *Anarchy, State, and Utopia* as representative.[1] (Indeed, since Nozick's book is rightly regarded by many as a sort of libertarian bible, I will be treating it as representative throughout this essay.) "Whether a person's actions are voluntary," Nozick writes, "depends on what it is that limits his alternatives. If facts of nature do so, the actions are voluntary. *I may voluntarily walk to someplace I would prefer to fly to unaided.*"[2] (I added those italics. The metaphor is so neat I wanted to make sure you didn't read past it.) If it is the conduct of others that limits a person's alternatives, Nozick notes, his actions are still voluntary, provided the other people's conduct was not wrongful. He illustrates this with the following inspired example:

> Suppose there are twenty-six women and twenty-six men each wanting to be married. For each sex, all of that sex agree on the same ranking of the twenty-six members of the opposite sex in terms of desirability as marriage partners: call them A to Z and A' to Z' respectively in decreasing preferential order. A and A' voluntarily choose to get married, each preferring the other to any other partner. B would most prefer to marry A', and B' would most prefer to marry A, but by their choices A and A' have removed these options. When B and B' marry, their choices are not made nonvoluntary merely by the fact that there is something else they each would rather do. This other most preferred option requires the cooperation of others who have chosen, as is their right, not to cooperate. B and B' choose among fewer options than did A and A'. This contraction of the range of options continues down the line until we come to Z and Z', who each face a choice between marrying the other or remaining unmarried. Each prefers any one of the twenty-five other partners who by their choices have removed themselves from consideration by Z and Z'. Z and Z' voluntarily choose to marry each other. The fact that their only other alternative is (in their view) much worse, and the fact that others chose to exercise their rights in certain ways, thereby

---

[1] Robert Nozick, *Anarchy, State, and Utopia* (New York: Basic Books, 1974).
[2] Ibid., 262.

shaping the external environment of options in which Z and Z′ choose, does not mean they did not marry voluntarily.[3]

The "no fraud" requirement also bears some clarification. Not every asymmetry in information between two contracting parties vitiates a contract. Not every instance of A not telling B something that might make B think twice or even desist from entering into a contract with A qualifies as fraud. Thus, for instance, in one famous nineteenth-century case that perfectly tracks libertarian views, a tobacco wholesaler who did not disclose to his customer that a tobacco embargo was about to come to an end and that the price of tobacco was due to fall imminently was not found guilty of defrauding the buyer.[4]

The requirement most in need of clarification and refinement is the libertarian's third one, having to do with "no third-party effects." This one quite clearly cannot be taken at face value. When A agrees to marry A′ in Nozick's example, this obviously has an effect on everyone else who would like to marry A′, but it is still not a problematic transaction. What the "no third-party effects" requirement really means to forbid is an agreement between two parties to violate the rights of a third party. Making agreements that adversely affect others is unobjectionable. It is agreements that amount to conspiracies—agreements to do jointly what one is not entitled to do singly—that are off-limits.

So much for what the libertarian believes about consent and freedom of contract. Let us turn next to his beliefs with regard to rights and responsibilities. These are a bit harder to nail down and summarize. The literature on rights is large, and interpretations of the concept of rights range widely. My own understanding of rights is going to be pretty much the one Nozick sets forth in *Anarchy, State, and Utopia*: "A line (or hyper-plane) circumscribes an area in moral space around an individual. Locke holds that this line is determined by an individual's natural rights, which limit the action of others."[5] These rights function as constraints on what others may do—"side-constraints" Nozick evocatively calls them, alluding to the idea of a mathematical function being maximized subject to a side-constraint. One of their salient characteristics, as Nozick sees it, is that one may not violate these constraints even if by doing so one is minimizing the overall amount of constraint-violation. In other words, if a judge is being pressured by an angry lynch mob to order the execution of an innocent prisoner, and he knows that unless he does so the crowd will go wild, will riot, and will kill many people who are as innocent as the prisoner, he still is not allowed to kill the prisoner. He cannot kill one innocent in order to prevent many more innocents from being killed by others. He cannot violate

[3] Ibid., 263.
[4] *Laidlaw v. Organ*, 15 U.S. (2 Wheat.) 178 (1817). For an excellent discussion of such cases, see Kim Lane Scheppele, *Legal Secrets: Equality and Efficiency in the Common Law* (Chicago: University of Chicago Press, 1988).
[5] Nozick, *Anarchy, State, and Utopia*, 57.

one person's rights in order to prevent others from violating many more persons' rights. To be sure, a utilitarian might well be in favor of such a preventive measure, Nozick notes, but a libertarian is bound to abhor it.

So far, I have only talked about rights. Where and how does responsibility enter the scene? It enters when we start to think about situations in which one person invades the rights of another, when he engages in what Nozick aptly refers to as a "boundary-crossing," a penetration of that "line or hyper-plane" circumscribing what Nozick essentially pictures as a person's plot or homestead in moral space. What constitutes such a boundary-crossing? Clearly not every causing of harm qualifies. When I let someone drown under circumstances where I could easily have saved him, I have caused him harm, but I have not committed a boundary-crossing. I cannot be held responsible for causing harm to someone by way of an omission. But that is just the simplest example of causing harm to someone without committing a boundary-crossing, that is, without being responsible for the harm one has caused. Here is a more complicated example: Suppose someone hurls a deadly object in my direction. I duck and as a result it is you, rather than I, who dies. Again, I am not guilty of a boundary-crossing for what I have done. I cannot be held responsible for the harm I have caused. To cause someone's death by ducking is not to invade his rights. And how do we know which ways of causing harm constitute boundary-crossings? That is something the theory of responsibility explores. The rules that make up the theory of responsibility have been investigated only slightly by libertarian thinkers; they have been investigated far more thoroughly by lawyers, judges, and legal scholars writing about criminal and tort law. To be sure, those writing about responsibility on the legal side do not especially think of themselves as working in a libertarian vein, but there is little doubt that most of the central ideas they are pursuing—like the distinction between acts and omissions or the meaning of self-defense—simply serve to flesh out the libertarian's intuitions about what constitutes a boundary-crossing. In the course of this essay, I will assume that the libertarian subscribes to most of those ideas.[6]

[6] Some people might take exception to my saying that by omitting someone's rescue I cause his death; a few might even object to my saying that by ducking I cause someone's death. There is a lively debate on the question of whether omissions ever cause anything. Some philosophers have tried to split the difference by distinguishing between negative and positive causation, and saying that omissions are only capable of the former. In this particular context I do not believe much hangs on the question. When I say "cause," I really only mean to refer to the presence of *some kind of causal relationship*, which I cannot imagine anyone would deny to exist between either an omission and an unprevented but preventable harm, or between a ducking and an unprevented but ducking-preventable harm. Note that when consequentialists talk about bringing about the best possible consequences, they mean by "consequences" events that stand in a *causal relationship* to prior decisions of the decision maker, but not necessarily events that were *caused* by them (if, that is, one uses "cause" in a narrower sense than *causal relationship*)—which is why they would blame me equally for a death which I acted to bring about and a death which I omitted to prevent, or for a death which I brought about by a shielding and a death which I could have prevented by not ducking. For a bit more discussion of this and some bibliographic references on the debate about whether omissions can be said to cause harm, see Shelly Kagan, *The Limits of Morality* (Oxford: Oxford University Press, 1987), 92–93.

As has become clear by now, the beliefs I impute to libertarians are extremely rudimentary ones, which they would find it very difficult to disavow. This should make it all the more surprising that these ideas turn out to be in conflict with each other. What I will do in the next three sections is to lay out three ways in which they conflict, by presenting three types of contracts in which the libertarian's consent-based intuitions would push him to approve of the contract and his responsibility-based intuitions would push him to condemn it. The libertarian will then find himself faced with three unpalatable alternatives. (1) He could just throw overboard his very basic, hard-to-resist intuitions about when consent is binding. (2) He could throw overboard his very basic, hard-to-resist intuitions about how responsibility is to be assigned. (3) He could try to steer a middle-course and try to develop some sort of artificial boundary between contracts in which he will let his consent-based intuitions prevail (which he will therefore approve), and contracts in which he will let his responsibility-based intuitions prevail (which he will therefore condemn). My guess is that (3) will prove to be the least unattractive alternative. That is hardly cheerful news for libertarians.

A word about how each of the sections that follow is organized: Each section starts with a concrete legal case in which the tension between "responsibility" and "consent" will prove to be critical. We will see how courts guided by "consent" have tended to approve the bargain in question and courts guided by "responsibility" have gone the other way. The consent-based line of argument will usually be very easy to see, the responsibility-based line of argument much harder. It will take the help of a highly stylized, ridiculously unrealistic law-school hypothetical to tease out the responsibility-based line. Each section concludes with a more abstract explanation of how the tension between consent and responsibility was at work in what went before.

II. The First Problem: The Case of the Preemptive Assassin
(On Contracts with Curiously Indifferent Victims)

There is a legal issue that has vexed courts since time immemorial, which I will call the puzzle of the Bad Good Samaritan. A motorist is stranded by the side of the road; the surrounding area looks nasty and dangerous, and there is little hope that he will be picked up by someone anytime soon. Then luckily and at long last another car happens by. It is a ramshackle and uninviting-looking vehicle. The car stops and the driver offers the stranded motorist a ride. Alas, he also warns him: the car he is driving is highly unsafe. Its brakes are giving out, its tires nearly bald, its seat belts unusable. All this the driver explains, as well as the fact that he has been drinking more than he should (which does not mean he is willing to surrender the steering wheel). Still, if the stranded motorist wants to hitch a ride, he is most welcome. Considering the alternatives, that strikes the stranded motorist as the sensible thing to do. Twenty minutes later, they encounter the carcass of an animal draped across half of the road. Because his brakes are defective, his tires slippery, and his mental acuity none too good, the driver does not manage to avoid the obstacle. A fatal accident ensues—fatal, that is, for the passenger, the stranded motorist. The driver survives. Is he guilty of recklessness? Can he be held liable for damages under the tort law? Can he be convicted of manslaughter under the criminal law? This kind of scenario is a pretty generic one. It is not hard to think of analogies: A stricken passenger on an airplane and an incompetent doctor who asks him to sign a waiver before being willing to help him. A homeless man and a slumlord who offers him accommodations in a shack that is in flagrant noncompliance with health and safety codes but still much healthier and safer than the places the homeless man had been frequenting.[7]

Courts have tied themselves in knots trying to figure out how to deal with these cases. To be sure, some judges have insisted the matter is really straightforward. They invoke freedom of contract: They point out that much of the time the stranded motorist, the homeless man, even the stricken passenger, will not be too incompetent to give a valid consent. After all, they are only doing what any rational person would do under the circumstances! The judges point out that neither force, nor fraud, nor adverse third-party effects are present to vitiate consent. Nevertheless, many courts have gone the other way and have refused to find the victim's consent in such cases valid. Alas, they have had a hard time explaining clearly and convincingly why.

What courts are here encountering, I will try to show, is one manifestation of the tension between the libertarian's ideas about responsibility and his ideas about consent. To be more precise, I will try to show that the judges who insist on disregarding the victim's consent and on holding the driver, the doctor, and the slumlord liable despite their victims' waivers, are guided by libertarian intuitions just as much as the judges who want to acquit them. But to see this will require some elaborate stage-setting. Consider the following far-fetched hypothetical, whose connection with the legal problem at hand will only emerge quite a bit further on.

The Case of the Preemptive Assassin. Mob Boss approaches me and asks me to carry out a contract killing for him. He offers me $5,000. While he is eager for me to take on the assignment, he assures me that he is by no means dependent on my assistance. He has at least two other anxious candidates waiting in the wings, as competent as I and only marginally more expensive. He tries to use this fact to put to rest any scruples I might have: The victim, he assures me, is a dead man already. He is either going to die by my hand or by the hand of some other assassin. My pangs of

---

[7] Kenneth W. Simons, "Assumption of Risk and Consent in the Law of Torts: A Theory of Full Preference," *Boston University Law Review* 67 (1987): 213–87, offers a superb examination of the legal discussions of these kinds of cases.

conscience, my refusal to wield the dagger, will not prolong his life by so much as a second. So am I free to take on the assignment, morally speaking, on the ground that, in a bottom-line sense, I will have done no harm? No, of course not. But let us try to be pedantically explicit as to why that is before moving on to the punchline of this example. Why, then, is it that despite the fact that my acquiescence in the Mob Boss's proposal makes no difference to the victim's fate, I should still be blamed for his death— provided it is I, rather than the assassins waiting in the wings, who wields the dagger?

The libertarian's most cogent reply would, I think, have to go something like this. Whereas to a utilitarian, results are the only thing that matters, to a libertarian the *way* in which a particular result is brought about is crucially important. I can cause death by failing to help or by acting to kill, but the causal relationship is different in each case, and that is critical, morally speaking. In fact, the difference between two ways of causing death can be incredibly minute and still matter hugely to one's moral responsibility. Or to put it differently, incredibly small differences in my causal relationship to a bad result can determine whether I have committed a boundary-crossing or not. To bring this out fully, consider a few examples in which these differences have been honed down to a hair's breadth.

1. I see V drowning in the ocean. I drag him ashore. I then change my mind about the rescue—he turns out to be someone I have always detested—and push him back into the sea, where he drowns. I leave him no worse off than I found him. Still, the law will (rightly) judge me more blameworthy than if I had just let him drown: I am guilty of murder. Dragging someone ashore and then pushing him back into the water is a boundary-crossing. Just leaving him there is not.

2. I see a friend of mine about to be hit by a heavy object. I could tell my friend to duck, in which case the object will kill the person standing behind him. I could also try to drag or lure that very same bystander—the third party standing behind my friend—into the path of the projectile. In other words, I could use him as a shield for my friend. In the former, the "ducking" case, I would be beyond reproach. In the latter, the "shielding" case, I would again be guilty of murder. The small, mechanical-looking difference between a "ducking" and a "shielding" here decides between whether there is or is not responsibility, whether there is or is not a forbidden boundary-crossing.[8]

3. Finally, consider a variation of an example first made famous by Philippa Foot and Judith Jarvis Thompson. In its original version, the example went like this:

> Edward is the driver of a trolley, whose brakes have failed. On the
> track ahead of him are five people; the banks are so steep that they

---

[8] The seminal article that first uncovered the ducking-shielding distinction is Christopher Boorse and Roy Sorensen, "Ducking Harm," *Journal of Philosophy* 85 (1988): 115.

will not be able to get off the track in time. The track has a spur leading off to the right, and Edward can turn the trolley onto it. Unfortunately, there is one person on the right hand track. Edward can turn the trolley, killing the one, or he can refrain from turning the trolley.[9]

Many people think that if Edward turns the trolley, he will be beyond reproach. He will not be blameworthy. He will not have violated anyone's rights. He will, to be sure, have caused the one man's death. But he will have caused it in a manner which, like causing-by-omission, or causing-by-ducking, does not constitute a boundary-crossing.

Now it is important to realize that the libertarian who approves of Edward's actions is not thereby endorsing the practice of sacrificing the one for the sake of the many. In general, he would view that sort of thing as beyond the pale. The libertarian would not, for instance, approve of carving up one person to use his heart, his lungs, and his kidneys to save five people who are in dire need of transplants. But the trolley case, libertarians say, is not simply another version of the transplant scenario. The trolley scenario has some special attributes which make sacrificing the one for the sake of the many in that case acceptable. Establishing just exactly what those attributes are has proved a bit of a challenge. Different proposals have been floated.[10] But that there is something special about the trolley case which makes the killing blamefree—that is widely accepted.

If we put together these facts—the fact that the libertarian would approve of turning the trolley and the fact that he would not approve of confiscating someone's organs for a higher purpose—we can produce a particularly powerful example of how crucial the manner in which I cause someone's death is for deciding whether I have committed a boundary-crossing. Imagine that when the brakes fail and Edward encounters the junction on the track, he lets the trolley run its course; he does not turn it away from the five and onto the one. Let us suppose that the trolley does not in fact kill the five. It only ends up injuring them severely. What is more, let us suppose that it injures them in a philosophically particularly interesting way: it destroys the heart of one, the kidneys of two, and the lungs of the remaining two. In other words, these five could be saved if we only had a spare heart, two spare kidneys, and

[9] Judith Jarvis Thomson, "The Trolley Problem," in Thomson, *Rights, Restitution, and Risk* (Cambridge, MA: Harvard University Press, 1986), 94–116.

[10] Frances M. Kamm, *Morality, Mortality*, vol. 2 (New York: Oxford University Press, 1996), ch. 6, is the most up-to-date and thoroughgoing examination of the trolley problem, and is quite amazing in its ingenuity. However, there is by no means universal agreement that the trolley case really is different from the transplant case. German criminal-law scholars generally seem to think there is no difference. See Ulfrid Neumann, "Rechtfertigender Notstand," in *NOMOS Kommentar zum Strafgesetzbuch*, ed. Ulfrid Neumann and Wolfgang Schild (Baden-Baden: NOMOS Verlagsgesellschaft Baden-Baden, 1997), commentary accompanying section 34 of the German criminal code, dealing with what Anglo-American law calls "necessity."

two spare lungs. At this point it occurs to Edward that perhaps the lone uninjured survivor on the other track should be killed after all to save the five. If he does so, would that be all right? No, of course not. Libertarians would regard this as an illegitimate boundary-crossing for sure. But note what this means: the very same sacrifice of the very same person for the very same five strangers can be brought about by redirecting the trolley but *not* by first letting the trolley run and then killing the one (perhaps less painfully!) for the sake of the five.

What these examples are meant to drive home is a somewhat unappreciated feature of libertarian morality, its path-dependence. To a libertarian, unlike a utilitarian, not merely the end result but the particular path by which it was reached is essential.[11]

So how does all of this relate to freedom of contract? How does it tie in with the alleged tension between responsibility and consent? Let us return to my original assassin example. Suppose that well in advance of my ever being hired as an assassin, indeed well in advance of my ever even contemplating such a career, I approach the person who much later turns out to be the victim with a proposal for a conditional agreement: "If it should ever happen that I (Leo) am offered an assassination assignment under circumstances in which a killing of you (the victim) would take place whether I agree to be the one doing it or not, will you (for a small sum perhaps) consent to my doing it?" The victim, it seems, might easily say yes. He would say yes because my wrongful conduct would have no bottom-line effect on him. To make it even more likely that he will say yes, I might offer to make sure that I will carry out the execution in a less painful manner than the Mob Boss's other potential assassins would. And, of course, I am sweetening the pot by offering the victim some money up front, here and now.

Should a contract like this one between me and the victim be enforceable? A libertarian, I would claim, should be torn about this. His intuitions about consent and his intuitions about responsibility here should find themselves at war with each other.

Let us start with the libertarian's consent-based intuitions. Those should lead him to say that the bargain between me and my potential victim is a highly beneficial transaction for both parties to it: The victim makes some money he otherwise would not have gotten, and he does not increase his chance of dying. And if he does die, it will be less painfully than otherwise. I, in turn, stand the chance of making some money through my fee from Mob Boss.

I can see only two consent-related reservations a libertarian might have about giving this transaction his blessing, and I think it likely that he would discard both of them on closer inspection. His first reserva-

---

[11] The depth and significance of path-dependence in law and morality are explored at length in my book *Ill-Gotten Gains: Evasion, Blackmail, Fraud, and Kindred Puzzles of the Law* (Chicago: University of Chicago Press, 1996).

tion might arise out of the extreme nature of the transaction: the victim is consenting to his own *death*. Even if one generally respects freedom of contract, bargains involving one's life are special. Not all libertarians feel that way, but an appreciable number certainly do. To make my point to them, I have to ask them to revise slightly the example I have used. Nothing in fact turns on life being at stake. That just happens to make the example more pristine and memorable. Libertarians who think such examples too extreme and peculiar should instead imagine that the crime that Mob Boss is contemplating is not an assassination but a bank robbery. What he asks me to do is not to kill someone but to crack a safe. And the contract I enter into with my victim is an agreement between me and a bank whereby I pay them a certain sum of money in return for the right to commit a bank robbery if in the future I am ever asked by Mob Boss to do so under circumstances where it is certain that the bank robbery is going to occur with or without my intervention. What's more, I promise the bank to make sure that no one is killed in the course of the robbery.

If a libertarian still has doubts about the legitimacy of the victim's consent—the victim in this case being the bank—that is probably due to the second reservation I alluded to. It might seem as though the victim in my examples is acting under duress. And duress, of course, vitiates consent. On closer scrutiny, however, I think a libertarian will conclude that there is no duress in these examples. To be sure, there is something here which some people might colloquially refer to as duress. But we already know from Nozick's marriage example involving A through Z that what gets described as duress colloquially might still be a voluntary choice by the libertarian's lights. The reason the libertarian initially feels tempted to say that my transaction is vitiated by duress is that it is entered into to escape the consequences of someone's wrongful conduct down the road. But many perfectly voluntary transactions are entered into to escape someone's wrongful conduct down the road. I buy a gun from a gunshop to escape an assailant sometime down the road. I buy insurance to deal with the repercussions of an assault sometime down the road. I enter into one of Nozick's famous protective agencies (his version of the embryonic state) to prevent an assault sometime down the road. Thus, on second thought, I think the libertarian would conclude that the bargain I strike with my potential victim is perfectly valid.

This is what would happen if the libertarian lets himself be guided by his consent-based intuitions. Things change radically, however, once he lets himself be guided by his responsibility-based intuitions. Responsibility, as we have seen, is for the libertarian a highly path-dependent affair. To be responsible for a boundary-crossing, it is not enough that the culprit has inflicted a harm; he must also have inflicted that harm by the right path. Harm inflicted by an omission (as opposed to an act), or by a so-called "ducking" (as opposed to a "shielding"), or by the simple diversion of a trolley from one group of victims onto a less numerous group of victims (as opposed to a carving-up following a trolley accident that was not diverted) does not constitute a boundary-crossing.

There is an aspect to this path-dependence that is easily missed. Victims are likely to feel very differently about the path by which harm is inflicted than philosophers, moralists, or judges. What I mean is this: Suppose we ask a victim whether he prefers to be harmed by an act or an omission, a shielding or a ducking, a carving-up or a diversion of the trolley—what would he say? We know what an impartial judge of the situation would say: he would prefer—morally speaking—the person who harms by omission, ducking, or trolley diversion, to the person who brings about the same harm by an act, by a shielding, or by a carving-up. But the victim's view of this is going to be different. If he is rationally selfish—if all he cares about is the bottom-line harm inflicted on him—he is likely not to care much about the path.

Indeed, we can state the point in a more extreme way: Suppose we are comparing two courses of actions that a harm-doer could pursue. He could *either* inflict a *less serious* harm by way of an act or a shielding, *or in the alternative* he could inflict a *more serious* harm by way of an omission or a ducking. A moral philosopher judging the situation would have to say that the infliction of the graver harm is the more moral course of action because of the path by which it is inflicted: omissions and duckings do not constitute boundary-crossings. The victim, however, is likely to judge the less serious harm to be preferable, despite the fact that it is inflicted by an impermissible path, one that constitutes a boundary-crossing. The victim would rather be subjected to a mildly harmful act than a super-harmful omission, or a mildly harmful shielding rather than a super-harmful ducking.[12]

Admittedly, this will not always be true. There might be some victims who think about harm directed at them in the same way a third-party observer would. There might be some victims who prefer being subjected to a grave harm by an omission rather than a milder harm by an act. They are likely to be the exception, however. And even those victims whose preferences are not totally of the rationally selfish kind, are unlikely to completely track a third-party observer's rules of responsibility in every respect. Even if a victim would prefer to be subjected to an omission-caused harm rather than an act-caused harm, he may not feel the same way about a shielding-caused harm versus a ducking-caused harm.

The foregoing raises this question: If victims do not much care about the particular path by which a harm is inflicted, why does libertarian morality care? If victims would prefer to be subjected to a mild act-induced harm rather than a grave omission-induced harm, why does libertarian morality judge the omission to be morally superior to the act?

[12] Further peculiarities about the way in which consent and path-dependence interact are explored in my *Ill-Gotten Gains*, Part II, examining the long-standing legal paradox of blackmail.

The libertarian's answer here is simple: What makes omission-induced harming morally superior to act-induced harming is that victims only have a moral claim—a right—to not being actively harmed. They do not have a moral claim to being aided; that is, they do not have a right to not being "omissively" harmed. The libertarian would say the same thing about the ducking-shielding distinction. Victims have a moral claim—a right—not to be harmed by a shielding; they have no such claim vis-à-vis a ducking. The victim's preferences in all of this are irrelevant. The rules that determine what constitutes a boundary-crossing have nothing to do with the victim's preferences.

Now consider again a situation in which I am thinking about inflicting harm on a victim by two possible paths. The first path is "forbidden"—it involves inflicting harm by an act or a shielding or a carving-up, or in some other manner which the victim has a right that I not use. The second path is permitted—it involves inflicting harm by an omission or a ducking or a trolley diversion, or in some other manner that the victim is not entitled to object to. Moreover, let us suppose that the second path would result in a slightly greater harm than the first. We now clearly understand that I may not use the first, the "forbidden" path, even if I know for sure that the victim would prefer me to do that rather than use the permitted path. That is because the victim's preferences are not what determines whether a path is forbidden or permitted; his rights do. Would it change things if the victim had, in the past, been very outspoken about his preferences, if he had stated repeatedly that he preferred a mild act-induced harm to a grave omission-induced harm, or a mild shielding-induced harm to a grave ducking-induced harm? Since his preferences are not what determines the moral acceptability of a path, it is hard to see that his declaration of his preferences should carry any weight. But if his public declaration of his preferences does not count for anything, why should it count for anything if he has struck a bargain with me, in which he consents to my inflicting harm on him by the forbidden route? The answer would seem to be—it shouldn't. Given what libertarians believe about responsibility, they should thus repudiate the bargain between me and my potential future victim.

One way of summarizing my point is to ask what the libertarian should say about a slight variation of my original example. Again, imagine that Mob Boss has approached me with the offer of $5,000 to carry out the assassination of the victim, giving me the familiar assurance that if I don't do it, someone else is standing ready to do so. I have made no prior agreement with the victim. Assume that I do, in fact, carry out the assassination. Now imagine further that in going through the victim's diary we find a curious diary entry to the effect that if his friend Leo ever were offered some money to assassinate him under circumstances where it was evident that somebody was going to assassinate him anyway, he hoped Leo would take it. Would that diary entry serve to exonerate me? I should think not. It does no more than establish something we already knew and did not care about: that the victim only cares about the bottom-line harm done to him, not about the route by which it is done. What if the victim had actually posted his diary on a website for the whole world to see? Would that change anything? Would that really exonerate me? Why should the publication of the diary entry change anything when we have already decided that the victim's preferences are irrelevant? This is how a libertarian should be led to reason by his beliefs about responsibility. And, of course, that starkly conflicts which the conclusions he is driven to by his beliefs about consent.

Let us now return to my original problem of the Bad Good Samaritan, the drunk driver with the unsafe car who stops to pick up a stranded motorist, warning him that he is drunk and that his car is unsafe. The logic of judges who acquit the driver is easy to understand. They simply let their consent-based libertarian intuitions guide them: The driver, though drunk and driving a defective vehicle, got the stranded motorist to willingly assume the risks associated therewith. Thus, the stranded motorist has nothing to complain about, and the driver cannot be blamed for any wrong. He owes no damages; nor can he be found guilty of manslaughter.

The logic of those judges who refuse to let the driver off is more elusive. They have never been able to fully articulate their reasoning. The argument I believe they are groping for is the one that I have stated to be implicit in the libertarian's responsibility-based intuitions. The relationship between the driver and the stranded motorist can be thought of as being quite analogous to the relationship between me and the victim in the "Preemptive Assassin" example. I have the choice of causing the death of the victim by two different routes: I can let him be killed by one of Mob Boss's substitute assassins or I can kill him myself. The drunk driver has the choice of imposing a great risk on the stranded motorist by two different routes: he can leave him by the side of the road to be assaulted by roving muggers, or he can subject him to his reckless driving. For the same reasons that the victim's consent in my "Preemptive Assassin" example will not serve to let me off the hook, the stranded motorist's assumption of the risk that the driver imposes on him will not let the driver off the hook. In short, if judges have not been able to decide how to deal with the problem of the Bad Good Samaritan, it is because they are rightly torn by two equally compelling sets of intuitions—those based on consent and those based on responsibility.

It may be worth stepping back for a moment and trying to see at a fairly abstract level what has brought "consent" and "responsibility" into collision here. Responsibility as the libertarian understands it is highly path-dependent: the same harm when inflicted by one route is prohibited, and when inflicted by another route is unobjectionable. Victims only care about end-results; they do not care about the route. Put those two things together—the path-dependence of responsibility rules and the victim's focus on the end-result—and you have an easy recipe for creating situations analogous to my "Preemptive Assassin" case. You simply need to imagine a situation in which someone could inflict a harm by two possible routes, a permitted and a prohibited one (in the "Preemptive Assassin" case: by letting others commit the assassination, or by carrying out the assassination oneself), and then imagine a contract between the harm-doer and the victim contemplating this situation in advance. If we truly believe in the path-dependence of responsibility, we are bound to feel very uneasy about the victim's advance consent exonerating the harm-doer.

III. The Second Problem: The Case of the Prescient Robbery Victim (On Contracts in Contemplation of a Wrong)

Let us take up, then, the second way in which consent and responsibility collide. Again, I will begin with a legal quandary in which that conflict turns out to play a pivotal role. We will see how a consent-inspired analysis of the quandary will drive the libertarian to resolve the quandary in one fashion and how a responsibility-based analysis of it will drive him to resolve it in precisely the opposite fashion. As in the previous section, the consent-based analysis will be the more obvious one. By contrast, it will take some effort—and the contrivance of the highly artificial "Case of the Prescient Robbery Victim"—to see the alternative, responsibility-based point of view.

Suppose that the Cosmopolitan Opera has hired a world-renowned singer for a three-year stint. They are paying her a munificent salary. Just as she is about to embark on her first season, she is approached by a competing opera house with an even better offer. She promptly relays this news to the director of the Cosmopolitan and asks him for a raise so as to bring her salary at the Cosmopolitan more into line with what she is being offered elsewhere. The director's initial reply is simple: "You are under contract with us for three seasons. You are pledged to sing for the salary in your contract. Whether another opera house is willing to pay you more is irrelevant. If you were to accept their offer, you would be in breach of the contract you have with us. I have no intention of paying you more than we agreed to in that contract." The singer replies: "I understand that I would be in breach of contract if I left. I have no intention of breaching. However I will be a very unhappy camper if you don't compensate me in line with my current market value. If I am unhappy I don't sing well. And if I don't sing well your audience isn't going to be happy either—and probably not very generous with donations. Think about it." "I understand," says the director, and he promises to raise her salary substantially, quite close to the amount the competing opera house is offering her.

Two and a half years elapse. During that time the director consistently pays the singer the promised higher salary. But when the last six months have passed and her final payment is due, he does something unusual: he subtracts from it the entire amount that he says he has paid her in excess of the original, contractually agreed-to salary. "But you promised to pay me more," the singer protests. "That was under duress," the director explains. "You were threatening not to put in the kind of performance you were required to put in under our contract. You were threatening not to give this job your best efforts. Faced with that kind of wrongful threat I had to promise you more. But you were engaging in highway robbery. I don't have to keep my promise to a highway robber."

What would a libertarian have to say about this kind of case? At first blush, he would, I think, have to agree with the director. The director did make his promise under duress. The contract modification entered into between him and the singer would therefore, by libertarian lights, not be valid.

Contrast this with what a utilitarian or an economist would say about this case. They might well recommend considering the director's promise of a higher salary to be binding. Not allowing it—by not enforcing it— would, in the long run, prevent many all-around beneficial bargains. If the contract modification between the Cosmopolitan and the singer were not allowed, what would happen—the economist would point out—is that the singer would pout and put in a worse performance. And that would be worse for both sides than the alternative—paying the singer more and getting a better performance out of her. To be sure, the economist would add that the matter is not entirely clear-cut. There are some unfortunate adverse consequences which would follow from allowing such contract modifications. If opera directors know that singers can always try to renegotiate by threatening to put in a worse performance, they might be unwilling to enter into long-term contracts with singers to begin with, since the contract is fully binding on the opera house without being fully binding on the singers, who can always back out of them by threatening a bad performance. Whether this further repercussion of allowing contract modifications makes them undesirable in the long run would depend, the economist would note, on a lot more specific facts, which we have not, so far, been given.[13]

It would thus appear that there is conflict between the way the libertarian would look at the question of contract modification and the way that an economist or a utilitarian would. This should not come as a great shock. There are many issues on which those groups do not see eye-to-eye. Utilitarians will often favor arrangements that maximize utility but entail the violation of rights: as we already saw, utilitarians might applaud carving up one person in order to use his heart, his kidneys, and his lungs to save the lives of five people in need of transplants, whereas a libertarian would never countenance such a thing. Economists are a species of utilitarian, bet-

---

[13] Varouj A. Aivazian, Michael Trebilcock, and Michael Penny, "The Law of Contract Modification: The Uncertain Quest for a Benchmark of Enforceability," *Osgoode Hall Law Journal* 22 (1984): 173–212; Robert A. Hillman, "Policing Contract Modifications under the UCC: Good Faith and the Doctrine of Economic Duress," *Iowa Law Journal* 64 (1979): 849–902.

ter called consequentialists—or, more precisely yet, welfare consequentialists. Unlike the utilitarians, they are not interested in maximizing utility pure and simple. What they want to maximize is welfare—which is only subtly different, but the difference is not worth exploring here. What is important is that by seeking to maximize welfare—by seeking to achieve efficiency—they appear to end up recommending many arrangements that involve what, from a libertarian point of view, looks unfair: boundary-crossings that make for efficiency, such as enforcing a contract entered into under duress.

We now come to the crux of the matter. It has become customary for economists to argue that this conflict between what an economist would do and what a libertarian would do about a legal or moral issue is more apparent than real. The economists' argument goes like this: "Suppose we announce up front that contract modifications are generally valid, even where they are obtained under certain kinds of arguable duress—such as the threat not to put on a good performance unless one is better compensated. (We might make an exception if the parties expressly stipulate in their original contract that no modifications will be allowed.) If this fact is known in advance, then the opera house enters into its contract with the singer fully appreciating the possibility of a renegotiation under duress. The opera directors can take precautions to protect themselves. They can refuse to hire singers who are likely to renegotiate. They can offer a lesser fee initially to make up for the fact that they may have to raise it down the road. They can avoid entering into a contract altogether. In any event, they understand the rules of the game. These rules are incorporated, as it were, into their understanding with the singer. Thus, it would be not only efficient but fair, even from a libertarian point of view, to hold the opera house to the contract modification."

This kind of argument is standard in the law-and-economics literature. It is the customary way in which economists seek to persuade the rest of the world that an efficiency-based recommendation can be reconciled with fairness. My contracts modification case is thus emblematic of an entire mode of argument. Libertarians appear, by and large, to swallow it. Indeed, the economists who make the argument will often regard themselves as being libertarians.[14]

The reason the libertarian finds the economists' argument so compelling is that it jibes very well with his consent-based intuitions. The libertarian believes that if someone gives his consent to what would otherwise be a boundary-crossing, that is, if he consents to an invasion of his rights, then it ceases to be a boundary-crossing—ceases to be an invasion of his rights. A theft is not a theft if the victim agrees to it: it then becomes a gift.

---

[14] This argumentative strategy figures especially prominently in the landmark treatise on corporate law by Frank Easterbrook and Daniel Fischel, *The Economic Structure of Corporate Law* (Cambridge, MA: Harvard University Press, 1991), especially in their treatment of so-called "Corporate Control Transactions" (chapter 5) involving what at first appears to be unfair arm-twisting of minority shareholders by the controlling majority.

An assault is not an assault if the victim agrees to it: it then becomes something akin to surgery. A rape is not a rape if the victim agrees to it: it then becomes love-making. Similarly, the libertarian reasons, a duress-induced contract modification is not the boundary-crossing it appears to be if it, too, was consented to in advance. If we make it the law that contract modifications are allowed (unless the parties expressly state the contrary in their original contract), then we have a form of advance consent and there is no boundary-crossing.

The argument for letting contract modifications stand is far more problematic, however, than the libertarian reckons. But that only becomes apparent once the libertarian starts paying attention to his responsibility-based intuitions. To see why this is so, we will have to turn to yet another extravagant hypothetical.

The Case of the Prescient Robbery Victim. A man is held up by a robber. The man happens to be wearing a very attractive wristwatch, which immediately catches the attention of the thug. The man is very attached to his wristwatch for sentimental reasons, and he pleads with the robber not to take it from him. What's more, he backs up his pleas with an offer. He tells the thug: "Come to my office tomorrow and I will give you $1,000 in cash." He actually writes out an IOU. Is this IOU binding? No, of course not. By the libertarian's lights, this is the most straightforward kind of nonbinding promise. It was extracted at gunpoint.

What would an economist or a utilitarian say about the question of whether this promise should be binding? He would say it depends. He would say that quite possibly it should be binding. He would point out that it is quite conceivable that robbery victims would, by and large, be better off if they were able to strike enforceable bargains at gunpoint. He would worry, of course, that allowing such bargains would serve to encourage robberies. He would also worry that it would enable robbers to extract from their victims more than just what they happen to be wearing at the moment: after all, the robber could try to get the victim to sign over all of his possessions, or even future income. But how substantial such worries are would depend a great deal on further background facts. In any event, the economist would not categorically rule out making some such bargains enforceable. In this, then, the economist very much parts company with his customary ally, the libertarian. The libertarian would say that although it might on the whole be eminently desirable for such bargains to be enforceable, that does not change the fact that it would be unjust to enforce them. Enforcing a forcibly extracted promise for the sake of the overall social good thus achieved is merely the familiar kind of utilitarian trade-off that the libertarian, with his commitment to rights, spurns.

Consider next a variation on my robbery hypothetical. Trying to persuade the robber to accept the promise of $1,000 in lieu of his watch, the victim takes a piece of paper out of his pocket that reads somewhat as follows: "To: Robber. From: Leo. In the event that I am held up at gunpoint and someone asks me to give up my watch, I hereby promise him that I shall pay him $1,000 by the next day, if he allows me to remain in possession of my watch. I make this promise now, prior to ever being held up, so that everyone understands that I make this promise of my own volition and without duress." Suppose the robber accepts this document, leaves the victim in possession of his watch, and shows up the next day at the victim's office to collect his $1,000. The victim at that point tries to renege on his promise. Can he? If we believe the promise extracted at gunpoint to be nonbinding, it is hard to see that much changes when the victim, rather than writing out his IOU, produces a piece of paper which he has drafted beforehand in contemplation of just such an event. It is his handing the paper to the robber that activates the promise; and since this activation occurs at gunpoint, it is hard to see how it can be binding.

Now suppose that the robber recognizes all this as well and refuses to accept the pre-drafted IOU. The victim reacts to this with the following statement: "I understand your concern. Luckily for us both, I learned some days ago that there was a robber prowling in the neighborhood. It occurred to me then that I might end up in just the situation I now find myself in and might be unable to convince you to strike a mutually beneficial bargain, because you would fear that I would use the defense of duress to get out of any promise I made to you. Fortunately, I took care of this problem in advance. I have circulated a statement to several of my friends, as well as several newspapers, promising to honor any promise I make to a robber. This means that no one will be able to argue that my promise is vitiated by duress, since I made it freely at a time when no one was putting a gun to my head." What happens if the robber accepts this new version of the IOU and the victim later tries to go back on it? Is he entitled to?

What the victim would argue is this: "It is true that I promised to pay a would-be robber $1,000 if he left me in possession of my watch. But I made that promise in contemplation of a wrong. That's not very different from making the promise under the direct threat of a wrong, as when the robber is actually pointing his gun at my head. The promise I made in advance of the robbery was prompted by the same fear that would lead me to make it in the course of the robbery itself. Just as I will naturally use false promises in the course of the robbery to convince the robber to leave me alone, so I will use false promises in advance of the robbery to attain the same goal. According to the robber, my obligation to him was activated when I handed over my IOU to him. But I handed it over under duress. That means that I activated the promise under duress. Promises activated under duress are generally considered invalid!" I find the victim's statement pretty persuasive.

It may help to get a better feel for the situation if we translate it into a slightly different setting. If terrorists take hostages and the authorities make certain promises to obtain their release, there is little doubt that those promises are not binding. The terrorists know this, and bargaining with them is correspondingly tricky. Imagine, however, that so far the

authorities have only heard rumblings of an impending hostage-taking.
They anticipate difficult negotiations. Because they fear being unable to
make convincing commitments, they announce a policy that any promises made to hostage-takers shall be binding even though made under
duress. Isn't it apparent that there would be nothing wrong morally with
striking a bargain with the hostage-takers and then blithely disregarding
both the policy and the bargain?

What lessons does the case of the prescient robbery victim hold for the
puzzle of contract modification with which I opened this section? The
libertarian's consent-based intuitions have led him to think that bargains
ostensibly tainted by duress are not really objectionable when the consent
was given *in advance* of the duress. What the case of the prescient robbery
victim shows is that such advance consent may not wipe out the duress
objection after all.

How exactly does this illustrate a tension between "consent" and "responsibility"? When the libertarian admits that duress is a defense against
the bindingness of a contract, he incorporates into his mental picture of
consent a notion deeply rooted in the theory of responsibility. What he
has done, in essence, is to apply in the contractual setting the basic rule
in the theory of responsibility, that one cannot be blamed for the consequences of actions performed under duress. Just as one cannot be blamed
for actions performed under duress, one cannot be held to bargains entered into under duress. In the theory of responsibility, the duress defense
is known to give rise to some mind-boggling complexities. By admitting
the duress defense into the contract setting, the libertarian has incorporated many of those complexities into his picture of consent. The case of
the prescient robbery victim is simply a manifestation of one of those
complexities.

Let me explain what duress-related complexities I have in mind. At
least since Roman times, moral theorists have been puzzled about what to
do with cases in which a defendant took actions in anticipation of the
possibility that he might find himself being pressured into committing
wrongful actions sometime in the future. This was known as the puzzle
of the *actio libera in causa*.[15] Here is a simple example. A famous news-

[15] A survey of the most significant scholarly, statutory, and case-law treatments of this
problem is to be found in Michael Hettinger, *Die "actio libera in causa": Strafbarkeit wegen
Begehungstat trotz Schuldunfaehigkeit? Eine historisch-dogmatische Untersuchung* (Berlin: Duncker
and Humblot, 1988). For two of the most important scholarly treatments of the topic, see
Joachim Hruschka, *Strafrecht nach logisch-analytischer Methode: Systematisch entwickelte Faelle
mit Loesungen zum allgemeinen Teil*, 2d ed. (Berlin: Walter de Gruyter, 1987); and Ulfrid
Neumann, *Zurechnung und "Vorverschulden": Vorstudien zu einem dialogischen Modell straf-
rechtlicher Zurechnung* (Berlin: Duncker and Humblot, 1985). In English, probably the most
recent explorations of the topic are Paul H. Robinson, "Causing the Conditions of One's
Own Defense," *Virginia Law Review* 71 (1985); my own *Ill-Gotten Gains*; and my "Playing By,
With, Around, Under, and Above the Rules: An Essay For and About Fred Schauer" (Festschrift
for Fred Schauer, forthcoming in 1999).

The literal translation of *"actio libera in causa"* is "an action free in its origin." It refers to
the fact that if I deliberately put myself in a situation of duress in which I then commit

paper heiress has heard rumors that a gang of kidnappers is thinking about abducting her and forcing her to commit certain crimes as a way of discrediting her famous family. The heiress rather likes the idea of thus getting to commit some crimes "for free." They would be "for free," she thinks, because she would be committing them under duress. She makes it a point to get rid of her bodyguards so as to make the kidnappers' job easier. In due course, she is in fact kidnapped and forced to participate in a bank robbery. Can she plead the defense of duress to the charge of bank robbery? There is a lot of debate about that. Some have argued that she loses the defense because she helped bring her situation about: for her to present a defense on grounds of duress is like the man who kills both his parents and then asks the court for mercy because he is an orphan. Other theorists interpret the case much differently: they say she is not required by law to keep bodyguards. Not having done anything wrong, why does she lose her duress defense? A vast literature has erupted over this problem—indeed, more generally, over the problem of actions taken in anticipation of some future excuse or justification. By making duress a defense against being held to a contract, the libertarian willy-nilly makes that entire debate relevant to determining whether there was or was not a valid contract. The case of the prescient robbery victim is but a special manifestation of this sort of problem.

IV. The Third Problem: The Case of the Arnold Schwarzenegger Fan (On Trip-Wire Contracts)

There are contracts in law that operate somewhat like trip-wires. When I buy a condominium in a building, I automatically become subject to certain rules set forth in the declaration of condominium, a document filed by the real-estate developer before the first apartment is sold. Typically that document imposes various restrictions on the way in which the purchased apartments may be used—"No home-office medical practices," it might say—and authorizes the formation of a home-owners association with the power to promulgate additional rules as they become necessary. By purchasing the unit, I have tripped a legal trip-wire; I have activated certain rules to which I previously was not subject. The same happens when I buy a share in a corporation: I automatically become subject to the rules laid down in the corporate charter. And it is largely the same when I move to another country: I automatically become subject to that country's laws. Such trip-wires turn out to harbor yet a third kind of difficulty for the libertarian's beliefs about consent and responsibility.

Imagine a court that has to face the following not altogether unrealistic set of cases:

---

criminal actions, those actions are not free in and of themselves, but they are "free in their origin," since I freely set in motion the chain of events that led to my eventually finding myself under duress.

1. I buy a condominium in an apartment building. The building is run by a rather puritanical home-owners association which has adopted rules that prohibit men and women from cohabiting unless they are married. Penalties for every day that a violation lasts are astronomical: several thousand dollars. Having purchased the condominium, I flout the rule. Are they entitled to charge me several thousand dollars for the violation as they want to?

2. I purchase a share in a corporation that has an unusual, but hardly extraordinary provision in its corporate charter which provides that anyone who acquires more than 40 percent of the corporation's shares is required to offer to buy all shares of the other (the minority) shareholders for a specified price. That price is set at some astronomical level, something like twice the price that shares have sold for at their best. At first, I buy only 30 percent of the shares, own them for a while, and collect dividends. Then I decide to increase my holdings to 40 percent. But I don't want to buy the remaining 60 percent at the astronomical price the charter prescribes. Should the company be able to force me to do so?

3. I take up residence in the secluded island of Draconia. The laws of Draconia provide that I must pay half of my wealth in taxes every year regardless of where it is held. Also, if I stay longer than six months, I automatically become a citizen and am required to serve a year-long term in the Draconian army. Should Draconia be able to do that?

Libertarian-minded judges and scholars have been inclined to answer yes to each of these questions. I made my bed, now I must lie in it. According to them, the trip-wire works, not just legally, but morally. I bought that condominium, acquired those shares, moved to that island, and thereby undertook obligations with which I am rightly stuck. It is not hard to see how the libertarian's consent-based intuitions would drive him to such a verdict.[16] As before, however, things start to look very different once we give our responsibility-based intuitions free rein. To jolt our intuitions in the right way, consider a further extravagant hypothetical scenario. (Not as extravagant, however, as it might seem at first, since it is based on an actual incident in the life of the magician Harry Houdini.)

The Case of the Arnold Schwarzenegger Fan. I approach Arnold Schwarzenegger with the following proposition. I have heard, I tell him, that people who pump iron develop washboard stomachs that make them impervious even to pretty severe blows. I would like to try that out—meaning, I would like to deliver as hard a blow against his stomach as I can muster, both to see what it would feel like and to witness the effect on him. "Sure," he says, "but it will cost you." How much? I ask. "One hundred thousand dollars," says he. Ridiculous, say I, I can't afford to

---

[16] See, for instance, Richard Epstein, "Covenants and Constitutions," *Cornell Law Review* 73 (1988): 906; Robert C. Ellickson, "Cities and Homeowners Associations," *University of Pennsylvania Law Review* 130 (1982): 1519; and Easterbrook and Fischel, *Economic Structure of Corporate Law.*

pay that much. "Well, then," says he, "you won't be allowed to hit me. It really is up to you." Thereupon I take aim and hit him in the stomach. He smiles. He is a little perplexed and then holds out his hand to be paid. I explain to him that I have no intention of paying him, that I don't consider myself to have entered into any contract with him, since I explicitly rejected his offer. In hitting him, I admit, I have committed a tort, an assault. And if he wishes, he can sue me for tort damages. But that, I point out, will net him considerably less than $100,000. Who is right? Do I, or do I not, owe Arnold Schwarzenegger his $100,000 fee?

If we take the position that libertarian-minded judges and commentators have found so compelling when considering my condominium case, my shareholder case, and my Draconia case, we would have to say that, of course, Schwarzenegger is entitled to his fee. Punching him parallels acquiring the apartment, the corporate shares, or residence in Draconia. If we say that by moving into that apartment, or by taking possession of those shares, or by settling down on that island, I have consented to paying the price tag which the home-owners association, the corporation, and the government of Draconia attach to those things, then it seems we also have to say that by throwing that punch, I have consented to paying the price tag which Arnold Schwarzenegger attaches to *that*.

So let us assume that this is what should happen; I should be required to pay the fee. But that position will turn out to have some very strange implications. Suppose that after scoring his big triumph with me, Schwarzenegger has the inspired idea of attaching a sign to the top of his car, which reads: "If you hit this car, it will cost you $100,000." Anytime somebody inflicts ever so slight a dent on his car, or even causes no dent at all but simply makes contact, he will now owe whatever amount Schwarzenegger thinks fit, rather than what the tort law would award. It could get even worse: Suppose others decide to imitate Schwarzenegger. Suppose, further, that two such cars, each carrying a sign naming some dollar figure, collide with each other. What now? Does each side pay the other whatever amount it happened to name on its sign? That seems bizarre.

You might try to get out of this problem by drawing attention to a difference between the car example and the original assault that I seem to have blithely passed over: the original assault case involved an intentional tort, the collision case involved negligence. Whereas intentionally hitting someone can be counted as the acceptance of an offer, negligently running into someone cannot. But that is a difference without a distinction. We can see this most easily by converting the original assault example into one involving negligence rather than intention. We could do that by changing slightly the request I make of Schwarzenegger. I tell him: "I would like to see what it would be like to take aim at a person and then try to pull back at the last minute. Of course that's a risky thing. I may not succeed in restraining my fist at the last minute as I plan to, in which case I might end up hitting you quite hard. Since the risk of my doing so would be quite substantial, I would be guilty of negligently having hurt you. So I ask that you relieve me of liability by assuming that risk—for a suitable fee." The fee Schwarzenegger names is, again, $100,000. I then reject those terms and do what I planned to do anyway, and end up hurting him. This example raises the same quandary as the original, simpler one, but it is analytically identical with the collision case. Granting Schwarzenegger his fee in this case would seem to entail also granting him his fee in the collision case. And that is disconcerting.

This, then, is the case against the enforcement of trip-wire contracts, against subjecting me to every rule of the home-owners association, the corporate charter, or the statute books of Draconia. If we do subject me to those, it would seem that we would also have to make me pay Schwarzenegger his stipulated fee for hitting him, and if we do that, it would seem we would also have to make me pay him for inadvertently bumping into his car. Since we balk at the latter, we should balk at the former. Analytically, the cases are completely parallel.

It is worth pausing and trying to see more abstractly how consent and responsibility end up making trouble for each other here. In essence, what is going on in all of the cases in this section takes this form: A says to B, "You may cross my boundary provided you meet a certain condition." B then crosses A's boundary, but without meeting the condition. If we take a consent-based approach, we would say to B: "You crossed A's boundary. That is illegitimate unless you meet A's condition. To make it legitimate, you must meet his condition." If we take a responsibility-based approach, we would say: "You crossed A's boundary. That is illegitimate, because you did not meet A's condition. Hence, you must pay him compensation." Paying compensation will usually involve something much less onerous than meeting the condition. That is what brings responsibility and consent into conflict.

In a way, the Arnold Schwarzenegger example displays the consent-responsibility tension at its purest. It is the law of contract—the body of law which makes it its business to refine and develop the libertarian's thinking about consent—that gives rise to the "trip-wire" approach, the rule according to which Schwarzenegger's attaching a price to an invasion of his rights makes the invader liable for that price. And it is the law of torts—the body of law which, in good part, refines and develops the libertarian's thinking about responsibility—that gives rise to the rule under which the invader feels entitled to refuse to pay Schwarzenegger's price. More crudely and simply put: The law of contracts is about consent. The law of torts is about responsibility. Any case in which contract and tort law collide, as they do in the Schwarzenegger example, is bound to be a headache for libertarians.[17]

---

[17] The disharmony between contract and tort law is a long-standing topic in legal scholarship. One of the most famous explorations thereof is Grant Gilmore, *The Death of Contract* (Columbus: Ohio University Press, 1974).

V. Conclusion

To be a libertarian is frequently taken to be synonymous with a virtu-ally unbridled commitment to freedom of contract. Libertarians generally support the validity of all contracts between competent parties, provided there is no fraud, no force, and no adverse effects on third parties. This essay has argued that there are other things which the libertarian believes in even more deeply—having to do with rights and responsibility—which should preclude him from being quite so wholehearted in his endorsement of freedom of contract. The liberty of contract, I have ar-gued, really isn't all that libertarian.[18]

Law, University of Pennsylvania

[18] The claim advanced in this essay is slightly less unprecedented than it would appear to be at first. Over the last few years—decades really—a literature has started to emerge which in different ways points in the same direction. None of the prior pieces in that literature that I know of make precisely the same points I make here, but they arrive at conclusions that have a distinct affinity with what I say. Here is a short list of some of those pieces: (1) In 1970, Amartya Sen published what has come to be known as Sen's Libertarian Paradox, according to which a certain very plausible understanding of rights is inconsistent with the Pareto principle; see Sen, "The Impossibility of a Paretian Liberal," *Journal of Political Economy* 78 (1970): 152–57. Inasmuch as voluntary bargains, struck in the absence of force, fraud, or adverse third-party effects, are Pareto-optimal, Sen was suggesting—as I am in this essay—that certain ideas we have about rights do not square with freedom of contract. The source of the tension he identified was a little different, however, from the sources I identify. On the other hand, he was not claiming the source he identified to be the only possible one. Sen's claim has been controversial. When Robert Nozick published *An-archy, State, and Utopia,* he thought he had a way of answering it. His answer did not satisfy Sen and appears to no longer satisfy Nozick either. I infer this from a passing, cryptic remark in a more recent book by Nozick, *The Nature of Rationality* (Princeton: Princeton University Press, 1993), in which he writes that "Amartya Sen's work on the Paretian liberal paradox shows that a very natural interpretation of the scope of individual rights and liberties and of how the choices of society should be rationally organized, cannot be easily fit together. These notions need a new structuring" (ibid., xv). Related to Sen's paradox and usually debated alongside it is Allan Gibbard's paradox; see Allan Gibbard, "A Pareto-Consistent Libertarian Claim," *Journal of Economic Theory* 7 (1974): 366–410. (2) Frances Kamm, in her recent book *Morality, Mortality,* vol. 2, ch. 11 ("Agreements"), advances arguments and examples that have numerous affinities with mine here. (3) John Broome, in *Weighing Goods* (Oxford: Basil Blackwell, 1991), and Isaac Levi, "Pareto Unanimity and Consensus," *Journal of Philosophy* 87, no. 9 (September 1990): 481–92, have argued for the unacceptability of the Pareto principle in bargains involving uncertainty when both parties to a bargain differ radically in their assessment of the pertinent probabilities. (4) In retrospect, the long-standing objections to hypothetical contracts can be taken to point in the same direction as this essay. (A particularly compelling discussion of those objections is to be found in Ronald Dworkin, *A Matter of Principle* [Cambridge, MA: Harvard University Press, 1985].) It is hard to read those objections and not wonder whether some of them couldn't be extended into arguments against actual, as opposed to merely hypothetical, contracts. (5) My own work on blackmail and related criminal bargains suggests that ideas about responsibility alone justify the ban on blackmail, and it indirectly suggests that, by similar logic, many other bargains should be treated as suspiciously as blackmail. (6) One can read the literature about the problematic nature of plea bargains and settlements as pointing in the same direction. See, e.g., Albert Alschuler, "The Changing Plea-Bargaining Debate," *University of California Law Review* 69 (1982): 652; Jules Coleman and Charles Silver, "Justice in Settlements," *Social Philosophy and Policy* 4, no. 1 (Autumn 1986): 103; and Owen M. Fiss, "Against Settlements," *Yale Law Journal* 93 (1984): 1073. This does not exhaust the list of convergent developments, but it should serve to provide a bit of context.

THE IRRELEVANCE OF RESPONSIBILITY

By Roderick T. Long

I. Responsibility Not the Concern of Law

Responsibility is often thought of as primarily a *legal* concept. Even when it is *moral* responsibility that is at issue, it is assumed that it is above all in moralities based on law-centered patterns and models that responsibility takes center stage, so that responsibility is a legal concept at its core, and is applicable to the realm of private morality only by extension and analogy.[1]

As a genetic claim about the historical origins of the concept, this account may well be true.[2] What I wish to suggest, however, is that, regardless of how our concepts may have originated, judgments of responsibility are most properly at home in the realm of private morality, and are out of place in the legal sphere.

By "responsibility" I mean, of course, more than mere *causal* responsibility, in the sense invoked when we say that the acid was *responsible* for the corrosion of the metal, or that an asteroid was *responsible* for the extinction of the dinosaurs. Judgments of *causation* are, of course, essential to the working of any legal system. But there is a narrower sense of responsibility, having to do with positive considerations of knowledge and control, as well as normative considerations of praiseworthiness, blameworthiness, and obligation; and it is responsibility in this sense that I maintain is *legally* irrelevant.

Let me quickly qualify this "legal irrelevance of responsibility" in two ways. First, I am using the phrase "legal" here in a fairly narrow sense as well. There is a broad sense in which any organized system for adjudicating disputes and securing compliance counts as a *legal* system, even if judicial decisions are enforced only by voluntary, nonviolent means such

---

[1] "It was in *this* sphere then, the sphere of legal obligations, that the moral conceptual world of 'guilt,' 'conscience,' 'duty,' 'sacredness of duty' had its origin...." Friedrich Nietzsche, *On the Genealogy of Morals*, trans. Walter Kaufmann and R. J. Hollingdale (New York: Vintage Books, 1989), 65.

[2] It does not necessarily follow, however, that a particular moral code's emphasis on responsibility will be proportional to the extent to which that moral code follows a legal model. Ancient Jewish literature (e.g., the Torah) famously embraces a more law-centered conception of morality than does ancient Greek literature, which is more virtue-centered; yet the concept of moral responsibility plays at least as central a role in the latter as in the former, if not more so; think of Agamemnon's and Oedipus's disavowals of responsibility (in Homer's *Iliad* and Sophocles' *Oedipus at Colonos*, respectively), or the examination of the conditions of voluntary wrongdoing in Gorgias's *Encomium of Helen*, Plato's Socratic dialogues, and Aristotle's *Ethics*.

as boycotts and other forms of social pressure. The late medieval system of commercial law known as the Law Merchant was of this character.[3] I certainly do not maintain that considerations of responsibility are necessarily out of place in every institution that could be described as a legal system in this broad sense. My concern is with legal institutions in the narrower sense of institutions authorized to use *force* to back up their legal judgments. (The nation-state is the most familiar example of this sort of institution, though not the only one.)[4] The limits of legal relevance, in my sense, are set by the limits on the legitimate use of force; that is, because I am here concerned only with law that is backed up by force, considerations of responsibility can be legally relevant only to the extent (if any) that the presence or absence of responsibility makes a difference to whether the use of force is justified or not.

The second qualification I wish to make is that it is only *for the most part* that considerations of responsibility are legally irrelevant, on my view. Hence, this discussion might more accurately (if less dramatically) be titled "The *Legal Near*-Irrelevance of Responsibility." But the respects in which responsibility turns out to be legally relevant after all are, I shall argue, largely peripheral, and certainly outside the primary context in which responsibility has traditionally been considered paradigmatically relevant.

II. A Normative Limitation on the Use of Force

My argument will appeal to the following normative principle:

(1) Every person has the right not to be treated as a mere means to the ends of others.

I conceive this right as what I have elsewhere called a BC-right.[5] That is to say, this right is analyzable into two components: a *duty* of everyone to treat the rights-holder in a certain way (the B component), and a *liberty* of

---

[3] For the Law Merchant, see Leon E. Trakman, *The Law Merchant: The Evolution of Commercial Law* (Littleton: Fred B. Rothman, 1983); Bruce L. Benson, "The Spontaneous Evolution of Commercial Law," *Southern Economic Journal* 55 (January 1989): 644–61; W. Mitchell, *Essay on the Early History of the Law Merchant* (New York: Burt Franklin, 1904); Harold J. Berman, *Law and Revolution: The Formation of the Western Legal Tradition* (Cambridge: Harvard University Press, 1983); and William C. Wooldridge, *Uncle Sam, the Monopoly Man* (New Rochelle: Arlington House, 1970).

[4] For other examples, see Bruce L. Benson, *The Enterprise of Law: Justice without the State* (San Francisco: Pacific Research Institute, 1990); Tom W. Bell, "Polycentric Law," *Humane Studies Review* 7, no. 1 (1991–92); and Albert S. Loan, "Institutional Bases of the Spontaneous Order: Surety and Assurance," *Humane Studies Review* 7, no. 1 (1991–92).

[5] Roderick T. Long, "Abortion, Abandonment, and Positive Rights: The Limits of Compulsory Altruism," *Social Philosophy and Policy* 10, no. 1 (Winter 1993): 166–91. The right under discussion here is explicated somewhat more rigorously there.

the rights-holder (or the rights-holder's agent)[6] to use force to ensure that such treatment is indeed accorded (the C component).[7]

If this right is to be coherent and universal, the exercise of the liberty-component must not violate the duty-component; so when Anita forces Juanita to refrain from treating Anita as a mere means, Anita's doing so must not count as an instance of Anita's treating *Juanita* as a mere means. If *every* use of force against another person were impermissible (as some pacifists maintain), then there could be no such thing as a *right* to be free from such forcible imposition, since the permissibility of a resort to force (if not on the part of the rights-holder, then on that of her agent, e.g., the state) is part of what it means for people to have *legal* rights—the sort of rights with which we are presently concerned.[8]

What precisely does principle (1) give us a right to? What conduct on the part of others is it permissible for us (or our agents) to enforce? I have argued elsewhere[9] that the most plausible specification of the principle expressed in (1) is:

(2) Every person has the right not to have her *boundaries violated*, and also not to have her *boundaries invaded* unless such invasion is necessary to end some wrongful boundary-invasion of hers, and such invasion is also not disproportionate to the seriousness of her boundary-invasion.

where the terms emphasized above are defined as follows:

(3) S's action lies within O's boundary if and only if S's action involves using O as a means (whether mere or nonmere) to the ends of others.[10]

(4) S *crosses* O's boundary if and only if S performs an action within O's boundary.

---

[6] I leave open the question of the extent, if any, to which rights-holders should be required to renounce the personal exercise of this liberty in favor of delegation to a particular agent, the state.

[7] I have elsewhere distinguished an A component as well: the moral permissibility of exercising one's right. This is distinct from the moral permissibility of enforcing respect for one's right. It would be legitimate to defend one's right to promulgate Nazi ideology, for example, yet not legitimate to exercise the right one is defending.

[8] Bear in mind that we are still operating with the narrow conception of "legal" here. Claims not legitimately enforceable might nevertheless count as "legal rights" under a system of voluntary law like the Law Merchant.

[9] Long, "Abortion," 170–76.

[10] Note that one can be used as a means without being used as a *mere* means; it is only the latter that constitutes a rights-violation. Some such distinction is necessary, if the prohibition on using people as mere means is not to forbid most human interactions. Crossing someone's boundary counts as using that person as a means, but one uses someone as a *mere* means just in case one's boundary-crossing transgresses principle (2). For more discussion, see ibid.

(5) S *invades* O's boundary if and only if S crosses O's boundary without O's consent.

(6) S *violates* O's boundary if and only if (a) S invades O's boundary and (b) invading O's boundary (in that way) is not necessary to end any boundary-invasion on O's part.

Notice that none of these definitions turns on whether the act in question is intentional. If I trespass on your boundary, the fact that I did not mean to do it does not make my action any less a trespass. Not all use is voluntary use. For example, a plant does not intentionally use water and soil, but it uses them nonetheless. Likewise, if I step on your face I am using your face as a support for my feet, even if I stepped on your face inadvertently (or was pushed).

Since I have previously defended the derivation of (2) from (1), I will not recapitulate that argument here. I did not then defend (1) itself, however;[11] and while I shall not undertake a full defense of (1) here, it is worth saying *something* in its defense, since the principle is hardly uncontroversial.

Although (1) may seem like a paradigmatically deontological principle, I think it receives its strongest support from Aristotle's ethics of virtue (though Aristotle himself did not draw such a conclusion). On an Aristotelian virtue-ethical account, right action is action that expresses the attitudes and dispositions appropriate to a flourishing human life,[12] where the latter is conceived as a life that gives primacy to the exercise of distinctively human capacities. A life aiming primarily at sensual pleasure, or at mere survival, is rejected as subhuman, since it focuses on capacities that humans share with the lower animals, rather than being organized around the exercise of distinctively human traits.[13] But superhuman lives are ruled out as well. Aristotle does urge us to strive for as godlike an existence as possible,[14] but he makes clear that our human nature places constraints on this goal,[15] and that actually becoming a god would not be a benefit for a human.[16] Hence, the best life for a human being is one that navigates between the extremes of subhuman and superhuman:

Man is a naturally political animal; and he who is without a polis by nature (and not through chance) is either base or superhuman. . . . He

<hr>

[11] I previously wrote only that "I shall not argue for the truth of (1), but I take it to be a plausible moral principle . . ." ("Abortion," 166 n. 2).

[12] An action need not actually be performed from virtue in order to express virtue, i.e., in order to be the kind of action that someone with the virtuous attitude would perform. For discussion, see Rosalind Hursthouse, "Virtue Theory and Abortion," *Philosophy and Public Affairs* 20 (Summer 1991): 223–46.

[13] Aristotle, *Nicomachean Ethics* (hereafter *NE*), 1097b25–1098a4.

[14] *NE*, 1177b26–1178a4.

[15] *NE*, 1178b5–7, 1178b33–1179a1.

[16] *NE*, 1159a6–12.

who is unable to share [in a political community], or who through
self-sufficiency has no need to, is no part of the polis—thus, either a
beast or a god.[17]

The Aristotelian virtues, too, can be seen as a mean between the subhuman vice of overvaluing, and the superhuman vice of undervaluing, our
vulnerable embodiedness. To err on the side of the beasts is to be excessively concerned with our animal nature, our physical desires and physical security; this is the error of the common people, whom Aristotle
regards as all too prone to take pleasure and material advantage as their
primary goals, and to neglect the possibility of higher values that may
require us to sacrifice comfort or even continued existence. To err on the
side of the gods, by contrast, is to treat human beings as disembodied
intellects for whom the animal nature is irrelevant; this is the error of
philosophers like Socrates who see knowledge and virtue as sufficient for
happiness, and dismiss external goods as unnecessary, aiming for a tran-
scendent self-sufficiency that is not an option for embodied beings like us.

> For he who flees and fears everything, and endures nothing, becomes
> a coward; and he who fears nothing whatever and approaches ev-
> erything becomes rash. And likewise he who indulges in every plea-
> sure and holds back from none is undisciplined, while he who flees
> them all, as boors do, is an insensible sort.[18]

> Sober-mindedness and indiscipline are concerned with those plea-
> sures that other animals also share in, which thus appear slavish and
> bestial. . . . Indiscipline seems to be justly reviled, since it belongs to
> us not as humans but as animals. . . . Those who fall short with
> regard to pleasures and take less enjoyment than they ought do not
> often arise; such insensibility is not human.[19]

> [Aristotle] used to say that some people are as stingy as if they were
> going to live forever, while others are as profligate as if they were
> going to perish the next day.[20]

In short, one set of vices places too much value, and the other too little,
on the animal side of human nature.

How, then, can it be shown that principle (1) expresses an attitude
appropriate to someone who is virtuous in Aristotle's sense? That is, how
can it be shown that (1) is the truly *human* attitude, that it neither falls
short of, nor exceeds, what can properly be demanded of our humanity?

---

[17] Aristotle, *Politics*, 1253a1–5, 27–33 (translation mine).
[18] *NE*, 1104a20–25 (translation mine).
[19] *NE*, 1118a23–1119a7 (translation mine).
[20] Diogenes Laertius, *Lives and Opinions of Eminent Philosophers*, V.i.20 (translation mine).
The point, once again, is that people who fall short of virtue place either too much or too
little value on their own vulnerable embodiedness.

Consider what Aristotle says about the political nature of human beings:

> Now that man is more of a political animal than the bee and every other gregarious animal is clear. For nature, as we say, makes nothing in vain, and among the animals only man has *logos* [reason, speech]. So while mere voice is an indication of pain or pleasure, and hence is found in other animals (for their nature reaches as far as this: having the perception of pain and pleasure, and indicating these to one another), *logos* is for revealing the advantageous and the disadvantageous, and so also the right and the wrong. For this is peculiar to man, as opposed to the other animals: to be the sole possessor of the perception of good and evil, of right and wrong, and the others. And a community of these makes a household and a polis.[21]

In other words, Aristotle identifies the distinctively human capacity for reason and speech as the basis of our being naturally political animals, for it enables us to pursue our goals through *discussion* with one another. Moreover, Aristotle famously regards *logos*, reason or speech, as the essential trait around which a flourishing human life must be organized.[22] This, it seems, is why Aristotle regards it as an essential component of a truly human life to deal with others *politically*, i.e., through reason and discourse—i.e., as conversation partners.[23] But such an ideal creates a strong presumption against the use of force, and in favor of relying on persuasion as far as possible. Aristotle indeed affirms that it is unjust to rule by force rather than persuasion, insisting that statesmen should be as dependent on the consent of their subjects as doctors and pilots are on the consent of their patients and passengers respectively.[24] I think, however, that Aristotle's insight points in the direction of a more radical critique of force than he is likely to have recognized. To deal with others by force is to act in a subhuman manner, like a beast of prey; we live a more human life (and therefore, in Aristotelian terms, a better life) to the extent that our relations with other people embody reason and persuasion rather than coercion.[25] Therefore, the need to avoid the bestial type of vice gives the virtuous agent reason to accept an obligation to respect other people as ends in themselves, rather than to treat them as mere means to her own

---

[21] Aristotle, *Politics*, 1253a7–28 (translation mine).

[22] *NE*, 1097b20–1098a18, 1168b29–1169a6.

[23] For a fuller presentation of this argument, see Roderick T. Long, "Aristotle's Conception of Freedom," *Review of Metaphysics* 49 (June 1996): 781–84.

[24] Aristotle, *Politics*, 1324b23–34.

[25] Cf. Lysias on the founders of Athenian democracy: "They believed that it was the way of wild beasts to be forcibly ruled by one another, but that the proper way for men was to define justice by law, to convince by reason, and to serve both by their actions . . ." (quoted in Kathleen Freeman, ed., *The Murder of Herodes, and Other Trials from the Athenian Law Courts* [Indianapolis: Hackett Publishing, 1991], 236). Both Aristotle and Lysias are thinking primarily of the choice of persuasion over force in the management of collective affairs, but the same principle seems to me to apply in the case of one-on-one interactions as well. (Cf. John Locke, *Second Treatise of Government*, II, 4–6.)

ends. If this high-level human end places a constraint on the pursuit of lower-level, animal ends, so be it.

This, however, gives us only the B-component of principle (1)—the prohibition on using the rights-holder as a mere means. This, by itself, does not entail the C-component—the permissibility of the rights-holder's (or her agent's) compelling others to comply with this prohibition. I suggest that what legitimates the C-component is the need to avoid the corresponding godlike type of vice, the pure pacifist position that requires the virtuous agent to cling to cooperation even when the other party abandons cooperation and resorts to aggression. The saintlike commitment to turn the other cheek accords less respect to one's own material needs than they deserve. Principle (1) can thus be seen as striking an appropriate balance—a Golden Mean—between subhuman aggression and superhuman pacifism.

But how does this principle affect the legal relevance of responsibility?

III. Two Kinds of Responsibility

The law is ordinarily expected to take cognizance of two kinds of responsibility. The first kind is *retrospective* responsibility, as when a person is held responsible or accountable for actions she has committed. In particular, the institution of *punishment* is supposed to aim at inflicting penalties only on those who have *responsibly* committed some sort of wrong or offense.[26] Wrongs committed through (nonculpable) ignorance, such as not knowing the gun was loaded, are regarded as having at least a strong claim to immunity from punishment, as are wrongs committed by external compulsion (for example, my injuring you because someone else forcibly shoved me into your path, tripping you) or by loss of ordinary mental control (as when an offender is judged "not guilty by reason of insanity"). In all these cases, the inflicting of legal punishment is held to be conditional on the defendant's responsibility for an action that has been committed. I call this kind of responsibility "retrospective" because it is backward-looking; it concerns an agent's relation to an event that has actually occurred (and so lies in the past).

This is the most familiar kind of responsibility, but we also use the term "responsibility" to describe an agent's relation to an action that has not yet occurred, one which the agent is able to perform, and may or may not perform; this is the kind of responsibility I call *prospective* responsibility. When someone says, "It is your responsibility to keep the cistern filled," it is this forward-looking kind of responsibility that is being invoked. This sort of responsibility seems to be a combination of authority and obligation; in the present example, having the responsibility to keep the cistern filled involves both having the *authority* to fill it (though not necessarily

---

[26] Even in cases of actions committed through negligence, the application of legal sanctions presupposes that the agent is responsible for being negligent.

the authority to enlist—much less conscript—others' aid in filling it) and being *obligated* to fill it.

These two kinds of responsibility—retrospective and prospective—are linked, in that the wrongs we can be held retrospectively responsible for are precisely those that it was our prospective responsibility to avoid. Prospective responsibility, too, is thought to be the proper province of law; part of the job of legal institutions is to require people to meet their responsibilities.

My contention, however, is that neither retrospective nor prospective responsibility is a proper concern of the law.[27]

IV. Retrospective Responsibility and the Law

Retrospective responsibility is thought to be crucial to legal judgment, primarily because the defendant's responsibility, or lack thereof, for committing an offense is thought to determine whether, and to what extent, it is permissible to inflict legal sanction or punishment. In other words, the standard view is that there are harms we may inflict on a responsible wrongdoer that we may not inflict on a nonresponsible wrongdoer.

This is the view I wish to challenge. My claim is not that the responsible and the nonresponsible must be accorded precisely the same treatment in every respect; the responsible wrongdoer may properly be the object of moral outrage and condemnation, of social ostracism, and so forth. What I do claim is that there is no use of *force* that is permissible against responsible wrongdoers but not against nonresponsible ones.

Let us first consider, then, what we are justified in doing to a nonresponsible wrongdoer; and then we shall see what more, if anything, may be inflicted on a wrongdoer who is responsible.

Consider two possible cases. In the first case, a nonresponsible wrongdoer commits a boundary-invasion; e.g., Erika, under hypnosis, stabs someone with a butcher-knife. In the second case, a nonresponsible wrongdoer commits no such boundary-invasion; e.g., Helga, under hypnosis, passes out Nazi leaflets on the street. In the latter case, although Helga is doing something wrong (I presume that promoting Nazism is wrong),

---

[27] My thoughts on this subject have been influenced by Randy E. Barnett, "Restitution: A New Paradigm of Criminal Justice," in Randy E. Barnett and John Hagel, eds., *Assessing the Criminal: Restitution, Retribution, and the Legal Process* (Philadelphia: Ballinger, 1977); Randy E. Barnett, "Pursuing Justice in a Free Society: Part One—Power versus Liberty," *Criminal Justice Ethics* 4, no. 2 (Summer/Fall 1985): 50–72; Randy E. Barnett, *The Structure of Liberty: Justice and the Rule of Law* (Oxford: Clarendon Press, 1998); Richard A. Epstein, *A Theory of Strict Liability: Toward a Reformulation of Tort Law* (San Francisco: Cato Institute, 1980); Michel Foucault, *Discipline and Punish: The Birth of the Prison*, trans. Alan Sheridan (New York: Vintage Books, 1979); Walter Kaufmann, *Without Guilt and Justice* (New York: Dell Publishing, 1973); Thomas Szasz, *Ideology and Insanity: Essays on the Psychiatric Dehumanization of Man* (Garden City: Doubleday, 1970); and Benson, *Enterprise of Law*. None of these authors should be associated with the precise views I defend here; the conclusions I defend are closest to those of Barnett, but my case for those conclusions comes from a significantly less consequentialist perspective than does his.

one cannot, in turn, inflict harm on her without violating her boundary and thus offending against principle (2).[28] Let us focus, then, on the first case, that of Erika, the nonresponsible boundary-invader. And suppose that Erika's boundary-invasion is wrongful; that is, either it is an outright boundary-violation and thus counteracts no aggression (she just stabs someone out of the blue) or else it is a boundary-invasion out of proportion to whatever aggression it counteracts (she stabs someone who stepped on her toe). What measures can permissibly be taken against her?

First, one may take defensive action against Erika, to repel or expel her from her victim's boundary. The fact that she is not responsible for her wrongful boundary-invasion does not alter the fact that she has committed it, and the C-component of the right specified in principle (2) licenses the use of defensive force against her. If it were wrong to use force against innocent threats, it is hard to see how the use of force could become legitimate simply by the addition of wicked thoughts to the minds of these threats; for we surely do not enjoy rightful jurisdiction over the contents of other people's minds.[29]

Second, one may restrain or imprison her if she poses a continuing threat to other people's boundaries. Why is this so? Suppose that I deliberately aim a rifle at your head and place my finger on the trigger. Are you permitted to take action against me in self-defense? I might claim that you are not; after all, I could say, I have not violated your boundary *yet*, and thus any violent response on your part would go beyond what is licensed by principle (2). But surely it is more plausible to say that by threatening you with my rifle I have already treated you as a mere means, someone who can be legitimately subjected to my ends. Thus, I have already violated your boundary, and you may respond with force.

But now suppose that my aiming the rifle at you is not deliberate; an uncontrollable epileptic seizure has caused me to jerk the rifle around to face you, and the next spasm is likely to cause my finger to depress the trigger. *My lack of responsibility does not cause my action to cease being a boundary-violation.* Thus, you still need not wait until I actually pull the trigger before using force in response. The broader moral is that if a person's pattern of behavior poses a sufficient threat to others, that person may justly be restrained[30] before she has taken any overt action against those others, regardless of whether she is responsible for her actions.

Third, one may force the nonresponsible wrongdoer to pay restitution to her victim. Here is the argument. If Anita breaks into Juanita's house,

[28] Notice that this principle rules out victimless-crime laws as impermissible. (Or at least, it rules out the *enforcement* of such laws.) I regard this as an advantage rather than a defect of my view.

[29] Cf. Long, "Abortion," 188 n. 46.

[30] By whom? Once again, I leave open the question of whether, and under what conditions, this right may be exercised by the victim (or third parties) or must be delegated to a particular institution.

Anita is illegitimately within Juanita's boundary and may properly be expelled. But suppose Anita leaves with Juanita's stereo. Since the stereo is Juanita's property, Anita is still within Juanita's boundary (and thus liable to justified coercion) until she exits Juanita's boundary by returning the stereo.[31] But suppose instead that Anita destroys the stereo; then she remains within Juanita's boundary until she replaces the stereo with a new one of equal value (or the closest equivalent possible under the circumstances). Moreover, she must also compensate Juanita for the period of time during which Juanita was deprived of the use of the stereo, since that lost time was, as it were, something belonging to Juanita but destroyed by Anita, and so Anita remains within Juanita's boundary until she gives it (or its equivalent) back. More broadly, Anita should be legally required to make good any harms she inflicts on others in violation of principle (2).

Note that in none of these cases does it matter whether Anita was responsible for her actions. If she entered Juanita's premises by accident, or was blown through the window by a tornado, she cannot use that fact as an excuse for not leaving now that she is able to do so. Likewise, if Anita took (or destroyed) Juanita's stereo inadvertently, her lack of responsibility for her action does not void Juanita's claim to compensation.

Now in some cases (e.g., homicide, permanent injury, or the destruction of irreplaceable heirlooms) it may be impossible to make full compensation. Since "ought" implies "can," full compensation is therefore not obligatory. But partial compensation is certainly possible, and so may legitimately be required.

It might be argued that since one remains in one's victim's boundary until compensation is paid, if one commits a crime[32] for which full compensation is inherently impossible, one remains in one's victim's boundary forever and thus may be subjected to coercion indefinitely, in effect becoming the slave of the victim (or, in the case of homicide, of the victim's family). This inference would be mistaken, however. Coercion of the perpetrator is justified by principle (2) only so long as it is needed in order to expel the perpetrator from the victim's boundary. If *no* amount of coercion will suffice to expel the perpetrator from the victim's boundary,

---

[31] I take it that a person's property consists in objects whose relation to that person is such that one cannot use the objects as means without thereby using the person as a means. This might be because the products of our labor are an extension of ourselves (a proposition dear to the hearts of both Lockean defenders of capitalism and Marxist theorists of alienated labor), or because, as Robert Nozick argues (*Anarchy, State, and Utopia* [New York: Basic Books, 1974], 169–70), my seizing the products of your labor is tantamount to forcing you to labor for me. If the stereo is the product of Juanita's labor (either directly, because she built it, or indirectly, because she bought it with money she earned), then Anita's appropriation of the stereo counts as an indirect appropriation of Juanita herself, and thus as a boundary-invasion.

[32] Or if one commits a tort—but one implication of the theory developed here is that the crime/tort distinction may be untenable. For a critique of that distinction, see Benson, *Enterprise of Law*; Barnett, "Restitution"; and Barnett, *Structure of Liberty*. The crime/tort distinction is the exception, not the rule, in legal history.

a policy of indefinitely prolonged coercion makes no contribution to such expulsion and so fails to conform to principle (2).

How much should be required in the way of partial compensation? What principle can be invoked to set an upper limit, even approximately, on the amount of restitution that can be mandated? Consider the clause in (2) that specifies that one's response to a rights-violation should not be disproportionate to the seriousness of that violation. (For example, although one has a right not to have one's foot stepped on, one does not have the right to use deadly force in order to prevent someone from stepping on one's foot—even if in the circumstances only deadly force would prevent the act.) The burdens imposed on the perpetrator by the restitution requirement, then, cannot be so onerous as to be out of proportion to the seriousness of the offense. For example, if a billionaire's million-dollar vase is broken by a fellow billionaire, the second billionaire may be required to pay full restitution to the first; but if the vase is broken by an indigent laborer, a million-dollar debt constitutes a greater burden (a lifetime of debt)—a burden which, in this case, is arguably out of proportion to the seriousness of the offense—and thus the amount of damages that can be demanded of the offender is far less.[33]

We can apply this principle to the problem of uncompensable wrongs: If we think of partial compensation for an uncompensable crime as *full* compensation for *part* of the crime, then compensation ceases to be mandatory as soon as its burdens become disproportionate to the seriousness (not of the entire crime but) of the portion of the crime for which the victim is being compensated. While this does not offer a clear-cut guide to judges, it does place some weight on the perpetrator's side to counterbalance the victim's demand for indefinite restitution in the case of wrongs that are not fully compensable. (I do not mean to suggest that it is possible in every case to *identify* by description a distinct compensable component of an uncompensable wrong. But it is possible for analytic purposes to regard the seriousness of a crime as being composed of portions, each of lesser seriousness, without needing to identify a particular aspect of the wrong action itself that corresponds to the degree of seriousness of each portion.)

I have argued that an innocent aggressor may be subjected to various sorts of permissible coercion, including defensive force, imprisonment, and compulsory restitution. If we define punishment simply as *imposing a cost on a person in response to the person's having committed an offense*, then it is sometimes permissible to punish the innocent—since defensive force,

---

[33] It might be objected that this solution violates the liberal principle of equality before the law. But demanding a million dollars from a billionaire and demanding a million dollars from a pauper do not strike me as cases of equal treatment. In any case, liberal jurisprudence has traditionally recognized the concept of bankruptcy, i.e., a limitation on the claims creditors can make on someone whose resources have been exhausted; and tailoring damages to a defendant's ability to pay seems to me an application of the same principle.

imprisonment, and compulsory restitution all count as costs imposed on the innocent aggressor in response to her aggression. In none of these cases, however, is it essential to the treatment in question that it be *felt* as a cost by the perpetrator, i.e., that it be unpleasant to the perpetrator. Disutility for the perpetrator is a foreseen, but not intended, result of the enforcement of rights.[34] Hence, it is importantly different from the kind of punishment with which we are most familiar (let us call it punishment-as-suffering) in which the disutility experienced by the victim is the main goal of punishment—whether on *retributive* grounds (the wrongdoer deserves to suffer), *deterrence* grounds (inflicting suffering on wrongdoers will discourage other wrongdoers from imitating them), or even *rehabilitative* grounds (discipline and hardship will make the perpetrator a better person). It is generally conceded that punishment-as-suffering is morally inappropriate when inflicted on wrongdoers who are not responsible. But does punishment-as-suffering become legitimate when the wrongdoer is responsible for her actions?

I claim that it does not. The only difference between the responsible and the nonresponsible wrongdoer is the presence of malicious thoughts in the former. But malicious thoughts by themselves are not boundary-invasions and do not fall within the jurisdiction of the law *except insofar as they make a difference to external behavior.* Accordingly, the presence of malicious thoughts cannot justify any *additional* coercive treatment beyond what is already justified without them:

> A restitutive theory of justice varies the level of reparations according to how serious a rights violation has occurred. . . . In contrast, a retributive theory requires that the sanction must be varied according to this factor and also according to how "bad" the offender is who committed the act. . . . This means that the criminal is liable not only for what he did but for *what he was thinking* while he did it. . . . [P]unishments for the mental state of the criminal—whether intention or motivation—can be justified within a rights theory only if one posits that someone has a right to a particular mental state or the particular thoughts of others. . . . [T]o extract more than what it takes to rectify the rights violation he inflicted is to violate the criminal's rights.[35]

[34] This claim needs to be qualified somewhat. In the exercise of defensive force, I may keep striking you because I know my blows cause you disutility and I hope they will accordingly motivate you to desist; or if I imprison you I may set up a device to give you electric shocks if you attempt to climb the prison walls, once again hoping that the disutility caused by the shocks will motivate you to stop trying to escape. In such cases the disutility is intended, not merely foreseen. In both cases, however, your discomfort is a means of controlling you, not an end at which the controlling process is aimed. For example, I cause you disutility in order to keep you imprisoned; I do not imprison you in order to cause you disutility.

[35] Barnett, "Pursuing Justice," 65–66.

As for deterrence, the difference between defensive force and deterrent force is that deterrent force inflicts disutility on the perpetrator not in order to affect the *perpetrator's* behavior but in order to affect *other* people's behavior. Deterrent force thus fails to satisfy the conditions laid down by principle (2).

Rehabilitative force is more like defensive force in that the focus is on affecting the perpetrator's behavior, but unlike defensive force, rehabilitative force typically goes beyond what is needed to protect any victims' boundaries and thus once more violates (2). It might be thought that rehabilitative punishment is consistent with (2) because it involves using the perpetrator as a means to her *own* ends rather than to the ends of others.

One way of responding to this defense of paternalism is to claim (a) that people's interests are constituted entirely by their preferences, and (b) that there is no reliable way to identify people's preferences beyond seeing how they are expressed in actual choices. Hence, it would be impossible to promote someone's good by coercively interfering with his or her choices, because whatever people choose for themselves is automatically good for them. This subjectivist argument is not the line of response I shall take, for I do not believe that either (a) or (b) is true. Instead, I shall appeal to objective features of human flourishing.

First, on an Aristotelian conception, liberty is an essential component of the human good,[36] so that while freedom of choice may not be *sufficient* for a flourishing life, it is nonetheless *necessary* for it.[37] Hence, paternalistic interference does not in fact advance the welfare of its recipient, and so is, in reality, a subjection of the recipient to the paternalist's own goals—a clear violation of (2). Second, paternalism also interferes with the well-being of the paternalist herself, since by forcing her preferences

---

[36] Long, "Aristotle's Conception of Freedom," 787–92. Aristotle himself did not take the value of liberty to rule out coercive paternalism, because he thought that the requirements of liberty (*eleutheria*) were satisfied by allowing consent *to* a political framework, even when very little freedom of choice (*exousia*) was permitted *within* that framework (ibid., 792–98). For a criticism of this view, see Roderick T. Long, "Immanent Liberalism: The Politics of Mutual Consent," *Social Philosophy and Policy* 12, no. 2 (Summer 1995): 1–31.

[37] On the Aristotelian view, self-directed activity is crucial to *eudaimonia* (human flourishing). As Jennifer Whiting observes:

> A heart which, owing to some deficiency in its natural capacities, cannot beat on its own but is made to beat by means of a pacemaker is not a healthy heart. For *it*, the heart, is not strictly performing its function. Similarly a man who, owing to some deficiency in his natural capacities, cannot manage his own life but is managed by means of another's deliberating and ordering him is not *eudaimôn*—not even if he possesses the same goods and engages in the same first order activities as does a *eudaimôn* man. . . . Aristotle's general identification of what it is to be human with rational agency is not altogether implausible—at least not to those of us who would prefer to trust our hearts to pacemakers than our deliberations and the pursuit of our ends to another, no matter how benevolent and wise he happens to be.

Jennifer Whiting, "Aristotle's Function Argument: A Defense," *Ancient Philosophy* 8, no. 1 (Spring 1988): 43–46.

on others, she is dealing with those others by coercion rather than cooperation, and thus is living a less human life.

As for retributive punishment, it is an even clearer violation of (2), since
punishment is a boundary-invasion,[38] and boundary-invasions can be
justified only as a means of stopping prior boundary-invasions, not simply to inflict suffering. But if the wrongdoer's responsibility or lack of it
makes no difference to what the legal system may permissibly inflict on
her, then whether or not one is retrospectively responsible for the wrongs
one has done is indeed *legally* irrelevant.

It might seem that considerations of responsibility are legally relevant
after all, because they affect our predictions of a malfeasor's future behavior, and thus our judgment as to what sort of restraint it may be
appropriate to impose. If, of my own free will, I kill a stranger just for fun,
then in addition to the legitimacy of exacting from me (partial) restitution
for the victim's family, it is permissible to lock me up, not out of retribution but because I pose a continuing danger to other people. Yet on the
other hand, if I kill someone because I nonculpably skid on unexpected
ice and hit the victim with my car, then while (on my theory) I still owe
compensation, the fact that my killing of the victim was caused by an
accident rather than by my free choice means that I do *not* pose a continuing danger to others and so should not be incarcerated.

In fact, however, responsibility itself is irrelevant to the difference between the two cases. What really matters is the likelihood of future offenses.
A criminally insane offender may justly be imprisoned, despite her lack of
responsibility, because her condition constitutes an ongoing threat to
others;[39] and, on the other hand, those who pose no further danger to

---

[38] At least, the sorts of legal punishments we are concerned with are boundary-invasions,
since they involve forcible impositions of various kinds. Peaceful, private sanctions like
boycotts, ostracism, and the like can be punishments of a sort, but are not boundary-
invasions, and thus may be imposed for retributive, deterrence, or rehabilitative reasons
without violating principle (2).

[39] It might be objected that my position, since it denies any legal jurisdiction over people's
mental states, cannot countenance treating wrongdoers as "ongoing threats," since such a
judgment makes reference to the wrongdoers' mental states. But my position is that any
causes predisposing people to violate others' rights may be considered as grounds for
restraining such people, be those causes mental states or epileptic seizures. It is not the fact
of the mental state itself, but its tendency to issue in action, that brings it within the law's
purview.

"The liberal conception of justice prohibits not only the unjustified use of force against
another, but the unjustified *threat* of force as well.... It is the right of self-defense that
permits persons to use force to repel a threat of wrongful harm before the harm occurs"
(Barnett, *Structure of Liberty*, 185).

If I point a gun at your head and start to play Russian roulette, you do not have to wait
till a shot is fired before taking defensive action. To impose on others a sufficiently high risk
of boundary-invasion is itself a boundary-invasion. Hence, preventive restraint can be justified. Needless to say, given the potential for mistake and abuse, the scope for preventive
restraint should be narrow. As Barnett writes, "I would limit the use of preventive detention
to those persons who have communicated a threat to others by their *past criminal behavior*.... I would wager that the odds of a crime being committed by someone who has
already committed a crime greatly exceed the odds of a crime being committed by one who
has never committed a crime" (ibid., 213).

others should not be imprisoned even if they are retrospectively responsible for their crimes.[40] It is not the responsibility as such that is relevant.

Retributivists will resist the idea that evil motives should not be taken
into account in the legal treatment of criminals. After all, we all recognize
the importance of motives and other inner states in our judgment and
treatment of other people generally; why shouldn't we take them into
account in legal contexts as well? My answer is that legal contexts involve
an element that is ordinarily absent from everyday interactions, namely
force. The imperative to treat other people as conversation partners rather
than as objects of manipulation creates an extremely strong presumption
against the use of force. The need to resort to force to defend one's rights
when an aggressor's actions render peaceful coexistence impossible is
sufficiently weighty to overcome the presumption; but using *more* force
than is necessary to protect one's boundaries is harder to justify, and the
presence of malicious intentions in the malefactor's head does not seem

---

[40] My position entails that an offender like Karla Faye Tucker Browne (an axe murderer
who was executed in Texas in 1998) should not have been kept in prison, let alone executed,
since (to all appearances) she had become rehabilitated, and so neither imprisonment nor
execution could pass the test of principle (2). More controversially, it entails that a participant in genocide like Adolf Eichmann should not have been imprisoned or executed, because despite an apparent *lack* of rehabilitation, he still posed no ongoing danger to others.
Browne and Eichmann would still owe compensation to the families of their victims, however.

The notion of compensation in the case of Eichmann in particular may seem ludicrous.
First, even those who accept the notion of partial compensation to the families of homicide
victims may wonder how an individual of average means could make any substantial
compensation to the survivors of the *millions* of victims to whose deaths Eichmann contributed. Second, even if Eichmann were the richest man on Earth, it may seem grossly insulting
to the victims of so great an evil as the Holocaust to ask them to accept payment in lieu of
the perpetrator's punishment.

But consider: Even on the retributive theory, there is no punishment for Eichmann that
would not be ludicrously inadequate to his crime. We cannot execute Eichmann six million
times. And even if such a sentence were physically possible, we could not carry it out
without becoming monsters ourselves.

For that matter, as a purely pragmatic point, we must recognize that if there were no legal
provision for punishing Eichmann, that would not mean that he could live in happy impunity. Someone like Eichmann, once his identity and location became known, would
almost certainly be the victim of private revenge; and the perpetrator of that revenge, if
unlikely to kill anyone else, would also have to be released. As Sade wryly suggests:

> Let us never impose any other penalty upon the murderer than the one he may risk
> from the vengeance of the friends and family of him he has killed. "I grant you
> pardon," said Louis XV to Charolais who, to divert himself, had just killed a man; "but
> I also pardon whoever will kill you."

Donatien-Alphonse-François de Sade, "Yet Another Effort, Frenchmen, If You Would Become Republicans," in *The Marquis de Sade: The Complete Justine, Philosophy in the Bedroom,
and Other Writings*, ed. and trans. Richard Seaver and Austryn Wainhouse (New York: Grove
Press, 1966), 296–339.

To some it may seem paradoxical that, after being so highly critical (too critical, many will
think) of public retribution, I should offer private retribution as in some instances a salutary
corrective. Let me clarify. I am not recommending retribution, either public or private. (I do
think private retribution is often more *excusable* than public retribution, but that does not
make it just.) My point is simply that, given human nature as it is, the threat of private
retribution would be a genuine one under the system I advocate, and that some of the
consequences of this fact are not unwelcome (as a deterrent, for example).

a weighty enough consideration to warrant a further suspension of the presumption against force. This is not to say that other forms of punishment, not involving force—e.g., ostracism and the like—might not be morally justified. Certainly we ought to treat responsible wrongdoers differently from nonresponsible ones, in all sorts of ways (some of which may be quite effective as deterrents, incidentally). What I deny is that the greater demerit of responsible wrongdoers is grounds for relaxing the very stringent presumption against the use of force.[41]

Rejecting the legal relevance of retrospective responsibility involves rejecting the time-honored legal standard of *mens rea* ("accountable mind"), which makes the imposition of criminal penalties depend on showing that the lawbreaker acted with intent. Dispensing with *mens rea* will strike many, particularly those of retributivist persuasion, as grossly counterintuitive.[42] Roger Pilon offers a retributivist defense of *mens rea*:

> Are we really to treat, by way of remedy, my accidentally hitting you with my automobile and my intentionally hitting you with a club as acts of the same kind? Is the *mens rea* element to be allowed *no* place in the calculation? Even if we include in the compensation due the

---

[41] A still weaker case for retribution, in my view, is the idea that punishment is needed to send a "message." "The act of punishment constitutes symbolic condemnation of the offender for his offense. As such it serves to uphold and enforce collective moral norms violated by the criminal." See Franklin G. Miller, "Restitution and Punishment: A Reply to Barnett," *Ethics* 88, no. 4 (July 1978): 359. I find the notion of *symbolic* or *expressive* violence a rather disturbing one. In any case, the need to express symbolic condemnation is hardly weighty enough to overcome the presumption against force, given the numerous other methods available for expressing symbolic condemnation.

[42] It should be noted, however, that our own legal system's commitment to *mens rea* is not unambiguous:

> Frequently, in the modern era, the Anglo-American criminal law has imposed liability without requiring the showing of a *mens rea* or guilty mind. . . . Criminal statutes are frequently silent on what sort of *mens rea*, if any, must be shown. . . . Although Sir William Blackstone, writing in the 18th century, asserted that the *mens rea* is an indispensable element of a crime, developments that have occurred largely since that time have created a considerable body of penal offenses in which no intent or other mental state need be shown. Absence of the *mens rea* requirement characterizes a few offenses like statutory rape, in which knowledge that the girl is below the age of consent is not necessary to liability, and bigamy, which in most jurisdictions may be committed even though the parties believe in complete good faith that they are free to marry. For the most part, however, absolute liability has been created by statutes defining offenses to which only slight or moderate penalties are attached. These offenses, sometimes called "public-welfare offenses," are most frequently concerned with economic regulation or with protection of the public health and safety. . . . The maxim *ignorantia facti excusat* ("ignorance of fact excuses") represents one aspect of the *mens rea* doctrine. . . . On the other hand, the Anglo-American law recognizes the maxim *ignorantia legis neminem excusat* ("ignorance of the law excuses no one"). . . . The doctrine that mistakes of law do not excuse seems reasonably supportable when the offense involves conduct which would be recognized as dangerous and immoral by any responsible adult. The matter is much less clear, however, when the case is one of a statutory offense prohibiting conduct that is not obviously dangerous or immoral.

Francis A. Allen, "Criminal Law," in *Encyclopedia Britannica*, vol. 6 (Chicago: William Benton, 1970), 765.

victim . . . special damage, including the costs of apprehension, trial, and legal fees for both sides, and general damages, including pain and suffering . . . there still remains a crucial element that these considerations do not touch. For thus far the compensation is identical with that ideally due the victim in a simple civil action. . . . The reduction of criminal wrongs to civil wrongs . . . or at least the addressing of criminal wrongs with civil penalties, bespeaks an all too primitive view of what in fact is at issue in the matter of crime. . . . For the element missing from the mere tort but present in the criminal act is the guilty mind. The criminal has not simply harmed you. *He has affronted your dignity.* He has *intentionally* used you, against your will, for his own ends. He cannot simply pay damages as though his action were accidental or unintentional. How would this right the wrong? . . . [H]ow would compensation make the victim whole again? For compensation does not reach the whole of what is involved—it does not reach the *mens rea* element. There is simply no amount of money that will rectify certain wrongs.[43]

It is quite true that restitution cannot always make the victim whole.[44] But punishing the perpetrator cannot make the victim whole either. Restitution at least goes some way toward making the victim whole, while punishment does nothing of the sort.

Pilon suggests that retributive punishment does satisfy the intent behind the requirement of making the victim whole, for it restores equality between the two parties:

The original act . . . creates a right in the victim (or his surrogate) to use the criminal as he himself was used. Only so will the parties be treated as equals. For only so will the *character* of the original act be reflected in the remedy. Money damages simply do not do this. It is the *using* of one person by another—this affront to the victim's dignity or integrity—that must be captured in the criminal remedy. Thus the victim's treatment of the criminal is equal in character to the treatment he himself suffered.[45]

I have two problems with this argument. First, in the case of restitution the intent is to restore equality by *making the victim better off at the expense of the perpetrator.* Retribution merely makes the perpetrator worse off without improving the prospects of the victim (unless the victim's lot is

[43] Roger Pilon, "Criminal Remedies: Restitution, Punishment, or Both?" *Ethics* 88, no. 4 (July 1978): 350–52.
[44] I would disagree, however, with Pilon's contention that in the case of intentional injury, no amount of restitution could make the victim whole. If Bill Gates were to empty a bucket of Jell-O over my head, and then sign over to me half his fortune by way of restitution, I would regard myself as more than adequately compensated for his action. (Bill Gates, if you're reading this, please take note.)
[45] Pilon, "Criminal Remedies," 355–56.

supposed to be improved simply by the experience of retributive satisfaction with the perpetrator's punishment). In any case, the point of
restitution is not to restore "equality" but to end the perpetrator's ongoing invasion of his victim's boundary.

Second, the notion that the remedy must have the same character as the
original offense (and so must be a harmful using of the criminal, as
opposed to mere financial compensation) has unsettling implications. For
it was a crucial aspect of the original offense that it was *unjust* and
excessive; that is precisely what is horrendous about it. So must not the
remedy too, if it is to share the character of the offense, be unjust and
excessive? The logic of retribution points in the direction, not of an eye for
an eye (for how could an eye justly taken be any match for an eye unjustly
taken?), but of two eyes for an eye, or a life for an eye.[46]

Pilon insists that because "the criminal intentionally used the victim for
his own ends, and against the victim's will . . . the criminal alienated his
own right against being similarly treated by the victim (or by anyone else
acting on behalf of the victim)."[47] But remember that the criminal's right
against being ill treated is grounded in the duty of others to live a life of
rational cooperation, and that this duty, in turn, is part of living a truly
human life. Thus, it is not in the criminal's power to alienate this right; it
consists in facts about other people's good that he cannot alter by any
action of his own.

Advocates of a deterrence theory of punishment will offer somewhat
different objections. From the point of view of deterrence, the difference
between responsible and nonresponsible wrongdoers is that the behavior
of the former (but not of the latter) is responsive to incentives, and therefore it makes sense to apply legal sanctions to the former but not to the
latter. The fact remains, however, that the prospect of having to pay
restitution certainly will have some deterrent effect, even if such deterrence is not the justificatory ground of the restitution policy.

It may be true that a greater degree of deterrence could be achieved
through a policy of punishment that goes beyond mere restitution. But
such a policy has a high moral cost, once we take into account the fact that
such punishment will be inflicted by fallible human beings. As Barnett
points out:

> [A]ny gains obtained by increasing sanctions beyond what is re-
> quired to compensate victims will inevitably increase the suffering
> of those innocent persons who have been wrongfully accused of

[46] One is reminded of the character Asineth in the novel *Hart's Hope*, a victim of terrible
injustice who takes a nevertheless excessive revenge. When told that vengeance is justified
only "if you avenge yourself on those who harmed you [and not, say, their loved ones], and
only if your vengeance is equal to the wrong done" (two conditions she is violating),
Asineth responds, "I was unjustly treated, and unless my vengeance is monstrously unjust
I won't be satisfied." Orson Scott Card, *Hart's Hope* (New York: Tor Books, 1983), 43–44.
[47] Pilon, "Criminal Remedies," 355.

crimes. . . . Every increase in the *level* of punishment to enhance deterrence of the guilty increases the harm inflicted upon the wrongfully accused. That is, once we assume—as we must if we want to be
realistic—the inevitability of enforcement error, a *rule* requiring punishment in addition to full compensation comes at the direct expense
of the innocent. In sum, absent perfect information, a strategy of
punitive deterrence requires that some people who are wrongfully
accused be sacrificed to deter more crime.[48]

Of course, my claim is that punishment-as-suffering is unjust even when
the person being punished is guilty. All can agree, however, that it is
unjust when the person being punished is innocent; and as long as punishment institutions are in the hands of human beings and not of angels,
there seems to be no way to gain the benefit of greater deterrence through
increased punishment without paying the cost of greater suffering for the
innocent.

My case against punishment-as-suffering is not a consequentialist one.
However, I do not take the view that pragmatic objections can be dismissed out of hand. If a virtue-based or rights-based position were to lead
to horrendous consequences when put into practice—if, for example,
restricting punishment to restitution were to lower deterrence so far as to
unleash a torrent of crime that only a more robust practice of punishment
could restrain—that would be, to my mind, a strong argument against it.
Social consequences are not the foundation of my position, but they are
not irrelevant to it either.[49] Once again, however, I do not see that the
threat of mandatory restitution (and, in the case of criminals who pose
serious ongoing threats, preventive restraint) is a negligible deterrent.
One must also keep in mind that the more severe a penalty is, the more
reluctant a jury may be to impose it; thus, increases in severity may be at
least partly offset by decreases in certainty.[50]

[48] Barnett, *Structure of Liberty*, 205, 228.
[49] One of the concerns of virtue is the public welfare; and one component of the public
welfare is the adherence to virtue. Thus, to my mind, neither the requirements of virtue nor
the requirements of public welfare can be defined in complete independence of one another.
To be sure, each has *some* independently definable content; but a full specification of both
will be a matter of coherence and mutual adjustment. The requirements of virtue put some
constraint on what can be regarded as genuinely in the public interest; but the reverse is also
true.
[50] Barnett (in *Structure of Liberty*, 234) offers additional reasons for regarding the restitution system as an adequate deterrent:

> Full compensation includes compensation for the costs of detection, apprehension,
> and prosecution. . . . In such a case it is likely that the subjective cost of making
> restitution will often exceed the subjective benefit gained from the crime. . . . Pure
> restitution can also increase the certainty of sanctions and their proximity to the
> offense. Restitution increases incentives for victims to report offenses and to cooperate
> with law-enforcement authorities. . . . Moreover, since the cost of making restitution
> increases as time passes [because enforcement costs continue to accumulate], even
> offenders will have an incentive to avoid prolonging the proceedings.

Let me consider a few other pragmatic objections to the implementation of a policy of pure restitution. A system in which wrongdoers pay money damages might seem to benefit the rich over the poor. I have argued above that justice can countenance demanding lower money damages of the pauper than of the billionaire, but there may still remain the concern that since the wealthy face a lower marginal utility of money, even the higher damages they pay may be an inadequate incentive to refrain from crime.

This objection is short-sighted, however, for it looks no farther than the point at which the rich malefactor gives restitution to the poor. The interesting question is: What happens next?

> [W]hat about wealthy criminals who could easily make restitution and go free? . . . [Some] worry that the wealthy will have little incentive to refrain from committing crimes in a system of pure restitution. . . . [This objection overlooks] the potential for reprisals that wealthy offenders, above all others, would have to fear in a system of restitution. For the amount previously paid in restitution could, if the victim or the victim's friends and family so wished, be used to make complete restitution for the commission of a like offense against the wealthy offender. While this may not seem an entirely attractive aspect of a system of restitution, it would nevertheless serve as a potential deterrent to wealthy offenders. Indeed, it might well provide a more effective deterrent than the likelihood that our current system will catch, successfully prosecute, and punish a wealthy offender. . . .[51]

I would add that to the extent that it *is* a successful deterrent, the threat of victim reprisal would generally not need to be implemented, thus mitigating its "unattractive aspect."[52]

---

[51] Barnett, *Structure of Liberty*, 181–83.

[52] I may seem to have solved one problem only to create another. Doesn't my position, by licensing this kind of private retaliation, open the door to a reemergence of the bloodfeud? I don't think so. First, my position does not *license* such retaliation; it remains a crime (or tort) against which the victim can legitimately defend himself. And second, Europe's actual experience with restitution-based systems suggests that the prospect of collecting compensation tends to tame the bloodfeud:

> [T]he fact that they would have to give up the restitution they had received as reparations would cause victims to consider long and hard whether they really want a reprisal. . . . I suggest that a less retributivist state of mind would likely result from a system in which victims and their families had to choose between accepting complete restitution or arranging for a reprisal as compared with a system in which government-authored punishment is the victim's only option. That the right of restitution—or composition—largely supplanted the blood feud in medieval Europe tends to support this suggestion. (Barnett, *Structure of Liberty*, 183–84)

Cf. David Friedman, "Private Creation and Enforcement of Law: A Historical Case," *Journal of Legal Studies* 8 (March 1979): 399–415; and Benson, *Enterprise of Law*.

Restitution, when it is awarded, goes to the victim—or, in the case of murder, to the victim's heirs. But what happens in cases where there are no heirs? Can friendless orphans be killed with impunity?

I suggest that this problem can be handled by making the right to restitution transferable, like any other property. In the restitution-based system of medieval Iceland, a victim of modest means could sell his claim to compensation (or part of it) to a wealthier and more powerful individual who was in a better position to extract compensation.[53] (This is perhaps not so different from hiring a lawyer on a contingency fee.) My proposed system would incorporate the idea of claims to restitution as transferable property, but with the additional feature that such claims would survive their possessor's death and, in the absence of specific heirs, become *abandoned property available for homesteading*. That is, the first person to claim the abandoned right by initiating a suit against the killer (thus mixing his labor with the right, as it were) would become entitled to compensation; and this would create the needed incentive for prosecuting murderers even when the victim dies without heirs.

Franklin Miller puts forward four problem cases for advocates of a restitution-based legal system. First, he asks, in the case of cruelty to animals, "to whom should restitution be paid?"[54] Well, it depends. Deciding the question of animal rights lies beyond the scope of my present project. But either animals have rights or they do not.[55] If they do, then compensation should be made to the animals. (Suit would presumably be brought by someone acting on behalf of the mistreated animal's interests; in this respect, animals would enjoy a legal status similar to that of young children. The recipient of the compensation might be a fund to provide care to the animal. If the animal is no longer alive, compensation might go to a homesteader, as in the case of friendless orphans.) If they do not have rights, then compensation should be made to the animals' owners; if the animals are rightless and unowned (or owned only by the person inflicting the cruelty), then no compensation is owed to anyone, and the act, while morally repellent, is perfectly legal. This admittedly leaves no room for the position, held by many, that animals have no rights but nonetheless deserve legal protection; but if animals indeed have no rights, then cruelty to animals is a victimless crime, and punishing victimless crimes

---

[53] Jesse L. Byock, *Medieval Iceland: Society, Sagas, and Power* (Berkeley: University of California Press, 1988).

[54] Miller, "Restitution and Punishment," 359.

[55] Does the presumption against force and in favor of persuasion extend to our relations with animals? I am inclined to answer along the following lines: In the case of animals with whom some cooperation is possible, where the choice between cooperation and compulsion is accordingly a meaningful one, there is a sense, albeit an attenuated one, in which animals count as conversation partners, and this probably licenses the extension to them of some rights, consistent with the limitations on their capacity that justify certain forms of paternalism. The extent of such rights may depend on the degree of cooperation and communication that is possible. Animals for whom very little along these lines is possible may accordingly be lacking in rights entirely (though this is consistent with our having other—non-rights-based, and therefore nonenforceable—moral obligations toward them).

is a clear case of a boundary-violation (i.e., a trespass on one rights-holder that is not a response to that rights-holder's trespass on another rights-holder) and thus runs afoul of the prohibition on using conversation partners as mere means.

Miller's second problem case is that of harm to public institutions. "The rights of private persons are not necessarily violated by instances of such conduct,"[56] so who is entitled to bring suit? Here I suggest that harms to large, dispersed groups could be handled by class-action suits. We have a precedent in ancient Athenian law, which, while not exclusively restitution-based, did treat crimes as torts to the extent that all legal actions against lawbreakers were initiated and conducted by individuals rather than public prosecutors. The closest Athens came to a crime/tort distinction was the difference between bringing a lawsuit on one's own behalf, to rectify a private wrong, and bringing a lawsuit on behalf of the wider public of which one is a member, to rectify a wrong affecting the community as a whole.[57] If possible, compensation should be paid to all the members of the affected group. When this is not practicable (if, for example, the group's members cannot be easily identified), their right to compensation can be regarded as an abandoned right that has been homesteaded by the person bringing suit.[58] A class-action suit could also be brought to ensure preventive detention, if warranted.

Miller's third problem case is that of attempts:

> Attempted crimes may not cause any harm to particular individuals. For example, a terrorist is apprehended planting a bomb in the men's room of an office building. Whose individual rights has the terrorist violated? Restitution to the owner of the building merely for trespass would be far out of proportion to the gravity of the act.[59]

But this case too could be handled by a class-action suit. Endangering the public at large is a violation of the rights of those persons so endangered,

---

[56] Miller, "Restitution and Punishment," 359.

[57] The distinction in ancient Athens between private and public suits was closer to that between ordinary and class-action lawsuits than between civil and criminal cases:

> To begin with, there was no public prosecutor. The State took no cognizance of any crimes, not even murder, unless committed against itself: that is to say, the State did not prosecute for offences now commonly regarded as committed against the community, but only for offences against the actual administration, such as treason or cheating the public treasury. Until Solon's day, prosecution was allowed only to the person injured or his next of kin; under Solon's reforms, any citizen who wished could bring an indictment against another. . . . Any Athenian citizen could bring a public action; but a private action had to be brought by the person directly interested, or . . . by his or her legal guardian. (Freeman, *Murder of Herodes*, 19–25)

[58] The homesteader who receives this compensation could, in turn, be the object of a class-action suit if it transpires that a feasible way of identifying and compensating the group was available but ignored. (A court might also explore the possibility of there being ways to compensate a group without identifying its members.)

[59] Miller, "Restitution and Punishment," 359.

even if no actual injury results. Once again, unless some practicable way of compensating the public can be found, compensation would go to the person homesteading the "abandoned" right to compensation by bringing suit. The same reply can be given to Miller's fourth case, that of reckless driving that endangers the public. (Similarly, if I subject you to a game of Russian roulette I am violating your rights.) Hence, I cannot agree with his conclusion that "[i]f we do not wish to give up such crimes, then we cannot accept a paradigm of pure restitution."[60] In short, none of the pragmatic objections to a purely restitution-based system seem to me serious enough to justify overturning the moral case against punishment-as-suffering that is mandated by the principle of respect for persons.

V. PROSPECTIVE RESPONSIBILITY AND THE LAW

I have thus far discussed the role of retrospective responsibility in a legal system. What about prospective responsibility? We often hear laments over the decline of personal responsibility, conjoined with calls for governmental action. For example, on the left, it is sometimes said that economic advancement for the poor is the responsibility of those more fortunate, who accordingly should be legally required, or at least encouraged, to donate their time and money to helping those who are less well-off—while on the right, it is sometimes said that economic self-advancement is, on the contrary, primarily the responsibility of the poor themselves, and hence that government welfare programs should be curtailed or eliminated. What are we to make of such claims?

Well, let us take the two specific claims I mentioned—that the welfare of the poor is the responsibility of the more affluent, and that the welfare of the poor is their own responsibility—and see what implications either, if true, might have for legal policy.

Suppose that the poor are (prospectively) responsible for their own economic welfare. Since this responsibility is a prospective one, it entails both the *authority* and the *obligation* of the poor to be self-dependent. Insofar as the poor have the authority to be self-dependent,[61] they are entitled to legal protection of the authority; but this is presumably because one could not interfere with that authority without violating principle (2). But what of the obligation—is it enforceable?

When this claim is invoked by opponents of welfare policies, it seems as though they are saying that the government should make sure that poor people meet this responsibility, rather than being allowed to escape it by getting government handouts. In fact, however, this cannot be what is meant; for those who make this claim do not, in fact, favor enforcing this responsibility. For example, if a poor person is denied public assis-

[60] Ibid., 360.
[61] As I am using the term "authority," one can have the authority to do X *without* necessarily having the authority not to do X.

tance, but finds private charities willing to subsidize her instead, opponents of welfare programs will not generally call for the state to *forbid* her to accept this private assistance. They may believe that it would be *better* for her to shoulder her own burdens rather than becoming dependent on charity, so they do believe that her welfare is her own prospective responsibility, morally speaking; but they clearly do not regard this responsibility as properly enforceable, or else they would be seeking to outlaw private welfare programs, not just public ones.

If pressed to explain the difference, they will probably point to the fact that contributions to private charity are voluntary, while public welfare programs are funded by compulsory taxation—so their real objection is to treating the taxpayers as mere means to the ends of the welfare recipients, a reason that has nothing to do with welfare recipients' alleged prospective responsibility for their own welfare.

My point is this: When opponents of welfare programs advocate changes in the law to make poor people "responsible" for their own welfare, it may *sound* as though they are committed to the position that prospective responsibility is legally relevant. As I have tried to show, however, a closer examination of their position shows it to carry no such commitment.

Consider now the contrary proposition, that the economic welfare of the poor is the responsibility of the rich(er). Should this obligation to the poor be legally enforceable? This depends on the grounds of the obligation. Suppose the argument is simply that the rich have a duty of compassion to the poor. If the rich then refrain from fulfilling that duty, they may be behaving reprehensibly, and may accordingly be subject to moral condemnation and various sorts of noncoercive social sanctions; but by merely failing to help the poor they have not invaded the poor's boundaries, and thus may not be coerced consistently with principle (2). As I have argued elsewhere,[62] positive rights are inconsistent with (2) *unless* those positive rights can be plausibly interpreted as necessary for the implementation of the more basic negative right not to be treated as a mere means.

If, instead, the case for the obligation is that the more affluent owe their position to their *exploitation* of the poor, then their status constitutes a wrongful invasion of the poor's boundaries, and principle (2) thus licenses compulsory restitution to the poor. In that case, the responsibility to help the poor is enforceable, but only because it is a special case of (2); the poor's positive right to assistance is derivative from and parasitic on the negative right not to be exploited.[63] Certainly the responsibility to respect people's boundaries is enforceable; that is just what (2) says.

Yet even here, it is not precisely *as* a responsibility that this responsibility is enforceable. Suppose Scrooge owes his wealth to unjust exploi-

---

[62] Long, "Abortion."

[63] For the purposes of the present discussion, I do not (thank goodness!) have to determine what precisely exploitation consists in or whether every case of exploitation constitutes a violation of principle (2).

tation of Cratchit, so that he owes Cratchit compensation. Yet suppose further that Scrooge is currently senile or in a coma, and is unable to understand or act on this obligation. In that case, compensating Cratchit is not Scrooge's prospective *responsibility*, strictly speaking; for our prospective responsibilities are the things we can be held retrospectively responsible for failing to do, and Scrooge is not a responsible agent. He may now bear the retrospective responsibility for not compensating Cratchit *earlier*, when he was still a responsible agent; but he has no *prospective* responsibility now (for he will have no retrospective responsibility tomorrow for his failure to act today). Yet Scrooge's lack of prospective responsibility toward Cratchit does not mean that a court cannot legitimately demand a transfer to Cratchit of some of Scrooge's assets; if Cratchit is legally entitled to restitution from Scrooge, Scrooge's mental state is irrelevant. Prospective responsibility is simply not the law's concern.

VI. EXCEPTIONS

I have said that both retrospective and prospective responsibility lie outside the legitimate scope of the law. There are a few cases, however, in which it does seem to me that legal institutions should take cognizance of issues of moral responsibility. None of these exceptions, however, seriously affects the central point of my argument.

The first exception derives from principle (2)'s provision that one's response to a wrongful boundary-invasion must not be disproportionate to the seriousness of the invasion. This proportionality requirement places a restriction on what we may do in defense of our rights. I cannot blow you away with my bazooka even if that is the only way to prevent you from planting an unwanted kiss on my cheek; nor, if you swallow my diamond ring, is it permissible for me to rip your stomach open (thus killing you) in order to retrieve it.[64] But although principle (2) licenses the use of appropriate force against innocent threats,[65] such use of force does seem a more serious matter, morally, than a like use of force against threats who are not innocent; that is, the case for using force against

[64] The proportionality requirement does not mean that a defender must never inflict a greater injury than that threatened by the aggressor, however:

> It might be objected that killing can never be a proportionate response to any threat short of death. But our concern is with proportionality in moral seriousness, not proportionality in physical effect; to claim that a defensive killing can be morally proportionate only to a threat of death is to assume, between aggressive force and defensive force, a moral symmetry difficult to square with [principle (2)]. (Long, "Abortion," 187)

[65] And arguably against innocent shields as well. (For the distinction between innocent threats and innocent shields, see Nozick, *Anarchy, State, and Utopia*, 34–35.) If I strap a baby to my chest and then go after you with a machete, so that you cannot defend yourself without injuring or killing the baby, it seems to me that in invading your boundary I have brought the baby into your boundary, and you are in your rights to respond; the invader of the baby's boundary is not you but myself.

innocent threats, though it can often be made, will always be *more difficult* to make, all else being equal, than the case for using force against a noninnocent threat. The use of force is an evil, and there is always a presumption against resort to it, though this presumption can often be defeated; force against the innocent is (again, all else being equal) a greater evil than force against the noninnocent, and thus the presumption that must be overcome is greater.[66] It is likely, then, that there will be cases in which it is the aggressor's responsibility or lack of it that makes the difference between a defensive response's being legitimate or illegitimate, and in such cases responsibility does become legally relevant.

The second exception is that there are arguably cases in which whether an action is a boundary-invasion or not depends on whether the agent is responsible or not.[67] Suppose that Caesar is fleeing from the murderous Brutus, only to find his path of escape blocked by Cassius. If Cassius is deliberately cutting off Caesar's only way out, then he is an accomplice in Brutus's attack; his blocking the exit is something that is coordinated with the attack and helping it succeed, and thus is a boundary-invasion.[68]

But now suppose Cassius is no part of the assassination plot, but simply happens to be passing through the door when Caesar reaches it, causing Caesar to pause long enough for Brutus to reach him. Physically this situation may appear indistinguishable from the first; but Cassius's innocence, and the lack of coordination between his actions and those of Brutus, seem to make his act no longer a boundary-invasion. After all, he had every right to walk through the door when he did. In this case, then, responsibility becomes legally relevant, because the presence or absence of responsibility changes the nature of the act.[69] (Note, however, that this exception does not affect the vast majority of cases in which an action can be determined to be or not be a boundary-invasion irrespective of the agent's mental states.)

The third exception is that persons who (temporarily or permanently) lack the capacity for responsible choice (e.g., young children, comatose patients, and the mentally ill) are treated differently in the law, in that other people are allowed to make decisions for them. How is this provision to be squared with my earlier rejection of paternalism?

---

[66] Likewise, I am inclined to think, for the same reason, that the case for force against innocent shields faces even *greater* obstacles than the case for force against innocent threats, and thus has an even more stringent presumption to overcome. Most instances of "collateral damage" in warfare do not, in my judgment, come anywhere near to passing such a test.

[67] The following type of example was suggested to me by David Boonin-Vail.

[68] Whether it is also a boundary-violation will depend on whether Brutus and Cassius are right in regarding Caesar as an intolerable threat to Roman freedom.

[69] Even so, we may wonder whether it is indeed Cassius's responsibility, rather than the coordination of his action with Brutus's, that is doing the real work. Suppose Cassius had walked through the door innocently, but did so because Brutus had asked him to come through at a particular time (without telling him why); or suppose Cassius had been insane, and so had participated in the assassination plot intentionally, but not responsibly. In these cases the coordination with Brutus seems enough to change the significance of Cassius's act, despite the absence of responsibility.

I would suggest that what licenses paternalistic treatment of children is not the mere fact that children *benefit* from such treatment (for foolish adults might benefit from paternalistic treatment as well). Rather, the crucial point is that children lack the *capacity* to govern their lives by reason (while foolish adults may possess that capacity even if they do not exercise it). Just as we are justified in making medical decisions for comatose patients if we have good grounds for thinking they *would* consent to certain kinds of treatment if they were in possession of their faculties (so that, rather than overriding their will, we act as *agents* for them because they cannot currently express their will), so too we may legitimately act as agents for persons whose capacities for rational decision-making are not completely blocked (as they are in a comatose patient) but simply *diminished*, through intoxication, mental illness, or, in the case of children, incomplete maturation. A child's guardian is his *agent*, treating the child as the child would want (so far as can be determined) to be treated if his capacities were undiminished.[70] Thus, what justifies paternalism is not benefit but counterfactual consent.[71]

Hence, one may make decisions for another person *if* that person's capacity for responsible choice is impaired. Since a person's right to act as an agent depends on the absence of responsibility in the principal, responsibility is relevant to the legal question of what rights a person has.

The fourth exception involves contractual obligation. Contract law might seem an utter contradiction to my thesis, for entering into a contract seems to involve taking on a legally enforceable prospective responsibility, which is impossible if, as I claim, prospective responsibility is not the concern of the law. But I think this objection confuses moral responsibility with legal obligation. Suppose I give you twenty dollars, on the condition that you mow my lawn (and you accept it on that understanding). I have transferred my title to the twenty dollars conditionally; that is, the money is yours only on the condition that you mow my lawn. If the condition fails to be met, title to the money reverts to me, and you are within my boundary until you vacate it by returning the money (plus damages for the inconvenience you have caused me). Thus, we have a case for contract

---

[70] The standard of counterfactual consent will presumably overlap considerably with the standard of the child's welfare, but the two will diverge, especially as the child grows older. Diminished capacity is, after all, a matter of degree, and as the child matures, the case for regarding his *expressed* will as an accurate reflection of his counterfactual will grows steadily stronger.

[71] Cf. Roderick T. Long, "Beyond Patriarchy: A Libertarian Model of the Family," *Formulations* 4, no. 3 (Spring 1997), 29. This account provides an explanation for why guardianship rights (specifically, the right to make decisions about what happens to the child) and guardianship duties (specifically, the duty to care for the child's welfare) come bundled together as they do. It is because we are justified in acting as a person's agent (and thus substituting our judgment for his) *only when* the decisions we make are those to which the person would (so far as we can determine) consent if unimpaired.

enforcement that makes no reference to responsibility, but only to the fact of a boundary-invasion.[72]

Where responsibility does become relevant, however, is in determining the *competence* of agents to enter into contracts in the first place. If my rational capacities are diminished, so that I, as it were, am unqualified to act as my own agent, then I am not competent to transfer over to you my title to the twenty dollars in the first place. Thus, a court, in determining whether a boundary-invasion has taken place, will have to take account of whether the transfer of title was successful, which will, in turn, sometimes depend on establishing whether one (or both) of the parties involved is a responsible agent. This is then a variant of my second example, in that while the law is concerned with boundary-invasions rather than with the mental states of the persons involved, there are occasional cases in which the mental states make a difference to whether something is a boundary-invasion or not.

I have listed four kinds of cases in which the law may legitimately concern itself with questions of responsibility; no doubt there are more. The legal irrelevance of responsibility is thus not complete. Nevertheless, the kinds of examples I have given are fairly peripheral to the central cases where responsibility has traditionally been thought to be the concern of law. Hence, these exceptions do not seriously affect my main thesis.

VII. Conclusion

The determination of responsibility is widely regarded as one of the central tasks of any legal system. But the life appropriate to a rational, political animal is one that involves renouncing the use of force except in response to the aggressive force of others. Hence, the presence or absence of responsibility on the part of the wrongdoer makes no difference to the degree of force that may legitimately be used in response to her; no more force may be used against a responsible aggressor than against a nonresponsible one, since only aggression licenses retaliatory force, and the responsible aggressor commits no greater amount of aggression than the nonresponsible one. If my argument is correct, then all legal practices imposing greater costs on responsible wrongdoers than on nonresponsible ones stand condemned as unjust.

Philosophy, Auburn University

---

[72] For an argument that enforcing the contract should mean requiring you to pay me, rather than requiring you to mow the lawn, see Randy E. Barnett, "Contract Remedies and Inalienable Rights," *Social Philosophy and Policy* 4, no. 1 (Autumn 1986): 186-95.

ON RESPONSIBILITY IN SCIENCE AND LAW

By John Staddon

I. Introduction

Respon'sible, liable to be called to account or render satisfaction: answerable: capable of discharging duty: able to pay.[1] The old Chambers's dictionary gives a behavioristic view of responsibility: in terms of action, not thought or belief. "Lust in the heart" is not equated to lust *in flagrante*. It is this view I shall explore in this essay, rather than the more subjective notion of *moral* responsibility, as in, "I feel moral responsibility (i.e., *guilt*) for not doing anything to save the Tutsis [Hutus, ethnic Albanians, etc.]." My presumption is that responsibility implies capability: you cannot be held responsible for something over which you have no control (Hutus, ethnic Albanians, etc.). There is obviously uncertainty in some cases—where control is less than total, where the degree of potential control depends on our own efforts, where we cannot know if we have control until we try to exert it, etc. The relation between responsibility and degree of control is a separate topic which I shall not treat here.

Responsibility in the behavioristic sense is also *social*, we are responsible *to* some person or group,[2] and therefore it goes beyond the individualistic focus of most psychology and psychiatry. I equate "behavioristic" with "scientific" because it is generally agreed that science deals only with "third-party-confirmable" concepts, "public knowledge" in J. M. Ziman's phrase.[3] I will contend that responsibility in law traditionally has been, and should be, behavioristic, concerned with intersubjectively verifiable actions. I will argue that responsibility and determinism are not antithetical but mutually supportive ideas; that factors affecting responsibility, such as drugs and mental and physiological conditions, may be the occasion for increased or decreased penalties; and that the decision to be made in such cases is not scientific but moral. I will conclude, *contra* some modern authorities, that there is no opposition between science and law.

---

[1] *Chambers's Twentieth Century Dictionary* (London: Chambers, 1959). There is very little new that can be said on the topic of this essay—every idea has its antecedents, and an essay that attempted to cite them all would be impossible to write, to read—and to print. I have done my best to reference key items, taking comfort from Alfred North Whitehead's aphorism "Everything of importance has already been said by someone who did not discover it."

[2] Some talk of "responsibility to oneself," but this is metaphorical, usually employed to disguise selfishness ("I'm doing it for me") as altruism ("I'm doing it for someone else").

[3] J. M. Ziman, *Public Knowledge: An Essay Concerning the Social Dimension of Science* (Cambridge: Cambridge University Press, 1968).

II. Responsibility and Determinism

Generations of introductory psychology students have learned that human behavior is governed by causal laws, that it is *determined*. Their teachers often go on to assert that responsibility and determinism are mutually exclusive, that if a man's[4] behavior is entirely caused by his personal history (especially if that history is tragic or aberrant) he cannot be held fully responsible for his actions. Several observers have noted that this idea of diminished responsibility is usually not extended to positive accomplishments. Great achievements are rarely dismissed as the inevitable by-product of a felicitous upbringing, even though failures and misdeeds are frequently excused by a bad one. The opposition of determinism to responsibility, promoted persuasively by psychologists of all stripes, from radical behaviorist B. F. Skinner to psychoanalyst Karl Menninger,[5] provides a supposedly scientific basis for the "abuse excuse." In the notorious Menendez case, for example (in an unprovoked attack, the Menendez brothers murdered both their wealthy parents), defense attorneys introduced testimony about a history of child abuse. Defense lawyers routinely contend that beating of the child may excuse murder by the adult.[6] The scientific assumption that behavior is causally determined has gradually led to a widespread feeling that the concept of personal responsibility is a holdover from an earlier and less sophisticated age, when people lacked the insight into the springs of human action now afforded by modern psychology and psychiatry.

This view does not withstand analysis. I will argue that determinism and responsibility are not contradictory but mutually supportive ideas. About human behavior we are not that much wiser than our ancestors. The advances in psychology, while interesting and even important (especially to psychologists), are, in many respects, little better than Penelope's knitting: for every three steps forward, when we learn something new, we go one or two steps backward—and forget something old. The role of childhood experience in the adult behavior of any particular individual is largely a mystery and (I will argue) is in any case irrelevant to the innocence or guilt of the Menendez brothers and others like them.

A. The argument against personal responsibility

The argument against the concept of personal responsibility runs something like this. To hold a man responsible, he must, in principle, be able

---

[4] For simplicity and on the basis of historical precedent—and because most criminals are male—I use the masculine generic.

[5] Karl Menninger, *The Crime of Punishment* (New York: Viking Press, 1968); B. F. Skinner, *Beyond Freedom and Dignity* (New York: Bantam Books, 1971).

[6] See Alan Dershowitz, *The Abuse Excuse* (Boston: Little, Brown, 1994), for an entertaining description of the creative flights of the legal profession in this direction. See D. L. Horowitz, "Justification and Excuse in the Program of the Criminal Law," *Law and Contemporary Problems* 49 (1986): 109–26, for an account of some of the legal aspects.

to have acted other than as he did—he must have the power of choice, must have "free will." But human behavior is, in fact, determined; hence, human beings cannot be held responsible.

There seem to be two meanings of "free will," an objective meaning and a subjective meaning. The objective meaning has to do with predictability, and control. If behavior is completely predictable under all circumstances—like the position and velocity of moving bodies—it makes little sense to say that it could have been other than it was: "predictable" can be equated with "determined." If we can predict in detail what someone will do, we may well conclude that his behavior is not free, no matter what he feels about it. By this criterion, human behavior is pretty determined; just ask any long-married couple how well they can predict each other's behavior.

Determinism is also defined objectively in terms of *control*. If we can affect something in a predictable way by our own actions, then its behavior is, by definition, determined. Human behavior is notoriously affected by, *controlled*[7] by, outcomes. If I offer you a choice between two boxes, one containing $1,000, the other a piece of coal, I can confidently predict your behavior. Conversely, penalties that are both extreme and certain will likely have a deterrent effect. As we will see in a moment, this kind of determinism is not contradictory to the idea of responsibility, but essential to it.

The subjective meaning of free will has to do with how a person feels. No matter how well Joe Bloggs's wife can predict his behavior, Joe himself probably feels perfectly free. In other words, subjective and objective meanings of free will need not, and in general do not, coincide. The feeling of freedom can perfectly well coexist with perfect predictability and perfect determinism.[8]

It is worth noting that introspection can reveal our behavior to be determined in at least the following sense: we may feel free to choose how we achieve our goals, but in general we do not feel free to choose the goals themselves. It is notoriously difficult to decide *not* to like tobacco or sweet things. The set of "reinforcers," in behaviorist jargon, is largely predetermined. We may choose not to seek some goals, but that is only because they are subordinate to others (we decide not to smoke, not because we cease to enjoy smoking, but because we want to avoid lung cancer). Usually, felt "free will" resides not in our choice of goals so much as in the means we choose to attain them.

[7] This is Skinner's term—but see note 27.

[8] Note that the contrary proposition, that we are, or could be, aware when our behavior is determined, leads to endless regress: because we are not then aware that our awareness may itself be determined. Note also that *failure* to predict does not imply *absence* of determinism. The behavior of a chaotic system like the logistic map becomes less and less predictable further and further into the future, even though it is perfectly deterministic, for example.

Society ·and the law have no interest in subjective feelings (we are not yet in the era of George Orwell's "thought police"). B. F. Skinner's influential criticism of free will takes the objective view for granted: "In the traditional view, a person is free. He is autonomous in the sense that his behavior is uncaused. He can therefore be held responsible for what he does and justly punished if he offends. That view, together with its associated practices, must be re-examined when a scientific analysis reveals unsuspected controlling relations between behavior and environment."[9] Thus, for Skinner, and for most other psychologists, as well as many in the legal profession, determinism ("unsuspected controlling relations") equals lack of free will, which equals no responsibility for one's actions. Or, to put the same thing in the opposite way: unpredictable, hence uncaused, behavior equals free will equals responsibility. If all behavior is determined, then, by definition, in any given circumstance, no man could have acted other than as he did. Hence, man does not have free will; hence, he cannot be held accountable, he is not responsible.

B. What does responsibility mean?

This is an odd argument, because it defines a responsible person in such a way that the usual sanctions (i.e., rewards and punishments) become ineffective, and hence irrelevant. If the behavior of a responsible person were indeed "uncaused," if such a man could, in principle, act in a completely unpredictable way, it is hard to see what purpose would be served by holding him accountable, that is, by delivering reward or punishment consequent on his actions. For example, suppose that a man were constructed in the following way: at a choice point, when he might behave well or ill, he routinely decides at random, by tossing a mental "coin." Sometimes he will behave well and sometimes badly; he has "free will," as far as any external observer can tell—at least in the sense that his behavior cannot be predicted and has no (external) cause (i.e., it satisfies Skinner's definition of free will). But it would make no more sense to hold such a man accountable than to blame the weather for spoiling your picnic. Why? Not because he is unpredictable—even if the weather were perfectly predictable, we still would not blame it for failing to fit in with our plans. The reason we would not blame such a man, I will argue, is because his behavior, like the weather, is *not responsive to contingencies of reinforcement*.[10] It will make no difference, to "random man," or to others

---

[9] Skinner, *Beyond Freedom and Dignity*, 17.

[10] Daniel Dennett, *Elbow Room* (Cambridge, MA: MIT Press, 1984); Michael Levin, *Why Race Matters* (New York: Praeger, 1997), 172 and 318 *et seq.*; John Staddon, "On Responsibility and Punishment," *The Atlantic Monthly*, February 1995, 88–94. I describe the concept of contingency in more detail below.

like him (i.e., to what I will term his *deterrence group*), whether he is rewarded or punished. His future behavior will be the same. Consequently, a man who does not respond to reward or punishment cannot be held responsible. You might as well punish a paving stone for tripping you or a cloud for making you wet. I conclude that equating "responsible" with "possessing free will" and with "uncaused behavior" is false. The behavior of a responsible man cannot be "uncaused," because he must be able to learn from the consequences of his behavior. I therefore propose that the first meaning of responsibility is *the ability to respond appropriately to reward and punishment*.

Ability to learn from consequences does not exhaust what we mean by "responsible," however. The second meaning of responsibility is social. Responsibility is responsibility *to* something or somebody—to the state or to your family, for example. An orphan Robinson Crusoe without hope of rescue or future human encounter can be responsible to no one.[11] More on the social aspect in a moment. I will argue that both aspects, sensitivity to reward and punishment and the social aspect, are essential to the legal concept of responsibility.

Uncertainty—A red herring. The physics of chaos and uncertainty are sometimes used to recapture free will and to evade the conclusion that human behavior is determined.[12] The argument has particular appeal to physicists,[13] because chaos theory, Heisenberg's uncertainty principle, and quantum mechanics, all show that the idea of perfect predictability is wrong in physics. As I just tried to show, the evasion is unnecessary. The key point for free will and responsibility is not predictability but sensitivity to reward and punishment.

There is a paradox, however, that I will explore further in a moment. Sensitivity to reward and punishment depends on variability in behavior, which implies some degree of unpredictability. The paradox is that the predictability of behavior conferred by reinforcement learning (i.e., learning guided by reward and punishment) depends on initial *un*predictability. In trial-and-error learning, the organism must first behave more or less at random, but as the correct response is discovered, behavior becomes more predictable. Sensitivity to contingencies (see below) makes behavior predictable, but not (by definition) unalterable. Hence, an organism driven entirely by stimulus-response instincts cannot be held

[11] He may feel remorse for past misdeeds, but he is responsible to no one for his actions on the desert island.

[12] In fact, for many practical matters, chaos theory is not relevant. Space shuttles and geostationary satellites achieve their orbits through Laplacean calculations. The "physics of the macroworld," as it is called, *is* pretty much predictable. And we have no solid evidence that human behavior, at the gross level that is important for much of public policy, is unpredictable either.

[13] See, for example, Roger Penrose, *The Emperor's New Mind* (Oxford: Oxford University Press, 1990).

responsible—not because its behavior is predictable, but because it cannot be changed by experience.

C. The social aspect

A dog, a lunatic, and an infant are all sensitive to reward and punishment, yet we would not want to call them responsible beings. Fido may learn to stay off the Aubusson if he is consistently punished for doing so, but he lacks *something*. What is it?

Since the M'Naghten rule defining the insanity defense,[14] it has been thought that though he be guilty of committing the *act*, a man cannot be found guilty of the *crime* if he did not know the act was wrong. But "knowing it is wrong" is only part of the story. "Knowing it is wrong" can be detected in an objective way *after* the act, in animals as well as in humans. Many a dog-owner can recognize the "guilty" behavior of his pet after it has transgressed. A criminal lunatic may know his behavior is wrong (or at least, punishable) and may show it by trying to conceal evidence of the crime and perhaps showing remorse when caught. But neither dog nor man may be deterrable in the normal way. These examples show that "knowing it is wrong" does not by itself confer responsibility; the social component, the ability to be deterred, is also necessary. The issue here is not one of reward and punishment only, but of the ability to understand the contingency in advance. The dog will learn to stay off the rug, but we have no way to tell it in advance to stay off. Much the same holds for infants and lunatics. We may reward and punish them so that their behavior may be improved; but we do not expect them to learn from instruction or example. Punishing one dog will not improve the behavior of the canine community as a whole. Others cannot learn from the fate of the guilty. In a community that lacks the capacity to learn from instruction or example, punishment cannot *deter*.

In sum, responsibility has both an individual and a social component. The individual component has to do with the capacity to adapt to contingencies of reinforcement. The social component[15] has to do with the capacity to be deterred by the prospect of punishment and encouraged by

---

[14] In 1843, Daniel M'Naghten murdered Edward Drummond, secretary to Sir Robert Peel, the British Prime Minister who was M'Naghten's intended victim. M'Naghten contended that his mission was guided by the "voice of God." This trial yielded the M'Naghten rule: insanity is proved if the defendant was "labouring under such a defect of reason, from disease of the mind, as not to know the nature and quality of the act he was doing; or if he did know it, that he did not know he was doing what was wrong." See, for example, L. Livermore and P. Meehl, "The Virtues of M'Naghten," *Minnesota Law Review* 51 (1967): 789–856.

[15] I term this component *social*, even though it represents a capacity of individuals, because it depends on the uniquely human ability to learn about consequences through signals (signs, language) rather than only from direct experience.

the anticipation of reward. Normal adult human beings possess both components; infants, many animals, and some lunatics possess the individual component but lack the social component; still other animals, and severely deranged human beings, lack both.

III. THE CONCEPT OF CONTINGENCY

A. Reinforcement contingency

Reinforcement contingency is the behavioral psychologist's term for the relation between what an organism does and what, of consequence, happens to it. What must a man do to get the food, the money, or the girl? Reinforcement contingency is equivalent to the economist's equally technical term *objective function*.[16] Rational-choice economists[17] and naive reinforcement theorists usually end the story there. For both, once the contingencies are set, the behavior is perfectly determined. If the hungry pigeon must peck a key ten times to get a bit of food (a fixed-ratio 10 schedule of reinforcement), it will inevitably learn to do so and go on to develop the characteristic stereotyped pattern of behavior. If single women are paid substantial amounts of child support, they will have more children and the rate of illegitimacy will increase.[18]

It is hard to overestimate the pervasiveness of the idea of reinforcement contingency in human social thought. It is, after all, far from a novel idea, and it has led to practices that are generally very effective. Think, for example, of the behavioral technology involved in the workings of the great sailing ships, especially the great warships of the eighteenth and early nineteenth centuries. A single "ship of the line" might carry a thousand men, each a cog in a vast machine, to work a hundred guns and control dozens of sails in a coordinated way to attack an enemy or ride out a storm. Without habits of automatic obedience and mindless skill, such ships must soon have perished—and, of course, many did. But most did not, weathering storms, reefs, and lee shores that all posed extraordinary risks for cumbersome vessels entirely at the mercy of external forces. The rewards and often severe punishments that maintained this efficiency are well known and often deplored. Yet without them, the tight control necessary to the survival of large sailing ships alone for months on

---

[16] See, for example, J. E. R. Staddon, "Operant Behavior as Adaptation to Constraint," *Journal of Experimental Psychology: General* 108 (1979): 48–67, and other papers in that issue, for many examples of the relations between psychological and economic concepts.

[17] Or, at least, neoclassical economists. There are other varieties that take a broader view (e.g., Armen Alchian, Brian Arthur, Ludwig von Mises).

[18] It is, of course, irrelevant to the economic argument whether support payments actually reward childbearing or simply remove a disincentive. Charles Murray has provided a pathbreaking analysis of this and related issues: see Murray, *Losing Ground: American Social Policy: 1950–1980* (New York: Basic Books, 1984).

the high seas might well have been impossible. On a less heroic scale, the behavior of car drivers is quite sensitive to the penalties for motoring infractions. British drivers seem to pay little attention to speed limits, for example, because penalties for speeding are rarely enforced; but drivers in those U.S. states that stringently enforce speed limits are much more careful, even when the limit is well below what most would judge safe. All governments know the power of the tax code to boost some activities (like house ownership in the U.S., and agriculture in the European Union) and inhibit others (like alcohol and tobacco consumption).

Contingencies do not always work as intended, however. The failures are of two kinds: either the subject is smarter than the experimenter, or the reverse. Examples of the first kind are tax "loopholes." A provision designed to facilitate one kind of activity is turned to unintended uses by ingenious tax-avoiders. As the fraction of the national treasure taken in by governments has increased over the past century, and as the central state has assumed responsibility for ever-wider segments of national life (from national defense to day-care), tax law has become a Darwinian contest in which laws are drafted for one set of purposes and then used by tax-payers to further a quite different set.

But contingencies may also fail because the subject is dumber, or more constrained, than the experimenter thinks he is. Pigeons (and even, alas, many human beings) cannot learn calculus, for example; and no matter how rewarding the reinforcement schedule, a bird that must get its food only by forming derivatives will starve. Thus, there are capacity limita-tions: pigs cannot fly and ants cannot speak. But there are also limitations of a more subtle kind. For example, raccoons can easily manipulate small objects, and so many years ago some associates of B. F. Skinner's, Keller and Marion Breland,[19] who had gone into the animal-training business, tried to train a raccoon to put a wooden "coin" into a large piggy bank. They used the usual method of "shaping"—training by rewarding suc-cessive approximations to the target task: first reward touching the coin, then reward picking it up, then reward moving to the piggy bank, and finally reward insertion of the coin into the bank slot. In this way, the raccoon eventually learned to get food reinforcement by putting the coin into the bank. Very soon, however, the behavior disintegrated. Instead of putting the coin into the slot, the raccoon began to hold it in its paws and "wash" it in the characteristic way that these beasts do with small bits of food. By behaving thus with the token "food" the animals failed to make the correct, rewarded response, and hence blocked their access to real food. The Brelands called this "irrational" misbehavior *instinctive drift*

[19] K. Breland and M. Breland, "The Misbehavior of Organisms," *American Psychologist* 16 (1961): 661–64. See J. E. R. Staddon and V. Simmelhag, "The 'Superstition' Experiment: A Reexamination of Its Implications for the Principles of Adaptive Behavior," *Psychological Review* 78 (1971): 3–43, for a theoretical account of the phenomena described in the text.

and discovered many other examples with other species. In every case, the "reinforced" behavior was superseded by an "instinctive" reaction that interfered with the behavior required by the reinforcement contingency and thus prevented delivery of the reinforcer.

Procedures that present painful stimuli (aversive schedules) provide many other examples. For instance, if two rats, strangers to each other, are placed together in a cage and intermittently shocked through the floor, they will attack each other, and this will prevent them from learning to press a lever to prevent shock delivery. Even isolated rats find it difficult to learn an avoidance response because the shock induces instinctive reactions, such as "freezing," that interfere with lever pressing. Most surprisingly, many animals can actually be trained to produce painful stimuli. After an appropriate training history, cats and monkeys will press a lever that occasionally produces painful electric shock.[20]

The failures of human aversive control are legion. For example, many of the British penal colonies in Australasia incorporated amazingly sophisticated systems of (usually aversive) behavioral control. Some worked satisfactorily; many did not. Norfolk Island, a tiny speck in the Pacific, provides examples of both sorts. Under the regimen of Major Joseph Anderson (in charge from 1834 to 1839), for example, five men might get 1,500 lashes between them before breakfast—for crimes like "singing a song" or "robbing the earth of its seed" (not planting corn properly). "Deranged by cruelty and misery, some men would opt for a lifetime at the bottom of the carceral heap by blinding themselves, thus, they reasoned, they would be left alone."[21] The only convict to leave a record of life on the island at this time wrote of Anderson's even more brutal predecessor James Morisett:

> If you endeavour to take out of [a prisoner] that manly confidence which ought to be cherished in every civilized human being, you then begin the work of demoralization; and it will end in the very Dreggs of debasement and insensibility to every species of integrity and decency, and eradicate every right feeling in the human breast. You make him regardless of himself, and fearless as to the consequences of doing wrong to others.[22]

Clearly, aversive contingencies can fail if they are too severe. The reason? The "misbehavior" effects mentioned earlier. As in the rat example,

[20] See Werner K. Honig and J. E. R. Staddon, eds., *Handbook of Operant Behavior* (Englewood Cliffs, NJ: Prentice-Hall, 1977), for many of these examples.

[21] Robert Hughes, *The Fatal Shore* (London: Collins, Harvill, 1987), 481.

[22] Laurence Frayne, "Memoir on Norfolk Island," *NSW Colonial Secretary Papers*, vol. 1 (re. NSW 1799–1830), Ms. 681/1, ML, Sydney, 25–26.

punishment that is excessive produces behavior that competes with the behavior the punisher desires, and thwarts the intended effect of the punishment regimen.[23] Punishment that is perceived as unjust also elicits reactions (usually aggressive) other than those intended.

It is noteworthy that Norfolk Island was also the site of a much more moderate regime that resembles, in almost every particular, the modern behavioral psychologist's *token economy*, still widely used in such mental and remedial institutions as remain after the closures of U.S. institutions in the 1970s and 1980s. This regime was put in place on Norfolk Island between 1840 and 1844 by one Alexander Maconochie: "Let us offer our prisoners, not favors, but *rights*, on fixed and unalterable conditions."[24] Called the "Mark System," Maconochie's scheme involved sophisticated scheduling of both positive and negative reinforcement.[25] Good behavior was rewarded with "marks" that went toward a reduction of sentence: 6,000 marks were equivalent to a seven-year sentence, 7,000 to a ten-year sentence, and 10,000 to a life sentence—a nonlinear scale corresponding roughly to the disutility of each sentence. Marks could also be exchanged for goods, they were "just wages, and will equally stimulate to care, exertion, economy and fidelity."[26] By all accounts, the Mark System was reasonably successful during its short life, but it was, in the end, stymied by Britain's need for Norfolk Island to be a place where "[f]elons . . . have forfeited all claim to protection of law," the deterrent *ne plus ultra* for intractable villains. Maconochie's humane system failed to meet *this* objective.

B. Contingency versus cause

Despite their many successes, then, we must conclude that reinforcement contingencies by themselves do not always allow us to predict[27] behavior. Why? The simple philosophical reason is that explanation in

[23] Literature provides many vivid examples in which the threat of severe punishment fails to achieve the desired behavior. For instance, in the seventeenth-century play *Surgeon of Honor*, by Spanish writer Calderon de Barca, the clown-servant Coquin is given the ultimatum that he must make the King laugh—or else have all his teeth pulled out. This particular reinforcement contingency is more likely to leave Coquin toothless than the King in fits of mirth.

[24] Hughes, *The Fatal Shore*, 499.

[25] Negative reinforcement is the removal of an aversive stimulus (for example, reducing the convict's time of servitude); positive reinforcement was provided in Maconochie's scheme in the form of goods (such as food, tobacco, and clothes) that could be bought with "marks." "Time off for good behavior" is an impoverished modern version of Maconochie's "marks."

[26] Ibid., 500.

[27] "Control" in Skinner's misleadingly forceful terminology. The effects of contingencies are always limited by the means organisms have for adapting to them; hence, "predict" is a more accurate term than "control."

terms of contingency is *teleological*.[28] To explain behavior by the maximization of utility (the economic idea of *rationality*)—or in terms of its consequences in general—is to explain it in terms of its ultimate goal, not its proximate causes. To say that men act rationally (should they ever do so) is not to say what rationality *is*. As is well known, means are always finite; hence, behavior is not always optimal.[29] Economists have proposed various fixes for optimality analysis, such as H. A. Simon's "bounded rationality"[30] (the idea that people will settle for results that are "good enough," though not necessarily "the best") and others. But given the richness of human behavior, none is really adequate. Indeed, in the long run, the only satisfactory solution is to abandon the whole idea of contingency as an explanation and look directly for the proximal causes, the mechanisms, of behavior.

We are a very long way from that point. However, there is an intermediate approach which preserves the insight that behavior is usually guided by contingencies, but which can prevent us from falling into the trap of teleological determinism. I have called this the *Darwinian metaphor*.[31]

Contingencies reward and punish, but they can only reward and punish *what has actually occurred*. In other words, they can only *select* from what is offered by the subject. Moreover, rewards and punishments have two kinds of effects: they select, yes, but they also have what I will call *direct* effects[32]—for example, shock-elicited fighting and freezing, "washing" of the food-associated tokens, and others. Problems arise if the direct effects of rewards and punishments conflict with their selective effects.

The general process of learning through contingencies of reinforcement (operant learning) is illustrated schematically in Figure 1. The fan of lines indicates the *repertoire* of behavior at a given time. The particular response

[28] More precisely, such explanation is *teleonomic*, in C. S. Pittendrigh's sense (see Pittendrigh, "Adaptation, Natural Selection, and Behavior," in *Behavior and Evolution*, ed. Anne Roe and George G. Simpson [New Haven: Yale University Press, 1958]).

[29] There are extensive discussions of these issues in the biological literature. See, for example, J. Maynard Smith, "Optimization Theory in Evolution," *Annual Review of Ecology and Systematics*, 1978: 31–56; J. F. Oster and E. O. Wilson, "A Critique of Optimization Theory in Evolution," in Oster and Wilson, *Caste and Ecology in the Social Insects* (Princeton, NJ: Princeton University Press, 1978), 292–315; J. E. R. Staddon, *Adaptive Behavior and Learning* (New York: Cambridge University Press, 1983); J. E. R. Staddon, "Optimality Theory and Behavior," in John Dupré, ed., *The Latest on the Best: Essays on Evolution and Optimality* (Cambridge, MA: Bradford/MIT Press, 1987), 179–98; John Staddon, *Behaviorism: Mind, Mechanism, and Society* (London: Duckworth, 1993); and J. E. R. Staddon and J. M. Hinson, "Optimization: A Result or a Mechanism?" *Science* 221 (1983): 976–77.

[30] H. A. Simon, "Rational Decision Making in Business Organizations," in *Advances in Behavioral Economics*, vol. 1, ed. L. Green and J. H. Kagel (Norwood, NJ: Ablex Publishing, 1987). (This was originally Simon's 1978 Nobel lecture.)

[31] Staddon, *Behaviorism*.

[32] These direct effects need not be *immediate*. Instinctive drift follows the laws of Pavlovian (rather than operant) conditioning and takes some time to develop. The point is that what I am calling "direct effects" are effects of antecedent, not consequent, events. Psychologists sometimes use the term *elicited* for these effects.

Environment

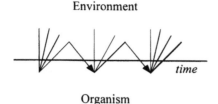

Organism

FIGURE 1. Learning through contingencies of reinforcement.

that has some (reinforcing) consequence ends in a black arrow, which leads from the behavior back to the organism, symbolizing the effects of the consequence on the repertoire in the next instant of time. Notice that the set of rays is a little different after the first "reinforcement." The process continues and, if the contingencies are working effectively, the repertoire will eventually be dominated by the desired, "target" response.

Nevertheless, it is always the organism that "proposes" and the environment that "disposes." If, as sometimes happens, the repertoire elicited by the reinforcer fails to contain the desired behavior, training will fail—as it so often did on Norfolk Island, where the extremity of punishment produced despair and resentment, rather than productive action. The lesson? We must take as much account of the direct effects of our reinforcers as of their selective effects. The error of rational-choice economists and radical behaviorists alike was to ignore the direct effects almost entirely.[33]

IV. RESPONSIBILITY, PUNISHMENT, AND THE AUTHENTIC SELF

In the world of politics, "accepting responsibility" often means nothing more than saying "I accept responsibility," but in the real world, it means paying a cost or accepting a punishment for failing in some obligation. The obvious policy question, therefore, is: How efficacious *is* punishment, both individually and as a deterrent?

Psychologists and psychiatrists, both behavioristic and otherwise, have answered (almost)[34] with one voice: punishment ("aversive control," in Skinner's terminology) is not effective. The reasons vary. The touchy-feely types, for example, argue like this: "Any of us who were raised in

---

[33] This actually gives too much credit to the economists, who were entirely uninterested in dynamics, process, etc.

[34] The work of Sarnoff Mednick, who tracked the careers of criminals with and without a history of consistent punishment for their crimes, is a notable exception. For these individuals, punishment was evidently a strong deterrent; see, e.g., P. A. Brennan and S. A. Mednick, "Learning Theory Approach to the Deterrence of Criminal Recidivism," *Journal of Abnormal Psychology* 103 (1994): 430–40.

the traditional patriarchal system have trouble relating because we've been 'mystified' to some degree by an upbringing that compels obedience and rules by fear, a raising that can be survived only by a denial of the authentic self."[35] What this kind of New Age vaporing really means is far from clear; but the echoes of Jean-Jacques Rousseau are plangent. The general ideas seem to be: (a) each of us has an "authentic self," akin to Rousseau's "noble savage"; (b) the authentic self is intrinsically free and good; but (c) it is corrupted by conventional authority—the "patriarchal system," "rule by fear," etc. ("Man is born free, but is everywhere in chains," and so forth.)

Each of these notions is doubtful. Proposition (a) assumes that each of us has an identifiable essence. No proof is offered, perhaps because none is possible. What difference would it make if there were no "authentic self"? How can such a self be identified? Does a serial killer like Jeffrey Dahmer have an authentic self? Is that self a serial killer or something better? If the former, can we hold up the authentic self as an ideal? If the latter, how do we know? This brings us to proposition (b): supposing there is an authentic self, how sure can we be that it is in every case socially desirable? Answer: We cannot. The novel *Lord of the Flies* is at least as likely to be an accurate picture of man's true nature as *Peter Pan*. And with respect to proposition (c), the evidence is also contrary to Rousseau's view. Nothing is more self-centered, amoral, and uncaring than a baby. Civilization depends upon inculcating, not always by positive reinforcement, altruism and conscience in little beings that begin with few vestiges of either. (The process was imperfectly successful in the case of Rousseau himself, as we know, since he forced his illiterate common-law wife to put all their offspring into foundling homes so they should not distract her from devoting full attention to *him*.)

So much for pop psychology: what thinks the mental-health profession? There are strong economic reasons for professional psychotherapists to downplay aversive control. Hence, it is no surprise to see little support for it within the profession. "Clients" usually seek psychotherapy voluntarily. Indeed, the therapist must live by his ability to attract them. There must be rewards for undergoing psychotherapy. If therapy were generally effective, the reward would be obvious: a cure.[36] But the evidence in favor of "the talking cure" is, in fact, tenuous. The best that can be said is that although average mental health (however measured) after therapy is much the same as before, the variance has increased; that

[35] John Bradshaw, *Lear's Magazine*, January 1993, 42.
[36] Seventeenth-century diarist Samuel Pepys was willing to be "cut of the stone" (probably a gallstone), sans anesthetic, because without the operation, death was certain. Depressives will tolerate the pain of electroconvulsive shock because the treatment, crude as it is, often provides relief. People will accept pain from a therapist if their condition is dire and they believe relief is probable.

is to say, some patients get better, but an equal number get worse.[37] Lacking the ability to cure reliably, psychotherapists must give their patients some other reinforcer to keep them coming. Generally speaking, a regimen that emphasizes punishment and discipline[38] will fail to please. Since no profession can for long embrace beliefs that threaten its own existence, it is natural that hostility to aversive control has come to be the received wisdom among psychotherapists.

It is also worth noting that the professional psychotherapist has an obligation *only to his patient*. The impact of his work and his ideology on others and on society at large is not part of his role. If, as I will argue, judicial punishment is most important for its social effects, we should not be surprised to find little acknowledgment of this fact in the mental-health profession.[39]

Skinner and his school argued against punishment for another reason. Like Sigmund Freud and Karl Menninger, Skinner was a master at waving the banner of "science" whenever his arguments began to violate common sense. He did not reject punishment because it is morally wrong, which would be a defensible, if controversial, view. Like all behavioral scientists, he believed he had rigorously excluded morality from his work. Instead, he defended an ostensibly absurd position by asserting that "science shows" it to be true: he argued that aversive control must be rejected because it doesn't work.

Skinner's argument boils down to two points: punishment is ineffective because when you stop punishing, the punished behavior returns; and punishment provokes "counterattack." Both have proved either to be wrong or to apply with equal force to positive reinforcement. The correct

[37] A critical discussion of psychotherapy, particularly psychoanalysis, that is both knowledgeable and entertaining is experimental psychologist Stuart Sutherland's description of his own treatment for mental-health problems: *Breakdown: A Personal Crisis and a Medical Dilemma* (London: Weidenfeld and Nicolson, 1976). A more recent critique is to be found in Terence W. Campbell, *Beware the Talking Cure: Psychotherapy May Be Hazardous to Your Mental Health* (Boca Raton, FL: Upton Books, 1994). It is not just capitalist insensitivity that makes the bean-counters who run health maintenance organizations reluctant to pay for mental-health benefits. The cost-benefit calculations are not favorable.

[38] As induction into some religious orders—a sort of psychotherapy, one might suppose—used to do.

[39] This myopia seems to be characteristic of all the "caring" professions. Some readers may recall the objections of physician Dr. Marcia Angell, editor of the *New England Journal of Medicine*, to a government-funded study that proposed to compare very low doses of anti-HIV drugs with a no-dose control group, as part of an effort to find an inexpensive treatment for endemic AIDS in sub-Saharan Africa; see Marcia Angell, "Tuskegee Revisited," *Wall Street Journal*, October 28, 1997. Her objection: that some experimental subjects received no treatment. The fact that no subjects were injured, that the value of the "treatment" given to experimental subjects was conjectural, and that the results of the study might benefit millions, carried no weight. Her attention was entirely focused on the fact that the control subjects (under the "care" of the experimenters, in her view) received no treatment. (See John Staddon, letter to the editor, *Wall Street Journal*, November 11, 1997, for a contrary view.)

160 JOHN STADDON

conclusion is that evidence from the experimental laboratory is pretty neutral in deciding between reward and punishment. They both have their advantages and disadvantages: punishment is better for suppressing behavior; positive reinforcement is better for generating behavior; some aversive schedules have more persistent effects than any schedule of positive reinforcement;[40] and so on. There is no scientific argument for the abolition of punishment.

A. Judicial punishment

If it were not for the Gallows, some men are of so cruel a nature, as to take delight in killing men—more than I should to kill a bird.
—Thomas Hobbes[41]

Legal scholars normally identify two purposes for judicial punishment: retribution and deterrence.[42] These two ideas are not, in fact, as distinct as they sound, because retribution, the public sense that justice has been done, itself constitutes a deterrent to potential malefactors. I will assume, then, that deterrence is the chief function of judicial punishment.[43] Does punishment really deter? The argument is clouded by ideology—many people are ethically opposed even to just punishment, and most people are opposed to "cruel and unusual" punishment. And it is, in fact, strictly

[40] In the animal laboratory, the most persistent behavior is generated by *shock-postponement* schedules. These work by delivering brief, painful electric shocks at fixed intervals. The next shock can be postponed for a fixed time by pressing a lever or making some other operant response. Well-trained animals respond frequently enough to avoid all shocks, and may continue to do so indefinitely, long after the shock generator has been disconnected. No schedule of positive reinforcement produces such persistent effects. (It is an interesting sidelight on the nexus between policy advice and laboratory science, that the inventor of this procedure is nevertheless a passionate opponent of aversive control in public policy; see Murray Sidman, *Coercion and Its Fallout* [Boston, MA: Authors Cooperative, 1989]).

[41] In John Aubrey's *The Life of Mr. Thomas Hobbes of Malmesburie*, in *English Biography in the Seventeenth Century*, ed. Vivian de Sola Pinto (London: Harrap, 1951), 188.

[42] The commonest form of punishment, incarceration, serves a third purpose: prevention of further offenses by the criminal during his prison time. Incarceration of repeat offenders can be very effective in reducing crime rates (see, e.g., E. H. Methvin, "Mugged by Reality," *Policy Review*, July 1997, 32–38). But the control here is physical, not behavioral.

[43] Many legal theorists have argued for the contrary view. Most recently, Michael Moore (see *Placing Blame: A General Theory of the Criminal Law* [Oxford: The Clarendon Press, 1997]) has argued persuasively and at length that "[o]f the possible functions for criminal law, only the achievement of retributive justice is its actual function" (78–79). I have no space here to contest this position. Suffice it to say that: (a) Achieving consensus on what *is* retributively just is likely to be even more difficult than getting agreement on what minimizes general suffering. (b) The near-universal agreement that punishment for attempted murder should be less than for successful murder strongly supports the idea that judicial punishment should have a retributive component and not be based on deterrence only. But (c) punishment certainly *does* deter, so it seems unwise to formulate criminal-justice policy without taking this element into account.

impossible to decide the issue *conclusively* by the methods of science. We cannot do experiments on human society, so arguments about the deterrent effect of (for example) the death penalty must always be inconclusive. Did the murder rate decrease in State X when the death penalty was imposed? If the answer is "yes," the objection by death-penalty opponents may well be that the penalty was imposed only because the murder rate at the time was unusually high—and would be expected to fall anyway (because of "regression to the mean"), and thus that fall was not caused by the penalty. But if the answer was "no" (the murder rate increased), the objection by death-penalty proponents will be that the rate would have been even higher without the penalty—or that an increased penalty takes time to have an effect ("Let's look five years down the road . . ."), and so on. These arguments cannot be ruled out. The problem is that in the real world, murder rates are affected by many things in addition to the penalties for murder. And in any case, the causation goes both ways: penalties affect crime rates, and crime rates affect penalties. I propose that we just assume that judicial punishment has *some* deterrent effect, and then ask how such punishment should be sensibly applied. We can then come up with a very simple, utilitarian view of personal responsibility.

The utilitarian view is that the purpose of legal punishment is to minimize the total amount of suffering in society, the suffering caused by crime as well as the suffering caused by punishment. The concept is simple: if theft is punished by amputation, the level of theft will be low, but the suffering of thieves will be very high, higher perhaps than is warranted by the reduction in theft.[44] On the other hand, if murderers go free, the level of murder will be high, and the pain of the innocent will hardly be compensated by the euphoria of the killers. We may argue about how to measure suffering and how to assess the effect of a given level of legal punishment for a given crime, but the utilitarian view[45] of punishment seems reasonable enough. It is consistent with the fundamental principle that government exists not to empathize with individuals (although empathy is integral to the political process), but to act *for the welfare of society as a whole*.[46]

---

[44] Philosophical economists have pointed out that utility cannot be compared between individuals: even President Clinton cannot really "feel my pain." Nevertheless, such comparisons are essential to any utilitarian analysis of social effects. In practice, most writers seem to assume a highly nonlinear scale that effectively rules out extreme ("cruel and unusual") punishments. John Rawls's influential *A Theory of Justice* (Cambridge, MA: Harvard University Press, 1971) also argues for this view.

[45] See Cesare Beccaria, *An Essay on Crimes and Punishments* (1764; Stanford, CA: Academic Reprints, 1953), for what seems to be the earliest statement of this view.

[46] "Why worry about whether the degree of suffering imposed on the criminal is appropriate to the crime?" some might ask. "Why not just minimize the suffering of victims?" One reason is that just retribution probably cannot be excluded as a component in criminal justice, even if it is probably not the only component. Another is that without including the suffering of the criminal in the utilitarian equation, we can raise no principled objection to a colleague of mine who, only half-joking, proposed the death penalty for littering.

In the utilitarian view, the case for *individual* responsibility rests entirely on the beneficial *collective* effects (on the sum total of human suffering) of just punishment. It does not rest on philosophical notions of individual autonomy, or on personal intent, or on anything else at the level of the individual—other than normal sensitivity to reward and punishment. The idea that the law is somehow concerned with the mental state of the accused, rather than with his susceptibility—and the susceptibility of others like him (his deterrence group)—to judicial sanctions, is a recent error which is aided and abetted by the myopic individualism of the mental-health profession.

Surprisingly, perhaps, traditional legal practice agrees with the utilitarian view. Only when punishment is likely to be completely *in*effective as a deterrent does the law limit its use. If a criminal is insane—which is to say that he is not sensitive to rewards and punishments in the ways I described earlier—he is not found guilty. If a prophetic angel had whispered in the ear of Lyle Menendez, "If you shoot your mother, you will die," and if Lyle had believed the angel, but shot anyway, then he is *not guilty*. (Although I would hope we would lock him up anyway, as dangerously insane.)[47] But if, in the jury's estimation, he would have heeded such an angel, then he is *guilty*, because he was indeed responsible for his action in the only way that makes judicial sense.[48] More on this topic in a moment.

"Not guilty" is also the verdict if injury is the unintended result of an action that a reasonable person would expect to be harmless: if the politician's wife turns on a light that then gives an assassin a clearer view, the law would not implicate her in her husband's death—because, not knowing the risk, she could not have been deterred by legal penalties for putting someone at risk. "Guilt" is established not so much by the act itself, as by the potential of punishment to deter the act. Notice that this definition skirts the difficult issue of "motive" even as, in most cases, it comes to a conclusion similar to that which would be reached if we did consider motive (for example, a maid, complicit in the assassination plot, might be deterred under such circumstances, because her knowledge of the risk makes her liable; thus, she would be judged guilty). Traditional law is objective in a way that recent psychotherapeutically inspired distortions (e.g., the *Durham* decision; see below) are not.

[47] What about the individual who is sensitive to punishment in the normal way, but is willing to disobey the law anyway because he disagrees with it? Mohandas Gandhi and Nelson Mandela, but also Oliver North and Leon Trotsky, come to mind. Such individuals will naturally fail the deterrence test. Consistency implies that they should therefore be treated as irresponsible, but dangerous, like a mentally ill person. And indeed, political prisoners are often treated in this fashion, restrained indefinitely but not necessarily punished in any other way (cf. Mandela's long-term incarceration, the indefinite house-arrest of the Burmese opposition leader Aung San Suu Kyi, etc.).

[48] A skeptic might ask: "Well, if he would have heeded the angel, why did he shoot?" The obvious answer is: "Because he thought he wouldn't be caught—or, he thought that if he were caught, he could get off." The belief that a crime will go undetected or unpunished is, of course, a major "root cause" of crime.

B. *What about rehabilitation?*

The utilitarian view of punishment and responsibility leaves the criminal largely out of the picture; he figures only as one among a multitude. The focus is on society at large. But what *about* the poor felon, his suffering and his future? For much of this century, with rising public interest in both mental health and redemptive religion, the fate of the criminal has often been at center stage. In this, as in so many other things, Ann Landers[49] is a touchstone for popular opinion. She recently cited with approval the work of influential psychiatrist Karl Menninger as the last word on the subject of judicial punishment. What were his views? In a word: incredible.[50] Menninger, more concerned with the criminal than the victim, called punishment a crime, argued that criminals are a creation of the law-abiding (who "need" someone to punish!), and believed criminality to be a form of mental illness. To Menninger, criminals should be *treated*— rehabilitated—not punished. He would not have been sympathetic to any view that legitimates punishment.

This is, in some respects, an understandable position. After all, the victim in murder cases is not present and cannot testify, whereas the accused, neatly groomed, remorseful, and perhaps even subject to recent religious conversion, plucks at the heartstrings of the *simpatico* juror. Many are therefore drawn to Menninger's apparently humane position. What are we to say to them? Just this: The issue is simply a matter of numbers. Unfortunately, like most social and political issues, we don't know the numbers and cannot find them with certainty. But we can at least understand what it is we need to know. Granted that our aim is to minimize total suffering, we need to know: (a) What is the probability that a typical criminal can be rehabilitated? (b) How much will he be improved by treatment, compared to his previous state: that is, how many crimes will he commit after a "cure" versus how many would he have committed without it? (c) How much effort (people, facilities) must society devote to rehabilitation? (d) Could these resources be better employed elsewhere: that is, what is the opportunity cost? But the critical question is the last one: (e) How many potential crimes by others would be deterred by punishing this criminal rather than rehabilitating him? (You may recall that this was the question that killed Maconochie's reforms on Norfolk Island.)

The best answers to the first four questions seem to be: (a) low, especially if he has a history of recidivism; (b) not much; (c) a lot; and (d) yes—all with a high degree of uncertainty. But the answer to the last question, with somewhat less uncertainty, is "several." That is, by punishing one criminal for one crime, we are likely to prevent several others.

---

[49] Ms. Landers, now in her eighties, has been writing an advice column syndicated in hundreds of U.S. newspapers for more than forty years.

[50] Menninger, *The Crime of Punishment* (*supra* note 5).

Even if our criminal is not rehabilitated at all, therefore, punishment may be a very good deal for society. And anything that weakens punishment's deterrent effect, including even a very successful effort at rehabilitation, may be a bad deal. Without just punishment, the level of suffering in society may well be higher than with it. Dr. Menninger's view is not so much softhearted as softheaded.

V. Diminished Responsibility

I have discussed some cases of diminished responsibility—children, the insane—that can be understood simply. But there are others that require more analysis. How is responsibility affected by drugs? By a mental-health "disorder"? By "false consciousness"? In some cases, scientific analysis suggests concrete solutions, but in others, analysis can only reduce the question to issues that are, at bottom, political and moral, not scientific.

A. Drugs and responsibility

Not all drugs impair behavior: tobacco, for example, is addictive but does not in any way diminish responsibility. For the purpose of the present discussion, we can ignore drugs that do not affect behavior. With regard to behavior-altering drugs, we need to distinguish between those that are addictive and those that are not. Alcohol, for example, is not addictive for most people, but does impair judgment. The alcoholic may, in his drunken state, be responsive to reward and punishment, as the infant and the idiot are, but he clearly lacks the social component I referred to earlier. The drunk cannot make an accurate assessment of the consequences of his actions. *In his drunken state*, his responsibility is diminished. But someone not addicted to alcohol can both understand the connection between drunkenness and diminished responsibility and be deterred by suitable contingencies from drinking alcohol at inappropriate times—before driving, for example.

For the alcohol addict, it is otherwise. He cannot be deterred from drinking in the same way as the nonaddict. He may continue to drink inappropriately even in the face of extreme penalties. He is, in fact, not fully responsible. What should be done? First there is the problem of distinguishing between addicts and nonaddicts. Is addiction an all-or-nothing condition, for example? If it is, the problem is simpler, provided we have a reliable litmus test. If it is not, if addiction is a matter of degree, then the possibility arises that the number of "addicts" is dependent on the level of punishment. If punishment is severe, there will be fewer addicts than if it is lenient. But suppose addiction is all-or-nothing, and addicts can be reliably identified. Should alcohol be kept from them entirely, and if so, how? Since we cannot predict in advance what the general consequences of different policies will be, and since all of them are likely to conflict with some widely held moral beliefs (such as the intrinsic value of personal freedom, for example), these are political and moral questions not to be settled here.

And finally, what of the individual who has never tasted alcohol, who is neither an addict nor a social drinker? How should he be treated? Clearly, given the right contingencies, he can be deterred from sampling an unknown delight; but the penalties may need to be severe to deter a majority of potential drinkers.[51] Because we (so far) cannot tell in advance who the potential addicts are, many individuals will be severely punished who would not go on to become addicts and would not, therefore, pose a threat to others. Is it fair to punish severely individuals engaged in behavior that, *for them*, is not potentially dangerous? Is it even fair to punish potential addicts, given that their addictive potential is not their fault? Once again, we are in the realm of politics and moral philosophy, facing questions that go beyond the ambitions of this essay.

B. Psychological disorder

Drug addiction may or may not be all-or-nothing, but mental disorders obviously come in myriad varieties, from the clearly insane and incompetent to some of the characters in Woody Allen movies who, in past ages, might have been questioned as to their morals but not their health. Now all are subsumed under the heading of "mental-health problems." Unfortunately, the classification of mental disorders is not a science. The American Psychiatric Association's *Diagnostic and Statistical Manual of Mental Disorders* (DSM), the bible for mental-health professionals, is a strange mixture of science, fashion, politics, and the economics of the medical profession.[52] In the words of a *sympathetic* commentator: "[N]ew disorders do not represent claims to fresh biological knowledge. Which is to say that yes, a particular mental disorder is whatever the DSM says it is."[53]

DSM "disorders" may not represent biological knowledge, but all too often they do represent arguments for diminished responsibility. "The Devil made me do it" is no longer acceptable, but syndromes from PMS to "road rage" are now routinely offered as mitigating circumstances in

---

[51] Of course, prohibition is one solution to this dilemma. But again, nonaddicts are punished needlessly by being deprived of a harmless (for them) enjoyment. Is the greater good served? What about personal freedom, which is also a good? Again, these questions go beyond practical science.

[52] See, for example, Herb Kutchins and Stuart A. Kirk's recent exposé *Making Us Crazy: DSM—The Psychiatric Bible and the Creation of Mental Disorders* (New York: The Free Press, 1997); and L. J. Davis, "The Encyclopedia of Insanity—A Psychiatric Handbook Lists a Madness for Everyone," *Harpers Magazine*, February 1997.

[53] Larissa MacFarquhar, "Diagnosis: Totally Sane—The DSM Isn't Crazy in the Slightest, A Review of Kutchins and Kirk," *Slate* (internet magazine), November 12, 1997.

criminal trials. When does a mental disorder diminish responsibility, and what should be done about it?

Once again, normal susceptibility to the effects of reward and punishment suggests an answer. If the individual is so disordered that he is not deterred by the prospect of punishment, then his responsibility is diminished. But (it may be objected) surely we have merely shifted the problem. What is "normal susceptibility"? What is "normal punishment"? Even a very disturbed individual might well be deterred by the prospect of a severe punishment, severe enough to be unacceptable to most people. We have, in fact, already encountered this problem, in connection with drug addiction. In the case of mental disorders, however, we know that there are grades of susceptibility—of "self control,"[54] to use an older terminology. Indeed, quite apart from supposed mental illness, we know that there are individual differences in susceptibility to punishment, as there are in everything else. So the question of mental illness boils down to this: How are we to deal with individual differences in "self control"?

We can distinguish three cases, differing in the way that individual differences are identified, and in the accuracy with which people can be categorized: self-identification; identification by behavioral test; and identification by "markers."

Self-identification. Most straightforward is the case of the repeat offender. An individual who breaks the law repeatedly, and is caught and punished, is clearly less susceptible to deterrence than average. And the law accommodates this difference by increasing the punishment for repeated offenses. This method is self-evidently valid and is not controversial. Notice, however, that the reduced sensitivity to contingencies demonstrated by recidivism is not taken as a *mitigating* factor, but as a reason to increase the level of punishment. The opposite is true for mental disorders, which are always proposed as mitigating factors.[55]

Identification by behavioral test. It is conceivable that a psychological test, like an intelligence test, could be devised to identify people who are less likely than average to respond to normal deterrents. Perhaps some of

---

[54] There is a more technical meaning for self-control, as capacity to delay gratification (i.e., impulse control), which is treated at length in an elegant experimental literature. (See, for example, George Ainslie, *Picoeconomics* [Cambridge: Cambridge University Press, 1992]; and Howard Rachlin and Leonard Green, "Commitment, Choice, and Self-Control," *Journal of the Experimental Analysis of Behavior* 17 [1972]: 15–22.) I intend the simpler meaning—susceptibility to deterrence—here.

[55] There is a category of diminished responsibility that is the mirror image of the repeat offender. The repeat offender is, by definition, insufficiently deterred by punishment. The complementary category is people who are excessively encouraged by reward. It may seem odd to see such people as less responsible than average, but this is apparently the view of a colleague of mine who recently termed payments to a public lottery an "implicit tax." Granted that a tax is "a contribution exacted by the state: anything imposed, exacted or burdensome," to call voluntary and presumably pleasurable participation in a lottery a tax is, on its face, absurd—unless you feel that people who play a lottery cannot control themselves—are not fully responsible. This category is not yet fully accepted in the legal arena ("compulsive gambling" and "sex addiction" as mental illnesses are contenders, I suppose), but its time will probably come.

the disorders identified by the DSM fall into this category. But the DSM has other purposes, and only the most extreme diagnoses, "paranoid schizophrenia," "dementia," etc. (those which place the individual in the conventional category of "crazy") are generally agreed to mitigate criminal guilt.

Even if tests for milder degrees of insensitivity could be devised, however, it is by no means clear what should be done with them. Take, for example, the case of the hyperactive child, that is, one who suffers from so-called "attention deficit hyperactivity disorder" (ADHD).[56] Such children are often identified because they present discipline problems. In the past, schools used more severe punishments than are permitted now; and punishments were applied not just to misbehavior, but also for failure to learn. Perhaps this move toward a kinder, gentler schoolroom is a change for the better, but one certain result is that less-amenable children may now misbehave or fail in a way that they would not have under stricter discipline. For some (how many?) children, the ADHD diagnosis has, in effect, shifted a self-identified insensitivity to normal reinforcement contingencies from the "repeat-offender" category—which justifies upping the level of punishment—to the "mental-illness" category, which justifies medication.

It is easy to see why society is suspicious of punishment of children. The practice is obviously open to abuses, even if the disciplinarians are entirely without malice. Consider two hypothetical children. Child A is simply at the "insensitive" end of the normal distribution of sensitivities, but child B has real mental problems. The problem is that the two children can often be distinguished only by the fact that child A does eventually learn to behave, whereas child B does not, even when punishments have reached unacceptable levels.[57] In other words, by the time one can tell the difference, child B has received cruel levels of punishment. The problem is where to draw the line. It is not to be drawn at "zero," by eliminating punishment altogether (which is the aim of many educators), because the educational cost to the class as a whole outweighs the cost of mild punishment of miscreants.[58]

The ADHD diagnosis is now used to identify child B without raising his level of punishment to unacceptable levels. But it was not designed for this purpose. The bias in the mental-health profession against punish-

[56] See, for example, M. D. Rapport, "Attention-Deficit/Hyperactivity Disorder," in *Handbook of Psychological Treatment Protocols for Children and Adolescents*, ed. V. B. Van Hasselt and Michel Hersen (Mahwah, NJ: Lawrence Erlbaum, 1998), 65–107, for the current view on this fluid category.

[57] There are, of course, many more dimensions to the problem than simply punishment and reward. The child is sensitive to all sorts of aspects that cannot easily be quantified: Is the punishment just? Is the teacher to be respected? To be believed? What is right and wrong? Will my parents support me or my teacher? How about my friends? And so forth. The effects of these aspects, which may deflect the expected effects of reward and punishment, come under the heading of the direct effects of reinforcement contingencies, discussed earlier.

[58] See Murray, *Losing Ground*, for a thoughtful discussion of this problem.

ment, and feeble discipline in most public schools, means that the diagnosis is rarely tested against the obvious alternative—that the kid just needs tougher discipline. Hence, it is probably applied far too widely. Perhaps psychologists in the future can come up with valid tests not just for "attention deficit" but for sensitivity to reasonable discipline.[59]

There is a strange variant of the psychological-syndrome justification that occasionally pops up in the literature dealing with personal responsibility, and that is a version of the Marxist notion of "false consciousness." I encountered this idea most recently in discussions with a radical feminist who insisted that some 25 percent of college women are victims of rape—even though most questionnaires have come up with much smaller numbers. It turned out that she had a much broader version of rape than I did. It included (for example) consensual sex while both parties are drunk. Most would assume that responsibility in such cases is shared, if not exactly equally, between the man and the woman. But the argument is offered that because women have been oppressed in U.S. society (i.e., conditioned in certain ways) they are likely to say "yes" when they mean "no,"[60] and to feel coerced by their boyfriends, even in the absence of physical threat. Often, "victims" see things more clearly in the morning—or after spending a few sessions with a support group[61]—when they realize that they were not really responsible for what happened. So, they must have been raped.

Responding to an apparent rise in spousal abuse, the legal systems in some states seem to echo the view that women have diminished responsibility. For example, on being notified of a "domestic dispute" where physical violence is *possible*, police are often obliged to arrest the man, even if the woman protests, whether or not there is evidence of coercion or intimidation. The woman is assumed to be not responsible, as if she were a child or a mental defective.[62] When may the law legitimately treat a normal adult as if he or (more usually) she were a child? This is a topic that requires separate treatment. I mention it here just for completeness.[63]

Identification by "markers." The third way that individual differences in susceptibility to normal reinforcement contingencies are assessed is via

---

[59] "Repeated misbehavior" is a valid measure of insensitivity to discipline, of course, and those who failed this test used to be segregated in "reform schools," but this practice has fallen out of favor. I am arguing that some fraction of ADHD children probably belong in the "reform school" category.

[60] The traditional self-serving male chauvinist view is, of course, the opposite.

[61] David Mamet's play *Oleana* presents a vivid picture of this scenario.

[62] See Cathy Young, "Domestic Violations," *Reason*, February 1998, 23–31.

[63] The entertainment media have certainly picked up on this theme. Two examples: When asked by a television reporter about his simultaneous affairs with two sisters and their mother, English political charmer, aristocrat, and self-confessed rake Alan Clark recently responded: "Whatever happened to free will?" The answer seems to be that for women it has been, to some degree, suspended. And in the popular movie *As Good as It Gets*, the misanthrope romance novelist played by Jack Nicholson, when asked how he writes believable female characters, responds: "I think of a man. Then I take away reason and accountability." *Plus ça change . . .*

markers. Markers can be overt or covert. Overt markers are usually hard-to-alter visible characteristics correlated with the trait in question. The most obvious examples are sex, age, and race. But police "profiles" often use other less invariant features such as dress, grooming, type of car in relation to type of driver, and so on, as ways to maximize the efficiency of "stops." Thus, males are stopped more often than females, young males more often than old males, and black males more often than white, because men are more likely to commit most crimes than women;[64] young men more likely than old men, etc.

Classification by markers is controversial, perhaps because "race" is one of the markers. What bearing does it have on the concept of responsibility? Just this: that young men are evidently less susceptible to normal deterrents than old men, men are less susceptible than women, and so on. The obvious implication is that punishments for young offenders (all other things being equal) should be more severe than for older offenders. This is a conclusion that is probably not acceptable, for reasons that go beyond simple deterrence. Nevertheless, it has guided practice in times past. Fifty years ago in England, for example, so many strokes of the birch were given to young offenders for different classes of crime, but corporal punishment of older men was rare. Notoriously, blacks were, in the past, subjected to much more severe, physical penalties than whites for the same crime, because of a belief that they were less sensitive to punishment. Conversely, the execution of reformed murderer Karla Faye Tucker in Texas in 1998 serves as a reminder that women are, even now, much less often subjected to extreme penalties than men are. The usual explanation offered is "chivalry" by the male establishment. But the practice could equally well be justified on grounds of women's greater sensitivity to negative contingencies, as proved by their lower rates of (most kinds of) crime.[65]

Science has added another dimension to the "marker" question by beginning to discover *covert* features, such as genotype and physiological characteristics, that are correlated with crime. For example, recent work by a variety of neurologists, psychologists, and psychiatrists suggests that a history of child abuse coupled with measurable neurological damage strongly predisposes people to violent crime.[66] Malcolm Gladwell writes that psychiatrist Dorothy Lewis and neurologist Jonathan Pincus "believe

[64] Women tend to lead men in a few crimes, such as poisoning and embezzlement; otherwise, men are well ahead, particularly in violent crime.

[65] The bald fact of lower crime rates by women leaves open the question of how this comes about. The Darwinian metaphor offers two possibilities that are not mutually exclusive: women are less likely to initiate crimes (i.e., show less behavioral variation of this type); or they are more responsive to punishment. The two might be distinguished by comparing the recidivism rate for men and women comparably punished for comparable crimes. (Of course, women might first-offend less often than men because they are more readily deterred by the *prospect* of punishment—i.e., they may exhibit more of the social aspect of responsibility.)

[66] For a survey, see Malcolm Gladwell, "Crime and Science: Damaged," *The New Yorker,* February 24, 1997, 132–47.

that the most vicious criminals are, overwhelmingly, people with some combination of abusive childhood, brain injuries, and psychotic symptoms . . . and that while each of these problems individually has no connection to criminality . . . somehow these factors together create such terrifying synergy as to impede these individuals' ability to play by the rules of society."[67]

To use an example cited by Gladwell: An apparently normal individual was offered an orange juice by the nurse in his doctor's office and at once reflexively flung it back at her, damaging her eye; when asked why, he responded: "The orange juice was warm," adding, "I don't know what got into me." Such a person clearly lacks normal self-control, and indeed this particular individual had suffered severe brain damage in an accident; before the accident, his behavior had been normal.[68] On the other hand, another case cited by Gladwell is that of serial hate criminal Joseph Paul Franklin. Franklin wounded black civil-rights lawyer Vernon Jordan in 1980 and shot and paralyzed pornographer Larry Flynt in 1978, but he also carried out at least one less-famous murder at a synagogue in St. Louis. His preparations for the latter crime were meticulous. He bought the rifle through a for-sale ad (so the purchase could not be traced); he rode a bicycle from his parked car to the synagogue; he filed off the gun's serial number; and so on. His efforts to avoid detection prove that he knew that what he was doing was illegal if not wrong—and they also show his fear of judicial punishment. Yet Dorothy Lewis diagnosed him as a "paranoid schizophrenic," basing her diagnosis largely on a history of severe child abuse, and despite his lucidity in interviews and his own view of the insanity defense as "hogwash."[69]

These two cases seem to me very different. In the first case, there is a demonstrable accident, correlated with a clear change in the behavior of the same individual. Moreover, even after the accident, the individual might have been medicated or even trained to restrain himself. Nevertheless, responsibility is clearly diminished. Science might perhaps say how and when such a person is dangerous. Deterrence is clearly not an issue; once the individual is known to be abnormal, normal individuals no longer fall within his deterrence group. Given a known level of danger, what should be done to protect society from such a person is again more a political than a scientific matter.

Franklin, on the other hand, gave every evidence of being sensitive to the contingencies of the law. If punishment had been certain, he would probably not have committed his crimes. He is clearly "abnormal," just because most people don't engage in murder as a hobby. But most people don't keep snakes as pets, which is not to say that herpetologists should

[67] Ibid., 134–35.
[68] Ibid., 138.
[69] Ibid., 134.

be treated differently by the law from everybody else. There are several policy possibilities. *If* we believe that Franklin and others like him can be conclusively identified before they commit their crimes (which is by no means certain), we can institute screening programs to convert these covert markers into overt ones. The best we can hope for, in all probability, is that our tests are about as accurate as the overt markers of age, gender, and sex. But then, what do we do? Lock these folk up before they can kill? Does anyone seriously propose that we lock up young black men, just as a precaution? Perhaps science will bail us out by finding some kind of medication for some of these conditions, although this raises the specter of a Brave New World manipulated by drugs.[70] But medications usually have side-effects, and the side-effects are suffered by the individual, whereas the benefits of the treatment are conferred on others. Who will make potential criminals take their medicine? Who is responsible if they do not? (The medication problem is already well-known, since, e.g., it afflicts many homeless people.)

The other possibility is that we cannot accurately identify potential criminals in advance. After all, many victims of child abuse and many with damaged brains lead blameless lives. How, then, should we treat those individuals who do commit horrible crimes? Here the deterrence argument seems to me the overriding one: "'There was a man,' remarked Captain Eliot, 'who was sentenced to death for stealing a horse from a common. He said to the judge that he thought it hard to be hanged for stealing a horse from a common; and the judge answered, "You are not to be hanged for stealing a horse from a common, but that others may not steal horses from commons."'"[71]

VI. SCIENCE AND LAW

James Q. Wilson, one of our most astute observers on the relations between law and social science, recently took up the issue of responsibility in his influential little book *Moral Judgment*. First, he describes a scientific criticism of the M'Naghten rule—that it assumes people are either insane or not: "Mental health is not a bipolar state—crazy or sane—but a continuum, a matter of degree. . . . That criticism is good science but bad law. It is good science because it points out that all behavior is caused; it is bad law because it implies that to the degree a person's behavior is caused, he is not responsible for it." And later: "The *Durham* decision was the effort of one court to do the impossible—make the law mirror sci-

---

[70] C. S. Lewis, in a prophetic essay, points out the dangers of medicalizing crime—and argues for a retributive theory of punishment; see Lewis, "The Humanitarian Theory of Punishment," in Lewis, *God in the Dock—Essays on Theology and Ethics*, ed. Walter Hooper (Grand Rapids: Eerdmans, 1970); Lewis's essay was originally published in *20th Century: An Australian Quarterly Review* 3, no. 3 (1948).

[71] Patrick O'Brien, *The Mauritius Command* (New York: W. W. Norton, 1977), 210.

ence."[72] (In the *Durham* case of 1954, Monte Durham had received a medical discharge from the Navy for psychiatric reasons. After his discharge, he had been in and out of prisons and mental hospitals for fraud, robbery, and other crimes. By current psychiatric standards, Durham was a psychopath. This case broadened the legal definition of insanity beyond the M'Naghten rule and gave a great boost to testimony from psychiatrists and psychologists.)

The forces that Wilson is battling are real. For example, he goes on to cite Judge David Bazelon, a good friend to mainstream psychology,[73] who "[i]n the *Durham* case . . . said that a person was not responsible for his or her actions if they were the product of a mental disease or defect."[74] This change in the M'Naghten rule turned out to be (Surprise! Surprise!) "unworkable," in Wilson's words; but "[p]sychiatrists liked the decision; now there was virtually no criminal trial in which their testimony would not be relevant." Wilson concludes that this will not do, but offers no solution beyond the injunction "that we let neither science nor compassion decide legal precepts."[75]

Wilson's comments set up an opposition between science and law that seems to me utterly unjustified. The science to which Wilson refers is not so much bad science, as poor philosophy. The first part of this essay set out the reasons why the concept of responsibility *requires* a certain kind of determinism, namely, the capacity to adapt in a predictable way to reinforcement contingencies. The latter part argues that reduced susceptibility to conventional contingencies—one aspect of the fact that mental health is a continuum—can as well lead to the need for increased severity of punishment as to mitigation. Wilson writes: "One may be so depressed, enraged, or panicky as to do things one would not ordinarily do."[76] What does science say? Science indicates only that *either* severer penalties may be needed to deter people in one of these conditions, *or* that they should be regarded as mitigating factors. Which is chosen depends not on science but on the values of the culture. For example, suppose a man is enraged because he catches his wife in bed with another man, and shoots the other man (or the wife). In the culture of France, this case used to be thought to involve such an extreme provocation, such a violation of the husband's rights, that homicide was both understandable and excusable. The husband was not thought to be responsible in such a situation; homicide in such cases was treated much like self-defense elsewhere. Verdict: innocent. But in most Anglo-Saxon countries, a verdict of at least "manslaugh-

[72] James Q. Wilson, *Moral Judgment: Does the Abuse Excuse Threaten Our Legal System?* (New York: Basic Books, 1997), 36–37.
[73] David L. Bazelon, "Veils, Values, and Social Responsibility," *American Psychologist* 37 (1982): 115–21.
[74] Wilson, *Moral Judgment*, 37.
[75] Ibid., 112.
[76] Ibid., 36.

ter" would be rendered. The provocation would be considered only partial mitigation.

In modern American culture, certain categories of assault, such as wife-battering, are regarded as especially heinous, partially, perhaps, because men are so easily provoked to violence against their wives—the evidence being testimony from women's groups and a growing number of spousal-abuse cases. The result has been that in many states, the penalties for such crimes are now more severe than for other kinds of assaults: the "up the punishment" option. So-called "hate crimes" are another example where punishment for the same act (e.g., assault) is especially severe if the motive is thought to be racial, ethnic, or religious prejudice. There are several reasons for this policy, but one of them is surely the prevailing view that racial hatred is an emotion that is especially easily aroused,[77] and so must be met with exceptional deterrence.

What has science to say about these disparities? Why is a predisposition to act taken in some cases as mitigation (the self-defense model) and in others as reason for greater punishment (the wife-battering or hate-crime model)? The degree of deterministic causation may be the same in both kinds of cases. The differences between the legal penalties reflect not scientific but cultural and moral differences. There is not, and cannot be, opposition between good science and good law.

VII. Conclusion

Responsibility is a behavioristic concept, because responsibilities are discharged by action, not thought. The idea that if behavior is causally determined a man cannot be held responsible for his actions is false. Responsibility depends on a degree of determinism, namely, predictable response to contingencies of reward and punishment (*reinforcement contingencies*).

Responsibility, behavioristically defined, has two components: sensitivity to contingencies of reinforcement; and the ability to learn from instruction and example (deterrence). Normal adults possess both components (although there are individual differences); children, animals, and the mentally ill lack one or both.

Contingencies of reinforcement are not determinative. Reinforcement and punishment have direct effects ("misbehavior") as well as selective effects; hence, they do not always work as intended. Consequently, attempts to control crime solely by increasing or decreasing levels of reward and punishment may not work as planned.

---

[77] This view is, apparently, mistaken, since hate crimes are neither common nor increasing in frequency; see James B. Jacobs and Kimberly Potter, *Hate Crimes: Criminal Law and Identity Politics* (New York: Oxford University Press, 1998).

The problem of "diminished responsibility" boils down to how we should deal with individual differences in sensitivity to contingencies. Individual differences are either intrinsic, or traceable to external causes such as drugs or upbringing (or both). They can be identified via behavior (repeat offending), behavioral tests, or overt and covert markers. In most cases, however, moral and political[78] considerations determine whether diminished responsibility is treated as mitigation (e.g., "mental defect") or leads to increased penalties (e.g., the repeat offender).

Contrary to some authorities, I argue that there can be no conflict between science and law. The role of science is to understand what *is* the case and what is possible. The role of law is to decide what *should be* the case and what should be done, within the limits set by science, politics, and morality.

Experimental Psychology, Duke University and
the University of Western Australia

---

[78] I do not add "legal," because I assume that law is a product of science, politics, and morality, not an independent entity. But this view may not be generally held.

RESPONSIBILITY AND THE ABUSE EXCUSE*

By Michael Stocker

I. Introduction

Does a woman's being repeatedly battered by her husband excuse her killing him while he was asleep? This and similar questions are often dealt with by asking a more general question, "Should we accept *abuse excuses*?" These questions engender a lot of heat, but little light, in the media and other public forums, and even in the writings of many theorists. They have been discussed as if there is a typical abuse excuse we can examine in order to examine abuse excuses in general. Similarly, the question of whether we should accept abuse excuses has often been discussed as if it is simple and straightforward. But there is no one typical abuse excuse, and the question of whether to accept such excuses is neither simple nor straightforward. There are many different abuse excuses, many different circumstances in which they are deployed, and many different sorts of concerns motivating their use. In this, abuse excuses are just like other, well-accepted excuses, such as self-defense.

Nonetheless, the whole category of abuse excuses is often discussed, and rejected, in terms of one or a few abuse excuses. These are often particularly silly or egregious examples—often with dire consequences sure to follow if they are accepted. This combination is used to "show" that no abuse excuses should be accepted.[1] Somehow it is not noted that similar "arguments" would "show" that no excuses at all should be accepted: for every sort of excuse—from the very best to the very worst, whether an abuse excuse or not—can be used stupidly or egregiously, with dire consequences if it is accepted. In all cases, we need to examine, not just broad categories of excuses, but particularized cases of them— and, if there are any, sensible and probative examples of them.

These points are so obvious, as are the particularizing factors we need to take into account, that we must ask how they are so often ignored or

---

* My warmest thanks for their invaluable help are owed to Elizabeth Hegeman, John Draeger, and Erik Schmidt; to other members of my Spring 1998 Syracuse University seminar on responsibility; to the other contributors to this volume; and to its very helpful editors.

[1] Alan Dershowitz, *The Abuse Excuse and Other Cop-Outs, Sob Stories, and Evasions of Responsibility* (Boston: Little, Brown, and Co., 1994) is not the most egregious of the works which purport to show this, but it is a good place to start. Moreover, it provides a useful list of new excuses that Dershowitz and many others find so objectionable. A good source on the complexities of abuse excuses and similar excuses is the symposium in the Spring 1996 issue, volume 57, of the *University of Pittsburgh Law Review*.

forgotten in discussions of abuse excuses. One suggestion is that at least many of those who do this are not interested in answering the question "Should we accept abuse excuses?"—at least not in ways that a political, legal, or philosophical theorist would be interested in answering it. Rather, they are concerned to use it as a weapon in an ongoing cultural, social, and political struggle—often conducted through polarized, invective-filled shouting matches put forward as debates. They use that question and their "answers" to it to jeer at abuse excuses, to "argue" that these excuses are too dangerous, too destructive of responsibility—all the while exhibiting or pandering to punitiveness, rigidity, and self-righteousness, coupled with a clear preference for the ways things used to be when, or would be if, abuse excuses were not accepted or even advanced.

To be sure, not all opponents of abuse excuses are so thoughtless (nor are all proponents sufficiently thoughtful). In his recent book *Moral Judgment: Does the Abuse Excuse Threaten Our Legal System?*,[2] James Q. Wilson shows himself to be clearly among the more thoughtful, calmer, less vitriolic, and less alarmist opponents of allowing abuse excuses. Some of his comments might reassure those who complain that our system is letting off anyone who can find, or trump up, an abuse excuse or a similarly objectionable excuse. Speaking of abuse excuses and other objected-to excuses, he writes:

> New defenses are being introduced, but few of them lead to killers being acquitted; at most, theories about the mental state of the defendant may lead to verdicts of manslaughter rather than murder, and even that occurs only infrequently.

And:

> Professor Alan Dershowitz has compiled a list of some of the newer [defenses], including drug or alcohol addiction, battered woman syndrome, black rage defense, XYY chromosome defense, mob mentality defense, pornography defense, posttraumatic stress disorder, premenstrual stress syndrome, rape trauma syndrome, steroid defense, and urban survivor syndrome.[iii] New ones appear regularly. Richard Delgado and David Bazelon have proposed the "rotten social background" defense.[iv] Dershowitz echoes the feelings of many Americans when he complains of our increasing resort to "the abuse excuse" and other "cop-outs, sob stories, and evasions of responsibility."

This list is, I think, greatly exaggerated. Many of these excuses, defenses, and syndromes have not worked for the defendants who raised them. Colin Ferguson was convicted of murder for shooting

² James Q. Wilson, *Moral Judgment: Does the Abuse Excuse Threaten Our Legal System?* (New York: Basic Books, 1997).

several passengers on the Long Island Railroad despite his lawyers' claim that he was a victim of racism venting black rage. No man in this country has persuaded a court that having an extra Y chromosome excused his criminal act, nor has any man been able to beat a rape charge on the grounds that he had been reading pornography. The bodybuilder who said that his use of steroids explained why he killed his girlfriend did not convince the jury. It is impossible to find a court in which a person charged with possessing heroin got off because he argued that he was an addict.[3]

Wilson's moderation and level-headedness give us good reason to think that we can make some headway in understanding abuse excuses by studying his objections to them. I will argue against many of his views; but my real goal is not to take on his claims. It is to take off from them, to use them as introductions to topics that need further discussion. Further, for all I will be concerned to argue, his practical prescriptions and diagnoses may well be right. I think that having pursued the following discussion, we will be in a better position to make judgments about the relations between responsibility and the abuse excuse, not just about Wilson's views on these relations.

This essay is arranged as follows. Section II presents a list of factors that must be taken into account for a sound understanding of abuse excuses in general and for particularizing these excuses. Section III discusses Wilson's claim that we should not allow abuse excuses into trials because that would lessen individual responsibility. Sections IV and V examine Wilson's argument against admitting abuse excuses because they require jurors to explain, not just to judge, the behavior of defendants. Section VI shows the importance of emotions for good and bad judgments and describes how we harm our understanding of abuse excuses if we focus simply on trials for felonies.

II. Constituting and Particularizing Factors

I turn now to the list of factors we need for an adequate study of abuse excuses. We need a catalog and discussion of the various abuse excuses—

---

[3] The first quote is from ibid., 3, the second from ibid., 23–24. (Insofar as clarity allows, page references will henceforth be given in the text.) The internal notes are Wilson's. Note iii refers to Dershowitz, *The Abuse Excuse*, 321–41. I will follow Wilson in, perhaps misleadingly, calling all these new, controversial excuses, *abuse* excuses, even though only some have to do with abuse.

Note iv refers to Richard Delgado, " 'Rotten Social Background': Should the Criminal Law Recognize a Defense of Severe Environmental Deprivation?" *Law and Inequality Journal* 3 (1985): 9; and to David L. Bazelon, "The Morality of the Criminal Law," *Southern California Law Review* 49 (1976): 385. These two essays are reprinted in *Justification and Excuse in the Criminal Law*, ed. Michael Louis Corrado (New York: Garland, 1994). Bazelon's article is discussed briefly below.

for example, long-term battering by one's husband, being a victim of incest, coming from a rotten social background. So, too, we need a catalog and discussion of other excuses that seem similar to abuse excuses (and not simply in terms of the ire they raise): for example, the XYY chromosome defense, the mob mentality defense, and the steroid defense, as discussed in Dershowitz's instructively named book, *The Abuse Excuse and Other Cop-Outs, Sob Stories, and Evasions of Responsibility*. We must discuss how abuse excuses are similar to and differ from these other excuses. And we must discuss how these two sorts of excuses are similar to and differ from well-entrenched, generally accepted excuses, such as self-defense, mistake, and coercion. The discussions of similarities and differences will have to include both the content and the probative value of the various excuses.

We need, further, to discuss which crimes, torts, forms of misbehavior, and other wrongs abuse excuses are intended to excuse—e.g., killing the batterer, flagrant promiscuity, inappropriate or antisocial behavior. We must also discuss the hoped-for and the actual or likely effects of offering these excuses: a lessening of the charge or of the penalty, or rehabilitation outside of jail, or being honored for having survived such abuse. We need, also, to discuss the above elements and combinations in terms of when the excuse is offered and to whom it is offered—e.g., speaking of abuse excuses in the legal processes, in initial police investigations, in deliberations about whether to indict, in evidence presented to the jury or judges trying the defendant, in determining the contours of a sentence. We need, further, to discuss in what forums other than trials abuse excuses can be raised—e.g., disciplinary proceedings within a university, family groups, between friends or coworkers. So, too, we need to discuss the social, moral, and policy effects of using such excuses—e.g., a bolstering or a weakening of confidence in the justice of, say, the legal system. For this last issue and others, we will need estimates of how frequently abuse excuses will be used in these various proceedings, both absolutely and in comparison with other excuses.

We must discuss how the abuse excuse is supposed to excuse—e.g., by showing damaged, deformed forms of thought, emotion, and action, or by showing considerations of rectificatory justice that give special entitlements. This requires further individuation of excuses in terms of the different ways different excuses can work—e.g., suffering from years of incest can result in psychological damage encompassing, forming, and deforming large areas of one's psyche; the damage from a single rape is almost certainly likely to be quite different. So, too, we need to discuss the different ways the "same" excuse can work—e.g., some battered women, suffering from "learned helplessness," kill their batterer only after having "snapped" or "broken down," as a desperate measure to allow them to escape.[4] They may be able to advance excuses based on damaged forms of thought and emotion. And some battered women develop guile and heightened vigilance, and kill at a time of their choosing, when they decide that they have had too much. They may be able to advance excuses based on considerations of justice and self-respect;[5] or based on considerations of threat and self-defense similar to those available to kidnapped people who kill their captors in order to escape or even simply in the course of escaping.[6] The problems occasioned by conflating or not recognizing these and other differences are like the problems of not particularizing abuse excuses. This is hardly surprising: in important ways, these differences make for different abuse excuses.[7]

It would be useful to know why abuse excuses have recently come to the fore—to see whether there are, for example, new social factors that explain both the emergence and the nature of these excuses. And it would be useful to know the extent to which social stereotypes figure in and perhaps disfigure debates over these excuses. As Donald Alexander Downs writes:

> [M]any women's characters, situations, and reactions to stress simply do not fit the BWS [battered-woman syndrome] mold, especially if the women do not conform to images of womanhood prevalent in the white middle class; . . . Sharon Angella Allard contends that BWS encourages unprincipled racial stereotyping: "The theory incorporates stereotypes of limited applicability concerning how a woman would and, indeed, should react to battering. To successfully defend

[4] On learned helplessness, see Lenore Walker, *Terrifying Love: Why Battered Women Kill and How Society Responds* (New York: Harper Collins, 1989). Other references can be found in Donald Alexander Downs, *More Than Victims: Battered Women, the Syndrome Society, and the Law* (Chicago: University of Chicago Press, 1996).

[5] For self-respect and justice considerations, see Benjamin Zipursky, "Self-Defense, Domination, and the Social Contract," *University of Pittsburgh Law Review* 57 (1996): 579.

[6] See Richard A. Rosen, "On Self-Defense, Imminence, and Women Who Kill Their Batterers," *North Carolina Law Review* 71 (1993): 371.

[7] For harmful conflations and omissions of this sort, see Elaine Showalter, *Hystories: Hysterical Epidemics and Modern Media* (New York: Columbia University Press, 1997). Downs holds that (many of) those who link learned helplessness and the battered-woman syndrome make this error by not discussing other outcomes of the syndrome and what led to it. But from what he writes, it is unclear whether they hold that learned helplessness is the only outcome, or whether, for other reasons, they focus only on that outcome. Downs, himself, comes close to making this error. As one of his central criticisms of explanations of behavior in terms of learned helplessness, he writes that battering is often accompanied by "*heightened reason* with which the battered women perceive impending danger" (*More Than Victims*, 5). But he does not show how the outcome of heightened reason in some battered women tells against learned helplessness being an outcome in some other battered women. (Downs here cites Julie Blackman, "Potential Uses for Expert Testimony: Ideas toward the Representation of Battered Women Who Kill," *Women's Rights Law Reporter* 9 [1986]: 231. Downs also cites Blackman, *Intimate Violence: A Study of Injustice* [New York: Columbia University Press, 1989].)

herself, a battered woman needs to convince a jury that she is a 'normal' woman—weak, passive, and fearful. . . . Race certainly plays a role in the cultural distinction between 'good' and 'bad' woman. The passive, gentle white woman is automatically more like the 'good' fairy princess stereotype than a [b]lack woman, who as the 'other,' may be seen as the 'bad' witch."[8]

To understand these last issues, as well as many of the earlier ones, we require many disciplines, including psychology and psychoanalysis, history, sociology, economics, criminology, and cultural studies. And we need philosophical and other theoretical understandings of excuses and justification, justice, sociality, and community.

I doubt that these are all the elements we need to take into account to give sound answers to the question "Should we accept abuse excuses?" or even to the question "Should we accept this fully particularized abuse excuse?" And obviously, only some of them can be taken up in the space of a single essay. But the very fact of their number and variety is useful: it shows us that there is no one abuse excuse, no one way abuse excuses may be deployed, and no one question about accepting abuse excuses. Sound reasons for accepting a particular abuse excuse raised by a particular person facing a particular charge need not be sound reasons for accepting this or another abuse excuse in other circumstances. This must be kept firmly and clearly in mind. (In what follows, I have tried to do this, even when, for ease of exposition, I write about "*the* abuse excuse," or talk about abuse excuses *quite generally*, or do not differentiate *abuse* excuses from other new, controversial excuses.)

III. Abuse Excuses and the Diminution of Responsibility

Above, I claimed that an understanding of abuse excuses requires a sound background in history. To bear this out, and for other reasons that will become apparent, I will offer a fascinating, very instructive quote from Wilson (I will discuss some, but not all, parts of this quote immediately below and at other places in this essay):

As late as 1660 an English jury was restricted to either ordering a convicted felon hanged or returning him to the community with a brand on his thumb.[iii] For lesser offenses, the man might be whipped. By 1800 [there was also] . . . incarceration [and] . . . transportation. . . .

---

[8] Downs, *More Than Victims*, 8, citing Sharon Angella Allard, "Rethinking Battered Woman Syndrome: A Black Feminist Perspective," *UCLA Women's Law Journal* 1 (1991): 193–94, 206, which in turn quotes Shirley Sagaw, "A Hard Case for Feminists: People v. Goetz," *Harvard Women's Law Journal* 10 (1987): 256 n. 21. See also Beth Ritchie, *Compelled to Crime: The Gender Entrapment of Battered Black Women* (New York: Routledge, 1996).

J. M. Beattie, who has carefully traced trials during this period, notes that these awkward choices did not become serious ones so long as the crime rate was relatively low. . . .

[When] crime rates began to rise . . . people had to take seriously the effectiveness of the death sentence. When they did, they began to find it both odious and ineffective. A parliamentary commission heard middle-class Londoners testify that with execution the penalty for countless crimes, they were unwilling to bring charges against shop-lifters and thieving servants.[iv] . . .

. . . Professor Martin J. Wiener has shown that the crime wave that struck England in the 1820s and 1830s was met by moderating pen-alties (the death penalty was abolished for all offenses save murder and treason) but making those that remained more certain [by, *inter alia*, the creation of an effective police force].[vi] . . . All of these changes lightened the burden on unguided jurors. . . . Prosecution was made easier, punishment more certain, and penalties more predictable. "The guiding vision of this reconstructed system of criminal justice," Wiener has written, "was that of the responsible individual."[viii] . . . "A cru-cial supposition underlying early Victorian attempts at law reform was that the most desirable way of making people self-governing was to hold them, sternly and unblinkingly, responsible for the con-sequences of their actions."[ix] . . .

The early Victorians wished to hold man responsible and so viewed him as choosing between crime and duty: to them the central prob-lem was to deal with a fallible human nature that too easily gave way to lust, greed, and impulsiveness. By the end of Victoria's reign, however, the crime rate was declining, and this atmosphere of rela-tive social peace seemed conducive to the view that crime resulted more from social injustices than personal failings. Accordingly, En-gland began to broaden the range of excuses and make punishment less certain; as crime rates declined, prison sentences grew shorter.[x] The English had come to think that a people were not entirely re-sponsible for their actions, that crime was socially caused and not personally chosen. . . .[9]

There are a multitude of ways this historical account might be used to help us understand abuse excuses. People given to explaining the present

---

[9] Wilson, *Moral Judgment*, 72–75. The internal notes are Wilson's. Note iii refers to J. M. Beattie, *Crime and the Courts in England, 1660–1800* (Oxford: Clarendon Press, 1986), 618; note iv refers to ibid., 630. Note vi refers to Martin J. Wiener, *Reconstructing the Criminal: Culture, Law, and Policy in England, 1830–1914* (Cambridge: Cambridge University Press, 1990); notes viii and ix refer to ibid., 48. Note x refers to Douglas Hay, "Crime and Justice in Eighteenth-and Nineteenth-Century England," in *Crime and Justice*, ed. Norval Morris and Michael Tonry (Chicago: University of Chicago Press, 1980), 2:57.

and predicting the future in terms of similarities with the past will be concerned to discuss which of these phases of English society are most like where we are now. So, too, they might well be interested in determining which legal changes and provisions are most like allowing or disallowing abuse excuses. For my part, I am not inclined to do this. I am too unsure of the soundness of what seems to be the methodological, background claim: that societies in general, or the societies of England and the United States, are composed of only a few elements that, when arranged in similar ways, result in similar outcomes.

I do think, however, that we can draw many useful conclusions about abuse excuses here and now. One is the great complexity of legal changes and accompanying social changes. Another is that accepting new excuses and modulating the severity of punishment are not always dangerous, and do not always lessen a sense of responsibility. Indeed, they may have precisely contrary results. A closely related conclusion is that a severe and rigid regime of responsibilities and penalties can go hand in hand with a lesser sense of responsibility, and a more moderate and modulated regime of responsibilities and penalties can go hand in hand with a greater sense of responsibility. Thus, we need argument, evidence, and reasons to hold or to deny that allowing abuse excuses would be harmful, beneficial, or neutral.

Wilson and others believe that the effects would be, overall, harmful—primarily because allowing such excuses will lead to people feeling and being less responsible. We can take them as holding that to allow abuse excuses "would encourage people to underinvest in foreseeing the likely results of their actions and would thereby weaken the support the law gave to the creation of self-governing people" (Wilson, 73). What are their reasons for holding this, and how good are those reasons?

Some theorists, though not Wilson, advance such "reasons" as the following: Potential miscreants, seeing how a skillful lawyer can deploy an abuse excuse, will be less deterred by legal penalties; and other potential miscreants, because they have accepted the probative weight of abuse excuses, will feel less strongly that it is their responsibility to resist temptations to act illegally.

I see various problems with this line of argument. First, as already noted, the fact that an excuse can be used misleadingly, deceptively, or improperly, does not tell against its being a sound excuse—nor does the fact that it is difficult, even impossible, for others or the accused to tell whether the excuse is being used honestly and properly. Here we must remember that these problems afflict almost every, perhaps every, excuse, including coercion, self-defense, and mistake. These, too, can be used misleadingly, deceptively, or improperly; and it may often be difficult, if not impossible, for others or the accused to tell whether the excuse is being used honestly and properly.

Second, for these claims about the dangers of allowing abuse excuses to get much of a grip, it must be assumed that their effect will be considerable: it must be assumed, for example, that despite clear evidence of guilt, because of the abuse excuse, the verdict will have to be "Not guilty," or the sentence will have to be, say, a short period in a rehabilitation center or a small fine, perhaps conjoined with not-very-onerous public service. Put polemically, the assumption backing this worry is that the defendant will get at most a slap on the wrist, perhaps conjoined with a pat and a hug.

Other outcomes of allowing abuse excuses make these concerns far more difficult to accept. Consider, for example, a reduction of a charge from first to second degree murder; or an acquittal on the charge of first degree murder, coupled with a conviction on the charge of second degree murder; or a reduction of a sentence from a maximum of fifteen years to a maximum of ten. It is difficult to see how these outcomes support the concern that giving weight to abuse excuses will, or is likely to, help open the flood gates.

A correlative worry expressed by Wilson and others (or a different way of putting much the same worry) has to do with what they think is an important role of the law: to stiffen our moral backbone, make us less prone to give in to temptations—to sustain and even increase our sense of responsibility (Wilson, 27–28).

If our backbones are not stiff enough, this may be unexceptionable. But where people are already too stiff, greater flexibility and looseness, not greater stiffness, may well be what is wanted. Taking some examples from outside the law and its concerns, we could think of perfectionists who excoriate themselves or others, not just for imperfections, but for "failure" to live up to exacting standards, even where success is humanly impossible. We should also think of those who blame themselves, holding themselves too responsible, for too much. Here we might think of a parent, often a mother, who overly subordinates her own interests to those of her children—who does "everything" for them, and yet blames herself for not doing enough.

Turning now to some cases of concern to the law, we could hardly do better than to consider these passages from Wilson:

> "The guiding vision of this reconstructed system of criminal justice," Wiener has written, "was that of the responsible individual." The criminal law was increasingly expected to hold people accountable: [As Douglas Hay writes:] "A crucial supposition underlying early Victorian attempts at law reform was that the most desirable way of making people self-governing was to hold them, sternly and unblinkingly, responsible for the consequences of their actions." (Wilson, 73)

And:

> Not only were the British slow to accept the idea of excuses, but they also kept in place rules that made it difficult to ascertain the mental state on which such excuses would depend. There was no clearly stated insanity defense until 1843. (Wilson, 73–74)

I think we are right to accept insanity as an excuse. Correlatively, I think that considerable wrong and harm was done to the insane and to others, perhaps to society quite generally, by holding the insane "sternly and unblinkingly, responsible for the consequences of their actions." If this is right, these passages immediately show that we would make a serious evaluative error in thinking that every increase in a sense of responsibility is to be applauded and every decrease deplored.

Making much the same point, some people take or are given far too much responsibility. Some feel responsible, and try to take responsibility, for "everything," for the whole world. (Almost certainly, this is a form of wildly extreme grandiosity, extending well into the realm of severe psychological disorder, perhaps even paranoid fantasy.) And some people ascribe or attribute far too much responsibility to others. Here we could remember how the Nazis and other anti-Semites held the Jews responsible for "all" or "nearly all" defects in society, and how some Jews came to accept this responsibility.[10]

What's more, we should take up some concerns of the psychiatrist James Gilligan, formerly medical director of Bridgewater, Massachusetts, State Hospital for the Criminally Insane and director of mental health for the Massachusetts prison system. In his *Violence: Our Deadly Epidemic and Its Causes*,[11] Gilligan argues forcefully that much criminal violence and violent criminality is traceable to the shaming administered by (as I would put it) our society's punitive, self-righteous, and very stiff moral-legal backbone. There is a strong suggestion in Gilligan that letting up and loosening up can certainly be good.

Further, as many of us have seen in classes, both as students and teachers, and in family groupings, backbones and necks can be too stiff, and too much responsibility can be given or taken. Not only can these be wrongs in themselves—e.g., wronging those who are put upon—they often lead to the disruptive "need" to stand up to authority, and to negativism, lack of compliance, defiance, and rebellion.

In the examples I have just given, and in others that Wilson is concerned with, what may be wanted is a decrease in a sense of responsibility and an increase in letting others take over or share the responsibilities—

---

[10] See, e.g., Jean-Paul Sartre, *Anti-Semite and Jew* (New York: Schocken Books, 1976).
[11] James Gilligan, *Violence: Our Deadly Epidemic and Its Causes* (New York: G. P. Putnam, 1996).

not to mention, a pleased and glad, rather than a guilty, acceptance of pleasures and temptations.

What is wanted quite generally—for oneself, relations, institutions, and society—is a proper sense of responsibility, not just the greatest possible sense of responsibility. What is wanted is a moral backbone that is neither too stiff nor too flexible. It is possible to look to the law to adjust matters either way. Thus, it is of considerable interest to ask why in certain times and places, including our own, those who look to the law for adjustments often err on the side of over-stiffness. Perhaps this is because of the way the law is structured or what it is best suited to accomplish at those times and places. Or perhaps this is due to the hopes and fears, or the authoritarian character, of those who look to the law to make corrections in stiffness.

It may be objected that I have failed to note a crucial phrase in Wilson's claim, thus failing to note that he and those he quotes are not talking about the greatest possible amount of responsibility. Rather, they are concerned with people accepting responsibility, being "responsible for the consequences *of their actions*." The thought here is that the insane, Jews, and many of the others mentioned above should not have accepted or been ascribed responsibility to the extent that occurred, precisely because those "areas" were not the consequences of their actions.

This might go some way toward mitigating my criticism of those who hold that the acceptance of abuse excuses would be harmful; but it does not go very far. To see why, let us consider what Stephen J. Morse writes about a closely related issue in his essay "The Twilight of Welfare Criminology: A Reply to Judge Bazelon," criticizing Bazelon's account and subsequent use of the "rotten social background" abuse excuse in his essay "The Morality of the Criminal Law." Morse writes:

> A person's behavior is a matter of harder choices and easier choices. But behavior is a matter of choice. Unfortunately, Judge Bazelon obscures the question by use of the words "free" and "unfree," and thus masks the complex relation between compulsion and condemnation.
>
> The Judge wishes to admit into evidence all possible testimony about the causes of the defendant's behavior so that the jury can decide whether the defendant was unfree and not deserving of condemnation. This view assumes, of course, that a vast range of factors made a defendant's choices so hard that it is unjust to condemn him. But which choices are too hard? There is no bright line between free and unfree choices. Harder and easier choices are arranged along a continuum of choice: there is no scientifically dictated cutting point where legal and moral responsibility begins or ends. Nor is there a higher moral authority which can tell society where to draw the line. All society can do is to determine the cutting point that comports with our collective sense of morality. The real issue is where society

ought to draw the line of responsibility—and by whom it should be drawn.[12]

I take Morse to be rejecting, not the "rotten social background" abuse excuses, but Bazelon's account of them in terms of causal factors—in particular, Bazelon's view that the causal determination these excuses show precludes or diminishes responsibility. I further take Morse to be holding that if these excuses do excuse, they do so not by showing causal determination, but by showing that the agent's choices are harder than can be reasonably and morally required of a person—where, further, this hardness is not understood in terms of causality, but in terms of evaluations of the person acting under such burdens. (We need not inquire whether Morse would replace Bazelon's view that causal determination is incompatible with freedom and responsibility—'incompatibilism' in philosophical terms—with a version of compatibilism, or, more exactly, with a position reminiscent of, as will be discussed below, Aristotle's or Peter Strawson's.)

Morse is, of course, talking about what precedes action. But it is easy enough to apply his argument to what follows from action—in particular, to vexing questions about what the consequences of a person's action are and for which of these the person should feel, be, and be held responsible. Consider, for example, a person who was mugged while walking innocently down a city street; or a woman who was raped because, as her attacker put it, she was wearing "enticing" clothes. I would agree with Morse in holding that a scientific study of causes cannot help us here. "Scientifically speaking," walking down the street and wearing such clothes help cause the crimes, in that they arouse certain desires and thoughts in potential attackers. In turn, again "scientifically speaking," those crimes and the harms suffered by the victims must be counted among the effects of their (the victims') actions.

Now, some juries have accepted those conclusions, especially in cases of rape—perhaps on the ground that the victims provoked their attackers, "asked for it," or "had it coming." On the substance of these jury decisions, my view is that they are vicious nonsense. On the issue of looking to science to tell us what we are responsible for, by telling us what our acts cause, I agree with Morse that "[t]he real issue is where society ought to draw the line of responsibility."

Morse's comments also tell against a claim Wilson presents (it is unclear whether he endorses or just reports it) that seems to join Bazelon in the essentially incompatibilist view that causality precludes responsibil-

---

[12] Stephen J. Morse, "The Twilight of Welfare Criminology: A Reply to Judge Bazelon," *Southern California Law Review* 49 (1976); reprinted in, and quoted from, Corrado, ed., *Justification and Excuse in the Criminal Law* (*supra* note 3), 550–51. The Bazelon article, cited in note 3, also appears in the Corrado volume.

ity: "The English had come to think that a people were not entirely responsible for their actions, that crime was socially caused and not personally chosen. . . ." I would join Morse in asking why it should be thought that a crime's having social causes is incompatible with the agent's being responsible for it. (Whether there are significant issues about being *entirely* responsible requires that notion to make sense—which I am not sure it does.)

If I had the time, I would also join Cornel West in arguing, as he does in *Race Matters*,[13] that there need be no incompatibility at all between accepting responsibility, even full responsibility, for a crime and at the same time advancing an abuse excuse. The purpose of offering that excuse here would not be to argue for a diminution of culpability or responsibility, and perhaps not even a reduction in punishment, but to get other sorts of appreciation and consideration. However, because of the amount that still needs to be said about Wilson and his objections to abuse excuses, I will continue to join him and others in considering abuse excuses from the perspective of eliminating or reducing culpability, responsibility, or punishment.

My conclusion so far is that even from the policy perspective, Wilson has not made out his claim. He has not given us much, if any, reason to think that admitting abuse excuses would *decrease* our sense of responsibility. Nor has he, contrary to his goal, given us materials showing that admitting abuse excuses would *increase* our sense of responsibility—as modulating and moderating criminal penalties in Victorian England seems to have increased people's sense of responsibility. Nor, for that matter, has he given us much, if any, reason to think that admitting abuse excuses would lead to an inaccurate or misleading sense of responsibility. As I see matters, it still remains to be seen which, if any, changes in our practice and sense of responsibility will result from allowing abuse excuses— although it seems plausible to think that different abuse excuses in different situations may well have different effects. Moreover, the evaluations of these changes still remain to be made—although it seems plausible to think that different abuse excuses in different situations may well lead to different evaluations.

IV. JURORS SHOULD JUDGE, NOT EXPLAIN

Let us now turn to another strand of Wilson's arguments against admitting abuse excuses: that they involve jurors in trying to explain, rather than judge, the defendant's behavior. He writes:

> When a jury *judges* a defendant it considers his or her mental states only to the extent necessary to establish the existence of one or an-

---

[13] Cornel West, *Race Matters* (New York: Vintage Press, 1994).

other of a small list of excusing or justifying defenses, such as insanity, necessity, or self-defense. But when a jury *explains* the defendant's actions, it searches for a full account of the factors—the motives, circumstances, and beliefs—that caused them. (Wilson, 90)

There should be no disagreement that abuse excuses typically involve explanations concerned with an "account of the factors . . . motives, circumstances, and beliefs." What would serve better than such an explanation in presenting the abuse and arguing that it grounds an excuse? Nor should there be any disagreement that at least many abuse excuses are *new* excuses and thus do not appear on our "small list of excusing or justifying defenses, such as insanity, necessity, or self-defense."

Some brief historical claims will help us to see what we should make of the absence of abuse excuses from that "small list." As already noted, Wilson observes that "[t]here was no clearly stated insanity defense [in British law] until 1843." In his book *With Justice for Some*, George Fletcher describes the great changes that have occurred in what counts as self-defense and in its force as an excuse. Discussing the development of the common law in Britain over the past four hundred years, he writes:

If the defender had retreated to the point at which his back was "against the wall" and he had no further means of evasion, his slaying in self-defense was excused—wrongful and unlawful but exempt from ordinary criminal punishment. It was called *se defendendo*, and at least until some time in the 19th century the slayer suffered the forfeiture of his property as a sanction. Because he was not to blame for his act of self-preservation, however, his life was spared.[14]

These comments should be read along with Wilson's comment that "[t]here was no clearly stated insanity defense until 1843." Together they show important improvements made to our legal system—by allowing such "new" excuses as self-defense and insanity. The issue about abuse excuses should not be that they are absent from our "small list" of excuses. It should be whether people are, thereby, harmed, wronged, treated unjustly—and whether, if they are, the magnitude of this is large enough to justify recognizing those excuses.

To pursue the argument in a different way, consider the claim some make that self-defense should be an admissible excuse since it is such a natural reaction. I have trouble understanding the claim of naturalness (and thus its force). Legitimate forms and legitimate targets of self-defense vary both grossly and in nuanced ways from culture to culture and even within a single culture. Historically, slaves and other low-born people often lacked any right to escape or forcefully defend themselves

[14] George Fletcher, *With Justice for Some* (New York: Addison Wesley, 1995), 19.

against their masters and betters. And many who (as they saw matters) lacked the right of self-defense did not try to escape or strike back. In our society, many adult children think that they may duck blows from an enraged parent, but should not strike out at the parent. So, too, many people who are practicing Gandhian nonviolence do not try to escape or strike back. Thus, both how one acts in self-defense, and how much of an excuse it is, seem to be cultural, social, and moral issues, not issues of nature and causality. As Morse said on a related matter: "The real issue is where society ought to draw the line of responsibility."

Let us now turn to Wilson's objection that if jurors are concerned with such explanations, that concern "will lead juries to excuse the act or mitigate the punishment" (Wilson, 90) where they should not. This claim is partly empirical: that explanations result in leniency and mitigation. It is also partly evaluative: that they do so too much.

Turning to the empirical issue, I would start by registering a worry about Wilson's targeting *explanations* as the cause of the (supposed) increase in leniency and mitigation. The explanations he asks us to consider are presented as essential features of abuse excuses and similar excuses. These explanations are presented precisely to help excuse the defendant. I want to suggest that we have no way to tell whether their (supposed) success is attributable to their being good and moving excuses or to their being offered by means of explanations. It thus seems that in order to examine Wilson's claim that a jury's being concerned with explanations increases leniency and mitigation, we would have to examine what happens (or would happen) if the prosecution or a neutral party offered an explanation "of the factors—the motives, circumstances, and beliefs" surrounding a defendant's actions—but now with the goal of showing the defendant to be guilty (or for some other purpose).

It might be said that it "just stands to reason" that abuse excuses and their attendant explanations improperly increase leniency and mitigation. One reason for this relies on some such thought as "To know all is to excuse all" or the thought that explanations will preclude condemnations. I see little reason to accept these thoughts.[15] At times, to understand better is to hate more. This is what happened to the psychiatrist Willard Gaylin, when, through a series of interviews, he came to understand the murderer Richard Herrin better, and came to see him not just as a disturbed young man, but as an evil being.[16]

Sometimes, of course, in getting to know others better, one sees them to be more and more like oneself. Let us, then, briefly consider jurors who learn of the difficulties and temptations the defendant faced and remem-

---

[15] The issues discussed in this paragraph and the next two (through the quote from Vladimir Jankélévitch) are drawn from Michael Stocker and Elizabeth Hegeman, *Valuing Emotions* (Cambridge: Cambridge University Press, 1996), 214–17.

[16] This is described in Willard Gaylin, *The Killing of Bonnie Garland* (New York: Penguin, 1983).

ber that they also faced similar difficulties and temptations. This may increase leniency and mitigation; perhaps these people are moved by thoughts such as: "There but for the grace of God go I." But some people become harsher the more they see others as similar to them. Here we might think of those who remember—fiercely, perhaps with pride, perhaps with indignation—that they struggled and overcame their own difficulties without any excuses. They now *demand* the same high performance from others, again without any excuses.

And there are also people who react harshly toward others they see as similar in order to separate themselves from those others. Describing how this last phenomenon can work, Vladimir Jankélévitch (as presented by Paul Berman in his instructively entitled "The Other and the Almost the Same") writes:

> You are almost like me. The similarity between us is so plain that in the eyes of the world you are my brother. But, to speak honestly, you are not my brother. My identity, in relation to you, consists precisely of the ways in which I am different from you. Yet the more you resemble me the harder it is for anyone to see these crucial differences. Our resemblance threatens to obliterate everything that is special about me. So you are my false brother. I have no alternative but to hate you, because by working up a rage against you I am defending everything that is unique about me.[17]

These last comments have been about the empirical effects of allowing explanations. The issues concerning evaluations of these effects are at least as tangled. If we suppose that explanations encourage jurors to see the defendants as more and more like themselves, we must also suppose that before those explanations, the jurors did not see similarities to such a degree. Though this supposition is near enough tautological, it has important implications for us. It shows the importance of asking: "What are the conditions for jurors to have a more accurate understanding of the defendant?" and also "What are the conditions for jurors to be more likely to make better evaluations and sounder decisions about the defendant?"

I am not concerned to suggest that the more jurors know, the better their decisions are likely to be. I think that view may well be more a matter of a hopeful sensibility than a canon of science or ethics. Further, in the contemporary United States and elsewhere, defendants, victims, and other concerned parties often have the right to require juries to proceed without full information, because they have the right to exclude certain facts from the jury's consideration. (This is discussed below.)

[17] Paul Berman, "The Other and the Almost the Same," *New Yorker* 70 (February 28, 1994): 62.

V. Other Reasons For Jurors Not to Engage in Explaining

I want now to consider some other reasons to allow or disallow abuse excuses because they involve explaining. The issues, here, quickly become very tangled, but even some brief sketches may be useful. (These sketches do not derive from Wilson. I have already discussed his reasons.)

One reason that might be offered for disallowing excuses has to do with a particular view of acts. On this view, acts are nothing, or very little, more than physical happenings. Since this is what acts are, this is all we can legitimately be concerned with in judging guilt or innocence. For such judging depends simply on whether or not the person did the act; and that, in turn, depends simply on physical states. Taken as a piece of metaphysics, this view is unacceptable. We can see why by examining two weaker, and somewhat more plausible, versions of it.

The first is that *every act* involves, even if it is more than, a physical state. Some philosophers accept this view. However, I reject it, precisely because it denies the possibility of purely mental acts, such as thinking, perhaps enviously, perhaps with lust, of one's neighbor's spouse.

The second version has it that every act *the law is concerned with* involves, even if it is more than, a physical state. Many theorists argue for this by arguing that if the law is concerned with nonphysical aspects of acts, then it can be interested in judging and punishing thoughts. This seems to require that the distinction between physical states and thoughts is exhaustive. I am unsure whether it is. Here we could consider many cases of criminal omissions, especially where there is mere forgetfulness or inadvertence. So, too, we could consider cases where the crime is owning a car or house in which illicit goods are found, having been put there by someone else without the knowledge or consent of the charged person.

For our purposes, the real defect in these three claims—the very strong one and the two weaker ones—is that even if all acts the law is concerned with involve a physical state, at least many go beyond this. Consider a case where my hand comes into contact with your face—a physical state (or a happening, a continuum of states). To understand (and even just to identify) what I did, it is vital to know whether this was merely the result of an epileptic seizure, or was done in an attempt to "snap" you out of your hysteria, or in an attempt to insult you, or in an attempt to wound (or perhaps kill) you. What is done—what my act is—depends essentially on these "further" characterizations. To sustain the view that acts are nothing but physical states would require showing that an attempt to wound, say, is nothing but a physical state. And that seems hopeless. (I am not talking, one way or the other, about mind-brain relations. They are at entirely different levels of inquiry and discourse.)

There is an evaluative cousin to this metaphysical view. It holds that, for evaluative reasons, "account[s] of the factors—the motives, circumstances, and beliefs—that caused" an act cannot be relevant for assessments of the act or of the person who performed it. Put in terms of our present inquiry, the claim would be that there is nothing in an abuse excuse that could bear on the evaluation of what the person is charged with doing. This might gain some support from the philosophical doctrine that act evaluations and agent evaluations are so unrelated that what is relevant for the one cannot be relevant for the other. Under the sway of that doctrine, we might be invited to note—and draw the expected conclusion from the fact—that what is mentioned in abuse excuses has to do only with what bears on the evaluation of the agent and not also of the act.

This evaluative cousin, however, seems mistaken at every step. Trials are concerned with evaluating what, if anything, was done by the defendant and also with evaluating the defendant for doing it: for example, a trial may be concerned with both whether I struck you and whether I did so in self-defense. Further, what is shown by an abuse excuse and its attendant explanation is important for evaluating both the act and the agent.

Finally, there are many varied and important connections between act and agent evaluations. To summarize some conclusions from my essay "Act and Agent Evaluations":[18] In some cases, an act's evaluative character is due to the agent's evaluative character: to act with malice is to act maliciously; enacting a bad intention or motive, such as malice, can, as such, be wrong and bad. The grounds for both evaluations can be the same: for example, driving while drunk makes the driving wrong and shows the drivers to be uncaring, even bad, people. Further, some evaluations are conjointly act evaluations and agent evaluations: to act supererogatorily is at once to do more than is morally required and to do so with morally good intentions.

Let us now turn to some more positive reasons for thinking that those explanations Wilson would exclude from consideration by jurors should not be so excluded. For the first set of these reasons, I would call attention to the claim made by many theorists that such explanations give us materials which are essential for making assessments of responsibility, guilt, and innocence. As Peter Strawson argues in "Freedom and Resentment,"[19] assessments of, say, harms typically require knowing the agent's meaning and state of mind and character—knowing, for example, whether a hurtful remark was meant as an insult or was merely a matter of clumsiness and inattention. Similarly, as Morse notes, we often need to know how hard a choice was for a person. Quite generally, these theorists hold that in order to judge, we first need to explain and understand, and

---

[18] Michael Stocker, "Act and Agent Evaluations," *The Review of Metaphysics* 27 (1973): 42-61. This is discussed further in Michael Stocker, *Plural and Conflicting Values* (Oxford: Oxford University Press, 1990); and in Stocker and Hegeman, *Valuing Emotions*.

[19] Peter Strawson, "Freedom and Resentment," *Proceedings of the British Academy* 48 (1962): 187-211.

that action and choice must be understood and assessed by reference to character.[20] Often this is held as an explicit Aristotelian doctrine.[21]

It is important to note that the more plausible of these character-involving views do not hold that evaluations of character can, in any simple way, be "transferred" to an act. In particular, they do not hold that whatever is done by a person of good (bad) character is good (bad). So, too, the more plausible versions of these views do not simply rest with, and often do not even accept as relevant, the agent's meaning or how hard the agent found it not to do the act in question. As Aristotle says:

> [T]here seem to be some acts which a man cannot be compelled to do, and rather than do them he ought to submit to the most terrible death: for instance, we think it ridiculous that Alcmaeon in Euripides' play is compelled by certain threats to murder his mother![22]

As this shows, even theorists who hold character-involving views about act evaluations are able to hold that whether an excuse is successful depends not just on character, but also on the charge. Correlatively, it also shows that such theorists can hold that whether an excuse is successful depends not just on the excuse (e.g., what the person has to endure), but also on the value and importance of what the excuse is needed as a defense against.[23]

I am not claiming that all judgments of acts or agents require a concern with character and character-involving assessments. And clearly, in some cases we may be barely concerned, if we are concerned at all, with character. Initially, at least, a victim might reasonably be completely uninterested in assessing why the harm was done and may be interested only in the fact that it was done: "I don't care why he did X (e.g., hit or humiliated me). I care only that he did it. He is to be punished for that." And clearly, victims and their families might, again reasonably, think that the harm and wrong done to them have been disregarded or dishonored if, because of an abuse excuse, the defendant is acquitted or given only a light penalty. I do not want to comment on the force of this last claim. But we

---

[20] See, for example, Michael S. Moore, "Choice, Character, and Excuse," *Social Philosophy and Policy* 7, no. 2 (Spring 1990): 29–58; Peter Arenella, "Convicting the Morally Blameless: Reassessing the Relationship between Legal and Moral Accountability," *UCLA Law Review* 39 (1992): 1151; and Arenella, "Character, Choice, and Moral Agency: The Relevance of Character to Our Moral Culpability Judgments," *Social Philosophy and Policy* 7, no. 2 (Spring 1990): 59–83. Moore's article and Arenella's "Character, Choice, and Moral Agency" are reprinted in Corrado, ed., *Justification and Excuse in the Criminal Law.*

[21] For Aristotle, see *Nicomachean Ethics*, Book III, chs. 1–5, especially ch. 2. See also Nancy Sherman, *The Fabric of Character* (Oxford: Oxford University Press, 1989); and Susan Sauvé Meyer, *Aristotle on Moral Responsibility* (Oxford: Blackwell, 1993).

[22] Aristotle, *Nicomachean Ethics*, Book III, ch. 1.

[23] See, for example, ibid., Book III.

should note, first, that "victims' rights" movements have had considerable influence on policies on these issues; and second, that many of the issues surrounding the admissibility of abuse excuses also surround the admissibility of statements by crime victims and their families describing the suffering and loss the crime caused them.[24]

As we have seen, these issues about character and its importance for evaluations of acts and agents are very complex, making it hard to come to any definitive or even definite conclusions. In light of the importance and merit of various character-involving accounts, however, I think we should not accept views that, like Wilson's, would simply preclude explanations making reference to character.

I want now to turn to another reason to allow abuse excuses and their attendant explanations. As Wilson notes, prior to the English reforms discussed above, there was widespread jury-nullification and refusal to prosecute—precisely because it was felt that the punishment, death, did not fit the crime. The only means open to victims of crimes, prosecutors, and jurors to modulate the penalty (not to make it fit the crime, but to make the fit better) was to preclude conviction, by acquitting or refusing to prosecute. We, too, should be concerned with how well the punishment fits the crime. And I do not see how we will be in a good position to know this if we do not examine, or even listen to, an account, ideally a "full account of the ... motives, circumstances, and beliefs" that were involved in a particular person's performance of a particular (perhaps illegal) act.

My point here is not just that where there can be a lack of fit between crime and punishment, it is a good thing (from a policy perspective, say) for there to be room to maneuver, to have technicalities or loopholes that, even if they really have nothing to do with that lack of fit, can nonetheless be exploited to prevent punishments that do not fit the crime. (In the contemporary United States and many other jurisdictions, and in pre-reform England, this would be in addition to the power of a jury to engage in blatant, outright jury-nullification.) My point here is also that the lack of fit, or appropriateness of fit, between crime and punishment can be exposed by explanations of defendants' behavior and character.

It might be objected that this "doctrine" would encourage jurors and others in the legal process to substitute their judgment for that of legislators and judges—in deciding what punishment fits the crime, perhaps by first deciding, as in the case of some mercy killings, what punishment is deserved and then finding a crime for which that punishment is appropriate. But this doctrine need not encourage jurors and others to do what legislators and judges do. In a good (or good enough) society, jurors should undoubtedly see laws as creating very strong presumptions—this

[24] My thanks are owed to Alvin Goldman for raising this latter point.

punishment for that crime. But even in such societies, this is only a very strong, not an irrebuttable, presumption.

VI. Emotions, Trials, Felonies, and Other Wrongs

Using drunkenness as an example of an unacceptable excuse, Wilson writes that "allowing drunkenness as a defense . . . is simply a way of inventing a doctrine of partial excuse for a common human failing toward which many jurists have acquired, over the last century, a certain personal sympathy" (Wilson, 100–101). Making a similar claim, again using drunkenness as an example, he also writes: "[W]e risk taking a principle (the need to assess the guilt or innocence of an accused person) and modify[ing] it with a preference" about how to deal with intoxication (Wilson, 87). I will simply call attention to the fact that he suggests—as perhaps anyone might, to stress a polemical point—that principle is on his side and that those who disagree do so out of "a certain personal sympathy" or a "preference." For my part, I have found principles aplenty on all sides of the question of how intoxication (whether of the occasional, social drinker; the alcoholic; or anyone in between) should bear on criminal behavior.

Now is not the time to discuss these principles.[25] Nor is it the time to discuss to what extent and in what circles intoxication does arouse sympathy or, say, contempt. What I would have liked to discuss, but have the space only to mention, is this: I agree that insofar as certain stories, considerations, and facts, such as those that might be presented in explanations, are likely to encourage or discourage sympathy or contempt, there are good policy reasons to be careful about how they can be presented. Not allowing them to be presented in court is only one way to exercise care here. Another is getting jurors and others to take care to see whether or not these considerations give good grounds for sympathy or contempt. They must also see whether their antecedent sympathies and antipathies are being played with.

Here I would make several other points. First, however justified the charge is that abuse excuses play on a jury's sympathies, it is clear that playing on our sympathies and antipathies is a major feature of current "debates" about abuse excuses. Thus, many opponents (and proponents) of admitting abuse excuses play on and encourage tendencies toward self-righteousness and punitiveness, coupled with (and often fueled by) hyperbolic worries.

Second, that sympathies can be played with is no reason to exclude them from trials. As noted earlier, most, if not all, forms of argument—

---

[25] See, e.g., Norman Care, *Living with One's Past: Personal Fate and Moral Pain* (Lanham, MD: Rowman and Littlefield, 1996).

whether or not they involve emotions—can be played with. I know of no way even to estimate the proportion of mistakes we make because of faulty, misleading "reason" as compared with the proportion we make because of faulty, misleading emotions. I do know, however, that many errors are made on account of both. Further, as I see matters, we have no reason to think that the best, or even a good, strategy to reduce errors will preclude emotions, while accepting "dry reason." I also believe that the best reasoning and the best reasoners use and require emotions.[26]

That we must take care to get the right information and to handle it well is a commonplace. But this commonplace, especially in light of Wilson's worries, raises very important issues for two closely related, and currently very prominent, philosophical accounts of responsibility: Aristotle's in the *Nicomachean Ethics*, and Strawson's in "Freedom and Resentment." The two accounts share a core view that responsibility is constituted by, and in this sense secondary to, certain emotions and emotional reactions: people are responsible because they are the proper objects of certain emotions and emotional reactions, such as indignation, blame, or pity. As Strawson argues, there is no state characterizable as free from causality that grounds or allows for responsibility or the correctness of, say, reactions of indignation or resentment. To be held responsible just is, say, being the object of some such emotion. Many other philosophers think this is at best paradoxical, and probably just wrong. On their view, for those emotions to be probative, they must be warranted, and this depends on people being responsible for what the emotions are about.

I do not want to enter this dispute here, except to note the following. Those who would tend toward Aristotle's and Strawson's views must contend with the issue, in general and in particular cases, of which emotions under which conditions are probative for which judgments. Aristotle and Strawson are well aware of this, and they do discuss some of those conditions. On their view, my indignation (or my seeming indignation) at your knocking me down goes little, if any, distance toward showing that you are responsible for knocking me down if my emotional responses would not be modified by certain excuses—for example, that it was not you but someone else who lurched into me, or that you were thrown against me, or that you were coerced into knocking me down, or that you reasonably believed that the only way to stop me from harming you or an innocent third party was to knock me down.

As our discussion of Wilson shows, however, this is not enough. We need to ask Aristotelians and Strawsonians such questions as: What restrictions, if any, are there on the knowledge or belief "base," the ground, of these attitudes? Can we know too much, not merely what is irrelevant, but what is all too likely to mislead us? Are there special restrictions on

---

[26] On these points, see Stocker and Hegeman, *Valuing Emotions*.

what we can or should know, depending on where and to what end a person's responsibility is in question?[27]

The last question refers to what might be improperly prejudicial, such as information about a defendant's criminal record or a victim's sexual history. This question also refers to what might be invited by—and what might invite us to fall into or adopt—different relationships and forms of concern. I am thinking here of what Strawson calls an *objective* concern, a concern to treat or manipulate others, as differentiated from a *reactive* concern, a concern to live directly and openly, as a person with other people. Further, we need to ask these and similar questions in regard to different times and stages of trials and other enterprises. What would be inappropriate to mention during the trial might be admissible, and indeed very important, at sentencing hearings.

Turning now to issues canvassed under the heading of *moral luck*, we need to ask Aristotelians and Strawsonians about the importance of background conditions.[28] I do not know if they would be equally justified, but I would expect there to be different emotions and attitudes toward the "same" crime in a time of peace and plenty than in a far harder, more desperate time. Similarly, we need to ask about the importance of what other people do. Again, I do not know if they would be equally justified, but I would also expect there to be different emotions and reactive attitudes toward the "same" crime depending on, say, whether it is seen as a lone occurrence or, instead, as one of a "wave" of such crimes. How would Aristotelians and Strawsonians deal with these different emotions and attitudes, and different occasions for emotions and attitudes? Are they all probative, and equally so? Or are some to be preferred to others, in general or for particular purposes?

To bring out some other, though related, issues about abuse excuses, let us consider a psychoanalytic vignette presented by Christopher Bollas and David Sundelson, who describe a patient who has talked about fantasies of killing his wife. He is further described as

[a] sexually impulsive patient . . . [who] might dress seductively and talk [with his analyst and others] of sexual relations. . . .

Did this patient really intend to kill his wife? The analyst at first thought this was simply one of the innumerable dares the patient gave to himself, but over time became less certain, eventually reaching the point where he [the analyst] actually thought it might happen. . . . In the end it was quite clear that this patient was terrified of

---

[27] On these issues, see Alvin Goldman, "Epistemic Paternalism: Communication Control in Law and Society," *The Journal of Philosophy* 88 (1991): 113–31.

[28] I have been helped here by Arenella's discussion of Strawson, in "Convicting the Morally Blameless," 1535–44.

aggression and was certain that if he entertained the violent parts of his personality he would be torn into pieces. His defense against such fears had been consistently to act out in a mildly provocative way that earned him a repeatedly negative response from co-workers and acquaintances.[29]

Suppose, now, that this person is charged with either a successful or an attempted killing of his wife. His state, as just described, is not itself an abuse excuse, but let us suppose that, as is likely, it is explained by a history of abuse. Does that state and its attendant abuse excuse do much, if anything, to excuse him for trying to kill or succeeding in killing his wife? In at least most circumstances, I think the answer will have to be some sort of "No"—perhaps simply "No" or "Hardly at all."

However, in regard to other charges and other forums, I think that his abuse excuse can indeed provide a sound defense. Suppose that he is brought before a governmental tribunal dealing with hostile workplaces or sexual harassment on the job, having been charged with being inappropriately sexually provocative. Or suppose that he is brought before the grievance board of his employer, or that a coworker, face-to-face and completely unofficially, tells him reprovingly that he is sexually provocative.

I find it easy in all these latter cases to complete the story in ways which show that his state and attendant abuse excuse should be taken into account and should be accorded considerable weight. For my claim, it is not important whether the state and the excuse would lead to exoneration, or just a reduction in the severity of any punishment, or a change in the nature of the sentence from, say, a fine to counseling—or, in the case of the individual coworker, whether they would lead to a lessening of blame, objection, or distaste. What is important is that against such a charge in any of these last forums, this excuse would have a strong probative force.

One conclusion here is that how this person's state and closely related abuse excuse should fare as a defense for attempted or successful murder shows little about how it should fare as a defense for some other wrong, and conversely. Another conclusion is that we severely limit our understanding of abuse excuses if we focus simply on felonies. A third, closely related, conclusion is that we severely limit our understanding of abuse excuses if we focus simply on trials.

By "trials" I mean full-blown, state-run criminal trials. Other sorts of trials may be far more accepting of abuse excuses. (Of course, some trials, such as those concerned with violations of strict-liability codes, may be far less accepting of abuse excuses.) Consider a school tribunal dealing

---

[29] Christopher Bollas and David Sundelson, *The New Informants: The Betrayal of Confidentiality in Psychoanalysis and Psychotherapy* (Northvale, NJ: Jason Aronson, 1995), 80–82.

with an infraction of a not very serious school code by a youngish student. Here, an abuse excuse might carry a lot of weight in assessing both what was done by the student and what should be done to or for the student.

Similarly, we could consider the trials, or proceedings, of "diversionary justice" programs, as are now (in 1998) used in Australia and Scandinavia. In these "trials," defendants—typically younger ones accused of less serious crimes—instead of undergoing the more usual trial, and instead of facing imprisonment or fines, are "diverted" to discussions with law-enforcement personnel, social workers, and the like, and also with victims. These conferences are intended to help the defendants understand factually and emotionally the nature and gravity of what they did, focusing on its illegality and its effect on victims; on what led them to commit the crimes; on how they can make restitution to the victims; and on how they can turn their lives around and reintegrate themselves into society.[30] It is difficult in the extreme to see how abuse excuses and explanations incorporating them would, could, or should be excluded from such proceedings.

To conclude this section, let us consider one final case, a case that involves no trials of any sort, but does involve abuse excuses. This is a case of a middle-aged woman who, because of early abuse, cannot bring herself to disagree with another person because she is so fearful of the other being angry at her—so fearful that she would, she says, rather die than be in conflict. Clearly, she can harm and wrong many people due to this. For example, she does not—she cannot—stick up for her children, take their part in fights with others. She is not even able to stand up to her adolescent children, not even to set needed limits. She commits no felonies or other crimes and is not on trial. But there are still harms and wrongs that need to be excused. An abuse excuse, making reference to her early abuse and how that affected her, may well provide a strongly probative excuse.

As this case helps us see, especially when conjoined with the other cases we have considered, whether abuse excuses can be allowed can depend on whether there is simply a wrong to be excused or a formal or informal charge that has been laid and must be answered. So, too, it can depend on where a charge is heard and what sort of trial or form of judging a charge involves.

These last comments also suggest an obvious, further point with a useful implication for issues about abuse excuses. The point is that our legal processes are required to do a multitude of difficult jobs, virtually all at once: for example, decide on which crime, if any, has been committed;

[30] My thanks are owed here to Judge Angela Karpin of the District Court, New South Wales, Australia.

decide what the punishment should be; and give proper weight to society's and victims' concerns. The implication is that it is nearly inevitable that if an abuse excuse engenders a problem at one place, it will likely engender a different problem or none at all at a different place. So, for example, there is little, if any, reason to think that an abuse excuse could or should lessen or modify a victim's justified outrage in the ways and to the degree that it might properly lessen or modify the proper punishment for the crime.

VII. CONCLUSION

What, then, is my overall and final answer to the question "Should abuse excuses be allowed?" The answer I am most confident about is that, as posed, that question is very unhelpful. It obscures nearly everything that must be examined: the vast range of abuse excuses, the many different ways they can be used, and so on, as detailed throughout this essay.

Wilson's primary concern was with policy questions about, and objections to, allowing abuse excuses. His central theme was that to allow them would undermine responsibility. I have argued that he has not sustained his case. He has not given us much, if any, reason to believe that people will hold themselves or others less responsible if abuse excuses are admissible in legal proceedings. He has not given us much, if any, way to evaluate the status quo or possible changes in our sense of responsibility — for example, whether and how we should hold ourselves or others responsible where there are abuse excuses. Nor has he even given us much, if any, reason to think that jurors should judge, not explain, the behavior of defendants — and especially that they should not explain such behavior in terms of abuse excuses and other character-based factors.

Most of my arguments against Wilson did not find him mistaken; they found only that he had not made out his case. Indeed, the bulk of this essay, whether devoted to Wilson or to other topics, was concerned with what must be done if we are to understand, and to make out any case for or against, abuse excuses in general or particular ones.

I end, then, close to where I started — acknowledging the great difficulties in saying something at once clear, brief, and sensible about abuse excuses, taken generally or fully particularized. It seems to me that almost everything still remains to be done on the multitude of questions about abuse excuses. Some solace might be drawn from the fact that, quite generally, we face these difficulties when confronting difficult and contentious issues in morality and law.

Philosophy, Syracuse University

WHY CITIZENS SHOULD VOTE:
A CAUSAL RESPONSIBILITY APPROACH*

By Alvin I. Goldman

I. Some Rationales for Voting

Why should a citizen vote? There are two ways to interpret this question: in a *prudential* sense, and in a *moral* (or *quasi-moral*) sense. Under the first interpretation, the question asks why—or under what circumstances—it is in a citizen's self-interest to vote. Under the second interpretation, it asks what moral (or quasi-moral) reasons citizens have for voting. I shall mainly try to answer the moral version of the question, but my answer may also, in some circumstances, bear on the prudential question. Before proceeding to my own approach, let me briefly survey alternatives in the field.

Many theorists approach the issue from an *economic* or *rational-choice* perspective, and they usually have in mind the prudential question. On a standard version of this approach, it is considered rational for a citizen to vote if and only if the expected personal benefit of voting exceeds the expected cost. Confronted with a choice between two candidates, C and C', a prospective voter should ask how much he values getting his more preferred candidate as compared with his less preferred one. This difference in value should be multiplied by the probability that his ballot, if cast, would change what would otherwise happen. The resulting expected value should then be compared with the expected cost of voting, which might include the time lost from work, and the inconvenience of traveling to the polling site, standing in line, and so forth. Voting is prudentially rational if and only if the expected benefit exceeds the expected cost. Most theorists who analyze the subject from this angle conclude that it is rarely rational for a citizen to vote, especially in large elections. The expected benefit from voting is usually quite small because the probability of casting the deciding ballot in large elections is tiny. The expected cost of casting a vote, on the other hand, is not insignificant.[1]

* I am indebted to Tom Christiano, Holly Smith, and Ellen Frankel Paul, for valuable discussion and suggestions. Christiano's pointers to relevant literature on voting rationales were especially helpful.
[1] William Riker and Peter Ordeshook have estimated the probability of an individual voter being decisive to the outcome of a U.S. presidential election as $p = 10^{-8}$—that is, a 1 in 100,000,000 chance. See Riker and Ordeshook, "A Theory of the Calculus of Voting," *American Political Science Review* 62 (March 1968): 25. Perhaps the earliest formulation of the economic approach is due to Anthony Downs, *An Economic Theory of Democracy* (New York:

A different version of the expected-value approach incorporates the benefits that would accrue to the entire electorate, not merely to the voter himself. Derek Parfit argues that the benefits to the entire populace of electing the superior candidate must be taken into account, and the magnitude of these collective benefits, even when multiplied by the voter's tiny probability of being decisive, might make the expected benefits substantial.[2] Parfit's analysis is presumably addressed to the second interpretation—the moral or quasi-moral interpretation—of the "Why vote?" question.

A second possible moral rationale for voting is the *Kantian* approach. According to Kant's categorical imperative, one must not act according to a principle (maxim) which cannot be willed to become a universal law.[3] Thus, the Kantian approach would lead us to ask whether one can will it to become a universal law that everybody abstains from voting when it does not suit his or her personal economic calculus. Since the upshot would obviously be unacceptable for political democracy, the Kantian approach would not allow citizens to abstain on grounds of personal inconvenience. Presumably, according to Kantianism, only the general practice of voting can be universalized, and that is why one should vote. It is difficult to find full-fledged endorsements of the Kantian theme in the recent literature, but Paul Meehl comes close.[4] He says that you cannot get people to go "rationally" to the polls unless you introduce some sort of quasi-Kantian principle with a distinctly ethical content.[5]

A third rationale for voting is the *expressivist* rationale. Geoffrey Brennan and Loren Lomasky give the following motivating examples.[6] When you send a get-well card to a hospitalized friend, you do not expect the card to effect a therapeutic outcome. When a sports fan goes to the stadium to cheer for his team, he does not expect his scream from the bleachers to enhance the probability of his team's winning. These are "expressive" acts; they express certain desires or preferences of the actor, without any accompanying assumption that they will *cause* the desired outcome. Similarly, Brennan and Lomasky suggest, voting for candidate

---

Harper and Brothers, 1957), ch. 14. Downs formulates matters in terms of the "party differential" rather than the differential between the two individual candidates, but this difference is incidental.

[2] Derek Parfit, *Reasons and Persons* (Oxford: Clarendon Press, 1984), 73–75.

[3] Immanuel Kant, *Foundations of the Metaphysics of Morals*, trans. L. W. Beck (Indianapolis: Bobbs-Merrill, 1959), 39.

[4] Paul Meehl, "The Selfish Voter Paradox and the Thrown-Away Vote Argument," *American Political Science Review* 71 (March 1977): 11–30.

[5] Ibid., 13. Later, Meehl sketches his favored rationale as follows: "I would say that some sort of prima facie obligation or obligation vector exists for me as a voter to participate in the electoral process, relying on the general principle that unless people do, the system won't work . . ." (ibid., 21).

[6] Geoffrey Brennan and Loren Lomasky, "Large Numbers, Small Costs: The Uneasy Foundation of Democratic Rule," in *Politics and Process: New Essays in Democratic Thought*, ed. Geoffrey Brennan and Loren Lomasky (Cambridge: Cambridge University Press, 1989), 49–50.

A can be a bona fide and appropriate expression of support even when one knows that the effect on the outcome is miniscule. Stanley Benn endorses the expressivist approach in the following passage: "I am suggesting, in short, that political activity may be a form of moral self-expression, necessary . . . because one could not seriously claim, even to oneself, to be on [the side of the right] without expressing the attitude by the action most appropriate to it in the paradigm situation."[7]

I shall not try to assess the merits of these approaches in any detail. I shall not pick a quarrel, for example, with the economic analysis of whether and when it is prudent to vote. However, voting might be morally commendable even if it is not prudent. Nor shall I spend time evaluating the three foregoing approaches to the morality of voting. Although each has its difficulties, I believe, it is not essential for me to prove them wrong. This is because the approach I favor is not necessarily a rival to these other approaches; in principle, they could all be legitimate rationales for voting.

The approach I favor—a novel approach, as far as I know—may be called the *causal responsibility* approach. The first claim of the causal responsibility approach is that a voter can make a partial causal contribution toward the election of a given candidate even if he is not a swing or decisive voter. Even a non-swing voter can *help* elect a winner. Second, voting in favor of the actual winner counts as a greater causal contribution to her election than merely abstaining. Thus, if the election of a given candidate would be a (socially) *good* outcome, a person can earn more "credit" by helping to produce that outcome than by sitting on the sidelines. Conversely, if an election might result in a *bad* candidate being chosen, potential voters who sit on the sidelines may not escape partial blame for that possible outcome, should it occur. They could contribute (more) toward the defeat of that candidate by voting for a rival; and their failure to do so may carry with it some culpability or blameworthiness. They do not avert such blameworthiness or culpability simply because their vote would not have been a decisive, or swing, vote. So potential voters should vote either to help produce a good outcome or to avoid a bad one.

Exactly what kind of credit or blame is in question here? Is it *moral* credit and blame, or some other kind? This is an issue I shall not try to settle fully. Certainly in some cases moral credit or blame may be apt. In legislative voting and popular referenda, there may be votes on policies that are morally desirable or objectionable; failure to help enact or defeat such policies would be morally culpable. Similarly, in some elections one candidate may be morally inferior to a rival. A voter's failure to contrib-

[7] Stanley Benn, "The Problematic Rationality of Political Participation," in *Philosophy, Politics, and Society, Fifth Series*, ed. Peter Laslett and James Fishkin (New Haven: Yale University Press, 1979), 310.

ute as much as possible to the election of the morally preferable candidate
may be a moral blemish. More commonly, credit or blame might be in
order that is less clearly of a moral stripe. Consider the election of a chair
for a social club or professional organization in which neither candidate
is morally superior to the other but one is vastly more competent than her
rival. She would advance the collective interests of the social entity much
more than the rival. If a potential voter, knowing who would be the better
officer, nonetheless declines to vote, this might be regarded as a socially
irresponsible or socially culpable omission. Is it a *morally* culpable omission? I doubt it; but it does seem to be culpable in a *quasi-moral* sense. In
either case, the voter's culpability seems to arise in part from the fact that
his action causally influences the outcome. The first step that needs to be
taken, then, is to establish that voting or abstaining, even when one is not
a prospective swing voter, can nonetheless involve causal responsibility
for the outcome. This problem will occupy me for a large chunk of the
essay.

II. Overdetermination and Causal Responsibility

According to one view of causation, a particular vote causes a particular electoral outcome only if a different outcome would have eventuated
if that vote had not occurred. This is a *simple counterfactual* analysis of
event causation. More generally, the theory says that event c causes event
e just in case c and e actually occur but if c had not occurred e would not
have occurred. A theory very close to this is advocated by David Lewis.[8]
Lewis does not require precisely this counterfactual, because he says there
might be a causal chain from c to d to e such that d would not have
occurred without c, and e would not have occurred without d, yet e might
have occurred via a different causal route than through c. These types of
cases, however, do not matter for the analysis of voting. So I shall write
as if Lewis's account were equivalent to the simple counterfactual analysis. This analysis deals fairly adequately with acts of voting which are
decisive. If the citizen had not voted as he did, the outcome would have
been different (a tie, at any rate, if not a victory for a different candidate).[9]
Such a case will qualify as a cause of the actual electoral outcome under

---

[8] David Lewis, "Causation," in Lewis, *Philosophical Papers*, vol. 2 (New York: Oxford
University Press, 1986).
[9] The term "swing vote" perhaps suggests a vote that tilts the outcome either toward one
candidate or toward the other; it does not suggest a tie as a possible outcome. In the present
context, however, we want to consider possible abstentions as well as votes for different
candidates. And a decision to abstain rather than vote could change the outcome from a
victory for one candidate to a tie—perhaps requiring a run-off election. (For that matter,
even switching a vote from one candidate to another can result in a tie, when the number
of votes is even.) The counterfactual analysis also invites consideration of abstentions. If a
citizen votes for candidate X and we ask, "What would have happened if the citizen had not
cast this vote?," one possible scenario is that the citizen abstains rather than votes for an
opposing candidate.

the simple counterfactual analysis. But wherever a citizen's alternative action would not be enough to single-handedly cancel the outcome, his vote will not qualify as a cause of the outcome.

So much the worse, I say, for the simple counterfactual analysis. It is a defect of this account that it restricts causation to these cases. All but a few large elections are decided by a margin of more than one vote. In all of these cases, the simple counterfactual account implies that *no* voter's action is a cause of the outcome. But surely some of the votes—at least those cast for the actual winner—exercised *some* causal influence toward the outcome. Compare this situation with two others. Consider a firing squad with ten members who all fire simultaneously at a victim and all hit their mark. Is it not bizarre to declare that none of their individual actions has any causal influence on the outcome? Moral responsibility for the death is presumably contingent on playing at least some causal role in the death, so if we declare each shooter causally irrelevant to the death, we commit ourselves to absolving each shooter from any moral responsibility. That seems misguided. Any prospective murderer could then protect himself against culpability by recruiting an accomplice to commit the crime simultaneously. Analogously, suppose that ten friends are recruited to push a car out of a snow bank, when three would suffice for the job. If all ten push simultaneously, the car's being freed does not depend counterfactually on the pushing of any one. But surely this is a case in which each exerts *some* causal influence, and each deserves some degree of credit and thanks, which are presumably predicated on his partial causal responsibility.[10]

Both civil and criminal law support the view that in these types of (concurrent) overdetermination cases, each separate set of sufficient conditions qualifies as a cause.[11] Where two defendants ride their motorcycles past the victim's horse, which is startled and injures the victim, each defendant causes the injury, despite the sufficiency of the noise from each motorcycle to have done the job. Where two defendants independently stab or shoot the victim, who dies of loss of blood, each is liable for the victim's death.

Lewis groups these types of cases under a category he labels "symmetric overdetermination."[12] He says that these are cases in which common sense does not deliver a clear answer as to whether the individual act causes the outcome, so theory can safely say what it likes.[13] This strikes me as wrong, or at least inadequate. Although it may not be clear that

---

[10] In other cases, of course, credit or thanks might be given for mere *effort*, even if it makes no causal contribution. In this case, however, the effort plays a causal role; it is not merely fruitless effort.

[11] I draw the examples that follow from Michael S. Moore, "Causation and Responsibility," elsewhere in this volume. Moore, in turn, cites Richard Wright, "Causation in Tort Law," *California Law Review* 73 (1985): 1775–98, as an excellent discussion of such cases.

[12] See David Lewis, "Postscripts to 'Causation'," in Lewis, *Philosophical Papers*, 2:193–212.

[13] Ibid., 194, 212.

these are cases of "full" causation, they are at least instances of a weak
species of causation, call it *partial* causation, or *contributory* causation, or
causal *influence*.[14] Lewis points out that in cases of symmetric overdetermination we can always find a larger event that qualifies as a cause, an
event that consists in the "sum" of the various causes.[15] Returning to our
earlier examples, the sum of the ten shootings or the ten pushings will
satisfy the counterfactual analysis, even if the individual shootings or
pushings do not, because the death would not have occurred without the
ten shootings, and the freeing of the car would not have occurred without
the ten pushings. This *may* be right, but it does not go far enough.[16] A
satisfactory theory must also assign some causal influence to the individual shootings and pushings; and a satisfactory theory must assign causal
influence to individual acts of voting even in wide-margin elections where
no single vote is decisive.

Another approach to the theory of causation, which seems more promising for our purposes than the simple counterfactual approach, is presented by J. L. Mackie.[17] Mackie considers the example of a fire started by
a short-circuit. The short-circuit combines with other conditions, such as
the presence of flammable material, the absence of a suitably placed
sprinkler, and so on, to constitute a complex condition that is sufficient for
the fire. Also, the short-circuit is an indispensable part of this complex
condition; the other parts of this condition, in the absence of the short-
circuit, would not have produced the fire.[18] Mackie calls this an INUS
condition: an *insufficient* but *necessary* part of a condition which is itself
unnecessary but *sufficient* for the result. Thus, in typical cases, a cause is an
indispensable part of a sufficient condition.

This formulation would nicely handle standard election cases in which
the margin of victory is more than one. Consider an electorate of 100
persons, all of whom vote in a given election in which Jones defeats Smith
by a 60-to-40 margin. Let citizen Z be one of those who votes for Jones. Is
Z's ballot a (partial) cause of Jones's victory? If we focus on all 60 votes
for Jones, which is a condition sufficient for Jones's victory, Z's vote does
not meet the INUS requirement. Although Z's vote is part of that 60-vote
condition, his vote is not a *necessary* or *indispensable* part of that sufficient
condition. The other 59 votes for Jones still suffice for Jones's victory, even
if we subtract Z's vote. Let us instead consider any set of 51 actual votes

[14] In a similar spirit, Louis Loeb offers an account of causation that includes overdetermining causes. See his "Causal Theories and Causal Overdetermination," *Journal of Philosophy*
71, no. 15 (1974): 525–44.
[15] Lewis, "Postscripts," 212.
[16] I say it "may" be right because it is not entirely clear. If the ten pushings had not
occurred, would *no* pushings have occurred? Not obviously. Perhaps five pushings would
still have occurred, which would have been sufficient to free the car.
[17] J. L. Mackie, "Causes and Conditions," *American Philosophical Quarterly* 2, no. 4 (October
1965): 245–64.
[18] Ibid., 245.

for Jones, including Z's vote. Such a set of 51 votes is also sufficient for Jones's victory, and Z's vote is a necessary or indispensable part of that sufficient condition (given the 100-member electorate). Z's vote is indispensable because if his vote is subtracted from the 51—that is, if it is left open what Z will do—a Jones victory is not guaranteed. So Z's vote does satisfy the INUS condition.

It is true, of course, that any other set of 51 Jones votes, not including Z's vote, is also sufficient for Jones's victory. Z's vote is not an indispensable part of *those* sufficient conditions. But if the INUS approach is going to authorize overdetermining causes to qualify as causes, this should not matter. It should be enough that a given event is an indispensable member of *some* sufficient condition for the effect. It is not clear that Mackie himself means to allow this. In the fire example, he adds the requirement that "no other sufficient condition of the house's catching fire was present on this occasion."[19] This seems intended to exclude overdeterminers as causes, and would thereby exclude wide-margin electoral results from having any causes. This follows, at any rate, if "another sufficient condition" means any sufficient condition not identical with, but possibly overlapping, a selected one. For reasons already adduced, however, this addendum is unfortunate, precisely because it would exclude overdeterminers from qualifying as causes. This is especially unfortunate relative to our project of analyzing the concept of *partial* or *contributory* cause (as opposed to the concept of "*the* cause," for example). We do better to work with the initial formulation I took from Mackie, not the final formulation he provides.

To clarify how the INUS analysis works, let us ask whether someone's vote for Jones could ever serve as a partial cause of an opponent's victory. Setting aside "indirect" effects—for example, one's own vote influencing the votes of others—the answer is no. If Z votes for Jones but Smith wins by a 60-to-40 margin, there is no (actually present) condition sufficient for Smith's victory of which Z's vote is an indispensable part. To be sure, there is the set of votes consisting of 51 votes for Smith plus Z's vote for Jones. That set is sufficient for Smith's victory. But even if we subtract Z's vote for Jones, the remaining votes are still sufficient for Smith's victory.

What about abstentions? Can they qualify as partial causes under the INUS approach? Yes. But it depends on whether the number of potential voters is even or odd. If the number is even, an abstention can satisfy the INUS condition; if the number is odd, it cannot. To illustrate, consider first a 100-person electorate. Suppose Z abstains and Jones wins by a 59-to-40 margin. Consider the set of decisions consisting of 50 votes for Jones plus Z's abstention. This set of decisions suffices for Jones's victory, because only 49 potential voters remain and they cannot prevent Jones's

[19] Ibid.

victory. If we subtract Z's abstention, however, there is no longer a guarantee of Jones's victory. Because 50 voting decisions are still open, there could be a tie. So Z's abstention is an indispensable part of the originally designated set of conditions for Jones's victory. In the case of an odd-numbered electorate, however, this scenario cannot happen. To illustrate, consider a 101-person electorate. Where Jones wins with a minimum of 51 votes, we can consider a set consisting of 51 Jones votes plus Z's abstention. This suffices for Jones's victory; but subtracting Z's abstention, there is still enough to guarantee Jones's victory. So Z's abstention is not an indispensable member of such a set.[20]

Proceeding from this analysis, let us ask what can be said to citizen Z who is deciding whether to vote in a forthcoming election. Suppose he knows *how* he will vote if he votes at all but has not yet decided *whether* to vote. Assume that candidate Brown, for whom Z would vote, is indeed the best candidate in the race.[21] Here is what we can say to citizen Z, to justify his voting: "If you vote for Brown and Brown wins, you will deserve partial causal credit for her victory. If you vote for Brown but her (inferior) opponent Johnson wins, you will be absolved from any causal responsibility for Johnson's victory. A tie is possible but so improbable that it can be ignored. Thus, if you vote, you are guaranteed either partial causal credit for a good outcome or no causal discredit for a bad outcome. On the other hand, if you abstain from voting, there is no guarantee that either of these scenarios will transpire. If there is an even-numbered electorate, you will earn partial causal credit by abstention in case Brown wins, but you will also earn partial causal discredit if Brown loses. If there is an odd-numbered electorate, you will earn neither causal credit nor causal discredit. So in terms of causal credit or discredit, you are better off voting than abstaining."

If we adopt the INUS approach to causation, then, we have a rationale for voting in terms of causal responsibility. It is not as smooth and intuitive as one might like; and therefore in the next section, I shall propose an alternative approach. We see, however, how at least one familiar approach to causation provides a basis for rationalizing voting in terms of causal responsibility.

[20] There are a number of objections to Mackie's INUS account. One of them is that it requires causation to feature sufficient conditions, and this ostensibly implies that there is no causation without determinism. This is too restrictive, as many writers point out. Causation can take place even in chancy situations, where merely probabilistic laws hold sway. See Patrick Suppes, *A Probabilistic Theory of Causality* (Amsterdam: North-Holland, 1970); Nancy Cartwright, "Causal Laws and Effective Strategies," *Noûs* 13 (1979): 419–37; Wesley Salmon, *Scientific Explanation and the Causal Structure of the World* (Princeton, NJ: Princeton University Press, 1984); and Lewis, "Postscripts," 175–84. I concede this point, and therefore grant that the INUS account is not fully comprehensive. In the context of voting, however, we do not need to worry about probabilistic causation. Wherever an electoral outcome occurs, some set of votes is sufficient for the outcome. So the analysis sketched above is adequate for present purposes.

[21] For simplicity, I assume an election with a single race.

I should emphasize that this type of rationale requires certain explanations, qualifications, and/or provisos. Let me introduce these qualifications by reversing the earlier assumption that the candidate for whom citizen Z plans to vote is the superior candidate. Suppose instead that Z's preferred candidate Brown is the inferior candidate. Does Z still have good reasons to vote? In other words, should a citizen vote whether or not his preferred candidate is the objectively best choice? Or should he vote only when the preferred candidate is objectively best?

First let us ask what might be meant by the phrase "objectively best candidate." Elsewhere[22] I have suggested that if candidate A would produce a set of outcomes higher on the preference-ordering of a majority of citizens than the set of outcomes candidate B would produce, then A is a democratically better candidate than B. This is one possible way to give content to the phrase "objectively best candidate," though others, of course, might be proposed. Now a voter might be said to have *objectively good reasons* to vote for a certain candidate if that candidate is objectively best. But what if a citizen does not know, and indeed has no idea, which candidate is objectively best? Should such a citizen still be encouraged to vote rather than abstain?

On the approach I favor, citizens should not be encouraged to vote, *full stop*. Instead they should be encouraged first to gather enough information and then to vote. The point of becoming informed, of course, is to increase the probability of making a good choice, that is, of choosing the objectively best candidate.[23] The upshot is that voting is not necessarily and without qualification a desirable or dutiful act. Consider an uninformed citizen, late on election day, who has no time to become informed before the polls close, but wonders whether he should vote. The present approach would not justify his voting. In this respect, the present rationale differs from both the Kantian and expressivist approaches, which presumably urge people to vote under all circumstances. I do not regard it as a defect of the current rationale that it has this qualified aspect. I am unconvinced that a person ought to vote, or has a duty to vote, even when he is both uninformed and no longer has time to become informed.[24]

Even if a voter collects substantial information about the candidates, he might still be wrong about which would be the best one to elect. Can he still have good reasons to vote under this scenario? Here I introduce the notion of *subjectively* good reasons to vote, which I define in terms of what a voter is *justified* in believing about the candidates, rather than what is

---

[22] Alvin I. Goldman, *Knowledge in a Social World* (Oxford: Oxford University Press, 1999), ch. 10.

[23] The types of relevant information to gather would not be exhausted, of course, by campaign promises and accusations against one's opponent. Other relevant types of information would include each candidate's past experience and track record, her party affiliation and supporters, and so forth.

[24] The critical role of political information in producing good outcomes is elaborated in my *Knowledge in a Social World*, ch. 10.

true of them. Citizen Z's information might *justify* him in believing that Brown is the best candidate in the race, even if she is not. Z would then be justified in believing that by voting for Brown he would either achieve partial causal responsibility for the election of the best candidate or at least avoid all causal responsibility for the best candidate's defeat. His being justified in believing this gives him subjectively good reasons to vote for Brown.

Which class of reasons is more important, one might ask, objective reasons or subjective reasons? Which class of reasons is crucial in determining whether a citizen really should vote? These questions have no answers, I submit. The question of whether a person should vote is simply ambiguous as between an objective sense of "should" and a subjective sense of "should." There are simply two distinct questions here, and there is no reason to expect one of them to take precedence over the other. The important thing, for present purposes, is that in *each* sense of "should" our account shows why citizens will often be in a situation in which it is true that they should vote.

III. VECTORIAL AND CONVENTIONAL CAUSAL SYSTEMS

Although the INUS analysis of causation provides one basis for justifying a decision to vote, that analysis does not adequately capture the intuitive difference in causal role between voting and abstaining. I shall try to do a better job of capturing that difference by introducing another model of causation: the *vectorial* model. This is not intended to be a general analysis of causation, for it applies only to a restricted subset of causal relationships, which I shall call *vectorial causal systems*. Electoral systems are prime examples of such systems.

A vectorial causal system is a system in which states and state-changes result from the interplay among forces that can be represented as vectors. A simple illustration of a natural vectorial system is a tug-of-war. Forces are exerted on a rope in opposite directions, and movements of the rope— and of participants clinging to the rope—are the results of the sum of the vectorial forces. When an element in a vectorial causal system moves in a given direction, this is because the sum of the forces on that element are positive in that direction. This sum is computed from three kinds of forces: (1) forces that are positive in the direction of movement, (2) forces that are negative in the direction of movement, and (3) forces that are zero in the direction of movement.[25] Finally, when thinking about the causation of a given movement, we think of each positive force as a *contributing*

---

[25] John Staddon points out that these forces can be treated as *scalars* rather than *vectors*, because there is just one dimension of movement, and forces can be treated as either positive or negative along this dimension. In election cases, however, at least in races where there are more than two candidates, the scalar approach will not work. In any case, the term "vector" is here used loosely to depict an interplay of conflicting forces.

factor in the production of the movement, each negative force as a *counteracting*, or *resisting*, factor in the production of the movement, and each zero force as a *neutral factor* vis-à-vis the production of the movement.

Elections are what we may call *conventional* vectorial causal systems. Given the conventions of vote counting, a vote for candidate C is a positive vector vis-à-vis C's possible election. A vote for a rival candidate is a negative vector vis-à-vis C's possible election. And an abstention from voting is a zero vector vis-à-vis C's (and anybody else's) possible election. Now how should we link vector forces with event causation in electoral contexts? The following seems plausible. If the target candidate actually wins, each vote for her is a partial cause of her victory; but neither votes against her nor abstentions from voting are partial causes of her victory.

When we turn to an *agent's* causal responsibility, however, things are a little different. When we address the responsibility of an agent, we take into account all of the options available to him. We consider not only the options he chooses but those he could have chosen instead. If an available option is not chosen, but would have exerted a causal influence had it been chosen, this is certainly germane in assessing the agent's responsibility. Suppose citizen Z votes for candidate C, but C loses nonetheless. Is Z in any way responsible for C's defeat? No. Z did everything in his electoral power to elect C, so he cannot be held responsible.[26] Now suppose that Z abstains and C loses. Here Z can certainly be held partly responsible for C's loss, because an option available to Z—namely, voting for C—would have been a counteracting causal factor vis-à-vis C's loss. Thus, an abstention certainly opens an agent to charges of causal responsibility, despite the fact that the agent's act of abstention does not qualify as an event-cause of the outcome (under the vectorial model of causation). Of course, this analysis can be flipped on the other side. If an agent can be held partly responsible for a candidate's defeat by virtue of his abstention, shouldn't he equally be held partly responsible for a candidate's victory if he abstains? After all, he *could* have voted for a rival candidate but did not. This seems to me plausible, as long as we insist that an abstainer bears *less* responsibility for C's victory than someone who actually voted for C. That seems a clear implication of the vectorial model of causation. Obviously, a positive vote exerts greater causal influence toward a victory than an abstention, and that should weigh heavily in assigning responsibility.

Let us now link this responsibility-based approach to the rationale for voting that can be offered to citizens. The story is similar to the one presented at the end of Section II, but without the complications encountered there (e.g., those relating to odd- or even-numbered electorates). If Brown is the superior candidate, then Z's voting for her rather than

---

[26] There may be ways to influence the outcome above and beyond one's personal vote, for example, by persuading other voters. But this goes beyond the present subject.

abstaining places him in the following position. If Brown wins, Z will have had greater responsibility than an abstainer for the election of the better candidate; if she loses, Z will have had no responsibility for her loss. Furthermore, if Z is justified in believing that Brown is the better candidate, then he is justified in believing that he will have some measure of responsibility for the victory (or no responsibility for the loss) of the better candidate if he votes for Brown. Thus, Z has either objectively good reasons to vote for Brown, or subjectively good reasons, or both.

At this point an important objection must be confronted. The cases I have discussed of overdetermining causes are instances of what Lewis calls "symmetric" overdetermination, where all the redundant causes occur simultaneously. In the case of voting, though, many of the votes occur in sequence. Moreover, by the time many voters cast their ballots, the outcome has already been decided. This is particularly striking in the case of presidential elections in the United States, where several time zones are involved. By the time voters in California or Hawaii go to the polls, the earlier-voting states may already have determined the victor. How can voters in these later-voting districts rationalize their voting? Do their votes really qualify as partial causes of the outcome (even if they vote for the winner)?[27] Are they really responsible for the outcome?

These voting cases, the objection continues, are instances of what is commonly called causal *preemption*. In preemption, an event c_1 occurs and actually causes e, but another event, c_2, also occurs and would have caused e if it were not preempted by c_1. As Lewis puts it: "There is the beginning of a causal process running from the preempted alternative to the effect. But this process does not go to completion."[28] An example would be a case in which a would-be assassin sets a timer to fire a gun at an intended victim at the stroke of midnight. A moment before midnight, another assassin shoots and kills the victim. Here intuition dictates that the preempted alternative is not a cause at all of the victim's death. Nor is the agent who sets the timer responsible for the death. Doesn't this equally apply to voters who cast their ballots for Brown but who get preempted by earlier votes for Brown which suffice for her election?

To deal with this objection, we need to make greater use of the notion of a conventional causal system, introduced earlier in this section. A conventional causal system is one in which causal upshots are defined or stipulated by social conventions. For example, property ownership is conventionally conferred and changed as a function of various symbolic acts. When two people make certain verbal utterances and money is exchanged, this conventionally causes the transfer of ownership of some item of property from one individual to the other. Elections are another

---

[27] Thanks to Tom Christiano for calling my attention to this problem and for highlighting its importance.
[28] Lewis, "Postscripts," 199.

prime example of a conventional causal system, in which certain types of outcomes are conventionally stipulated to result from assorted collections of voting acts.

An important feature of conventional causal systems is that the time of an outcome is one of the conventionally determined elements. Certain types of sales, for example, do not go into effect until a certain time period has elapsed after the main transactions, to allow a party (especially a buyer) to reconsider. Similarly, I contend, elections standardly feature a certain conventional element with respect to time. Even if voters cast their ballots at different times on election day (or through earlier absentee ballots), the system conventionally abstracts from this actual or "natural" order and considers all the votes on an equal basis. This is reflected in the fact that the votes are not *counted*, and have no conventional causal up-shot, until all votes in a given electoral district are cast, that is, until the polls close. Nor does the order of counting make any official difference. For these reasons, the temporal asymmetry among different votes is officially voided or obliterated by the conventions of the electoral process. In the United States House or Senate, for example, a roll-call vote is completed even if the outcome is clear long before the last vote has been voiced. This is because, officially, votes are not counted or "registered" until all have been voiced. Because of this conventional feature, the causal impact of a late vote is not really preempted by a collection of early votes. From the official, conventional perspective, they are all simultaneous; hence, their causal statuses are perfectly symmetric.[29]

Admittedly, this conventional perspective is obscured by national elections featuring different time zones, or by different poll-closing times among districts within the same time zone. All such cases, I would say, are flawed executions of the traditional conceptualization of elections. The idea behind a democratic election is that all votes should have equal weight, and that idea is, to some degree, undercut by counting some people's ballots before other citizens have had an opportunity to vote.[30]

IV. Objections and Replies

The heart of my (quasi-) moral rationale for voting is that one stands to earn more "credit" for helping to elect the best candidate or stands to avoid "discredit" for letting the best candidate lose. But, it may be asked,

[29] There are, to be sure, all sorts of deals made by members of Congress that depend upon voting order. This is not the occasion to enter into a close analysis of what such deals imply or presuppose.

[30] It might be objected that not all votes do have equal weights under all systems. For example, under the American system of electing presidents, the electoral college, not all citizens' votes count equally. However, this is not a clear instance of unequal weights. The electoral college involves a two-step system, in which citizens first choose electors who then choose a president. In the race for any given elector, all votes count equally; and in the race for president, all electors' ballots count equally.

who is handing out this credit?[31] Other citizens? God? What I mean to say, in saying that a voter "earns credit" for voting, is that the voter attains a certain (quasi-) moral status, whether or not anybody else knows about this status or does anything about it. Analogously, if someone (appropriately) fulfills a promise to a deceased friend or relative, he thereby attains a certain moral status, whether or not anybody else knows of his promise-keeping or compliments him for it. People of certain persuasions may doubt that the prospect of attaining a certain moral status would be very *motivating* for prospective voters. I am inclined to disagree with these doubts; but, in any case, I have not yet claimed that the rationale proffered here will necessarily succeed in motivating citizens. Insofar as I am interested in providing a (quasi-) moral rationale for voting, I merely wish to offer normatively sound reasons for voting, however successful or unsuccessful these reasons might be in motivational terms.

It is but a small step, however, from this normative rationale to scenarios that provide voting incentives. Citizens often disclose their voting actions or inactions to their friends and associates. A voter who informs his chums that he voted for their mutually approved candidate may be greeted with verbal approval (credit), whereas an acknowledgment that he did not manage to vote may be greeted with disapproval (discredit). These responses may arise precisely because friends and associates recognize the respective causal effects of voting and abstaining. If a citizen *expects* approval for voting and disapproval for abstaining, such an expectation creates an incentive in favor of voting.[32] Thus, insofar as my (quasi-) moral rationale underpins peer approval and disapproval, it can also indirectly affect a citizen's *prudential* rationale for voting. But I do not wish to make much of this.[33]

Let me return, then, to the moral rationale. Readers who are persuaded that causal responsibility gives a citizen a moral reason to vote might still want to know more about this reason; in particular, they might want to know how *weighty* it is. After all, voting is still somewhat costly, and it would be good to know how to weigh the moral value of helping elect a good candidate—especially when one's help is not essential—against the personal cost of voting. More generally, how is moral credit to be divided when there are more than enough contributors to a socially valuable outcome?[34] It would indeed be nice to have answers to these further questions, but I do not have them. This in no way suggests, however, that

[31] Thanks to Ellen Frankel Paul for highlighting this issue.
[32] In principle, of course, someone who votes for Brown might incur the wrath of those who oppose Brown's election. But a voter for Brown will probably have fewer associations with people who oppose Brown's election, and is less likely to inform them of his vote.
[33] Feeling as if one is part of a team that is working toward victory is undoubtedly a major factor in the psychology of political participation. But the integrity of team spirit derives from the fact that team members can all make causal contributions toward mutually sought outcomes.
[34] This question was properly urged on me by David Sobel.

my type of voting rationale is on the wrong track; it merely suggests (unsurprisingly) that more work is left to be done.

Personal cost, moreover, is not the only reason to abstain from casting a vote. At least two other considerations of an entirely different nature can also militate against voting. First, if both candidates in a given race are terrible, a citizen might wish to avoid complicity in electing even the lesser of the two evils.[35] Second, one might sometimes wish to abstain in order to "send a message" of some sort. For example, if a citizen objects to the placement of a questionable referendum on the ballot, he might express his opposition by means of abstention.[36] Once again, however, the fact that there are sometimes these kinds of reasons to abstain does not cut against the proposal that causal responsibility creates a positive reason to vote. Nor does it undercut the possibility that *normally*, if citizens become sufficiently informed, their on-balance reasons will favor voting.

The final objection I wish to consider concerns the epistemic conditions of citizens in the contemporary age of scientific polling and rapid communication. Given pollsters' predictions prior to election day, or the reports of exit polls on election day itself, a prospective voter may either know or be highly justified in believing that one of the candidates is a shoo-in and that his own vote will make no difference to the outcome. In the face of such knowledge or justified belief, how can the responsibility rationale properly move him? How can he incur moral or quasi-moral culpability by not voting?[37]

This line of argument restates the rational-choice perspective on the voting problem. No doubt it has intuitive appeal, but I do not think it deserves to be either the sole or the dominant perspective on the problem. According to the argument I have offered, when a prospective voter knows or justifiably believes that candidate X will win with or without his vote, this does not cancel his partial responsibility for the electoral outcome. If partial responsibility for the outcome gives him a reason to vote, as I have argued it does, the prospective voter's epistemic condition does not undercut this reason.

To appreciate the force of my reply, return to the firing-squad example. Suppose a member of a firing-squad offers himself the following argument: "People have counseled me not to shoot because then I won't incur any moral responsibility for the victim's death. But I won't incur any responsibility even if I do shoot. After all, I *know* that my comrades are all going to shoot, so the outcome will be the same whether I shoot or not. I cannot single-handedly change the outcome, so I won't be responsible. Therefore, I might as well shoot and not get in trouble with my superiors

---

[35] This consideration was suggested by Roderick Long and Susan Sauvé Meyer.
[36] David Schmidtz suggested this consideration.
[37] Thanks to Tom Christiano for pressing this problem on me.

for abstaining." This argument is unconvincing, because our criterion of moral responsibility is not tied to the make-a-difference, or decisiveness, criterion. Nor does knowledge that one will not make a difference to the outcome entail absence of moral responsibility. Our criterion of moral responsibility is tied to being a *contributing* (though possibly redundant) cause, not to being a *decisive* cause. A member of a firing squad who shoots (accurately) *is* a contributing cause of the victim's death. If he shoots, he does bear partial responsibility, although he could not have reversed the outcome by abstaining. *Mutatis mutandis*, the same applies to a voter. He can earn (more) moral credit by voting for the good candidate even if his vote is not decisive for victory; and he can incur moral culpability by abstaining even if his abstention is not decisive for the candidate's loss.[38]

Another possible objection by appeal to epistemic conditions might run as follows: "Even if you (Goldman) are right in claiming that partial causation rather than decisiveness is the crucial de facto ingredient in culpability, there is still a further, epistemic ingredient. To be culpable for an act or omission the agent must know, or be justified in believing, that this act or omission would instantiate that de facto ingredient. Do citizens satisfy this epistemic constraint?"

The answer to this is easy. Since citizens understand the conventional causal system that comprises the electoral process, it is pretty trivial for them to appreciate (at least at a tacit level) the causal role that their voting or abstaining will play in a given election. So the indicated epistemic condition, I suspect, is regularly met. Indeed, I am tempted to speculate that the reason so many people *do* vote, as a matter of fact, is precisely because of their grasp of the rationale offered here, including their grasp of the "contributing cause" role that their voting occupies within the system. As we saw earlier, if voting is approached from the standard economic or rational-choice perspective (which incorporates the decisiveness test), it seems irrational for most people to vote. From this perspective, it is perplexing why so many people do vote. The current approach offers a possible explanation of this phenomenon. Conceivably, then, the account presented here fulfills the dual function of both *normative* and *explanatory* theory. It can explain why people *should* vote (after obtaining sufficient information), and it can explain why people *do* vote (in fairly substantial numbers).

V. CONCLUSION

Political theorists have been hard put to explain why citizens should vote—or why they *do* vote—because the theorists have largely focused on

[38] Similarly, many commentators on the Holocaust morally censure people—especially people in official capacities—who failed to speak out against it at the time, even if such speech would not have single-handedly changed the outcome.

the expected consequences of an individual's voting versus not voting. This essay proposes a different approach to the problem.[39] It argues that citizens often have good reasons to vote because they bear partial responsibility for the electoral outcome. Even if an individual's vote is not decisive for a given candidate's victory, such a vote can still qualify as a partial cause of that victory. So a voter can earn moral or quasi-moral credit for an electoral outcome even if he is not a swing voter. Thus, the proper treatment of partial causation and causal responsibility provides the underpinning of a good rationale for voting. If citizens intuitively grasp this rationale—and it is not implausible that they do—it may also explain why they actually vote (a fair amount of the time).

Philosophy, University of Arizona

---

[39] Strictly, the causal responsibility approach I propose could be subsumed under the expected-consequences, or rational-choice, perspective. Suppose we view the state of being a partial cause of a good electoral result, or the state of deserving moral credit (or discredit), as themselves possible *outcomes* or *consequences* of voting or not voting. Then the approach I favor may just be a special case of the rational-choice framework. The choice matrix now confronting the voter will differ from the matrix that would exist under the standard analysis. In addition to the outcomes being different, the probability of getting a more preferred outcome from voting than from abstaining is no longer linked to the probability of being a swing voter. Even if one is not a swing voter, one's act of voting can raise the probability of one's earning more causal credit for a superior candidate's victory and of avoiding causal discredit for such a candidate's loss. If citizens value some of these kinds of outcomes over others to a sufficient degree, the new choice matrix might make it "rational" for them to vote on numerous occasions. Since the outcomes have a moral nature, however, it may be controversial whether the choices should be considered a matter of "prudence" or "self-interest." I do not try to address this issue here.

INSTITUTIONALLY DIVIDED MORAL RESPONSIBILITY*

By Henry S. Richardson

I. The Notion of Forward-Looking Moral Responsibility

I am going to be discussing a mode of moral responsibility that anglophone philosophers have largely neglected. It is a type of responsibility that looks to the future rather than the past. Because this forward-looking moral responsibility is relatively unfamiliar in the lexicon of analytic philosophy, many of my locutions will initially strike many readers as odd. As a matter of everyday speech, however, the notion of forward-looking moral responsibility is perfectly familiar. Today, for instance, I said I would be responsible for watching my nieces while they swam. Neglecting this responsibility would have been a moral fault. When people marry, they undertake responsibilities, of moral import, of fidelity and mutual support. When people have children, they accrue moral responsibilities to feed, rear, and educate them. Not all forward-looking responsibilities are moral. While finishing this essay, I have had to keep an eye on a number of my administrative responsibilities, and, while reading it, you may well be occasionally distracted by some of your own. The notion of a responsibility that we accrue or take on, to look out for some range of concerns over some range of the future, is, then, perfectly familiar. Because this common notion of forward-looking responsibility has not been integrated into recent moral theory, however, my philosophical discussion of it will initially seem strange.

For a preview of this strangeness and some further indication of what I will be discussing, we will do well to look at Jean-Paul Sartre's treatment of responsibility in *Existentialism Is a Humanism*.[1] In this evocative tract, which is concerned mainly to deny the availability of metaphysically objective foundations for any ethical claim, Sartre makes statements about responsibility that sound rather extreme. For instance, he says that anyone alive during World War II is responsible for that war. Indeed, his view

* Earlier drafts of this paper were presented at the Kennedy Institute of Ethics, the Philamore Moralphil Group, and the Toronto Chapter of the Conference for the Study of Political Thought. Those present on each of these occasions were most helpful. I owe special thanks to Ronald Beiner, Sarah Buss, Chad DeChant, Ezekiel Emanuel, Emily Hoechst, Agnieszka Jaworska, Joseph Kakesh, and Matthew McAdam—none of whom, of course, bear any backward-looking responsibility for what I say here.
[1] Jean-Paul Sartre, *Existentialism Is a Humanism*, in *Existentialism from Dostoevsky to Sartre*, ed. Walter Kaufmann (New York: Meridian–New American, 1956), 345–69. I owe the distinction between backward-looking and forward-looking responsibility to Michael Wolf, who suggested it as a way to make sense of Sartre's discussion of responsibility in this work.

is that everyone is responsible for every aspect of his or her life-situation. This statement about the war would indeed be totally absurd—and not in the piquant existentialist sense—if it meant that, looking back on those events spanning the European and Pacific theaters of war, any individual, even a pacifist, could be held to account for everything that happened. Sartre did love paradox, but in this case his message is not so ridiculous as that. Rather, he is writing about the perspective of someone during the time of World War II, someone who must decide how to live from that moment forward. "It is up to you to determine," Sartre is, in effect, telling this person, "what moral significance you will endow this war with. Will you engage in it as a patriot? Will you stand aloof as a conscientious objector or perhaps simply as a private citizen? How will this war figure in your conception of your responsibilities?"

I will be using "responsibility" in something like Sartre's forward-looking way. I could continually say "forward-looking responsibility," but that would be a bore; besides, it would be pleonastic to ask our teenagers to "please take forward-looking responsibility for doing the dishes after dinner." For the most part, then, I will simply use "responsibility" in this essay to mean forward-looking responsibility. Although I will often be talking about morality, forward-looking responsibility is a notion that obviously extends more broadly. Neither my responsibilities on the departmental lecture committee nor my son's responsibility for the dishes directly pose any moral issues.

While Sartre did use "responsibility" in this way, the forward-looking sense has not been much explored by philosophers. I seek first of all to provide some further elucidation of the notion of forward-looking responsibility, one that will explain why it is a theoretically useful moral concept. Once I have done that, I will be in a position to set out some alternative positions about the scope of individuals' forward-looking moral responsibility. While Sartre's view is not absurd, it is extreme. As against him, I will be arguing that instead of seeing every individual as being responsible for everything—prospectively, remember—we should recognize that our moral responsibilities are highly differentiated.

I am hoping that this claim will seem immediately plausible, or at least more plausible than Sartre's extreme position. We will not yet be in a position to begin assessing it, however, until we can specify more exactly what we mean by forward-looking moral responsibility. By the time I am done doing that, some readers may well wonder whether there is any such animal, after all. Because I have argued elsewhere, in effect, that there is forward-looking moral responsibility, however, I will here have to beg the indulgence of any readers who doubt this and ask them, if they are curious, to refer to my previous work.[2] Here, however, I am eager to

---

[2] See my "Beyond Good and Right: Toward a Constructive Ethical Pragmatism," *Philosophy and Public Affairs* 24 (1995): 108–41.

get on to an important and hitherto little-explored question, namely, how forward-looking moral responsibility is distributed over individuals. Does everyone have the same moral responsibilities, of this prospective kind? Or do the moral responsibilities of individuals vary systematically? Although I will focus on addressing this question of uniformity versus variability, I will not entirely ignore the existence issue. The evidence presented in Section II that common-sense recognizes a division of forward-looking moral responsibility will provide some support for the claim that there is any at all.

I will be arguing, then, that the scope of individuals' forward-looking moral responsibility does systematically vary. Specifically, I will show that moral responsibilities, in the sense of what we are asked, morally, to look out for, systematically vary on the basis of social institutions. It is because these institutions create something of a division of moral-deliberative labor that I speak of this forward-looking responsibility as "divided," and not just as varying. I do not mean for a lot to hang on the term "institution." I am using "institutional" in a very broad sense, in which a parent hiring a babysitter participates in a relatively enduring, if loosely organized, child-care institution. Similarly, a sociologist or anthropologist visiting my household would recognize the teenager's dish duty as part of a common bourgeois pattern. As these examples make plain, the social roles that I have in mind are by no means limited to professional ones or to roles defined by formalized rules. To the contrary, the idea of "taking responsibility for something" is important, in part, because it transcends rules, as we will see.

An obvious desideratum for any account of forward-looking moral responsibility is that it must explain why we need this additional bit of terminology. If all I am saying is that my son has a duty to do the dishes, why not leave it at that? Duty, after all, is a central and exhaustively explored moral concept. Why import a fuzzy existentialist notion if I don't have to? To see why, we will have to see how forward-looking moral responsibility involves more than simply the notion of duty. The idea of "taking responsibility" in a prospective context adds two crucial elements. The first is that one's duties are oriented around a set of specific concerns for which one is responsible. This aspect of forward-looking moral responsibility is present also in nonmoral cases, and I want to turn to a nonmoral case to illustrate it. Consider my babysitter. Once I go out, he is responsible for the children for the evening.[3] For what about the children is he responsible? Not their well-being, full stop. For the evening, I waive certain hopes about inculcating good table manners and combating mass-culture schlock. I expect the babysitter to be concerned with my children's well-being and safety, interpreted in a more

---

[3] I am grateful to Sarah Buss for suggesting the importance of thinking about taking responsibility for persons and things.

basic way than that. While I expect he will let it pass unnoticed if they chew with their mouths open and may allow them to watch more television than I would, I trust that he will neither let in any strangers nor allow the children to surf for pornography on the internet. He will put them to bed, but perhaps not precisely at their regular times. Helping with their homework is a gray area, and may require some explicit clarification. The job description of "babysitter," delimited along something like these lines, seems to be perfectly conventional, at least in my neighborhood. It involves a rough indication of those concerns relevant to my children for which the babysitter takes charge. But now, one might object, cannot this job description be captured by the language of duties (here, nonmoral ones)? To be sure, the list of duties will be hard to spell out, but that will also be true of any area of moral theory. To answer this objection, I need to bring out the second dimension of forward-looking responsibility.

The responsibility I am talking about is future-oriented, and the future is unforeseeable. It surprises us. An essential aspect of taking responsibility for something, prospectively, is undertaking to cope with surprises. To continue with my nonmoral example for a bit longer: Saying that the babysitter is responsible for the children for the evening is saying more than that a list of rules is incumbent upon him; it also implies that he will look out for the children in myriad unforeseeable circumstances. Furthermore—and this is central to my point in this essay—it suggests that he will bend or revise preexisting rules, within limits. Suppose I told him explicitly, "Never leave the house with the children." Still, it would not merely be reasonable of him to take them out if there were a fire or an armed intruder: it would be irresponsible of him not to do so. The language of responsibility, here, is not a lazy shorthand that could be replaced by a fuller spelling out of duties. Because the future always surprises us, and because concerns and rules end up clashing and harmonizing in ever-novel ways, it can be appropriate for the individual agent to revise his or her understanding of the preexisting rules relevant to his or her responsibility.

This general lesson applies also, as I will argue, to the domain of morality. The notion of forward-looking moral responsibility is theoretically valuable, and cannot be substituted for by talk of moral duty, because it captures the need to rethink moral rules that arises in many difficult moral situations. In ethics, too, I suggest, there are important rules, but ones that need to be utilized responsibly, where this means being prepared to bend or revise them in certain cases.[4] This, then, is the second element that the notion of responsibility adds to duty.

---

[4] My stress that there are important moral rules constitutes my disagreement with the main emphasis of recent virtue ethics, which would otherwise provide an interesting way of translating my talk of taking responsibility for a range of concerns. I will not try to argue for this aspect of my view here.

I will not stop to try to define the concerns distinctive of morality. Instead, I am content if the reader grasps that my account of "forward-looking moral responsibility" incorporates the two elements that came out in my description of the babysitter's role: first, orientation to a specific range of concerns (the basic welfare, safety, and health of the children); and, second, an authorization of some kind to depart from stated rules in order to serve those concerns. When I talk about moral responsibility in the remainder of this essay, then, I will be assuming that it carries these twin implications of looking out for a certain range of concerns and being authorized to bend or revise rules in light of them. Admittedly, the case of giving my son responsibility for doing the dishes does not immediately conjure up conditions under which any rules would be revised. I return to this sort of counterexample in the following section. Before we get there, though, some further explanation of the idea of revising rules is called for.

Let me stipulate, first of all, that by "moral rules" I shall, in this essay, mean principles accessible to human understanding and potentially efficacious in human affairs that state what ought or ought not to be done. I am not talking about such rules as those which the non-particularist moral objectivist may hypothesize as the truth-conditions of moral claims, whether or not those rules are accessible to us. Rules of this kind are a philosopher's fiction. If we let M be the set of all true propositions of morality, then no one, I suppose, has authorization to revise any of them.[5] True propositions are simply true. But set M does not sit on a shelf somewhere, available for our inspection. While I presume that moral statements do have truth values—are either true or false[6]—I am not sure what the point of hypothesizing about the set M might be. I do not here mean to get involved in a theory of moral truth.[7] Still, since I think that moral statements have truth values, I must concede that there is *some* sense in saying that, at bottom, our only task is to discover the true

---

[5] Not even God has such authorization, as Leibniz argued against Hobbes and other theological rationalists. In "Three Concepts of Rules," *Harvard Journal of Law and Public Policy* 14 (1991): 771–95, Michael S. Moore calls this set of true propositions of morality the "real rules." In addition to these, he suggests that there are also some "authoritative rules" which come into existence upon the valid exercise of certain "normative powers" (a phrase he takes from Joseph Raz, "Voluntary Obligations and Normative Powers: Part II," *Proceedings of the Aristotelian Society* 46 [1972]: 79–102); these are rules whose function is to modify the balance of reasons determined by the real rules. This pair of definitions strikes me as mutually incoherent. If the "real rules" state the truths of morality, then any modification of the balance of reasons that they determine would yield a moral falsehood, and hence would not represent a valid exercise of a moral power.

[6] In presuming the bivalence of moral truth-values, I bypass issues of vagueness, which might be relevant to moral statements in, for example, the ways explained by John Broome, "Is Incommensurability Vagueness?" in Ruth Chang, ed., *Incommensurability, Incomparability, and Practical Reason* (Cambridge, MA: Harvard University Press, 1997), 67–89.

[7] For the kind of view of moral truth that I would defend, see my "Truth and Ends in Dewey," *Canadian Journal of Philosophy*, supplementary vol. 24 (1998): 109–47. The account I give there downplays the importance of a correspondence to true principles, while not giving it up entirely.

propositions of morality. Particularists such as Jonathan Dancy would hold that few of these propositions will turn out to be general ones.[8] As long as we are metaphysically speculating, however, why not suppose that the elements of M could turn out to be highly conditional general statements, along the lines of: "If you have promised to watch someone's children and have also promised not to take them out of the house, but you hear an intruder ... , then you ought to ..." These propositions hypothesized by the metaphysician in order to discuss the truth-conditions of moral statements, however, must not be confused with the moral rules to which we currently have access and which shape our societies. Having mentioned this philosopher's fiction, I set it aside.

In defining forward-looking moral responsibility, I said that it implies authorization, within some delimited range, to revise any preexisting moral rules. If this just means that individual judgments work changes in the moral rules that are socially in force in a given society, the thesis would be, not logically trivial, but entirely platitudinous. What sociologist would deny that mores evolve as a result of individual decisions? Yet the point I am making cannot be put simply in terms of what moral rules are socially in force.[9] To articulate what matters, we must take account of what we think, that is, of the collectively reflective aspect of moral practices. This is an awkward requirement, for this essay strives *toward*—and hence cannot presuppose—a better understanding of our collective reflection about moral matters by means of an analysis of forward-looking moral responsibility. Hence, in explaining what I mean by "preexisting moral rules," I will, for now, abstract from the questions about the epistemic division of labor that will occupy me in the core of this essay, leaving the "we" temporarily uninterpreted. Accordingly, let us simply say that the "preexisting moral rules that bear on a given situation" represent our best assessment, at a given time, of what someone in that situation ought to do. Their fixity at a given time is important to my account here.[10] Since an individual's authorized revision of a rule could well, and indeed should, contribute to further collective reflection, any account of moral justification that referred to idealized social agreement (such as, for instance, Jürgen Habermas's theory of the "ideal speech situation")[11] could *incorporate* a place for the kind of authorized revision

---

[8] Jonathan Dancy, *Moral Reasons* (Oxford: Blackwell, 1993). Arguing that "the behavior of a reason ... in a new case cannot be predicted from its behavior elsewhere" (60), Dancy's particularism attacks the usefulness even of prima facie generalizations in ethics.

[9] Such social rules are the third sort that Moore distinguishes in "Three Concepts of Rules."

[10] Because these moral rules reflect the moral reflections of a group of people at a given time, they have the sort of "historical" existence usefully flagged by Moore in "Three Concepts of Rules," 776.

[11] Jürgen Habermas, *The Theory of Communicative Action*, trans. Thomas McCarthy (Boston: Beacon Press, 1984). In the ideal speech situation, all participants are equally situated and all opportunity for the use of threats is removed, so that what may prevail is "the forceless force of the better argument."

I am here contemplating. Now, obviously, I have left vague how our collective moral assessments are fixed and who is the "we." While this is a significant abstraction, we may leave it vague at this point, for my thesis will be that, no matter how we interpret "our best assessment," individuals will have authorization to revise it. If they did not have this authorization, remember, they would not have moral responsibility of the forward-looking type that I have defined.

It is difficult to keep this discussion from gravitating toward entirely general claims about *all* moral rules, but let me try. Although one of the views that I will be considering will hold that every individual is authorized to revise *every* preexisting moral rule—again, this seems to have been Sartre's position—my own interest is in making out the possibility that this authorization is interestingly and substantively delimited and that individuals in different roles and situations have different ranges of authorization to revise moral rules. Hence, accepting the possibility of authorization to revise moral rules—of forward-looking moral responsibility—does not immediately or necessarily carry along with it the further claim that *all* moral principles are equally subject to revision. I myself, for instance, find it hard to imagine circumstances in which anyone would have grounds for revising the principle that it is wrong to kill innocent children just for the fun of it.

The question, then, that I will pursue in this essay is whether moral responsibility (I will henceforth mean the forward-looking kind) is divided in some institutionalized, regularized way, or rather, except on an occasional or irregular basis, remains invariant across persons or roles. To my knowledge, the bulk of the Western philosophical tradition comes down on the latter side. I suggest that most moral theories that—unlike particularisms such as Dancy's—have given any prominence to rules (or general statements)[12] fall into one of two categories, each of which casts moral responsibility as invariant. In using the term "responsibility" in labeling these views, recall, I am using it in the forward-looking sense which implies a range of concern and a range of authorization to revise.[13] The two influential positions on forward-looking moral responsibility that rule out its varying with an individual's role are the following:

---

[12] I should note that while I think that many of our best assessments of moral issues are framed as statements that do not name any particular individual, and in that sense are "general," I believe that few of them are rightly described as universal generalizations stating that all persons in a given situation should act in a certain way. Rather, I think most of them are best understood as saying that persons in situations of a given kind should, *generally speaking*, act in a certain way. I defend this claim in "Specifying Norms as a Way to Resolve Concrete Ethical Problems," *Philosophy and Public Affairs* 19 (1990): 279–310. Our moral norms, that is, already reflect our awareness of our fallibility and of the possibility that they might be revised.

[13] While it would be a topic for another essay to explore the relationship between these positions about forward-looking moral responsibility and different positions on attributing moral responsibility in a backward-looking way, I will say something about this in the concluding section.

(A) *The no-responsibility view*: There is no such thing as moral responsibility of this kind. The moral agent's sole charge is to abide by her duties as elaborated in the moral rules; she has no authorization to revise the rules that state her duties.

(B) *The almost-unlimited-responsibility view*: Moral rules, with one exception, are merely heuristic; in every case, the moral agent's ultimate obligation is to do what is, overall, for the best (e.g., to maximize social utility or self-interest), departing from any other rule wherever necessary, in wholly unpredictable and irregular ways. The agent is free to effect whatever changes in the rules the ultimate standard would support.

In addition, there is Sartre's position, with which I began, which does indeed represent the extreme on this dimension, for it removes reference to any ultimate standard for the revision of rules:

(C) *The unlimited-responsibility view*: There are no moral rules or standards to which an individual owes any deference; in every case, an individual should and must reconsider and revise any moral rule whatsoever, and must do so without recourse to any underlying standard of moral justification.

As against all three of these views, I will be arguing for a view according to which moral responsibility is (typically or always) differentially divided:

(D) *The institutionally divided responsibility view*: The moral agent's responsibility depends upon regular features of her social situation and role, as shaped by the moral rules themselves, and carries with it delimited authorizations, varying systematically with her situation and role, to depart from (our preexisting best assessment of the) moral rules.

Note that I have given the possibility that moral responsibility is haphazardly divided rather short shrift, subsuming it (in one possible form) under the unlimited-responsibility view.

Although my intention is to recommend view (D) over the alternatives, my argument against its competitors will be very short. I have already noted the absurdity of Sartre's position (C). In the next section, I will lay out common features of morality that fit the idea of divided responsibility, thereby supporting (D) over the other three positions. In the remainder of the essay, I turn to the task of elaborating the divided-responsibility view, (D). In Section III, I discuss the historical origins of views (A) and (B), which are illuminated by J. B. Schneewind's discussion of the "divine corporation" model and the reactions against it.[14] Section IV then lays out an understanding of the system of moral rules that takes seriously the conclusion that we, and not God, are effectively in charge of it. This understanding will provide a way of fleshing out the much-desired middle ground between (i) the conception that moral rules are absolute, binding without exception as universal generalizations for all agents in the given circumstances, and (ii) the conception that moral rules are mere rules of thumb, subject at all times to being overridden by a direct appeal to considerations of the general good.[15] On the alternative conceptions of rules I have in mind here, by contrast, the rules will imply or involve an understanding of the considerations for the sake of which it is licit to revise them. Since these considerations vary with an agent's role, they constitute a principal reason why the authorization to revise is divided.

What can we say in general about how forward-looking moral responsibility is divided? Section V raises this question, arguing that some level of collective control is both inevitable and appropriate and that this problem is partly an epistemic one. Viewing moral institutions as on a continuum with political ones, I take up democratic governance as regulating and extending the institutional division of deliberative moral responsibility and explore the close relationship between morality and politics that emerges. In order to rebut the objection that central democratic oversight restores an indirect consequentialism, Section VI examines the division of policymaking responsibility in democratic governments. In the end, while these various considerations about intellectual history, the nature of rules, and the nature of government will lend support to (D), the divided-responsibility view, their main function will have been to fill out our understanding of it. I will have achieved my principal goal if I succeed in putting this neglected conceptual possibility on the table for discussion.

---

[14] J. B. Schneewind, "The Divine Corporation and the History of Ethics," in Richard Rorty, J. B. Schneewind, and Quentin Skinner, eds., *Philosophy in History: Essays on the Historiography of Philosophy* (Cambridge: Cambridge University Press, 1984): 173–91.

[15] In "Specifying Norms as a Way to Resolve Concrete Ethical Problems," I described such a middle ground by developing the idea that norms may be progressively specified. There, however, I did not address the natural follow-up question, "By whom?" The present essay tackles this last question. While it would seem natural to associate the two conceptions of moral rules in the text with deontological and consequentialist theories of right action, respectively, this would be a mistake. To begin with, a rule-consequentialist might support an absolutist approach to moral rules. More significantly, as I have argued elsewhere, the distinction between consequentialism and deontology hinges upon separating, for the purposes of deliberation, two classes of consideration, those pertaining to the good and those pertaining to the right. In "Beyond Good and Right," I argued that the deliberative separation of right and good cannot be maintained.

II. Common Sense Divides Forward-Looking
Moral Responsibility

Deliberative moral responsibility is differentially distributed in two respects: differently situated agents have (1) reason to be concerned with different ranges of consequences, and (2) differential authorization to revise or re-specify the rules that impinge upon them. To explain and bolster these claims, I present two examples, one focused on each of these two aspects of practical responsibility.

Medical doctors' duty to promote their patients' health illustrates specialized moral concern. Often, this duty will demand of them a complex effort to weigh the consequences of alternative actions. Since medicine is an art, there is no simple set of rules for producing health. Sometimes, indeed, this duty will argue in favor of relaxing some other duty, such as the duty to be truthful, as when being frank about a diagnosis would set the patient back. It is not the duty of the doctor, however, to be concerned with consequences more broadly—say with the economic consequences of a proposed therapy for the hospital or managed-care organization within which he or she works. Those are the concerns of the hospital managers. Indeed, except at the extremes, it is the doctor's duty not to consider these other sorts of consequence. Further, it is a doctor's duty to consider the consequences for each patient's health individually in making decisions about that patient, and not, or not generally, to consider the consequences for all patients collectively. Public health officials have to worry about those. Thus, the philosopher's "Organ Transplant Case," which assumes it is possible to save five patients by cutting up one healthy one and distributing the organs so obtained, cannot draw support for the transplanting from any general duty of doctors to consider the health of patients collectively. To be sure, there are occasions when doctors do consider patients' health collectively, most famously in triage situations. Importantly, however—to anticipate the discussion in Section V—these are typically situations in which this departure from individualized care is institutionally established and controlled by the emergency-room management or the army field-hospital command. Thus, while the pattern of these cases indicates that a medical doctor's moral authorization to pursue a patient's health is interestingly and varyingly hemmed-in by other constraints, we also see that the basic responsibility involved is delimited, as it is focused on individual patients.

While these constrained ways in which consideration of consequences is invited already imply that differently situated agents—doctors, hospital managers, public health officials, and people on the street—are differentially involved in deciding whether to depart from rules, such as the rule against lying, it does not yet indicate that such agents are involved in *revising* rules. Perhaps they simply set them aside. But authority to revise rules in a more constructive or productive way is part of moral responsibility of the prospective kind, as I have defined it. To see this side of it, consider the situation of justice within the family. Contrary to some communitarian thinkers, I do believe that justice has a place within the family.[16] One has a duty to be fair to one's children in the distribution of rewards and punishments. There are, however, strong moral reasons, grounded in autonomy and privacy, for allowing parents considerable scope in framing rules of their own that interpret and institute family fairness. Indeed, I think the situation of justice within the family is similar to that of justice at large as viewed by John Stuart Mill.[17] The two situations differ in that the family acts not for the general good, but for the good of the family members. Yet as in the case of justice at large, there is no substantive precept of justice which is not sometimes subject to suspension or revision by the family. Some families decide that each child should have literally the same sorts of opportunities, thus affording minimal ground for complaint. Others are more comfortable with contrasting and more roughly balancing activities, partly in order to minimize sibling competition. It does not seem plausible that there is only one permissible way of interpreting and realizing familial justice. Nonetheless, once parents have established some such policy, claims and duties of justice do grow up around it. In unpredictable ways, the way in which parents exercise their authorization to revise the policy affects what is true about their future obligations.[18]

With this preliminary understanding of the two main dimensions of deliberative moral responsibility in place, it becomes easy to see how the whole of morality may be cast in these terms. Consider the kind of case that plays a prominent role in W. D. Ross's theory. Ross held that we have multiple, distinct duties that we must use intuition to balance when they conflict. Exploring the question of what it is, exactly, that our duties require of us, Ross uses the illustration of the duty to return a book to a friend.[19] The point he makes using this example would translate naturally into the language of responsibility: your duty, he argues, is neither to *aim* to return the book nor to *post* the book but to *see to it that* the book gets returned. Your promise defines a certain responsibility, which will have different concrete implications if there is a postal strike. You have a re-

---

[16] For the claim that we should not understand family relationships in terms of justice, see, e.g., Michael Sandel, *Liberalism and the Limits of Justice*, 2d ed. (New York: Cambridge University Press, 1998).

[17] In chapter 5 of *Utilitarianism* (Indianapolis: Hackett, 1979), Mill argues that all of the common-sense precepts of justice submit, when they conflict, to adjudication on the basis of the good of all.

[18] The moral objectivist, of course, can accommodate this sort of phenomenon by imagining that the principles which constitute the moral truth-conditions contain many conditional clauses. Again, I am not concerned with this layer of metaphysics.

[19] W. D. Ross, *The Right and the Good* (Oxford: Oxford University Press, 1930; reprint, Indianapolis: Hackett, 1988), 42–45.

sponsibility to look out for the relevant consequence. If you become aware that the messenger carrying the book has become too ill to deliver it, you have a duty to find some alternative way to get it to your friend. If you have lost or destroyed the book in question, you have a responsibility to see to it that your friend gets another copy. If no other copy is available, it is up to you to determine how best to fulfill the responsibility the promise imposes. Should you buy the friend another, rarer book, or instead photocopy the one in the library? Ross's point, which, again, translates well to the language of forward-looking responsibility, is that because the future surprises us, someone on whom a duty is incumbent has a responsibility that extends both to looking out for the concern that provides the duty its point, if there is one, and to revising the initially understood terms of the duty, if necessary. Here is the answer to the question, raised in the first section, about how giving my son responsibility for washing the dishes fits my definition of forward-looking responsibility. If he noticed that the tap water suddenly started running a bilious yellow, he would be authorized to stop washing, as the underlying concern for hygiene would look to be ill served by continuing. The point, again, is that even such simple tasks involve a true element of responsibility.

These examples, from medicine, family life, and book-lending, should serve as sufficient reminders that we expect moral agents in different circumstances to be concerned with different ranges of consequences of their actions and that we typically also expect that this special concern will have significant implications for the ways these agents deliberate about what they ought to do, including the ways they specify the principles under which they are acting and the conditions that count as excuses or negating conditions. I also hope that they sufficiently call to mind the reasons to reject (B), the almost-unlimited-responsibility view, as well as (C), Sartre's more extreme view. Our common understanding of our moral duties hems us in more than these views allow. Yet, like my notion of divided moral responsibility, it also makes some concession in the consequentialist direction, for it allows that agents do rightly look out for *some* ranges of consequences. Why, then, have philosophers tended not to recognize the ways in which forward-looking moral responsibility is differentially distributed? To explain this, it will be useful to lay out a picture of the provenance of moral rules that would support (A), the no-responsibility view.

III. A Takeover at the Divine Corporation

The picture of moral rules that historically lent support to (A), the no-responsibility view, and against which (B), the almost-unlimited-responsibility view, was a reaction, is that of the "divine corporation." J. B. Schneewind has masterfully elaborated this conception to shed light on the history of philosophical ethics.[20] In the divine corporation there is a specialization of offices, but one that allows no scope for individuals to revise the rules defining them.

Schneewind asks us to imagine a very well run corporation, one with many branches and divisions. Corporation rules and the organization chart circumscribe the employees' roles. In a modern-day corporation, one would expect employees to take some initiative in generating new and improved ways to carry out their functions. Part of a division manager's job, we tend to think, is to exercise a reasonable discretion. But the moral corporation is different in three respects. First, whereas the purpose of modern-day corporations is generally obvious (it has something to do with profit), this is not so in the one we are considering, for its purposes are unknown to the employees. Despite this, the employees bear an abstract allegiance to those purposes, whatever they may be. Second, the rules of the corporation forbid discretion and initiative. One is required simply to follow the rules in most cases. Third, the CEO here would be one who would actually deserve a seven-figure salary, being infinitely better than any of the employees at running a corporation. Now, in such a setting, Schneewind invites us to think, there will be little reason for consequentially grounded departures from the rules. Even if one knew the corporation's important purposes, one would have to defer to the CEO's judgment; and besides, one does not know what ends to aim at.

The "divine corporation" label gives the parable away: this story is the theological background, Schneewind suggests, for understanding much of moral philosophy in the Christian West until the modern era. God works in mysterious ways and with an understanding infinitely better than our own. He has provided us with commandments and other rules that we had better stick by in our various stations of life, for we have no rational basis for trying to second-guess them.

Divine-corporation morality depended upon being able to take a form of moral life largely for granted. Particular moral roles—promisor and promisee, house-seller and house-buyer, slaveholder and slave—have to be assumed to be part of the divine plan, and the rules that define them have to be accepted as divinely laid down. Cicero's term for the duties incumbent on people by virtue of these roles illuminatingly links them to the parable's managerial metaphor: he called them *officii*.[21] Further, individuals have to be relatively deferential about their capacities to reason. On this view, then, while individual roles are differentiated according to circumstance, and these roles provide reason for being concerned with different ranges of consideration, there is no real division of moral responsibility, of the kind I am concerned with here. That is because individuals are given scant responsibility for the interpretation of moral

---

[20] Schneewind, "The Divine Corporation and the History of Ethics."
[21] Cicero, *De Officiis (On Duties)* (Cambridge, MA: Harvard University Press, 1975).

requirements. Instead, what is required of them is something more deductive or subsumptive: the mere recognition that their case falls under some previously given rule. There is no differential authorization to revise because there is simply no authorization to revise.

A relatively early crack in the foundations of this system came with the publication of Machiavelli's *Prince*. Taking deliberate aim at the version of this sort of view found in Cicero, Machiavelli noted that some information about the purposes of morality seems to be encoded in its precepts. If cruelty is wrong, then it seems that cruelty is a bad to be avoided; but then, he argued, should we not learn to use cruelty well so as to minimize cruelty in the long run? Machiavelli's argument represents a generalizable consequentialist strategy that tends to erode all differentiation of moral roles. Anticipating this century's discussion of the "paradoxes of deontology,"[22] Machiavelli's argument serves as a schema easily adapted to undercut almost any specific duty. It thereby tends to undercut putting stock in those duties, and instead encourages thinking about overall consequences.

Some of the subsequent developments in the history of Western ethics follow through on Machiavelli's consequentialist beginnings, while others react against this move; but none of the main developments have moved toward a division of moral responsibility. The utilitarian reformers (such as Bentham and Mill) undercut differentiation, while the deontological conservatives (such as Ross) denied the need for "managerial" discretion.

As Schneewind notes, Bentham epitomized the attitude of a social reformer for whom social practices were definitely not accepted as divinely instituted and to whom the overall purpose of human society seemed as plain as day. For Bentham, then, the social rules become simply useful instruments for furthering the "artificial identification of interests." As such, they may be manipulated by the reformer as the circumstances demand and as the statistical evidence indicates. Whereas Machiavelli presumes to infer something about the ultimate purposes of morality from some of its particular dictates, Bentham steps willfully into the divine shoes, taking over as CEO.

Most deontological views, by contrast, preserved something like the status that social practices had had, but without the theological backing of the traditional view.[23] Instead, the prohibitions of morality were sup-

---

[22] The so-called "paradoxes of deontology," as exemplified by Machiavelli's argument, elicit from the defenders of some moral prohibition the admission that violating that prohibition is bad. Their antagonist then concocts a situation in which the agent would produce less of that bad by violating the prohibition. See, e.g., Samuel Scheffler, "Agent-Centred Restrictions, Rationality, and the Virtues," in Samuel Scheffler, ed., *Consequentialism and Its Critics* (Oxford: Oxford University Press, 1988), 243–60.

[23] For the reasons given in Barbara Herman, "Leaving Deontology Behind," in Herman, *The Practice of Moral Judgment* (Cambridge: Harvard University Press, 1993), 208–40, I do not think of Kant as a deontologist.

posed somehow to stand on their own, without appeal to any purposes or ends. These deontological positions reacted in ostrich fashion to the collapse of divine-corporation morality. They made no attempt to show that following the rules of morality would best achieve the overall purposes of human society. Instead, they tried to explain how we can know these rules to be binding, wholly apart from any such showing. Perhaps we have a special moral sense, or perhaps the intuitions of "the best people" may be trusted. In either case, we are, in effect, supposed to be able to go on as we had when we thought God was running the show, even though we have seen the little men behind the curtain.

The picture of the divine corporation usefully highlights the fact that the no-responsibility view is most plausible when the detailed texture of daily life can be taken for granted. Cicero's "offices" are replete with details—about house-sellers' duty to report the presence of vermin, about slave-owners' duties of justice to their slaves—that reflect practices that we now know to be morally contested or contestable. The great transformations that produced the modern world, and the "disenchantment" of the world that they produced, have meant that neither any such set of practices nor their legitimacy may simply be taken for granted. Morality without contact with such details is uselessly abstract; but as soon as it is implicated in such details, morality must be seen as subject to our reasoned revision. If (our best assessments of) moral rules are revisable, that raises questions about how we should think about these rules.

IV. Three Concepts of Rules

What is the nature of moral rules, such that they give rise to differential responsibility? To answer this question, I will situate and defend a third concept of rules in between the two that were set out in John Rawls's influential 1955 paper, "Two Concepts of Rules." In that paper, Rawls's overall aim, unsuccessful in the eyes of most subsequent commentators, was to defend a form of rule-utilitarianism. He distinguished between justifying a practice, such as punishing or promising, and justifying a particular action falling under a practice. He glossed a "practice" as "any form of activity specified by a system of rules which defines offices, roles, moves, penalties, defenses, and so on, and which gives the activity its structure. As examples one may think of games and rituals, trials and parliaments."[24] While a practice could be justified in utilitarian fashion, the act falling under the practice would be justified by direct reference to its rules. One reason that it is doubtful whether utilitarianism can be contained in this way is that if a generalized utilitarian consideration of consequences were allowed at any level, it would have a tendency to

[24] John Rawls, "Two Concepts of Rules," *Philosophical Review* 64 (1955): 3–32. I am using "institution" roughly synonymously with Rawls's "practice."

erode any purported barriers embodied in the rules of practices; for it is always possible to address each action under a practice in directly utilitarian terms.[25] The reader should keep this erosive potential in mind as we go on to discuss more stable ways of allocating normative importance to practices. Rawls himself, of course, soon shifted away from trying to give a utilitarian account of just practices.

One of the reasons that Rawls's 1955 paper is so deep is that, in addition to making this distinction, it pressed for a philosophical explanation of why it had not been sufficiently noticed. His answer invoked the two conceptions of rules of his title, the "summary conception" and the "practice conception." The former reflects the views of many moral philosophers, especially those in the utilitarian tradition, who had tended to see rules as, in one way or another, summaries of behaviors or their causal tendencies. As in Mill's reply to the objection that there is no time to calculate consequences on every occasion when one must decide, this conception takes rules to sum up the past experience of mankind regarding what sorts of actions yield the best consequences.[26] For the rule to be so derived, it must be possible to describe the behaviors involved without making reference to the rule. With such a basis, "each person is in principle always entitled to reconsider the correctness of the rule and to question whether or not to follow it in a particular case."[27] On the practice conception, by contrast, it is not possible to describe the relevant behaviors except by reference to the rule, which is hence constitutive of the behaviors. Striking out and balking, Rawls noted, are two actions that depend, logically, on the practice of baseball. Constitutive rules of this sort, then, cannot be derived in the first instance by generalizing statistically from individual behaviors—while the individual behaviors which, when aggregated, make up a social regularity may be described without reference to any social practice. Only in the case of constitutive rules do we find such a dependence.

As someone engaged in the practice, Rawls suggested, one has no authorization to revise the rules that constitute it:

> To engage in a practice, to perform the actions specified by a practice, means to follow the appropriate rules. If one wants to do an action which a certain practice specifies then there is no way to do it except to follow the rules which define it. Therefore, it doesn't make sense for a person to raise the question whether or not a rule of a practice correctly applies to his case where the action he contemplates is a form of action defined by the practice. If someone were to raise such

---

[25] See, e.g., Joseph Margolis, "Rule Utilitarianism," *Australasian Journal of Philosophy* 43 (1965): 220–25; and David Lyons, *Forms and Limits of Utilitarianism* (Oxford: Clarendon Press, 1965).
[26] Mill, *Utilitarianism*, end of chapter 2.
[27] Rawls, "Two Concepts of Rules," 23.

a question, he would simply show that he didn't understand the situation in which he was acting.[28]

On the basis of this restrictive understanding of constitutive rules, Rawls set out a firm distinction between justifications of actions within practices, which are not consequentialist, and justifications of the practice as a whole, which may be.

Wholly apart from the consequentialist criterion for the justification of practices, which the present-day Rawls has renounced, there are problems with this account. Although Rawls briefly addressed some quasi-ontological issues about the generation of practices,[29] he did not pay sufficient attention to the substantive moral and practical issues involved in their institution. He recognized that we make the practices, but insisted that there is typically a sharp distinction among roles:

> If one seeks to question these rules, then one's office undergoes a fundamental change: one then assumes the office of one empowered to change and criticize the rules, or the office of a reformer, and so on. The summary conception does away with the distinction of offices and the various forms of argument appropriate to each. On that conception there is one office and so no offices at all.[30]

I agree entirely with Rawls's criticism, here, which tasks the consequentialist approach with eliding distinctions among offices; but Rawls's distinction between the law-giver and everyone else is too black-and-white. I seek to revise his account by making room for the Enlightenment theme that, as rational moral agents, we are each of us equally empowered to change and criticize the rules under which we live. This theme adds an egalitarian commitment to the conclusion of the divine corporation's collapse—the conclusion that we are in charge. Fully to reconcile this theme with Rawls's criticism of consequentialism will require the notion of a moral division of labor, to be set out more fully in Section V, according to which this empowerment to revise, while it always exists, is nonetheless limited, constrained, and specialized. It will also require recognizing the substantive sense in which morality depends upon democracy.

My aim, then, is not to discard Rawls's distinctions but to construct a "middle way" using elements from each of his extremes. In introducing the distinction between justifying a practice and justifying a particular act

---

[28] Ibid., 26.

[29] Note 23 on pp. 25–26 of ibid. discusses the fact that although the existence of a practice depends upon the existence of instances of behavior, the descriptions of the relevant behaviors are nonetheless conceptually dependent on the practice.

[30] Ibid., 28.

within a practice, he suggested that we may understand it in terms of two exemplary questions:[31]

1. Why do people put other people in jail?
2. Why was J put in jail yesterday?

These two perspectives sharply differentiate the formation of a practice from following it out. By contrast, I suggest the following exemplary question:

3. Should we put J in jail tomorrow?

Like the conception of moral responsibility I pursue in this essay, this question takes a forward-looking and practical or deliberative perspective, one which places a proposed action within the context of a practice. On this perspective, it is clear that cases might arise in which the circumstances would call for a revision of the practices of punishment, and this notwithstanding the fact that the question makes no sense without reference to the practices as they have existed hitherto.

Baseball and other professional sports are atypical institutions in the degree to which their rules are centrally controlled. For this reason, they do give rise to quite a sharp split between the roles of rule-follower and law-giver. No basketball player could by himself have instituted a new penalty in response to Wilt Chamberlain's dominance under the net; but the NBA could and did institute the goal-tending rule.[32] The "coulds" here are more political than conceptual, however. An individual player might have tried to stop the play and convince people to line up for a foul shot, he just would not likely have gotten very far in this effort. Hence, whether to try to do so is not a sensible practical question. Similarly, in pro baseball, a player will be wasting his time if he says to the ump, "Hey, let me have one more strike, here." In a family game, by contrast, the child at bat making the same plea may be gratified. Admittedly, family games proceed under different rules than the pros do; but I mean to highlight the other difference that operates here, namely, that the political mechanisms for controlling the rules in family games are different from the ones in pro games. In family ball, there is less of a sharp split between those who play the game and those who make the rules defining it.

Accordingly, the third conception of rules that I favor, which I will call the "participant conception," accepts Rawls's point that the description of alternatives is conceptually dependent on the preexisting practices, but refuses to accept that those practices have the final word when it comes to actions defined in their terms. In this, it responds reasonably to the

[31] Ibid., 5.
[32] Maggie Little suggested this example to me.

collapse of the divine-corporation idea. While the rules of a divine-corporation may be uncriticizable, those of human practices are not. Neither of the modern responses to the breakdown of the divine-corporation idea provides an acceptable answer to the question, "Who's in charge here?" Benthamite consequentialism represents the hubris of stepping into the shoes made for God. Deontological views attempt to avoid the question altogether, and hence end by retaining nothing of the old theology except its mysteriousness. The participant conception of rules, by contrast, takes it that we are in charge, but that our limited cognitive skills and managerial abilities mean that we would do best to maintain the kind of division of labor found in moral practices. Of course, what it is to "do best" here must itself be open to recurrent interpretation, for there is no obvious and simple overriding purpose.[33] There are, nonetheless, various human purposes to which we should differentially defer, in various social roles, when addressing questions about what we ought to do. We find ourselves engaged in complex and intertwined cooperative (and competitive) activities. Without taking the godlike stance of a designer of the whole system, we nonetheless should reconsider the rules of each activity, when reason arises, in a perspective informed by participation in that activity.[34]

I suggest, then, that human moral practices are more typically like promising or tag than like the Federal Rules of Civil Procedure or professional baseball, in that they authorize some limited revision by the reflective participant. This participant conception offers a distinctive picture of the authority of rules. On the summary conception, rules are valid merely because they capture a statistical generalization of what we individually do. On the practice conception, rules have an impersonal relation to us, constituting the practices defining our options for action. On the participant conception, rules are understood as reflecting the collective intentions whereby we have shaped the practices in which we act. These rules are to be respected as representing our previously formed judgments about how we ought to proceed. The participant conception accepts that many actions cannot be described except by reference to existing practices, but denies that this fact creates a sharp dichotomy between those of us who participate in the practices and the "law-givers" who create them. While there will indeed be important questions about the relationship between the "we" who are deliberating and the "we" who created the rules, there is only a weak presumption of deference, one which flows from a general respect for the judgment of others and from our commitment to being engaged in the enterprises (such as baseball or

---

[33] See my "Truth and Ends in Dewey," for a characterization of Dewey on "success" as similarly avoiding giving a criterion of action.

[34] I do not mean to imply that all human activities deserve deference; I am simply characterizing a stance intermediate between deontological quietism and consequentialist hubris.

the United States government) that they conceived and established. The reason I label this the "participant conception" is to signal the potentially sovereign role of individual deliberators without losing sight of the equally important fact that the individual is a participant in something, namely a practice.

It is these two aspects of the participant conception that contain the seeds of the idea of divided responsibility. Since the participants are not radically separated from the law-givers, they do have some potential authorization to revise the rules. That which they are participants in, however, gives some shape and limits to this authority. Parents attempting to set out an understanding of a fair allocation of advantages among their children are, by virtue of their participation in broad institutions of family and of justice, constrained (a) to look out for the fundamental interests of their children in so doing, and (b) to work with some one of the available broad conceptions of justice. Declaring that it is just to allocate the advantages among my children in whatever way maximizes my time on the golf course will be as laughable as attempting to declare my third strike a home run, even in a family ball game. Someone who has unlimited authorization to revise rules is not really a participant in them at all. Hence, it is built into the participant conception that while deliberators have some authorization to rethink the rules under which they are operating, their concerns as they do so and the range of revisions they may consider are shaped and limited by the practices in which they are participating.

While I believe that the participant conception of rules well fits the facts about how moral institutions appropriately change over time, I cannot begin to show that here. We may simply take it as a conception of moral rules that responds reasonably to the collapse of the divine-corporation idea, neither acquiescing to an uncritical acceptance of the automatic aspects of human social evolution nor arrogating to itself the social-engineering hubris of a Benthamite. Insofar as the participant conception of rules is attractive, it lends support to the idea that moral responsibility is divided; at the least, it helps explain what it means to say that it is divided. We should next ask how forward-looking moral responsibility *ought* to be divided.

V. DIVISION OF RESPONSIBILITY ON THE PARTICIPANT CONCEPTION

Having seen reason to reject both the no-responsibility view and the unlimited-responsibility view, we have before us a prima facie case in favor of seeing moral responsibility as divided. We are in charge, but there is no way for all of us to get together extra-institutionally to make our moral rulings. Rather, we inevitably rule morality through a complex and shifting mix of tacit and explicit institutions, from the recess dynamics of kindergartens to the International Court of Justice. Contrary to some philosophical individualists, I think it is perfectly licit to speak of what "we" judge and will.[35] Licit attributions of collective will, however, presuppose a normatively endorsed context of institutions in which that will is developed and stated. The "we" may be forged by a one-shot agreement, within a broader institution of promising or contract, to carry out some task together, or it may be part of a longer-term and more amorphous institution such as the monogamous family. To imagine some supra-institutional "we" that somehow speaks for human society as a whole is indeed to indulge in a dangerous philosophical fiction. While I will have occasion, shortly, to speak about the place of the popularly sovereign demos in revising moral rules, the same point holds about this way that we formulate our will. The popular will in a democracy cannot even be defined without making some normative and institutional presuppositions. Hence, the general conclusion is that although we are in charge of our moral institutions, we must rely on our moral institutions in taking charge. Since institutions do divide responsibilities, the participant conception of rules supports the idea of divided moral responsibility.

This conclusion, as well as my examples in Section II, have suggested that the division is intimately related to the moral rules as they are understood at any given time; but this notion is vague; and in any case, there is a lot more we might like to ask about how moral responsibility is divided. In the remainder of this section, I will say various unsystematic things in response to this question. While I positively resist the idea that there might be a criterion for how responsibility ought to be divided, I think that something illuminating can be said in general.

On the participant conception, rules are all, in certain ways and in certain contexts, subject to revision, because they are, after all, rules that we institute in the pursuit of our common and individual purposes. But who are "we," and how do we do this? Or how should we? I propose that we orient our answers to these questions by maintaining some important aspects of the old divine-corporation ideal, even while prescinding from the notion that human society is managed in detail by God. In particular, we may continue to understand morality as a society-wide cooperative enterprise marked by a highly differentiated division of labor. (I agree with Rawls that our commitment to justice carries the implication that we ought to try to regard society as a cooperative enterprise undertaken for mutual advantage.)[36] If this approach is appropriate, then we should expect the burden and the authorization of revising moral principles to be differentially distributed. But on what basis should it be distributed?

---

[35] See my "Democratic Intentions," in James Bohman and William Rehg, eds., *Deliberative Democracy* (Cambridge, MA: MIT Press, 1997), 349–82, for development of this point.

[36] Cf. John Rawls, *Political Liberalism*, enlarged ed. (New York: Columbia University Press, 1996), 15–22.

One initial and obvious point, which has been implicit in some of my examples, is that responsibility gets distributed on the basis of which moral rules impinge on someone. Someone who has never promised to return a book or take care of children will lack the relevant responsibilities. That he or she lacks the relevant duty is close to tautological. The interesting point, though, is that with these duties comes a responsibility, which (as I am using the term) includes some authorization to revise the way these duties are formulated or interpreted. It appears that the structure of moral rules is a structure that divides moral responsibility. All right; but what implications about the structure of morality can we draw from the ideal of properly dividing our moral responsibilities?

A quick review of the nature of morality as a social institution will support the claim that there can be no simple instrumental criterion for dividing morality's labor. What distinguishes morality from other spheres of cooperative activity, such as banking or bowling, is that it does not aim at achieving some specific good or fulfilling some concrete purpose. Rather, morality is concerned in general with the promotion of the good, or with seeing to it that we do what we ought. As an institution, even if not at the level of individual motivation, morality is concerned with categorical imperatives: not what ought to be done if we are to achieve some end E, but what ought to be done, period. While many specific moral prohibitions and rights presuppose certain purposes, we do also reason about what our ends ought to be. When we do so, we use the resources of morality—the traditions of moral philosophy and the tacit knowledge of our moral practices. Hence, while some recent philosophers have purported to identify "the object" or purpose of morality,[37] this must be a mistake. While the institutions of morality may be crucial, as Hobbes thought, to maintaining public peace, we also morally debate the conditions under which this concern for peaceable consensus ought to be subordinated to the protection of rights or commodious living. In short, any such identification of a specific function or purpose of morality as a whole is not only reductionist and over-simple but also falsifies a crucial fact about morality: that it is, in a modern secular society, the most important forum in which we reflect about the ends of human life. The institution of morality asks us to act rightly and live well, and doing these requires a proper orientation toward what is truly good; but since there is no mutually acknowledged ultimate end summing up what is truly good, the institution of morality cannot rightly be understood as promoting any single good. Such an understanding would skew and cut short the institution's important work of bringing us to a better understanding of our final ends.

This account of morality as an institution contrasts both with the divine-corporation idea and with Bentham's radical replacement for it. Both of

[37] See, e.g., G. J. Warnock, *The Object of Morality* (London: Methuen, 1971).

these older conceptions view the overall purpose(s) as fixed and given. On the divine-corporation idea, they are fixed outside of time, and inaccessibly to us, in the infinite mind of God. On the Benthamite conception, the fixed purpose is maximizing social welfare, and is simply obvious, there being no need or room to deliberate about it. The participant conception of rules rejects both of these reasons for denying to individuals any discretion in practical reasoning. It insists that our human purposes are in continual need of refinement, at least, if not of original articulation. One of morality's main functions is to facilitate this process of collective reflection.

If this is right, then the appropriate ways of dividing moral responsibility cannot be determined on a simple, instrumental basis. It is not like the problem of dividing a company's manufacturing labor so as to maximize expected profits. Lacking a fixed purpose outside of the institutions of morality, we have no choice but to begin *in medias res*, referring to the substantive content of the actual moral practices that we have in order to find a basis for understanding the division of responsibility that it imposes.[38]

The absence of an instrumental criterion also has another implication. It means that instead of being responsible to the idea of maximizing welfare or minimizing coercive disruptions, morality is responsible only to what it is that we actually ought to do. If we think about why we would reject any particular suggestion about "the object" of morality, prominent among the reasons will always be cases in which, we judge, a given proposal yields false implications about what we ought to do. Morality's retreat from identification with any specific end, therefore, is an expression of its commitment to a strong fallibilism about its answers.[39] On this account, then, moral deliberation may be understood as epistemically oriented; that is, it is oriented not toward the achievement of some nameable goal, but toward generating right answers about what we ought to do. The division of labor that it involves is, accordingly, an epistemic division of labor, one which, in part, divides the responsibility for determining what ought to be done among different people.

The case of justice within the family, discussed briefly in Section II, illustrates both of these phenomena and their interaction. Starting *in medias res*, we note that our shared moral beliefs include various substantive reasons for allowing parents considerable sway in interpreting the requirements of justice within the family. As I mentioned, these include

[38] There are other apparent possibilities. A Kantian view does not, offhand, suggest ways of dividing moral responsibility, in my sense, unless some specifically Kantian way of filling in the latitude of imperfect duties could be devised. An Aristotelian view, oriented in a not simply instrumental way around an ultimate end conceived of as activity, is perhaps more promising. I take the process I recommend in the text to be compatible with Aristotle's procedure.

[39] This is to describe morality in pragmatist terms: cf. Hilary Putnam, *Pragmatism* (Cambridge, MA: Blackwell, 1995).

reasons of privacy (a mainly negative, shielding norm) and of autonomy (a more positive, expressive norm). Reinforcing these are some epistemic reasons for supporting this decentralized division of labor. Justice within the family, as we understand it, ought to concern itself with the good of each family member while taking full account of the particularities of each. The kernel of truth in the communitarian resistance to speaking of justice within the family is that any approach to justice within the family that ignored the particularities of each family member would be deficient. Parents are far better placed than almost anyone else for making the necessary judgments about the claims of desert and of well-being presented by each of their children.

These two grounds for supporting parental autonomy in the interpretation of family justice also suggest two kinds of case in which this normal arrangement may be questioned. (1) Sometimes, we question it on the basis of some substantive moral principle (one with its own place within our practices, I might add, though this really adds quite little). Let me illustrate how parents' responsibility over how their children ought to be raised can be questioned on substantive grounds. Vivid cases of this kind arise in constitutional law. Do Jehovah's Witnesses have a right to withhold potentially lifesaving blood transfusions from their children? Do Amish parents have a right to keep their children out of public high schools? The latter question reached the U.S. Supreme Court in *Wisconsin v. Yoder* (1972).[40] The Court viewed the case mainly in terms of a clash between the free exercise of religion and the state's interest in educating all children. In terms that are more central to the division of moral responsibility, we may also interpret it as a case in which the parents' autonomy in controlling the lives of their children runs up against one of the most general moral functions that we expect families to fulfill, namely, that of producing cooperative and effective citizens. What conclusions one draws from this consideration against the parental and religious autonomy of the parents in this case, however, will rightly turn on how one specifies this republican function. Are the high-school years crucial to forming effective citizens? To answer this question, one would need to articulate one's conception of citizenship and what it involves. If citizens needed only to be able to articulate their own preferences, they would have relatively little need for completing high school. On the premise that citizenship centrally involves questioning authority, however, Richard Arneson and Ian Shapiro argue that the Court was wrong in *Yoder* to permit the Amish to withdraw their children.[41] Questioning authority, they persuasively note, is an ability best honed in later adolescence. While I recognize that unsettling potentially oppressive power is an important

[40] *Wisconsin v. Yoder*, 406 U.S. 205 (1972).
[41] Richard Arneson and Ian Shapiro, "Democratic Autonomy and Religious Freedom: A Critique of *Wisconsin v. Yoder*," in Ian Shapiro, *Democracy's Place* (Ithaca: Cornell University Press, 1996), 137–74.

function of citizens, the conception of moral responsibility that I am here seeking to flesh out suggests an additional role, one that also provides grounds for criticizing the Court's decision. Citizens, I suggest, need to be prepared to reflect and reason with others about what we ought to do. This is a highly complex skill and one that requires considerable education and a broad awareness of the conditions of modern life. On this sort of substantive moral basis, then, one might constrain the otherwise quite decentralized allocation of authority over families' practices of religious and moral education.[42]

(2) A different sort of ground for departing from this decentralized division of responsibility would refer, not to substantive moral principles or aims but to more directly epistemological grounds. Central to the case for allocating primary responsibility to the parents is that they tend to know their children intimately. Some parents, however—notably absent ones—do not. In cases where parents have abandoned their children or have severely neglected them, the state rightly steps in to reallocate discretion over their care.

We have arrived at the realization that the division of moral responsibility, even when highly decentralized, is subject to a centralized oversight. Substantive moral considerations may impinge to rebut the reasons for decentralization. Epistemic grounds that generally support decentralization may fail in a given case. We may add that morality, as we understand it, builds-in important requirements of publicity such that (to modify the statement of these requirements to fit the idea of divided moral responsibility) the revisions made by any moral agent ought to be defensible to and assessable by any other moral agent. Hence, the point of view of the moral public remains an important one, despite divided responsibility. Some will object to these points on the grounds that they presume an objectively collectivist perspective. In response, I note that promulgating and enforcing liberal rights is itself a collective project. As Rawls has recently observed, the "sphere of the family" is a precipitate of the basic legal arrangements of society rather than a set of institutions that can have its life—in anything like the form in which we know it—without the laws of marriage, divorce, inheritance, and others.[43] There is no escaping the fact that there are some broadly collective enterprises that frame other

[42] I realize that I have shifted, in this paragraph, from a first-person formulation to the impersonal. We start *in medias res* also with regard to the institutions (customary, legal, and otherwise) that are effective in changing our understandings of moral rules and the divisions of responsibility that go with them. In the case of a conflict between parents' control over the religious upbringing of their children and the collective interest in raising just citizens, the U.S. Constitution has given the Supreme Court a pivotal role in the second-order division of responsibility, the division of labor within the U.S. government defining the process that governs how issues of our moral division of labor are to be regulated. Still, what various of us laypersons, parents, and pundits come to think about these matters is not without influence.

[43] Rawls, "The Idea of Public Reason Revisited," *University of Chicago Law Review* 64 (1997): 765–807.

ones. Further, one of the central motivations of the participant conception of rules is to get away from the absolute precedence for centralized deliberation that marks the Benthamite view. The conception I favor recognizes the existence of cooperative projects at various levels without presuming that the whole collective ought to have deliberative responsibility over every part of each of its projects.

It is not an accident, though, that with the cases we have discussed in which familial autonomy breaks down, we arrive at matters on which public policy and constitutional doctrine speak. The law is the primary instrument whereby the sovereign collective gives shape to the moral division of labor within its territory. Tort law, for instance, allocates the burden of responsibility for deliberating about risks. As doctors are all too well aware, it also shapes the situations in which they set about deciding what ought to be done. On the participant conception, then, a question of pervasive importance for morality is: Who is in charge of setting public policy?

VI. MORAL DEMOCRACY

The right answer is: We, the people. To be sure, this answer requires some elaboration. Since my purpose here is to explore the ramifications of the novel idea of an institutional division of moral responsibility, let me continue, in a speculative mode, to describe how democracy looks if we take it to be a central layer in such an institutionalization of morality. While my discussion will gloss over many important distinctions and leave many loose ends, I should particularly like to recognize at the outset that the law evolves in other ways than by explicit democratic decision. As the case of the tort law indicates, we often come to govern our own affairs via institutions that change only slowly over time as they respond to a myriad of particular difficulties. Still, insofar as the common law, in its genius, still carries some residue of our feudal and aristocratic past, it is often appropriate for us to reconsider it. And for the cases of breakdown and conflict, which are what have brought us, in the present context, to the topic of public policy, self-consciously democratic means are invaluable.

It would be tidy and impressive if the participant conception of rules by itself could provide a transcendental argument for democracy. I do not think it can. There are too many other alternatives to the centralized determinations of a God or a Bentham. As with the family, we must start *in medias res*, and notice the various substantive commitments we have that provide a sufficient case for democracy. Among these are commitments to equality and fairness. As I and others have argued elsewhere, these commitments, properly understood, support a deliberative conception of democracy, in which citizens (as I would have it) are viewed as deliberating together so as to come to an agreement about what they aim to do together. This will have to include some spelling out of the various parts each will expect the others to play as the project gets carried out (some will pay higher taxes, others will have to contribute time, and so on).[44] What makes a conception of democracy deliberative, though, is that it views these determinations as subject to a standard of correctness or truth.[45] This means a standard that, in the manner of the standard of moral deliberation in general, is no specific goal or end, but rather the goal of getting it right, or of arriving at what really ought to be done. It is the standard of practical truth. Of course, all democracy, on any conception, will involve some deliberation; but conceptions that analyze democracy in terms of the satisfaction of individual preferences (such as Kenneth Arrow's social choice theory and Anthony Downs's economic theory)[46] make no room for anything but the most mechanical and strategic deliberation. By contrast, I take it that a crucial function of structures of democratic governance is to enable us to decide what our political aims should be and will be. Forging our political ends is the central task of democratic politics. An additional implication of seeing democracy as deliberative is that this task is an effort to determine what we ought to do. That is, democratic procedures do not simply settle, by their operation, what we ought to do; rather, they generate relatively trustworthy, but fallible, collective judgments about what we ought to do.

Even if a complete set M of true moral propositions exists, in some sense, it would be bizarre to suggest that our discovery of these propositions has been completed. If it had, we would better agree about what ought to be done and would better be able to formulate norms secure against exception. Instead, we seem, if anything, to remain in rather early stages of the development of moral knowledge. The question then arises as to what role there is in the discovery process for individual experimentation and discretion. Following out the Enlightenment theme I mentioned earlier, I would suggest that this role is enormous. When it comes to moral discovery, we are all presumptive equals. The reason for this is not epistemic but substantively moral: it is an aspect of the equal respect due to all persons that there should be this rebuttable presumption of equal moral competence. While there is a place for experts in moral theory, that place must be subordinated to a broader "democracy" of moral inquiry, in John Dewey's sense, an inquiry in which all have a place.[47] The salutary features essential to Dewey's conception of a democracy of inquiry are that (a) we are all conceived to be fallible and

[44] Cf. my "Democratic Deliberation about Final Ends," in progress; and Bohman and Rehg, eds., *Deliberative Democracy*.

[45] For an explanation of the sense—admittedly attenuated—in which this can count as a standard, see my "Truth and Ends in Dewey."

[46] Kenneth J. Arrow, *Social Choice and Individual Values*, 2d ed. (New York: Wiley, 1963); Anthony Downs, *An Economic Theory of Democracy* (New York: Harper and Row, 1957).

[47] For a convenient summary of Dewey's far-flung views on the democracy of inquiry, see Putnam, *Pragmatism*, 72–73.

(b) we are all conceived to have something to contribute. Rather than beginning to point toward a Habermasian "ideal speech situation," here, however, I seek to refer these contested matters to our actual moral and political institutions.

While I cannot derive democracy from the highly abstract conception of rules that I am here defending, I can point out that the notion of a division of moral responsibility answers well to the requirements of democratic deliberation, so understood. Because of the complexity and number of the issues faced by modern democracies, we each have no choice but to rely upon others to do some of the work of fixing on ends and otherwise deciding what we ought to do. Here we return to the division of deliberative labor itself. To arrive at a realistic understanding of democracy as being above all a deliberative enterprise, we will have to appeal to this notion of a cooperative division of epistemic labor, for policy matters are too variegated and complex to be handled in full detail by all of us together. Even if we were willing to devote all of our time to meetings, we would not be able to do it.

In the actual division of deliberative responsibility, accordingly, intricate relations of trust evolve. Suppose that I aim to form true opinions about what ought to be done about right-wing hate groups in the United States—a delicate issue because of the importance of freedom of expression. In doing so, I must rely on others to inform me about the seriousness of the threat. I may decide, for reasons of limitation of time, that I will trust the Anti-Defamation League to give me reliable information about this (understanding that they will not likely underestimate the dangers). Here I trust others as sources of information. More interesting are cases in which I trust others to harmonize competing concerns in appropriate ways. Perhaps, on the basis of their track record in the Skokie case, in which neo-Nazis asserted their right to march in a neighborhood full of Jewish concentration-camp survivors, and other cases like it, I decide to trust the American Civil Liberties Union (ACLU) to find reasonable compromises between free speech and the threat of right-wing bullying. (In fact, the Skokie case caused many to cease to trust the ACLU to draw an appropriate balance in this area.) Epistemic trust—trust involving the good of knowledge—is a necessary lubricant of the division of deliberative labor that is inescapable in the complex politics of modern society (if indeed it was not always inescapable). We must depend on others to provide us with reliable information and to suggest acceptable ways of specifying and reconciling political aims.

A division of normative responsibility is most obviously seen in the more formal aspects of government. The Supreme Court concerns itself with the rights spelled out in the U.S. Constitution. The Environmental Protection Agency concerns itself with protecting the environment. This specialization of deliberative concern is not always well understood. Recently, the U.S. Congress called for an "ethics investigation" of an official in the Small Business Administration (SBA) who was pushing for the weakening of environmental standards for petroleum storage facilities. He was accused of taking actions that were intended to favor chemical wholesalers and gasoline distributors. Yet as his supervisor declared, with at least strong surface plausibility, "he has done what his job description says he should do, which is to represent the interests of small business."[48] The reason that this is a licit moral defense of this kind of position is not that we want government to be a battleground of contending interest groups and are content to see environmental groups dominate one agency while their foes dominate another. The point, rather, is that we, through our elected representatives, have decided that, in addition to an agency devoted to protecting the environment, there should also be one devoted to looking out for small businesses. Accordingly, we created an institution, the SBA, which includes offices that carry out this role in various detailed ways. The enabling legislation for the SBA set certain rules to be followed— certain specific tasks to be performed, and so on—and contemplated that those filling the offices that it established would exercise discretion in carrying out these responsibilities. Yet it also set out some clear general purposes to shape the exercise of that discretion. The official of the SBA is not expected to fill out the areas left vague by legislation by turning to an impartial consideration of the general good. Instead, the SBA official is to deliberate with a special view to the interests of small businesses.

I take no position, here, as to whether these governmental decisions about what we ought to do should be seen as part of morality, or rather as a distinct branch of normative inquiry. That is a partly terminological issue. What I have argued is (1) that the institutional division of moral responsibility, even in the narrowest sense of "moral," turns out to depend upon governmental regulation in difficult cases, and (2) that the conduct of democratic government involves a division of responsibility of a kind similar to that which we found within what everyone would count as morality. In any case, whether we take the democratic layer to be part of morality's division of labor or rather say that the former is superimposed upon the latter, it does not follow from democracy's regulative role that the government's decisions are any more authoritative than anyone else's.

If I am right, then, we are and ought to be in charge of morality. Morality presumably first arose in a customary and wholly informal guise. Nowadays, however, we engage in some collective and central management of morality by making law democratically. The principal grounds for thinking that we *should* do things this way are the same ones that establish the importance of democratic control over other features of our

---

[48] *The Washington Post*, April 9, 1997, A7.

joint lives.[49] The law helps institutionalize and define smaller branches and groupings in which we continue to carry out the work of specifying morality's requirements and hopes. I have provided no basis for saying that the central level of management is the most important, only that it is the most central. This does, however, provide a basis for viewing politics as continuous with morality, and indeed as central to it.

VII. Conclusion

The traditional philosophical issue of moral responsibility that derives from worries about free will tends to pose the question in binary terms: Was the agent responsible for what he or she did, or not? The forward-looking, practical conception of moral responsibility that I have sketched here instead asks for a qualitative and substantive answer: For what is the agent responsible? How these two sorts of question are related will itself depend upon the answers to philosophical questions about the compatibility between free will and determinism. The sort of responsibility that the moral division of labor requires one to take does not depend upon free will. Instead, it obtains sufficient support from the centrality of deliberation in moral decision-making. If, as compatibilists such as Boethius and Hobbes held, to act with deliberation is to act freely, then any substantive answer to the second question generates a positive answer to the first. But we will expect that, to some degree, deliberative responsibility will be imposed upon us, as individuals, by the moral institutions into which we are born. Even if the ideals of deliberative democracy that I have sketched were to be fully realized, there is no question of hoping for or even postulating as desirable a state in which all ways of institutionalizing a moral division of responsibility have been reconsidered and recast by the present generation. I am sure that many of our inherited moral institutions are sound and that many true principles of morality have been obvious from the dawn of consciousness. While some of these may require forward-looking responsibility in their exercise, then, they might not stem from any past free exercise of will, whether collective or individual. Forward-looking and backward-looking moral responsibility, in other words, are largely but not wholly independent in concept and in fact.

We have seen how the notion of being responsible for a certain range of substantive moral considerations in certain contexts illuminates various aspects of morality. For one thing, it calls our attention to the fact that

[49] As Roderick Long has pointed out to me, there is a lot more that would need to be said here about the respective virtues of tacit evolution and democratic control. This is not the place to go into this debate, however; after all, I have not specified which issues should be subject to democratic control. I take it as obvious that *some* issues about what we should do—including among them some that will impinge upon moral institutions proper—should be democratically settled.

even within relatively circumscribed moral situations, ones governed mainly by just one moral principle, there is nonetheless important room for agents to deliberate. They need to consider possible exceptions and interpretations, to exercise judgment rather than mechanically applying a rule. In doing so, they need to take responsibility for a certain range of concerns. Rather than being authorized to interpret and amend the principle in light of the general good, they are typically asked to give special consideration to the ends embodied in the principle or otherwise incumbent upon them. We saw that the idea of taking responsibility in this specialized way helps explain how we reason about certain kinds of moral situations, such as that of maintaining justice within the family or treating patients "responsibly."

This notion of responsibility specialized to a certain range of consequences was incorporated into the participant conception of rules. We are participants because we must exercise deliberative judgment; but the participant conception is a conception really of rules, and not merely of rules of thumb, because no one is authorized to remake his or her entire moral situation directly on the strength of an appeal to the consequences. Here, it was not only Sartre's rhetoric that was wrong. We do not, as individuals, make our own moral situations; for even if we do take it that there is no theological or extra-human basis for ethics, there is nonetheless an important institutional one, which evolves slowly as intelligence gets applied to particular problems that arise. That we, thus, collectively make our situations from scratch I have just denied; and in any case, I have also just noted that individuals must submit to collective judgments in many moral cases.

One will naturally want to know why the moral life is this way, with this specialized division of deliberative responsibility. Schneewind's story about the collapse of the divine-corporation idea helps us construct one plausible explanation. Morality, on this view, is regarded as a vehicle for constituting and coordinating complex cooperative action, which has no simple overall purpose. This system lacks an all-knowing and wholly wise administrator. Hence, we must simply rely on each other to a considerable extent, and trust people to look after what they intimately know, love, or are paid to protect.

In any remotely well-ordered society, this trust is bolstered by some elements of morality that remain relatively unchangeable. A corollary of my thesis that moral responsibility is specialized is that it is delimited by the confines of morally defined roles. As I have already said, in effect, no role that I can imagine would license someone to revise the principle that it is always wrong to torture innocent children just for the fun of it. And if we are willing to relax a bit the logical inflexibility of this "always,"[50] we will find many other moral principles that commend themselves to us

[50] See note 12 above.

all in obvious ways.[51] These self-evident truths provide us with a basis for responding to tyrants and bigots who claim to be revising morality but are instead perverting it. Further, these truths define a layer of moral duties that each of us has in common, alongside the specialized moral roles we also inhabit. This makes it wrong to hide behind one's specialized role, denying backward-looking moral responsibility for something that one's specialized role required of one, as Adolf Eichmann did.[52] Indeed, it is in part because of our more generalized duties that we must exercise responsibility in fulfilling our special duties.

The whole system of divided moral responsibility, however, is dynamic. It changes in response to new aspirations and problems. While some of this change will be evolutionary and beyond human control in any form, I have suggested that ideally and to some degree it should be overseen by democratic deliberation. I have sketched a way of conceiving of policymaking in a democracy as of a piece with, and as setting the framework for, the division of moral deliberative labor in society. In this way, then, the idea of deliberative responsibility provides a new way to conceive of the relationship between ethics and politics.

Philosophy, Georgetown University

---

[51] There are obviously difficult issues about cultural diversity lurking here. For a powerful defense of the idea that some of morality's most basic truths are susceptible to multicultural consensus, see Martha C. Nussbaum, *Feminist Internationalism* (Cambridge: Cambridge University Press, forthcoming).

[52] I am grateful to Sarah Buss for raising this issue and example.

FATE, FATALISM, AND AGENCY IN STOICISM*

By Susan Sauvé Meyer

I. Introduction

A perennial subject of dispute in the Western philosophical tradition is whether human agents can be responsible for their actions even if determinism is true. By determinism, I mean the view that everything that happens (human actions, choices, and deliberations included) is completely determined by antecedent causes. One of the least impressive objections that is leveled against determinism confuses determinism with a very different view that has come to be known as "fatalism": this is the view that everything is determined to happen independently of human choices, efforts, and deliberations. It is a common fallacy, among students contemplating the implications of determinism for the first time, to argue: "But if everything is determined in advance, then it doesn't matter what we decide to do; what is determined to happen will happen no matter what." This argument fallaciously infers fatalism from determinism.

The Greek and Roman Stoics were the first self-conscious and un-abashed determinists. These were the philosophers who adhered to the sect (*hairesis*) established by Zeno of Citium (334–262 B.C.E.)—notably including Cleanthes (331–232 B.C.E.) and Chrysippus (280–206 B.C.E.) in the "early" period; Panaetius (185–110 B.C.E.) and Posidonius (135–50 B.C.E.) in the "middle" period; and Seneca (1–65 C.E.), Epictetus (55–135 C.E.), and Marcus Aurelius (second century C.E.) in the "Roman Period." (In antiquity, they were called "the Stoa," with reference to their original gathering place, a painted colonnade [*stoa poikilê*] in the Athenian marketplace.)

The Stoics also get credit for being the first to diagnose the fallacy of inferring fatalism from determinism. However, their name for their brand of determinism is εἱμαρμένη (*heimarmenê*, literally, what is allotted or apportioned), a term whose Latin translation, *fatum* (literally, what is decreed), is the root of our terms "fate" and "fatalism." This is not simply a confusing accident of nomenclature. In the Greek literary tradition predating the Stoics, fate (εἱμαρμένη, or more usually its cognate μοῖρα) is generally depicted as ensuring outcomes that are immune to human efforts to prevent them. For example, in the story immortalized by Sophocles in the tragedy *Oedipus Rex*, Oedipus is fated to kill his father and marry his mother, and ends up doing both these things despite both his and his

* For helpful discussion of previous drafts of this essay, I am grateful to the other contributors to this volume, as well as to an audience at McGill University, and to Ellen Frankel Paul.

parents' best efforts to the contrary. And at least one Stoic, Posidonius, is reported to have invoked other such "fatalistic" stories in support of the Stoic doctrine of *heimarmenê*.[1]

We therefore need to consider carefully the question of whether the Stoics were, after all, fatalists of a sort. This is what I propose to investigate in this essay. After surveying the evidence, I will argue that the Stoic thesis of fate is not, after all, a thesis of fatalism. To arrive at this conclusion, however, we will need to appreciate how different the Stoic brand of determinism is from more familiar, modern varieties. At the root of the difference is the Stoic conception of causation, which differs from modern philosophical accounts that typically take causes to be events. The Stoic notion of cause, I will suggest, better captures many of our pre-philosophical intuitions about causation, and has distinct advantages for thinking clearly about the implications of determinism for human agency and responsibility.

My discussion will focus on views of the early Stoics, especially Chrysippus. Since virtually all of the writings of the Stoics are lost, we must reconstruct their views by relying on the testimony of later writers—for example, philosophers such as Sextus Empiricus (second century C.E.) and Alexander of Aphrodisias (fl. 200 C.E.); biographers such as Plutarch (first to second centuries C.E.) and Diogenes Laertius (third century C.E.); anthologists and doxographers such as Aetius (circa 100 C.E.), Aulus Gellius (130–180 C.E.), and John Stobaeus (fifth century C.E.); and Judeo-Christian writers such as Philo of Alexandria (30 B.C.E.–45 C.E.) and the Christian bishops Clement of Alexandria (fl. 200 C.E.), Hippolytus of Rome (second to third centuries C.E.), and Eusebius (260–340 C.E.). Another important source is the Roman statesman Cicero (106–43 B.C.E.), who wrote extensive accounts of Stoic, Epicurean, and Academic philosophy in the two or three years before his death. Many of these sources are hostile to the Stoics and have polemical intentions that may distort the accuracy of their reports. For example, Cicero, on whose treatise *De Fato* (Cic., *Fat.*) I shall be drawing frequently, takes the stance of the so-called New Academy (skeptical heirs of Plato's original school) in criticism of the Stoics; and Alexander of Aphrodisias, in his *De Fato* (Alex., *Fat.*), the other major text I shall rely on, carries on an Aristotelian polemic against the Stoic doctrine of fate.[2]

---

[1] Daphitas is fated to perish by falling from a horse and so avoids all horses, but dies in the end by falling off a rock known as "the horse"; a man who is fated to die by water gives up his career as a sailor, only to drown by falling into a stream (Cicero, *De Fato*, 5).

[2] Greek and Latin texts from these and other sources are collected in Hans Friedrich August von Arnim, *Stoicorum Veterum Fragmenta*, 4 vols. (Leipzig: Teubner, 1903–1905), as well as, more recently, with English translations and philosophical commentary, in A. A. Long and D. N. Sedley, *The Hellenistic Philosophers*, 2 vols. (Cambridge: Cambridge University Press, 1987). Where possible, I will give cross references to von Arnim (SVF) and Long and Sedley (LS). Translations quoted will typically be from LS or from Robert Sharples, *Cicero: On Fate* (Warminster: Aris and Phillips, 1991); and Robert Sharples, *Alexander of Aphrodisias: On Fate* (London: Duckworth, 1983). All unattributed translations are my own.

II. Stoic Determinism

The Stoics state their determinist thesis by claiming that everything happens by "fate."[3] Everything that happens in the universe is fully determined, down to the last detail, by Zeus, who is none other than fate. This is not, however, the Zeus of legend and superstition, who intervenes in the natural world as a causal power distinct from it. Rather, Zeus is constituted by the natural world: he encompasses all the particular "seminal principles" (*spermatikoi logoi*) in the world, whose unfolding constitutes the course of the universe from its beginning to its ultimate conflagration.[4] Clearly the details of Stoic cosmology would be unpersuasive to most modern readers, even to determinists. But the crucial feature of the Stoic view, which entitles it to the label "determinist," is captured in the report of Alexander of Aphrodisias:

> In setting out the differences which exist among causes they [the Stoics] list a swarm of causes . . . but, given this plurality of causes, they say that it is equally true with regard to all of them that it is *impossible*, where all the same circumstances obtain with respect to the cause and that to which it is the cause, that a result which does not ensue on one occasion should ensue on another. For if this happened, there would be uncaused motion. . . . (Alex., *Fat.* 192.17–25 [LS 55N3], trans. Long and Sedley, emphasis mine)

Alexander, a hostile critic of the Stoic thesis of fate, claims that, on the Stoic view, the alternatives to fated outcomes are "impossible." The Stoics, however, traditionally objected to the use of this modal terminology in characterization of their position. Chrysippus, for instance, goes to some lengths to reject the claim that what is fated is thereby necessary, or that its alternative is impossible (Cic., *Fat.* 12–16). We can make sense of this denial by noting that according to the Stoic definitions of "necessary" and "impossible," which have to do with ability and impediment rather than the sufficiency of causes to determine their effects, the conditions Alexander describes (in effect: same cause, same effect) do not entail that the effect is necessary or its alternative impossible.[5] There are, however, many different notions of necessity, one of which arguably captures or

---

[3] Diogenes Laertius, 7.149 (SVF 2.915); Aulus Gellius, *Noctes Atticae* 7.2.15 (SVF 2.977); Cic., *Fat.* 21 (SVF 2.952; LS 38G), 41 (SVF 2.974; LS 62C); Alex., *Fat.* 164.17–20, 171.26–27, 181.8–9; cf. 210.15; Plutarch, *De Stoicorum Repugnatiis* (*St. Rep.*) 1050a (SVF 2.937).

[4] Diogenes Laertius, 7.135–36 (SVF 1.102; LS 46B), 7.148–49 (SVF 2.1132; LS 43A); Aristocles, in the writings of Eusebius, *Praeparatio Evangelica* (*Pr. Ev.*) 15.14.2 (SVF 1.98; LS 46G); Nemesius, 309.5–311.2 (SVF 2.625; LS 52C); Aetius, 1.7.33 (SVF 2.1027; LS 46A); Cicero, *De Divinatione* 1.126 (SVF 2.921; LS 55L3).

[5] I develop this point in detail in "Moral Responsibility: Aristotle and After," in *Companions to Ancient Thought*, vol. 4: *Ethics*, ed. S. Everson (Cambridge: Cambridge University Press, 1998), 221–40. I follow Michael Frede, *Die Stoische Logik* (Göttingen: Vandenhoeck und Ruprecht, 1974), 107–17, in reading Diogenes Laertius's account of the Stoic modal notions (Diogenes Laertius, 7.75 [LS 38D]).

corresponds to the sort of causal determination Alexander here describes. And the Stoics themselves would seem to concede the point in spirit, if not in word; for their various articulations of the thesis of fate are replete with metaphors for necessity. They describe fate as an inescapable (*aparabaton*), invincible (*akôluton*), and inflexible (*atrepton*) series of causes.[6]

For these reasons it seems quite accurate to classify the Stoic thesis of fate as a thesis of causal determinism: that everything that happens is the result of antecedent sufficient and fully determining conditions. We shall see later on that this classification fails to exhaust the content of the Stoic thesis, but for our present purposes it is sufficient to note that the Stoic thesis that everything happens by fate is, among other things, a thesis of determinism.

III. DETERMINISM AND FATALISM

The Stoic thesis of fate was subjected to vigorous criticism in antiquity. One of the standard charges against it was that if everything happens by fate, then nothing is up to us (ἐφ᾽ ἡμῖν, *eph' hêmin*). One way of formulating this objection was known in antiquity as the "Lazy Argument" (so named because it says the thesis of fate would license us all to be lazy):

> They [the Stoics] argue as follows: "If it is fated for you to recover from this disease, then you will recover, whether you call the doctor or not; similarly, if it is fated for you not to recover from this disease, then you will not recover, whether you call the doctor or not. But one or the other is fated; so there is no point in calling the doctor." This kind of argument is rightly named lazy and idle, since by the same argument all activity will be removed from life. . . . (Cic., *Fat.* 28–29 [LS 55S1], trans. Sharples)

The Lazy Argument fallaciously infers that if an outcome is antecedently determined, then nothing I do is necessary in order for it to occur. This is to infer fatalism from determinism. In criticism of the Lazy Argument, Chrysippus points out that even if something is fated, it still might require specific antecedent causes:

> "For," he [Chrysippus] says, "there are some cases that are simple, others complex. A case of what is simple is 'Socrates will die on that day'; whether he does anything or not, there is a fixed day for his death. But if it is fated that 'Oedipus will be born to Laius,' one will not be able to say 'whether Laius has slept with a woman or not'; the

---

[6] Aetius, 1.28.4 (SVF 2.917; LS 55J); Aulus Gellius, *Noctes Atticae* 7.2.3 (SVF 2.1000; LS 55K); Plutarch, *St. Rep.* 1056c (SVF 2.997; LS 55R2); Aristocles, in the writings of Eusebius, *Pr. Ev.* 15.14.2 (SVF 1.98; LS 46G).

matter is complex and 'co-fated'"—for that is what he calls it, because it is fated *both* that Laius will sleep with his wife *and* that he
will beget Oedipus by her. Just as if someone had said "Milo will
wrestle in the Olympic games" and someone else answered "So,
whether he has an opponent or not, he will wrestle," he would be
wrong, for "he will wrestle" is complex. For without an opponent
there is no wrestling. So all captious arguments of that sort can be
refuted in the same way. "Whether you call in the doctor or not, you
will get well" is captious; it is as fated to call in the doctor as it is to
get well. These cases, as I said, Chrysippus calls "co-fated." (Cic., *Fat.*
30 [LS 55S2-3], trans. Sharples)[7]

Two events are co-fated, it appears, if one of them is fated, and the other
is necessary for the fated event to happen. If calling the doctor is necessary for your recovery, then if your recovery is fated, so too is your calling
the doctor. It is fallacious to draw an inference from the assumption that
your recovery is fated to the conclusion (the "captious premise" of the
Lazy Argument) that it is fated to occur whatever you do or try to do.

So the Stoics do, in response to the Lazy Argument, make (or presuppose) a distinction between determinism and fatalism. But what sort of
fatalism are they contesting? We might distinguish *fatalism about outcomes*,
the view that outcomes (e.g., recovery from illness) are determined independently of anything we might try to do, from *fatalism about actions*, the
view that our actions (e.g., calling the doctor) are determined to occur
independently of what we decide or choose, or will.[8] The specific example
at issue in this version of the Lazy Argument addresses fatalism about
outcomes. The argument questions whether, under fate, events in the
world depend on our actions, not whether our actions are up to us.
Although Cicero discusses the Lazy Argument in a context in which the
general concern is whether, under the Stoic doctrine of fate, our actions
are not up to us, it is not explicit from the response of Chrysippus that he
reports here, what moral about human agency Chrysippus intends to
draw—how, if at all, he thinks his response applies to the question of
whether our actions, if fully determined, can be up to us.[9]

A natural way of applying Chrysippus's doctrine of co-fatals to the case
of agency is to take him to be saying that human decisions or willings (in
Stoic terminology, "assent" [*sunkatathesis*]) are necessary for our actions.[10]

[7] A similar report of Chrysippus's response to the Lazy Argument is in Diogenianus, in
the writings of Eusebius, *Pr. Ev.* 6.8.25–29 (SVF 2.998; LS 62F).
[8] Alexander of Aphrodisias explicitly infers fatalism about actions from Stoic determinism
(Alex., *Fat.* 179.8–20).
[9] I thank Satoshi Ogihara for emphasizing the importance of this point.
[10] For a detailed treatment of the Stoic account of the psychology of human action, see
Brad Inwood, *Ethics and Human Action in Early Stoicism* (Oxford: Oxford University Press,
1985).

Just as your recovery is co-fated along with your calling the doctor, your calling the doctor is co-fated along with your decision to call the doctor. Since, on this view, our actions depend on our choices or assents, and cannot occur without them, it is fallacious for the critic of Stoic fate to draw an inference from the premise that our actions are fated to the conclusion that we are fated to perform them independently of what we choose or will.[11]

Independent support for this interpretation comes from Calcidius (fourth century C.E.) and from Alexander of Aphrodisias. Calcidius, although a hostile critic, confirms that for the Stoics "the movements of our minds"— presumably assent, choice, and the like—are necessary for our fated actions:

> The movements of our minds are nothing more than instruments for carrying out fated decrees, since it is necessary that they be performed through us, by the agency of fate. Thus men play the role of necessary condition, just as place is a necessary condition for motion and rest. (Calcidius, *In Tim.* CLX–CLXI [SVF 2.943], trans. Long, "Freedom and Determinism," 177)

If these "movements of our minds" are necessary for our actions, then presumably they would be co-fated along with the actions. Alexander, in relating the Stoic account of what makes our actions up to us, confirms that the crucial fact, in the Stoic view, is that our actions happen through our assent:

> [Since] fate [brings] about movements and activities in the world, some through earth, if it so happens, some through air, some through fire, some through something else, and some also through living creatures (and such are the movements in accordance with impulse), they [the Stoics] say that those brought about by fate through the living creatures are "up to" the living creatures. . . . (Alex., *Fat.* 182.8–13, trans. Sharples, slightly altered)

(A few lines later [182.16], Alexander makes it clear that the "impulse" he refers to here involves "assent.")

We have reason to suppose, then, that Chrysippus and the Stoics held that our actions, although fated, are up to us, because they depend on our assenting to or willing the action. To hold this view is to disavow fatalism about actions. Of course, the obvious next move for the critic of determinism to make (particularly one who is concerned with human respon-

---

[11] The argument is interpreted in this way by A. A. Long in "Freedom and Determinism in the Stoic Theory of Human Action," in Long, ed., *Problems in Stoicism* (London: Athlone Press, 1971), 178, 196 n. 33; and in Long and Sedley, *The Hellenistic Philosophers*, 1:392; and by me in "Moral Responsibility: Aristotle and After."

sibility) is to concede that our choice, will, and assent do make a difference to our actions, but to complain that under the Stoic thesis of fate, these choices, willings, and assents would be fully determined by antecedent causes, and hence not up to us. This is a very different objection from that of the Lazy Argument, and we will consider Chrysippus's response presently (in Section IV). For the moment, however, I want to consider evidence that calls into doubt whether the Stoics maintained that our choices, willings, or assents really are necessary for our fated actions. Might they not be fatalists about actions after all?

For the first piece of disturbing evidence, we need turn no further than the text in which Cicero presents Chrysippus's response to the Lazy Argument, quoted above. As an example of a "simple" fated outcome (i.e., one not co-fated along with a necessary antecedent), Chrysippus gives the day of Socrates' death: "whether he does anything or not, there is a fixed day for his death" (Cic., *Fat.* 30). Given that Socrates died by drinking hemlock in prison, and that, in the tradition known to Chrysippus, he had the opportunity to escape and avoid the outcome, the claim that there was nothing he could have done to alter the day of his death has a decidedly fatalistic ring to it.[12] Although this example has direct implications only for fatalism about outcomes rather than about actions, the characteristically "fatalistic" aspect of the claim Chrysippus seems willing to endorse in this example raises the possibility that he thinks at least some of our fated *actions* are similarly overdetermined—i.e., that we are determined to perform them independently of whether we assent to them or not.

Indeed, there are at least two texts that seem to attribute just this view to the Stoics. First of all, the Christian bishop Hippolytus (second to third centuries C.E.), in his polemic *The Refutation of All Heresies* (*Ref. Her.*), writes:

> Zeno and Chrysippus affirmed that everything is fated with the following model: when a dog is tied to a cart, if it wants to follow it is pulled and follows, making its spontaneous acts (*to autexousion*) coincide with necessity. But if it does not want to follow, it will be compelled in any case. So it is with men too, even if they do not want to, they will be compelled in any case to follow what is destined (*to peprômenon*). (Hip., *Ref. Her.* 1.21 [SVF 2.975; LS 62A], trans. Long and Sedley)

The metaphor of the dog tied to the cart, attributed here both to the founder of Stoicism (Zeno) and to the intellectual giant of Stoicism's early period (Chrysippus), is easily interpreted as asserting fatalism about ac-

---

[12] Plato (*Crito* 44b–47a) portrays Crito as offering to help Socrates escape from prison before his death sentence is carried out. Socrates, who has just claimed that his death has been prophesied in a dream (44a–b), refuses.

tions: whether we want to or not, whether we assent to the actions or not, we will nonetheless do what fate has decreed we will do.

We cannot discount this evidence as simply distorted by the Christian Hippolytus's anti-pagan polemical intentions (although it is quite right to discount his use of "necessity" to refer to fate). For we have, preserved in the writings of a friendly source, the Roman Stoic Epictetus (55–135 C.E.), a quotation from Cleanthes, the third of the three major figures in early Stoicism. His *Hymn to Zeus* makes essentially the point attributed to Zeno and to Chrysippus by Hippolytus:

> Lead me, Zeus and Destiny,
> Wherever you have ordained me,
> For I shall follow unflinchingly.
> But if I become bad and unwilling,
> I shall follow none the less.
> —Epictetus, *Enchiridion* 53 (SVF 1.527; LS 62B),
> trans. Long and Sedley

What are we to make of these texts? Do they show that the Stoics subscribe to fatalism about actions—that human intentions, deliberations, choices, and assents (indeed, all of the psychological contribution that, on most views, makes us responsible for our actions) are in fact irrelevant to our actions? If so, then it would make Chrysippus's response to the Lazy Argument quite disingenuous: If the basic issue at stake is whether the thesis of fate entails that our actions are determined independently of our assents and wills, then Chrysippus's response would be that the inference is fallacious (even though, according to the Stoics, its conclusion would be true)! Attributing such a "fatalist" theory to the Stoics would also be clearly in tension with the reports of the Stoic account that what is up to us is what happens through us (Alex, *Fat.* 182.8–13, quoted above). But if the Stoics are not fatalists about actions, then what is the meaning of the metaphor of the cart and dog, and how are we supposed to understand the passage from Cleanthes' *Hymn to Zeus*? Are the Stoics simply inconsistent on this issue?

I propose that the key to understanding these two troubling passages in a way that removes the apparent inconsistency comes from solving another long-standing difficulty in the interpretation of the Stoic thesis of fate.

IV. Fate and Chrysippus's Causal Distinction

The problem involves a causal distinction that Chrysippus invokes in response to the objector who concedes that the Lazy Argument is "captious" (our actions do depend on our assents and willings), but insists

that since our assents and willings are themselves determined by antecedent causes, neither they nor our actions are up to us:

> The [critics of Chrysippus] argued as follows: "If all things come
> about by fate, all things come about by an antecedent cause; and if
> impulses do, so too do those things which follow on impulse; and
> therefore so too do assentings. But if the cause of impulse is not
> located in us, impulse itself too is not in our power; and if this is so,
> neither do those things which are brought about by impulse depend
> on us. So neither assentings nor actions are in our power." (Cic., *Fat.*
> 40 [LS 62C4], trans. Sharples)

The objector who makes an argument of this sort relies on the principle:

> (P) If the cause of X is not in our power (*in nobis*), then neither is X
> in our power.

Chrysippus's response is to distinguish between two sorts of causes, and
to concede that principle (P) applies to only one of them (Cic., *Fat.* 41–43).
He distinguishes between "auxiliary and proximate" causes, on the one
hand, and "perfect and primary causes," on the other (Cic., *Fat.* 41), a
distinction which seems to correspond to one elsewhere attributed to the
Stoics, between preliminary (*prokatarktika*) causes and sustaining (*sunek-
tika, contentiva*) causes.[13] Here Chrysippus illustrates the distinction by
pointing to the difference between the push that starts the cylinder rolling
(the auxiliary and proximate cause), and the cylinder's "own force and
nature" (*suapte vi et natura*, Cic., *Fat.* 43), which is the perfect and principal
cause of the rolling. Chrysippus, according to Cicero, says that the "auxiliary and proximate" cause is merely necessary for the effect, whereas the
"perfect and principal" cause produces the effect "by its own power and
nature" (Cic., *Fat.* 43). Thus, the Stoic distinction seems to map onto one
that Cicero himself makes between antecedent causes that are merely
necessary conditions and those that are genuine causes (Cic., *Fat.* 34–38).
So we may raid Cicero's own examples for further illustration: the rich
dress of the traveler may be the auxiliary and proximate cause of the
highwayman's robbery, but—adding in the example preserved in Aulus
Gellius (130–180 c.e.)—the robber himself is the perfect and primary cause.[14]
A reasonable approximation to an understanding of this distinction is that

[13] On this point, I agree with Michael Frede, "The Original Notion of Cause," in *Doubt and
Dogmatism: Studies in Hellenistic Epistemology*, ed. Malcolm Schofield, Myles Burnyeat, and
Jonathan Barnes (Oxford: Clarendon Press, 1980), and Richard Sorabji, *Necessity, Cause, and
Blame* (Ithaca, NY: Cornell University Press, 1980), ch. 4 ("Stoic Embarrassment over Necessity"), against Jean-Joel Duhot, *La Conception Stoïcienne de la Causalité* (Paris: Vrin, 1989),
167–80.
[14] Aulus Gellius, *Noctes Atticae* 7.2.6–13 (SVF 2.1000; LS 62D).

perfect and principal causes are internal causes of something's activity, while auxiliary and proximate causes are external precipitating factors.

Chrysippus's causal distinction allows us to identify two different versions of the principle on which the aforementioned objector relies:

(P1) If the perfect and principal cause of X is not in our power, then neither is X in our power.

(P2) If the auxiliary and proximate cause of X is not in our power, then neither is X in our power.

In the sort of example the objector has in mind, an external impetus (e.g., the sense-impression caused by the traveler's rich attire), prompts the impulse in the highwayman to rob the traveler; the highwayman assents to the impulse and then proceeds with the robbery. While the chain of causation passes through the highwayman's impulse and assent, making the robbery up to the robber (on the Stoic view), the impulse and assent ultimately have their source in something external (the objector insists); and thus they and the subsequent action are not up to the agent. Thus, the objector is relying on (P2). But Chrysippus will grant only (P1). Whether he is justified in rejecting (P2) is beyond the scope of the present essay. What is important for our concerns at the moment is that Chrysippus claims that the thesis of fate is irrelevant to the antecedent of (P1):

> When we say that everything comes about by fate through antecedent causes, we do not want this to be understood as "through perfect and primary causes" but as "through auxiliary and proximate causes.". . .
>
> If all things come about by fate, it does indeed follow that all things come about by causes that precede them (*causis antepositis*), but these are not perfect and primary, rather [they are] auxiliary and proximate. . . . (Cic., *Fat.* 41 [SVF 2.974; LS 62C], trans. Sharples)

Is Chrysippus claiming that the thesis of fate maintains only that everything happens as a result of preliminary (auxiliary and proximate) causes — i.e., precipitating external causes? In antiquity this seems to have been a familiar interpretation of Chrysippus's position, as the biographer Plutarch (first to second centuries C.E.) reports:

> He who says that Chrysippus made fate not the self-sufficient (*autotelês*) cause of these things, but only an initiating one (*prokatarktikon*) will show him being inconsistent with himself . . . [since Chrysippus] says that nothing is maintained or changes even in the smallest respect other than in accordance with the reasoning of Zeus, which is the same as fate. Moreover, he says the initiating cause is weaker than the self-sufficient one, and does not arrive at its goal

when it is overcome by others that rise up against it; but fate he declares to be a cause that is unconquerable (*akineton*) and cannot be hindered (*akoluton*) or turned aside (*atrepton*), himself calling it *Atropos, Adrasteia*, Necessity, and *Pepromenê*, since it imposes a limit (*peras*) for all things. (Plutarch, *De Stoicorum Repugnatiis* [*St. Rep.*] 47, 1056b [SVF 2.997; LS 55R], trans. Sharples)

While Plutarch doubts that Chrysippus could consistently have maintained such a thesis of fate (a problem to which we will return shortly), he does here show that it was a prevalent understanding of the Stoic doctrine. Indeed, Cicero himself, in another work, represents the Stoic thesis of fate as concerning only preliminary (or at any rate non-necessitating) causes:

Of this kind of cause, without which something is not brought about, some are inactive . . . ; others, however, *provide a certain beginning* for bringing about the effect, and contribute certain things that in themselves assist, even if they do not necessitate, as "meeting had provided the cause of love, love of disgrace." *It is from this kind of causes, linked together from eternity (ex aeternitate pendentium) that fate is bound together by the Stoics.* (Cic., *Topica* 59, trans. Sharples, emphasis mine)

And Aulus Gellius, in reporting what appears to be the same source used by Cicero's account of Chrysippus's causal distinction (Cic., *Fat.* 41–43), explicitly identifies Chrysippus's thesis of fate as something that assails us (specifically, our minds) from the outside (*omnem illam vim quae de fato extrinsecus ingruit*).[15]

To view fate as consisting entirely of external causes certainly seems to fit a natural reading of Chrysippus's metaphor of the dog and cart: external causes determine our actions regardless of our (internal) choices and assents. But this appearance may be misleading. For, as Plutarch points out, the sorts of causes that are within the scope of this restricted thesis of fate (the preliminary or merely necessary causes) do not have, on the Stoic account, the sort of causal efficacy that would yield the inescapability or determination that makes the Stoic thesis of fate determinist in the first place. Moreover, if fate consists of causes that are merely necessary for fated outcomes, but do not have in themselves the power to bring about the fated outcomes,[16] then it would also be incapable of the sort of fatalistic overdetermination invoked in the natural interpretation of the dog-and-cart image.

---

[15] Aulus Gellius, *Noctes Atticae* 7.2.6–13 (SVF 2.1000; LS 62D). Modern scholars who accept this interpretation include Frede, "The Original Notion of Cause," 239–41; Long, "Freedom and Determinism," 178; and Harold Cherniss, *ad loc.*, in *Plutarch's Moralia*, vol. 13, part 2 (Cambridge, MA: Loeb Classical Library, 1976); for additional references, see Sorabji, *Necessity, Cause, and Blame*, 82 n. 56.

[16] Clement, *Stromata* 8.9.33 (SVF 2.351; LS 55I).

Indeed, if the Stoic thesis of fate were simply the thesis that everything that happens is preceded by external causes necessary for its occurrence, then there seems little left for critics of the Stoics to disagree with. This is, in fact, what Cicero says, in his discussion of Chrysippus's application of the causal distinction to the thesis of fate:

> Since this is how Chrysippus explains these things . . . see whether [Chrysippus's opponents] are not saying the same thing. For Chrysippus too concedes that the proximate and contiguous cause of the assenting is located in the sense-impression, but not that this is a necessitating cause of assenting; and so he will not concede that, if all things come about by fate, all things come about as a result of necessitating antecedent causes. And again, those who disagree with him do assert that assentings do not come about without sense-impressions preceding them *[and so they] will say that, if all things come about by fate of such a sort that nothing comes about except by a cause having preceded, then it must be admitted that all things come about by fate.*
>
> From this it is easy to understand that, since both sides, when their opinion is explained and set forth, come to the same result, they disagree about words and not about the facts. (Cic., *Fat.* 44, trans. Sharples, emphasis mine)

Our puzzle seems to amount to this. Only if the thesis of fate ranges over both sorts of causes (perfect and principal or sustaining, on the one hand, and preliminary or auxiliary and proximate, on the other hand) does it seem to be genuinely deterministic. The Stoics clearly took their thesis of fate to be a determinist thesis. So why does Chrysippus restrict the thesis to apply only to auxiliary and proximate causes? Anthony Long and David Sedley, in *The Hellenistic Philosophers*, have proposed that Chrysippus's remarks in this context simply recommend a point of view from which questions of moral responsibility are best considered, rather than stating a substantive thesis of Stoic physical or causal theory.[17] While they are no doubt right about the relevance of the remarks to concerns in Stoic moral theory (which I discuss below, in Section VI), I would like to argue that Chrysippus's position here is also deeply rooted in Stoic physical theory. And once we understand this aspect of the Stoic thesis of fate, we will be in a position to understand how the relevant features of Stoic ethics, no less than the metaphor of the dog tied to the cart, are rooted in the Stoics' physical theory.[18]

---

[17] Long and Sedley, *The Hellenistic Philosophers*, 1:393. Duhot (*La Conception*, 168, 185) suggests that the distinction is entirely ad hoc for the moral question, and has no implications for the general Stoic theory of causality or of fate.

[18] The Stoics claim that physics has a foundational relationship to ethics: they liken physics, which they call the soul of philosophy, to the fertile field from which the fruits of ethics (surrounded by a wall of logic) grow (Diogenes Laertius, 7.40 [LS 26B3]).

V. Fate as the Connection between Causes

We can understand why Chrysippus restricts the thesis of fate to invoke only external, precipitating causes once we properly appreciate the Stoic notion of a causal chain. One of the most common Stoic definitions of fate is that it is a string (εἱρμός) or chain (ἄλυσις) of causes. In Latin this gets translated as a *series* of causes (*series causarum*). For example:[19]

> They say [fate] is a string of causes (εἱρμόν γοῦν αἰτίων). (Alex., *Mantissa* 185.5 [SVF 2.920])

> [Fate] is an order and series of causes (*ordinem seriemque causarum*), since the connection (*nexa*) of cause to cause generates things from itself. (Cic., *De Divinatione* [*Div.*] 1.125 [LS 55L; SVF 2.921])

As Alexander notes, the notion of causes being connected to each other "in the manner of a chain" (δίκην ἀλύσεως) is what the Stoics consider the essence of their doctrine of fate (Alex., *Fat.* 193.4–8).

How are we to understand this notion of a causal chain? It is natural, when thinking about modern varieties of determinism, to think of the causal chain as a temporal succession of events, each one caused (indeed determined) by the preceding event in the chain, and each the cause of the succeeding event. This cannot be how the Stoics understood the chain, however; for they do not understand causation as a relation between successive events, but as an interaction between bodies:

> The Stoics say that every cause is a body which becomes the cause *to a body* of something incorporeal. For instance, the scalpel, a body, becomes the cause *to the flesh*, a body, of the incorporeal predicate "being cut." And again the fire, a body, becomes the cause *to the wood*, a body, of the incorporeal predicate, "being burnt" (Sextus, *Adversus Mathematicos* [*Adv. Math.*] 9.211 [SVF 2.341; LS 55B], trans. Long and Sedley; emphasis mine)

On this analysis, causation is an interaction between two bodies—one of them the cause, the other the body affected (agent and patient, if you will)—that yields a result. Thus, although the Stoics are determinists, what they identify as the cause of a result is not a sufficient condition for it (since both the knife and the flesh are part of that sufficient condition for cutting, yet the Stoics call only the knife, not the flesh, the cause). This conception of causation as interaction rather than temporal succession is preserved even in Alexander's articulation of the precisely deterministic aspect of the Stoic theory: the same result occurs whenever all the cir-

---

[19] See also Cic., *Fat.* 19–20; Alex., *Fat.* 192.1, 193.6–7, 194.4–5, 195.14–15, 195.19, 196.2 (SVF 2.528, 2.914, 2.915, 2.917, 2.918, 2.933, 2.989); and Diogenes Laertius, 7.149 (SVF 2.915).

cumstances of "the cause and that to which it is the cause" are the same (Alex., *Fat.* 192.22–24, quoted in Section II above).

The Stoic account of cause and of the causal relation presents another barrier to construing the causal chain as a temporally extended sequence of events. Such a temporally extended sequence requires that the same thing can function as both cause and effect: cause of what comes later, and effect of what came before. But the Stoics put causes and effects in different ontological categories: causes are bodies while effects are "incorporeals" (Sextus, *Adv. Math.* 9.211). While the Stoics are considerably more generous than we moderns are about what they would count as a body (fevers and other conditions are no less bodily than more familiar candidates such as hammers and nails, flesh and knives), this generosity does not extend to effects; they explicitly state that the effect is not a body. Strictly speaking, a Stoic cause cannot have a cause, as Clement of Alexandria (fl. 200 C.E.) emphasizes:

> Causes are not causes *of* each other, but there are causes *to* each other. For the pre-existing condition of the spleen is the cause, not of the fever, but of the fever's coming about; and the pre-existing fever is the cause, not of the spleen, but of its condition's being intensified. In the same way . . . the stones in the arch are causes *to* each other of the predicate "remaining," but they are not causes *of* each other. And the teacher and the pupil are causes *to* each other of the predicate "making progress."
>
> Causes are said to be causes *to each other* sometimes of the same [effect], as the merchant and retailer are the causes to each other of making a profit; but sometimes of different [effects], as in the case of the knife and the flesh; for the knife is the cause to the flesh of being cut, while the flesh is the cause to the knife of cutting. (Clement, *Stromata* 8.9.30.1–30 [SVF 2.349; LS 55D], trans. Long and Sedley)

Thus, while it would not be impossible to articulate, using Stoic vocabulary and notions, the modern notion of a causal chain as a sequence of events,[20] there is a strong presumption against construing the causal chain invoked by the Stoics in this way.[21]

In what way, then, can causes, as the Stoics conceive them, be related in a string or chain? First of all, we might note that the notion of a string or chain is not itself a temporal notion; the temporal use of string or chain (as in the modern notion of a causal chain or chain of events) is a metaphorical extension of a nontemporal notion. The notion of a string (εἱρμός,

---

[20] Long and Sedley give such a paraphrase in *The Hellenistic Philosophers*, 1:343.

[21] This is not a new point. See Duhot, *La Conception*, 257–58; and Long and Sedley, *The Hellenistic Philosophers*, 1:343, although Long, in "Freedom and Determinism," 178, does attribute to the Stoics the view that effects become causes of future events.

series) applies nonmetaphorically to a string of beads in a necklace, and the notion of a chain applies directly to the links in a chain. The beads and the links are all bodies, and thus are candidates for being causes, on the Stoic view. And Clement himself names a causal relation that can obtain between them: they can be causes to each other (i.e., can have effects on each other). The beads in a necklace, like the stones in the arch specifically mentioned by Clement, stand in relations of mutual influence on each other. Each stone, bead, or link, has an effect on the others. Clement here mentions other examples of causes that have effects on one another: the fever and the disorder of the spleen, the merchant and the retailer, the teacher and the pupil.

I propose that this relation of mutual influence between causes is what links the causes in the Stoic causal chain. Support for this interpretation comes from the frequent explanation of the Stoic causal chain as involving connections between causes:

> [Fate] is an order and series of causes, since *the connection (nexa) of cause to cause* generates things from itself. (Cic., *Div.* 1.125 [LS 55L; SVF 2.921])

> [Fate is] a reciprocal connection of things reaching through eternity (*connexio rerum per aeternitatem se invicem tenens*). (Cic., *Fat.* fragment 2)

> Everything comes to be from a natural binding together and uniting (*omnia naturale conligatione conserte contexteque fiunt*). (Cic., *Fat.* 31)

The Stoics thus stress the interconnections of causes in their doctrine of fate. So it is not surprising that they often describe fate as an ἐπιπλοκή (*epiplokê*)—an "interweaving" or "web" of causes:

> These things are interwoven with each other (ἐμπέπλεκται ἀλλήλοις) in the manner of a chain (ἁλύσεως δίκην). (Alex., *Fat.* 195.14–15)

> Must we call the continuous interweaving (συμπλοκή) [of causes] "fate" . . . ? (Plotinus, *Ennead* 3.1.4 [SVF 2.934]; cf. 3.1.2, 3.1.7)

> The interweaving (ἐπιπλοκή) and following of these [causes] is fate. . . . (Aristocles, in the writings of Eusebius, *Pr. Ev.* XV, 816d [SVF 1.98; LS 46G2])

Indeed, even in the traditional metaphor of fate as an unwinding rope, the notion of interconnection is near the surface:

> All things happen by fate. . . . The passage of time is like the unwinding of a rope; bringing about nothing new and unrolling each stage in turn. (Cic., *Div.* 1.127 [SVF 2.944; LS 55O], trans. Long and Sedley)

Here the explicit message is of predetermination; but the metaphor is also of inter*connection*; for a rope consists of many individual fibers twisted together to form a unity. A rope is a εἰρμός (*heirmos*, string) of fibers. (Recall the archaic metaphor for fate/destiny as captured in the image of the spinning wheel—Homer, *Odyssey* 7.197.)

Understanding the thesis of fate as insisting on an interconnection or mutual influence of causes gives us some insight into the Stoics' identification of fate as the totality of the "seminal principles" (σπερματικοὶ λόγοι) in the world.[22] These "seminal principles" are the individual natures of particular things unfolding according to their own proper causal powers, which the Stoics classify as either "tenor" (ἕξις), "nature" (φύσις), or "soul" (ψυχή), depending on whether they are inanimate (e.g., stones), living (e.g., plants), or ensouled (e.g., animals).[23] It is because fate, on the Stoic view, consists of the sum total of these individual causal powers that Cicero describes it as "the fate of physics" as opposed to that of superstition (Cic., *Div.* 1.126 [LS 55L3]). As Alexander explains the Stoic view:

> They say that the very fate, nature, and rationale (*logon*) in accordance with which the all is governed is god. It is present in all things which exist and happen, and in this way uses the proper nature of all existing things for the government of the all. (Alex., *Fat.* 192.25–28 [SVF 2.945; LS 55N4], trans. Long and Sedley)

There are conceivably two ways in which fate could operate through all the particular natures of existing things. One way, the "Leibnizian" alternative, would have, as it were, wound up inside each substance fully and determinately all of the changes it would undergo and be involved in in the course of its history.[24] There would be no causal interaction in such a world. The "Newtonian" alternative is to suppose that there is interaction among existing things. What happens to each thing may sometimes be simply the result of its unfolding nature (whether soul, or tenor, or "nature" in the strict sense)—for example, that it should die at some time (if a living thing) or be held together (if physical). But a good deal of what befalls it is due, at least in part, to the causal interaction between it and other bodies.

The Stoics' emphasis on the interconnectedness of causes shows that they are concerned to articulate the second of these alternatives.[25] And their motivation is clear: this is what gives unity to the universe. Just as

---

[22] See references in note 4.

[23] For texts and discussion of this Stoic distinction, which cuts across the Aristotelian notions of nature and soul, see Long and Sedley, *The Hellenistic Philosophers*, section 47.

[24] Gottfried Wilhelm Leibniz (1646–1716) proposed that the basic substances in the world ("monads") did not interact with each other, but rather unfolded their individual natures in a pattern of "pre-established harmony." Leibniz had well-known disputes on this and other questions with followers of Sir Isaac Newton.

[25] By contrast, Duhot, *La Conception*, 187, denies that such "secondary" causes (secondary to the "sustaining" [*sunektikon*] causal role of Zeus) have any real causal efficacy, and explicitly suggests that the Leibnizian alternative captures the Stoic view.

its "tenor" holds together the physical parts of a simple body such as a stone, the Stoics hold that in general there must be a cause responsible for the holding together of anything composed of parts. Zeus, as the sustaining cause (συνεκτικὸν αἴτιον) of the universe, binds together into a unity by mutual causal influence the various bodies that are its parts.[26]

Just as a woven fabric is a unity, and not simply a collection of independent fibers that happen to be located in one place, so, on the Stoic view, the "web of fate" makes the individual parts of the world into a unity. As Alexander explains, one of the Stoic arguments for the thesis of fate is the argument for the unity of the universe:

> For nothing in the world exists or happens causelessly (anaitiôs), because none of the things in it is independent of, and insulated from, everything that has gone before. For the world would be wrenched apart and divided, and no longer remain a unity, forever governed in accordance with a single ordering and management, if an uncaused motion were introduced.... (Alex., Fat. 192.8–13 [SVF 2.945; LS 55N2], trans. Long and Sedley)

This is a surprising twist on the notion of "no motion without a cause." A barely determinist thesis, which posits sufficient antecedent conditions for every world state or event, would not imply the sort of unity of conditions that warrant calling it an order (taxis, kosmos). And note how prevalent are the terms for order in the Stoic discussions of fate, and their close alternation with terms for interconnection.[27] The Stoic view of the universe as an ordered unity with each part playing its role in relation to the whole, no doubt relates to their view of the universe as a living creature with a soul that gives it both life and unity. Indeed, one of the primary functions of the global cause, variously identified as the world soul, the seminal principle, Zeus, or fate, is, like that of all causes (in contrast with the passive bodies from which they are distinguished), to hold together, or make a unity of, the body to which it is a cause.[28]

Given the stress on reciprocal connection in the doctrine of fate, it is not surprising that the topic of reciprocal causation should have been of serious interest to the Stoics and their critics, and thus it is not an accident that a discussion of this topic survives in Clement. For mere determinists,

[26] On the Stoic sustaining cause, see Clement, Stromata 8.9.33.1–9 (SVF 2.351; LS 55I); and Galen, De Causis Continentibus 1.1–2.4 (LS 55F). On fate as the sustaining cause of the world, see Alex., Fat. 195.3, 195.23–24; cf. Alex., Mantissa 131.5–10 (SVF 2.448), 182.20, 185.7; and Plotinus, Enneads 3.1.4.5 (SVF 2.934).

[27] Cic., Div. 1.125 (SVF 2.921; LS 55L1); Aetius 1.28.4 (SVF 2.917; LS 55J); Aulus Gellius, Noctes Atticae 7.2.3 (SVF 2.1000; LS 55K); Alex., Fat. 192.1 (SVF 2.945; LS 55N); and Stobaeus, 179.1–12 (SVF 2.913; LS 55M).

[28] Plutarch, St. Rep. 1053b (SVF 2.605; LS 46F); ibid., 1052c–d (SVF 2.604; LS 46E); Philo, De Legibus Allegoriae 2.22–23 (SVF 2.458; LS 47P); Philo, Quod Deus sit Immutabilis 35–36 (SVF 2.458; LS 47Q); Philo, Quaestiones et Solutiones in Genesin 2.4 (SVF 2.802; LS 47R).

interest in this topic would be surprising. Indeed, it seems clear from the dialectical structure of Cicero's *De Fato*, that Carneades (mid second century B.C.E.), the Academic critic of Chrysippus to whom Cicero is here sympathetic, contrasts the Stoic view that our minds are subject to fate, with the view that our minds unfold according to their own causal natures without being impinged upon by anything external:

> [Reporting Carneades' position:] Just so, when we say that the mind is moved without a cause, we are saying that it is moved without an antecedent and external cause, not without any cause. Of the atom itself it can be said, when it is moved through the void by heaviness and weight, that it is moved without a cause, because no cause comes to it from outside. . . . Similarly in the case of the voluntary movements of the mind an external cause is not to be looked for; for voluntary movement has this nature in itself, that it is in our power and is obedient to us. And this is not without a cause, for the nature of that thing itself is the cause of that thing. (Cic., *Fat.* 24–25, trans. Sharples)

That is, Carneades proposes that the mind is like a Leibnizian monad, outside the interconnected causal fabric of the rest of the world.

Once we appreciate that the main point of the Stoic thesis of fate is to insist on the connections of causes in the world, and to deny that any cause acts in isolation from the rest of the causal nexus, then it should not be surprising that Chrysippus should articulate the thesis of fate by appeal simply to auxiliary and proximate causes (Cic., *Fat.* 41). To claim that everything that happens has an antecedent, external, precipitating cause is simply to insist that no cause operates in isolation from the rest of the causal nexus. For every perfect and principal cause, there is also an external, precipitating cause that affects it.

Chrysippus's claim initially struck us as a puzzling "restriction" on the thesis of fate, but that impression depended on the assumption that the causes cited in the thesis of fate must be total determining sufficient conditions for their effects. However, we have seen that the Stoics do not conceive of causes as sufficient conditions. The claim might also appear to be a "restriction" if we suppose that the thesis of fate is supposed to supply explanations of particular phenomena; in that case, it would indeed be strange for the perfect and principal cause of the outcome to be left out of the explanation. But there is no reason to suppose that the Stoics intended to use the thesis of fate in this way. To claim that something was fated to happen is not to offer an explanation of why it happened, an explanation that would be in competition with the local explanation citing the perfect and principal cause.[29] Rather, it is to point

---

[29] Plutarch (*St. Rep.* 1056d) seems to construe the thesis in this way.

to a feature that its explanation will have. To claim that something happened by fate is to place it, and its perfect and principal cause, in a
broader context, to show its place in the broader scheme of things. At a
minimum, it is to claim that that perfect and principal cause was connected, more or less directly, to the rest of the universe. The reason why
the thesis of fate, as Chrysippus articulates it in this context, does not
mention perfect and principal causes is because, in effect, it is a thesis
about the connections between perfect and principal causes: they are
auxiliary and proximate causes for each other.[30]

VI. Agency, Externality, and Morality

The Stoic and the modern determinist can agree on the thesis of determinism: given the totality of the causal conditions in the world at a
particular time, what happens subsequently is completely determined.
However, we have seen that the Stoic and the modern determinist have
very different ways of employing causal notions to articulate this view.
The modern determinist tends to construe causes as events, which are
linked together in an asymmetrical, temporally ordered sequence of cause
and effect marching inexorably from the past to the future. The Stoic, on
the other hand, views causes as bodies with active causal powers, and
views the unfolding of the universe as due, inexorably, to the activity of
these causal powers and their interaction with each other. Are there any
advantages to having the Stoic rather than the modern view? I would like
to point out several advantages to having the Stoic conception of causality
in mind when thinking about questions related to agency and moral
responsibility.

First of all, in much of our pre-philosophical thinking about causality,
especially as it applies to our own agency and responsibility, we do tend,
like the Stoics, to think of ourselves as causes.[31] We think that the person
who is fairly held responsible for an action or outcome must have caused
it. To think this is to suppose that a person (who is, of course, not an
event) is a cause. This perfectly ordinary way of thinking about causality
is not easy, in practice, to integrate with the view of causality as a sequence of events, and the worry becomes particularly acute when the
sequence of events is supposed to be deterministic. One may be tempted
to fall into an error characteristic of many worries about determinism—to
"look back over your shoulder" at the inexorable sequence of events that
the modern determinist thesis postulates, and to conclude with a sense of
powerlessness: you fear these events will "wash over" and engulf you

---

[30] I give a more extended defense of this interpretation of the Stoic thesis of fate in
"Chains of Causes: What Is the Stoic Thesis of Fate?" (unpublished).

[31] See, e.g., the essays in this volume by Michael S. Moore, Leo Katz, and Kenneth W.
Simons discussing legal responsibility.

like waves overcoming a struggling swimmer. The error here is to over-look the fact that you are yourself an ingredient in the events determining the outcome. The inexorable sequence of events is not a set of *external* factors that bear down on you and fully determine your choices from the outside. This error, in fact, amounts to the fallacy of inferring fatalism from determinism.

One might also be tempted, by the divergence between our intuitive understanding of ourselves as causes, on the one hand, and the philosophical view that causes are events, on the other hand, to postulate a *sui generis* kind of causation exercised by agents alone, in order to mark out the causal status we seem, from the first-person perspective, to have; that is, we might think we are capable of "agent-causation" as opposed to the garden variety of event-causation that operates in the rest of the natural world.[32] This is to adopt a view of agency as radically discontinuous with the causal processes in the rest of the natural world, which is metaphysically a very extravagant assumption. While we have seen that the Stoics distinguish many different types of causes (for example, perfect and principal, on the one hand, and auxiliary and proximate, on the other), they do not attribute to agents causal powers of a sort not at work in the rest of the natural world. Agents, no less than fire, knives, and other bodies, can be perfect and principal causes, as well as auxiliary and proximate causes.

But, one might object, only agents (unlike fire, knives, or other bodies) are morally responsible for their actions, and thus it is reasonable to suppose that they must exercise a distinctive type of causality. In response, the Stoics would likely reply that all bodies have distinctive causal powers (only fire burns, for example, and only acorns grow into oak trees), and the distinctive causal power of agents is virtue or vice. But, the objector will continue, if our virtuous or vicious activity is precipitated by external circumstances (as the thesis of fate affirms), then how can it truly be up to us? The thought of external causation naturally leads one to think of coercion or compulsion or hindrance, all of which are instances of external causal influence. But Chrysippus's distinction between causes is intended to address this objection. He points out that it makes a difference whether the external cause is a perfect and principal cause, as opposed to a mere triggering cause. Not all external causes are of the hindering or compelling sort. For example, the flesh neither hinders nor compels the knife's causation of the cutting. Thus, the mere fact that

---

[32] Roderick Chisholm, "Human Freedom and the Self," Lindley Lecture, 1964; reprinted in *Free Will*, ed. Gary Watson (Oxford: Oxford University Press, 1982), 24–35, articulates such a view, citing, as antecedents, Thomas Reid (1710–1796) and Aristotle (ibid., 24 n. 1). But Chisholm is mistaken in attributing to Aristotle the view that such active causal powers are a *sui generis* kind of causation distinct from what goes on in the natural order. I develop this point in "Self Motion and External Causation," in *Self-Motion from Aristotle to Newton*, ed. Mary Louise Gill and James G. Lennox (Princeton: Princeton University Press, 1994).

external causes precipitate our particular virtuous and vicious actions is not enough to establish that they compel us in a way that undermines our responsibility.[33]

The Stoic view of morality presupposes that the proper way of evaluating oneself or another in moral terms can be captured in the vocabulary of inner and external causes. Unlike their opponents, who take the salient feature about external factors to be whether they are part of antecedent fully determining conditions, the Stoics insist that what is morally significant about external factors (or "externals") is how one responds to them. One's response to externals (e.g., whether one robs the traveler or shares the road with him) displays whether one is virtuous or vicious.

Virtue, for the Stoics, concerns the correct use of and attitude toward externals. Specifically, it concerns one's orientation toward the so-called "external goods" (health, wealth, pleasure, family, reputation, etc.). The virtuous person's pursuit of these things (which the Stoics prefer to call "indifferents" rather than "goods")[34] differs from that of the nonvirtuous person in two respects. First of all, the virtuous person makes the correct choice or selection of which of these external objectives to pursue. A vicious person may err in being too greedy—for example, in pursuing more wealth or power than he should. Thus, he would differ from the virtuous person in how he responds to an external "triggering" cause (for example, an opportunity to gain additional wealth at the expense of proper care for his children).

A second way in which an agent's relation to externals is relevant to her virtue or vice concerns the attitude she takes toward the success or failure of her selected objectives. As the Stoics stress, the achievement of what we elect to pursue is not up to us; the external world, which we do not control, must cooperate if we are to succeed.[35] For example, we may decide, properly, to devote significant energy to raising children, with the hope of making them good people who lead successful lives. But such efforts can be frustrated by disease, death, and other misfortunes. This vulnerability of human endeavors to fortune gives rise to the additional dimension in which the virtuous person differs from the nonvirtuous. The virtuous person, while she will aim at the right sorts of external objectives, will care only about choosing or deciding correctly; therefore, she will not be distressed or grieved when external misfortune prevents her from achieving what she has decided to pursue.[36] The person who is

---

[33] I offer a fuller discussion and defense of Chrysippus on this point in "Moral Responsibility: Aristotle and After"; see also Long, "Freedom and Determinism."

[34] Diogenes Laertius, 7.101–5 (LS 58A, 58B); Cicero, De Finibus (Fin.) 3.32 (LS 59L); Stobaeus, 2.96.18–2.97.5 (SVF 3.501; LS 59M).

[35] Epictetus, Discourses 1.1.7–12 (LS 62K).

[36] Cicero, Fin. 3.20–22 (LS 59D), 3.32 (LS 59L); Cicero, Tusculanae Disputationes 5.40–41 (LS 63L); Epictetus, Discourses 1.1.7–12 (LS 62K); Galen, De Placitis Hippocratis et Platonis 4.5.21–26 (SVF 3.480; LS 65L); Alex., De Anima 2.164.3–9 (LS 64B); Seneca, Epistulae Morales 92.11–13 (LS 64J); Stobaeus, 2.76.9–15 (LS 58K), 2.96.18–297.5 (LS 59M).

less than virtuous, by contrast, may care not only about choosing well, but also about achieving what she aims at. So she will be distressed or suffer grief if, for example, her children die or other plans of hers do not succeed. In such circumstances, the difference between the virtuous and the nonvirtuous person lies in how the virtuous person responds to the external causal factors to which, according to Chrysippus, we are inextricably linked in the fabric of fate.

We might well be repelled by the Stoic doctrine of indifferents—the view that external goods are not truly good, and thus provide no grounds for grief or disappointment if we fail to obtain them. However, understanding the doctrine provides the key to interpreting the metaphor of the dog tied to the cart.[37] Aulus Gellius's version of Chrysippus's distinction between causes highlights how the vicious person's attitude toward external conditions (displayed in her emotions or passions) parallels the dog's position with respect to the cart. The salient difference between the scenario in which the dog follows the cart smoothly and willingly, and the scenario in which it follows with distress and resistance, is not that in the one case the dog's actions are caused by its assent, while in the other its assent is irrelevant. Rather, the salient difference between the scenarios is whether the journey is rough (full of distress and regret) or smooth (without regret or other passion):

> If our minds' initial makeup is a healthy and beneficial one, all that external force exerted upon them as a result of fate slides over them fairly smoothly and without obstruction. But if they are coarse, ignorant, inept, and unsupported by education, then even if they are under little or no pressure from fated disadvantages, they still, through their own ineptitude and voluntary impulse, plunge themselves into continual wrongdoings and transgressions. (Aulus Gellius, 7.2. [LS 62D2; SVF 2.1000], trans. Long and Sedley)

It is not the external factors, but the qualities of the person's own mind, that determine whether the agent's course through life achieves the "good flow of life" (εὔροια βίου, alternatively described as "living in agreement with nature"—ὁμολογουμένως τῇ φύσει ζῆν) which the Stoics identify as the goal of life, and which they claim only the virtuous person achieves:

> Zeno in his book On the Nature of Man was the first to say that living in agreement with nature (ὁμολογουμένως τῇ φύσει ζῆν) is the end, which is living in accordance with virtue. . . . So too Cleanthes in his book On Pleasure, and Posidonius and Hecato in their books On Ends [say the same thing]. . . . Therefore, living in agreement with nature

---

[37] The interpretation I offer here agrees with that sketched by Long in "Freedom and Determinism," 191-92.

comes to be the end, which is in accordance with the nature of oneself and that of the whole, engaging in no activity wont to be forbidden by the universal law, which is the right reason pervading everything and identical to Zeus, who is this director of the administration of existing things. And the virtue of the happy man and his good flow of life (εὔροια βίου) are just this: always doing everything on the basis of the concordance of each man's guardian spirit with the will of the administrator of the whole. . . . (Diogenes Laertius, 7.87–88 [LS 63C], trans. Long and Sedley)

The vicious person experiences a rough and uncomfortable passage through life, even an unwilling passage, due to her pursuit of inappropriate objects, or to her inappropriate concern for attaining these objects. By contrast, the virtuous person "does nothing which he could regret, nothing against his will, but does everything honorably, consistently, seriously, and rightly" (Cicero, *Tusculanae Disputationes* 5.81).[38] The inappropriate concern of the vicious person is expressed in emotions such as disappointment, regret, grief, and feelings of constraint and conflict. These passions have characterized philosophical portraits of vice since Plato and Aristotle.[39] The Stoics' distinctive variation on this familiar theme is to connect these portraits of virtue and vice to their physical theory, in particular their thesis of fate. We are part of the causal nexus of the world whether we like it or not. How we navigate among the externals determines whether our course of life will be the rough ride of the wicked or the smooth and pleasant flow of life characteristic of the blessed.

VII. CONCLUSION

Despite the potentially confusing nomenclature, and other initial appearances to the contrary, the Stoic thesis of fate is not a thesis of fatalism. Quite unlike the fatalist who claims that human efforts, wills, and deliberations are irrelevant to our actions, the Stoic insists that our actions are up to us because they do depend on our assents and wills, not simply on external causal factors. The Stoic view that our actions depend on our assents is a special case of the main thesis in their doctrine of fate. While that doctrine is a determinist thesis, its main point is to insist on the mutual causal dependence or influence of all things. This relation of mutual causal influence is what the Stoics have in mind when they say that fate is a chain of causes. This view, rather than fatalism, is behind the metaphor of the dog tied to the cart. It is also at the root of Chrysippus's apparent restriction of the thesis of fate to external causes (Cic., *Fat.* 41).

[38] Translated by Long and Sedley (LS 63M); cf. Epictetus, *Discourses* 1.12.20–21 (LS 65V); and Stobaeus, 2.155.5–17 (SVF 3.564, 3.632; LS 65W).
[39] Plato, *Republic*, Books VIII–IX; Aristotle, *Nicomachean Ethics*, Book IX, ch. 4.

While Long and Sedley point out correctly that the restriction is linked to Stoic moral theory, this is only part of the story. I hope to have shown that the insistence on external causes in the doctrine of fate reflects a deep and very important aspect of Stoic thinking about the causal structure of the world: any cause's activity is part of the interconnected causal nexus that the Stoics identify with fate. This interconnectedness is what holds the world together, in their view. To alter Hume's phrase, it is not simply causation but fate that is the cement of the universe.[40]

Philosophy, University of Pennsylvania

---

[40] David Hume, *An Abstract of a Treatise of Human Nature* (1740), in Hume, *A Treatise of Human Nature*, ed. P. H. Nidditch and L. A. Selby-Bigge, 2d ed. (Oxford: Clarendon Press, 1978), 662. In reporting the Stoic view, Philo explicitly uses the metaphor of glue or cement (*Quaestiones et Solutiones in Genesin* 2.4 [SVF 2.802; LS 47R]).

ULTIMATE RESPONSIBILITY AND DUMB LUCK*

By Alfred R. Mele

I. Introduction

My topic lies on conceptual terrain that is quite familiar to philosophers. For others, a bit of background may be in order. In light of what has filtered down from quantum mechanics, few philosophers today believe that the universe is causally deterministic (or "deterministic," for short). That is, to use Peter van Inwagen's succinct definition of "determinism," few philosophers believe that "there is at any instant exactly one physically possible future."[1] Even so, partly for obvious historical reasons, philosophers continue to argue about whether free will and moral responsibility are compatible with determinism. *Compatibilists* argue for compatibility, and *incompatibilists* argue against it. Some incompatibilists maintain that free will and moral responsibility are illusions. But most are *libertarians*, libertarianism being the conjunction of incompatibilism and the thesis that at least some human beings are possessed of free will and moral responsibility.

People sometimes wonder why philosophers who believe that determinism is false *care* about the compatibility question. Those who read on will find a partial answer that has a lot to do with *luck*. For introductory purposes, the sphere of luck (good or bad) for a person may be understood as the sphere of things having the following two properties: the person does not control them; even so, they affect his or her life.

There is in the literature on free will and moral responsibility a notion of *ultimate responsibility* that, by definition, requires the falsity of determinism.[2] Agents are possessed of ultimate responsibility only if they are causally undetermined sources of at least some of their decisions or choices. Believers in ultimate responsibility may link it to *moral* responsibility in a variety of alternative ways, including the following two. It may be held that some human beings are ultimately responsible for some of what they

---

*For written comments on a draft of this essay, I am grateful to Randy Clarke, Ish Haji, Bob Kane, Dave Robb, and the editors of this volume. I am indebted as well to audiences at Wayne State University and Uppsala University.

[1] Peter van Inwagen, *An Essay on Free Will* (Oxford: Clarendon Press, 1983), 3.

[2] See Robert Kane, *The Significance of Free Will* (New York: Oxford University Press, 1996); Kane, *Free Will and Values* (Albany: State University of New York Press, 1985); Martha Klein, *Determinism, Blameworthiness, and Deprivation* (Oxford: Oxford University Press, 1990); and Galen Strawson, "The Impossibility of Moral Responsibility," *Philosophical Studies* 75, no. 1 (Summer 1994): 5–24.

do and that no one is morally responsible for anything unless he or she is ultimately responsible for something or other (*strong UR*). Alternatively, it may be held that some human beings are ultimately responsible for some of what they do and that, even though moral responsibility does not require ultimate responsibility, ultimate responsibility and the moral responsibility it makes possible are more important or more desirable than any compatibilist species of responsibility (*modest UR*). Since few philosophers today believe that determinism is true, few philosophers are likely to advance arguments from the truth of determinism to the non-existence of ultimate responsibility. However, compatibilists and others are likely to wonder how agents can be any more responsible or free in indeterministic universes than in deterministic ones, other things being equal.[3]

Consider two hypotheses about our universe. (1) Either the universe is deterministic or it is indeterministic only in ways that have no significant bearing on human agency and responsibility. (2) The universe is indeterministic in ways that have a significant bearing on human agency and responsibility. Those who believe that at least some of us are possessed of ultimate responsibility accept (2). It is incumbent upon them to explain, among other things, why indeterminism does not *preclude* responsibility, a topic introduced in Section II.

Although I myself am officially agnostic about the dispute between compatibilists and incompatibilists, I take strong UR and modest UR to be interesting and important claims.[4] My aim in this essay is to ascertain whether ultimate responsibility is possible, what may be desirable about ultimate responsibility and incompatibilist freedom, and whether these things may reasonably be valued more highly by some people than compatibilist responsibility and freedom. In Section II, I explore a serious problem about the possibility of ultimate responsibility and incompatibilist freedom—a problem raised by considerations of luck. In Section III, I set the stage for Section IV's argument that some people may reasonably value ultimate responsibility and incompatibilist freedom. In Section V, I offer a solution to the libertarian's problem with luck.

II. A PROBLEM FOR LIBERTARIANS: LUCK

A familiar libertarian claim is that an agent performed an action *A freely* only if she was not causally determined to *A*. (If, as I believe, choosing is

---

[3] This is not the place for a detailed discussion of the connection between moral responsibility and free will (or freedom of choice and action). It suffices for my purposes to observe that it is typically held that only free agents possess moral responsibility. For clarification of this idea, see Alfred Mele, *Autonomous Agents: From Self-Control to Autonomy* (New York: Oxford University Press, 1995), 139–42.

[4] For a discussion of why I am agnostic about the main metaphysical issue that separates compatibilists from incompatibilists, see ibid., chs. 8 and 13.

a mental action,[5] freely choosing is a species of freely acting.) The notion of an agent's not being causally determined to do what she did may be articulated in terms of possible worlds. Here is an illustration from van Inwagen, a well-known libertarian:

> To say that it was not determined that [a certain petty thief] should refrain from stealing is to say this: there is a possible world that (a) is *exactly* like the actual world in every detail up to the moment at which the thief refrained from stealing, and (b) is governed by the same laws of nature as the actual world, and (c) is such that, in it, the thief robbed the poor-box.[6]

Now, in principle, as I have explained elsewhere, a libertarian may grant that agents sometimes are ultimately responsible for actions that they are causally determined to perform.[7] For example, a libertarian may hold that an agent who, partly through his own causally undetermined free actions, has made himself a person of a sort who now is causally determined to A, may be ultimately responsible for A-ing.[8] But even such a libertarian insists that an agent who is ultimately responsible for what he does at *t* either is not causally determined to do what he does at *t* or was not causally determined to do what he did at some relevant earlier time. To facilitate exposition, I introduce a pair of labels: *Basic instances* of action for which an agent is ultimately responsible are causally undetermined actions for which the agent is ultimately responsible. *Nonbasic instances* are causally determined actions, the agent's ultimate responsibility for which depends upon relevant past basic instances (in the same agent).

Return to the case of the petty thief. Given van Inwagen's description of what is required if the thief's refraining is not to be causally determined, one wonders how agents can be morally responsible for what they do when their actions are *not* causally determined. Van Inwagen imagines that "God has thousands of times caused the world to revert to precisely its state at the moment just before the thief decided not to steal" and that "on about half these occasions" the thief refrained from robbing the poor-box.[9] But then, one wonders, why isn't the thief's deciding to refrain from stealing in the actual world a matter of dumb luck, in which case he seems not to be morally responsible for deciding as he does? After all, he

[5] See Alfred Mele, "Agency and Mental Action," *Philosophical Perspectives* 11 (1997): 231–49.
[6] Van Inwagen, *An Essay on Free Will*, 136.
[7] See Mele, *Autonomous Agents*, 208–9.
[8] Robert Kane, a libertarian, adopts this position in *The Significance of Free Will*, 77–78. He endorsed a parallel position about *moral* responsibility for choices (but not about ultimate responsibility for choices) in his "Two Kinds of Incompatibilism," *Philosophy and Phenomenological Research* 50, no. 2 (Winter 1989): 252.
[9] Van Inwagen, *An Essay on Free Will*, 141.

might just as easily have decided to steal the money given exactly the same past up to the time of decision and exactly the same laws of nature: in about half of the divine "reruns," that is precisely what he does.

Van Inwagen suggests that in the actual world, the thief's "refraining from robbing the poor-box (R) was caused but not necessitated by" a certain desire/belief pair.[10] "R was caused by" this desire/belief pair (DB), and "DB did not have to cause R; it just *did*."[11] Van Inwagen suggests, as well, that in those reruns in which the thief steals the money, his stealing was caused by another desire/belief pair.[12] Suppose we grant this; even then, it looks like what the thief does is a matter of luck. It seems to be just a matter of luck that DB causes a refraining rather than that the other desire/belief pair causes a stealing. If the thief had a little randomizing device in his head—perhaps even a randomizer that is a "natural part" of his brain—that gives each of two competing sets of reasons an initial 0.5 chance of prevailing in his present situation, and then randomly issues in the prevailing of one set of reasons, the divine "reruns" would show the distribution that van Inwagen imagines they do.[13] (Picture the device as a tiny, genuinely random roulette wheel, half of whose slots are black and half red. The ball's landing on black represents the prevailing of the thief's reasons for refraining from stealing, and its landing on red represents the other reasons' prevailing.) But in that case, if the thief is not morally responsible for what the device does, it is hard to see how he can be morally responsible (or deserve moral credit or blame) for refraining from stealing in the actual world, or for stealing in the "reruns" in which he steals. At least, it is hard to see how his moral responsibility for refraining or for stealing can extend beyond his moral responsibility for his having the reasons he has at the time. And if his responsibility for having those reasons is supposed to derive from earlier undetermined actions of his (including decidings) in which a randomizer of the kind described plays a central role, the same problem arises at the relevant earlier times.[14]

Perhaps, if we had a relatively robust understanding of what is supposed to be involved in the making of causally undetermined decisions, we would be able to see why they—or some of them—should be regarded as having been made freely and as occurrences for which their agents are morally responsible. Van Inwagen admits that he has no indeterministic theory of free action or free choice.[15] However, in a recent book, another libertarian, Robert Kane, has offered a detailed account of the making of

---

[10] Ibid., 140–41.

[11] Ibid., 141.

[12] Ibid.

[13] Van Inwagen discusses the significance of behavior's proceeding from a "natural part" of the brain in *An Essay on Free Will*, 134–42. On this, see my *Autonomous Agents*, 197–203.

[14] The objection advanced in this paragraph does not depend upon the probabilities that van Inwagen mentions. On this, see my *Autonomous Agents*, 202–3.

[15] Van Inwagen, *An Essay on Free Will*, 149–50.

causally undetermined decisions, partly in response to the very problem sketched here.[16]

In basic instances of ultimate responsibility for a decision, on Kane's view, there is an internal conflict in the agent: for example, a conflict "between what an agent believes ought to be done and what the agent wants or desires to do."[17] If agents' choices or decisions "are not determined in such cases," Kane writes, they "might choose either way, all past circumstances remaining the same up to the moment of choice."[18] He adds:

> The choice in moral and prudential conflict situations terminates an effort (to resist temptation) in one way or another. What is needed is a situation in which the choice is not explained by the prior character and motives alone, or by the prior character and motives plus effort, *even if the prior character and motives can explain the effort*. If such a condition were satisfied, the agent's past character and motives would influence the choice without determining it.[19]

Kane goes on to say: "Some of the agent's reasons or motives (the moral or prudential ones) explain why the agent makes an effort to resist temptation, while others (self-interested motives or desires for present satisfactions) explain why it is such an *effort*."[20]

For Kane, "the effort of will (to resist temptation)" in instances of the kind in question "is (an) *indeterminate* (event or process), thereby making the choice that terminates it *undetermined*."[21] Given the indeterminacy of these efforts to resist temptation, Kane writes,

> one cannot say of two agents that they had exactly the same pasts and made exactly the same efforts and one got lucky while the other did not. Nor can one imagine the same agent in two possible worlds with exactly the same pasts making exactly the same effort and getting lucky in one world and not the other. Exact sameness or difference of possible worlds is not defined if the possible world contains indeterminate efforts or indeterminate events of any kinds. And there would be no such thing as two agents having exactly the same *life*

---

[16] In *The Significance of Free Will* (171–72 and 236–37 n. 1), Kane cites and responds to versions of the "luck" objection advanced in Bruce Waller's "Free Will Gone Out of Control," *Behaviorism* 16, no. 1 (Spring 1988): 149–67, and in Strawson's "The Impossibility of Moral Responsibility." For another useful formulation of the objection, see Thomas Nagel, *The View from Nowhere* (New York: Oxford University Press, 1986), 113–14.

[17] Kane, *The Significance of Free Will*, 126.

[18] Ibid., 127.

[19] Ibid.; Kane's italics.

[20] Ibid., 128.

[21] Ibid.

histories if their life histories contain indeterminate efforts and free choices.[22]

Earlier in his book, Kane had written: "If free will implies ultimate responsibility and underived origination, then it requires that some free actions must be undetermined. They must be capable of occurring or not occurring, given *exactly the same past and laws of nature*."[23] Evidently, he has backed off from this, partly in response to the worry about luck. Does he succeed in laying this worry to rest? I think not.

Consider my friend John. He believes that he ought to arrive on time for a committee meeting today but he is tempted to arrive late, as a modest protest. John tries very hard to resist his temptation, and he has a reasonable chance of succeeding. The committee meeting begins at noon in his building, and he tries to master the temptation right up to noon. His effort fails, however, and he decides to go to the meeting late, thereby making his modest protest. Is John ultimately responsible for the failure of his effort and for his decision to go to the meeting late?

Move to a nearby world with the same laws and with a very similar past—as similar as can be regarding John (or his counterpart), given that he sometimes makes indeterminate efforts of will, including the present effort. Here, too, the agent—call him John$_2$—believes that he ought to arrive on time for the meeting and is tempted to arrive late, for the same reason. Here, too, he tries very hard to resist his temptation, and his effort is indeterminate. But in this world he succeeds. He masters his temptation, decides a minute before noon to show up on time for the meeting, and does so.

If John failed where John$_2$ succeeded because the latter tried harder, or more intelligently, than the former to resist temptation, then we might be inclined to regard John as morally responsible for his failure and John$_2$ as morally responsible for his success. But this is not the line Kane pursues. Obviously, if John's and John$_2$'s cases are to be *basic* instances of ultimate responsibility, then, for Kane, the strength and intelligence of their efforts to resist temptation cannot be any part of something that causally determines the efforts' success or failure. Now, perhaps it can be said that the harder, or more intelligently, people try to resist temptation, the more likely they are to succeed, other things being equal. And it might be said as well that, even if it was not causally determined that a certain agent's effort to resist temptation in the service of a moral judgment succeeded, an agent who tried hard and intelligently to resist—thereby increasing the probability that he would choose to do what he judged best—and succeeded in so doing deserves moral credit for his successful resistance and for the associated moral choice, and is responsible for the success of the effort and for the choice. But what should be said, then, about a very similar agent who also tries very hard and very intelligently to resist a very similar temptation, but fails to resist it? On Kane's view, given that the agents' efforts are "indeterminate," it cannot properly be said that the latter agent (John, perhaps) tried exactly as hard and as intelligently as the former (John$_2$, perhaps). But given that the difference in outcome in the two cases—successful resistance and a subjectively morally proper choice in one, and unsuccessful resistance and a subjectively morally improper choice in the other—is not to be explained by a difference in the amount of effort or in the intelligence of the effort, this alleged implication of the efforts' being indeterminate seems to cut no ice.[24] It looks for all the world as if the unsuccessful agent had bad luck, in which case the successful agent had, at least, *better* luck than his counterpart. If it were not for John's having worse luck than John$_2$, John would have been in John$_2$'s shoes: he would have successfully resisted temptation.

Kane's appeal to the indeterminacy of an effort makes it more difficult to formulate crisply the "objection from luck" to libertarianism. But the spirit of the objection survives. If John's effort to resist temptation fails where John$_2$'s effort succeeds, and there is nothing about the agents' powers, capacities, states of mind, moral character, and the like that explains this difference in outcome, then the difference really is just a matter of luck. That their efforts are indeterminate explains why the outcomes of the efforts might not be the same, but this obviously does not explain (even nondeterministically or probabilistically) why John failed whereas John$_2$ succeeded.

I do not mean to single out Kane's work for critical attention. As I say in a dustjacket comment on his book, his "is, quite simply, the most thoughtful and detailed defense of libertarianism currently available." Any libertarian is faced with some version of the luck problem. And Kane admirably tries to resolve it. However, I suspect that the failure of his effort is due more to the nature of the problem than to any indeterminacy that his effort might have involved.

Libertarians rightly see determinism as precluding agents' having causally open alternatives—that is, alternatives consistent with their past and with the laws of nature. Traditional libertarians maintain that such alternatives are required for free will and moral responsibility. Indeterminism opens up alternatives of this kind, but it also raises a very specific worry about luck in connection with moral responsibility. If there are causally undetermined or indeterminate aspects of a process (e.g., deliberation or

---

[24] Timothy O'Connor suggests that the agents are in "states having the same properties within the same value *intervals*"; see O'Connor, "Why Agent Causation?" *Philosophical Topics* 24, no. 2 (Fall 1996): 156. However, Kane can reply that even if this is true, it is false that the agents try exactly as hard and intelligently, insofar as it is false that there is a precise degree of effort and a precise degree of intelligence that both attempts to resist temptation exemplify.

an effort to resist temptation) that issues or culminates in a choice—aspects that are present at the very time the choice is made and are directly relevant to the process's outcome—then, to the extent that the agent is not in control of these aspects, luck enters the picture in a significant way. John and John$_2$ may coherently be imagined not to differ in the control they exert over their respective efforts, or to differ in control only in ways that are themselves a matter of luck. But then John's succumbing to temptation, whereas John$_2$ successfully resists temptation, appears to be a matter of luck.[25] Again, if John had had John$_2$'s luck, he would successfully have resisted temptation. This is a perfectly general problem—a problem for any libertarian who locates the indeterminism or indeterminacy required for basic instances of ultimate responsibility in the making of a choice at the moment at which the choice is made.[26]

One may be tempted to conclude that ultimate responsibility is impossible. It may seem that in opening the door for the basic *ultimacy* of a choice by supposing that the choice is not causally determined, one inevitably lets in luck that precludes the agent's being morally *responsible* for the choice. Things are not always as they seem, however. To distinguish appearance from reality here, one needs, among other things, to ascertain what the value of ultimacy is in ultimate responsibility.

III. Ultimacy and Alternative Possibilities

It is natural to suppose that the "ultimacy" component of ultimate responsibility requires being able to act (including being able to choose) otherwise than one does. However, this supposition is questionable. Consider what Harry Frankfurt has called "the principle of alternate possibilities":

> *PAP.* A person is morally responsible for what he has done only if he could have done otherwise.[27]

---

[25] Notice that this does not imply, for example, that it is just a matter of luck that John$_2$ decided to go to the meeting on time. After all, his effort to resist the temptation to go late might have significantly increased the probability that he would decide to go on time. What is just a matter of luck is a certain comparative fact—that John$_2$'s effort culminated in this decision whereas John's terminated in a decision to go to the meeting late. John simply had worse luck than John$_2$ in this connection.

[26] We are disinclined to deem people responsible for the immediate consequences of their bad luck, unless they are somehow responsible for being subject to a pertinent instance of such luck. However, one who holds that John is not responsible for succumbing to temptation may nevertheless contend that John$_2$ *is* responsible for successfully resisting temptation. Consideration of the asymmetrical position on responsibility that this contention suggests—a position that Kane implicitly eschews (*The Significance of Free Will*, 179–80)—is beyond the scope of this essay.

[27] Harry Frankfurt, "Alternate Possibilities and Moral Responsibility," *Journal of Philosophy* 66, no. 23 (December 1969): 829.

If Frankfurt's well-known attack on *PAP* is successful, alternative possibilities of the kind that proponents of *PAP* typically have had in mind are not required for what I have called "basic instances" of ultimate responsibility, and hence are not required for ultimate responsibility at all.

Let me explain, starting with a famous example of Frankfurt's:

> Suppose someone—Black, let us say—wants Jones to perform a certain action. Black is prepared to go to considerable lengths to get his way, but he prefers to avoid showing his hand unnecessarily. So he waits until Jones is about to make up his mind what to do, and he does nothing unless it is clear to him (Black is an excellent judge of such things) that Jones is going to decide to do something *other* than what he wants him to do. If it does become clear that Jones is going to decide to do something else, Black takes effective steps to ensure that Jones decides to do, and that he does do, what he wants him to do. Whatever Jones's initial preferences and inclinations, then, Black will have his way. . . . [However,] Black never has to show his hand because Jones, for reasons of his own, decides to perform and does perform the very action Black wants him to perform.[28]

For the sake of specificity, suppose that what Jones decided to do was to steal from a certain poor-box. By hypothesis, Jones could not have avoided so deciding. If Frankfurt's scenario is coherent, then, other things being equal (e.g., Jones is sane and is not a compulsive thief), it is plausible that Jones is morally responsible for deciding to steal the money. After all, he decided on his own to do this, with no interference from Black. And, assuming coherence, this is plausible even though, at the time, Jones could not have done otherwise than decide to steal the money.

As I explained earlier, a libertarian may grant that agents sometimes freely perform—and are ultimately responsible for—actions that they are causally determined to perform. Such a libertarian may endorse a modified version of *PAP* which incorporates a historical condition—for example:

> *PAPh.* S is morally responsible for what he did at *t* only if (1) he could have done otherwise at *t*, or (2) even though he could not have done otherwise at *t*, the psychological character on the basis of which he acted at *t* is itself partially a product of an earlier action (or actions) of his which was performed at a time when he could have done otherwise.[29]

---

[28] Ibid., 835–36. In reproducing this passage, I deleted a subscript after "Jones."

[29] In *Autonomous Agents*, I suggest that libertarians should prefer a historical condition of this kind to *PAP* (208–9). Kane recently advanced a view of this kind (*The Significance of Free Will*, 39–43, 77–78).

However, if Frankfurt-style counterexamples to *PAP* are successful, they can succeed in alleged basic instances of ultimate responsibility as well. Indeed, one can imagine extended, *global* Frankfurt-style scenarios in which at any relevant earlier time, the agent performs action *A* "on his own" (where action *A* may be a "deciding") but could not have done otherwise than *A*, owing to the presence of a counterfactual controller.[30]

The coherence of Frankfurt-style examples has been called into question in recent years.[31] David Robb and I have developed a way of preserving the full force of this style of example while avoiding the problems with Frankfurt's own way of spinning the stories.[32] Space constraints preclude reopening the argument here. I will simply assume that a variant of Frankfurt's case does falsify *PAP* on a standard interpretation of alternative possibilities and forge ahead. (Although the position advanced in this essay does not *depend* on the coherence of Frankfurt-style objections to *PAP* and *PAPh*, the objections are useful in clarifying what some believers in ultimate responsibility might reasonably find valuable in such responsibility.)

My assumption requires a brief explanation. On a standard interpretation, the alternative possibilities at issue in *PAP* are alternative *actions*, including intentional refrainings and instances of deciding or choosing.[33] Moreover, these possibilities are actions like stealing from a poor-box and deciding not to steal from a poor-box, as opposed to more refined actions like "*S*'s stealing from a poor-box without having been made to do so by someone else" and "*S*'s deciding not to steal from a poor-box because Black made *S* decide not to do so." I have offered a more formal way of

[30] See Alfred Mele, "Soft Libertarianism and Frankfurt-Style Scenarios," *Philosophical Topics* 24, no. 2 (Fall 1996): 123–41. Cf. John Fischer, *The Metaphysics of Free Will* (Oxford: Blackwell, 1994), 214; Mele, *Autonomous Agents*, 141; Ishtiyaque Haji, "Moral Responsibility and the Problem of Induced Pro-Attitudes," *Dialogue* 35, no. 4 (Fall 1996): 707; and Kane, *The Significance of Free Will*, 42–43, 143. A "counterfactual controller" is an agent who would have successfully intervened under certain conditions but did not intervene in the actual circumstances.

[31] See James Lamb, "Evaluative Compatibilism and the Principle of Alternate Possibilities," *Journal of Philosophy* 90, no. 10 (October 1993): 517–27; David Widerker, "Libertarianism and Frankfurt's Attack on the Principle of Alternative Possibilities," *Philosophical Review* 104, no. 2 (Spring 1995): 247–61; Widerker, "Libertarian Freedom and the Avoidability of Decisions," *Faith and Philosophy* 12, no. 1 (Winter 1995): 113–18; and Kane, *The Significance of Free Will*, 142–43, 191–92.

[32] See Alfred Mele and David Robb, "Rescuing Frankfurt-Style Cases," *Philosophical Review* 107, no. 1 (January 1998): 97–112. For other replies to recent objections to Frankfurt-style cases, see John Fischer and Paul Hoffman, "Alternative Possibilities: A Reply to Lamb," *Journal of Philosophy* 91, no. 6 (June 1994): 321–26; John Fischer, "Libertarianism and Avoidability: A Reply to Widerker," *Faith and Philosophy* 12, no. 1 (Winter 1995): 119–25; and Eleonore Stump, "Libertarian Freedom and the Principle of Alternative Possibilities," in *Faith, Freedom, and Rationality*, ed. Jeff Jordan and Daniel Howard-Snyder (Lanham, MD: Rowman and Littlefield, 1996), 73–88.

[33] Depending on how refraining is to be understood, "intentional refraining" may be redundant.

articulating the standard interpretation elsewhere; the brief remarks just made will suffice for present purposes.[34]

Now, if *PAP* and *PAPh*, on the standard interpretation of alternative possibilities, are falsified by some Frankfurt-style cases, then a thief need not be able to have chosen otherwise than to steal from a poor-box in order to be morally responsible for his choice to steal and his stealing. Moreover, on the present assumption, he need not ever have been able to choose otherwise than he did at any point in his life, on the standard interpretation of choosing otherwise, in order to be morally responsible for his present choice and action. But notice that this is not to say that moral responsibility is compatible with *determinism*. For a traditional incompatibilist about determinism and moral responsibility, an agent's being deterministically caused to *A* suffices for his not being morally responsible for *A*-ing. So if Frankfurt-style cases are to persuade traditional incompatibilists that agents can be morally responsible for stealing from a poor-box, say, even though they could not have done otherwise, it must be a feature of these examples that the agents' stealing was not deterministically caused. In principle, a libertarian's incompatibilism might be motivated, not by the thought that determinism precludes our ever having been able to do otherwise than we did, but instead by the thought that in a deterministic world our actions (including our decisions) are ultimately causally ensured *consequences* of the laws of nature and states that obtained long before we were born.[35]

Consider the incompatibilist's "consequence argument" in this connection:

> If determinism is true, then our acts are the consequences of the laws of nature and events in the remote past. But it is not up to us what went on before we were born, and neither is it up to us what the laws of nature are. Therefore, the consequences of these things (including our present acts) are not up to us.[36]

Whatever the merits of this argument may be, the assumed success of Frankfurt-style cases at falsifying *PAP* and *PAPh* does not directly constitute a proof that the "consequence argument" is unsound. Theorists who hold that determinism is inconsistent with agents' actions being up to them in a sense required for moral responsibility and freedom might

---

[34] Mele, "Soft Libertarianism and Frankfurt-Style Scenarios," 126–27.

[35] Cf. John Fischer, "Responsibility and Control," *Journal of Philosophy* 79, no. 1 (January 1982): 24–40; Robert Heinaman, "Incompatibilism without the Principle of Alternative Possibilities," *Australasian Journal of Philosophy* 64, no. 3 (Fall 1986): 266–76; Klein, *Determinism, Blameworthiness, and Deprivation*, ch. 3; and Derk Pereboom, "Determinism al Dente," *Noûs* 29, no. 1 (Spring 1995): 21–45.

[36] Van Inwagen, *An Essay on Free Will*, 16. For detailed versions, see ibid., ch. 3; and Carl Ginet, *On Action* (Cambridge: Cambridge University Press, 1990), ch. 5.

consistently hold on to that belief while granting that Frankfurt-style cases do prove *PAP* and *PAPh* false.[37] Their grudge against determinism need not be that it precludes alternative possibilities (standardly interpreted). After all, there is a significant difference between Frankfurt-style counterfactual controllers and deterministic causes, even if both preclude alternative possibilities, standardly interpreted. The former play no role at all in *causing* the agent's choice, but in deterministic worlds actions do have deterministic causes.

Evidently, the truth of determinism would preclude the ultimacy component of ultimate responsibility simply in virtue of the fact that, if our world is deterministic, causally sufficient conditions for everything we do are present long before we are born. Ultimately, we and our actions would be deterministic products of states of the world in the distant past over which we had no control. Now, that does not bother me much; but perhaps it should, and it certainly bothers libertarians a great deal. If we can understand why someone might reasonably be bothered by the absence of the ultimacy component of ultimate responsibility, perhaps we can find a theoretically useful place for indeterminism in an ultimately responsible agent—in particular, a place where indeterminism does not bring with it responsibility-precluding *luck*.

IV. A Desire for Ultimacy

Normally, if an individual has an intrinsic preference that is neither incoherent nor otherwise irrational and that coheres with her beliefs and other preferences, we are inclined to be open-minded about that intrinsic preference, even if we ourselves do not share it. Suppose someone were to tell you that she intrinsically values possessing a kind of freedom that is not possible in a deterministic universe. She says that her life would hold more meaning or importance for her if she were to discover that she has this kind of freedom than it would if she were to discover that she has only compatibilist freedom. And she reports that she intrinsically values a certain kind of incompatibilist freedom as an essential constituent of a life that, by her own standards, would be more meaningful or important than a comparable life in a deterministic world.[38]

Intellectually curious and reflective person that you are, you want to hear more. You ask the woman, Wilma, what bothers her about determinism. She replies that although she takes the "consequence argument"

---

[37] In *The Metaphysics of Free Will*, Fischer argues that such theorists must resort to something akin to alchemy (ch. 7; see p. 141 for the alchemy analogy). For a reply, see my "Soft Libertarianism and Frankfurt-Style Scenarios."

[38] Cf. Kane, *Free Will and Values*, 178: "[W]hat determinism takes away is a certain sense of the importance of oneself as an individual. If I am ultimately responsible for certain occurrences in the universe, . . . then my choices and my life take on an importance that is missing if I do not have such responsibility."

(described in the preceding section) to be unsound, her worry about determinism resembles the worry voiced there. Again you would like to hear more, and Wilma kindly obliges.

Wilma says that she is attracted to what I have elsewhere called "soft libertarianism."[39] A brief statement of that position will prove useful. Traditional libertarians about freedom of choice and action and about moral responsibility are hard-line incompatibilists. They claim that these freedoms (which they believe at least some human beings possess) are incompatible with determinism, and they take the same view about moral responsibility. I call them *hard* libertarians. A softer line is available to philosophers who have libertarian sympathies. A theorist may leave it open that freedom and moral responsibility are compatible with determinism, but maintain that the falsity of determinism is required for *more desirable* brands of these things. This is a *soft* libertarian line, the line Wilma finds attractive. Soft libertarians would be disappointed to discover that determinism is true, but they would not conclude that no one has ever acted or chosen freely and that no one has ever been morally responsible for anything. The version of soft libertarianism that Wilma favors is relativistic: it maintains that at least some human agents are possessed of kinds of freedom and moral responsibility that are incompatible with determinism and are reasonably preferred *by at least some of these agents* to any kind of freedom or moral responsibility that is consistent with determinism.

Wilma reports that the thought of herself and her actions as links in a deterministic causal chain is somewhat deflating and that the truth of determinism is inconsistent with her life's being as important and meaningful as she hopes it is. The thought that she is an indeterministic initiator of at least some of her deliberative, intentional actions, however, coheres with the importance and significance she hopes her life has.[40] Asked to elaborate, Wilma observes that *independence* is among the things that some people intrinsically value. Some people value independence, in some measure, from other people and from institutions. Wilma values, as well, a measure of independence from the *past*. She values, she says, a kind of independent agency that includes the power to make a special kind of explanatory contribution to some of her actions and to her world — contributions that are not themselves ultimately causally determined products of the state of the universe in the distant past. She values having an explanatory bearing on her conduct that she would lack in any deterministic world. She prizes indeterministic freedom as an essential part of a

[39] Mele, "Soft Libertarianism and Frankfurt-Style Scenarios." In this paragraph, I borrow from p. 123 of that paper.

[40] In *The Significance of Free Will*, Kane contends that "the desire to be independent sources of activity in the world, which is connected . . . to the sense we have of our uniqueness and importance as individuals," is an "elemental" libertarian desire (98). Here I am following his lead.

life that she regards as most desirable for her. The kind of agency she hopes for, Wilma says, would render her decisions and actions personally more meaningful from the perspective of her own system of values than they would otherwise be. Although Wilma emphasizes that this kind of agency is essential to the kind of meaningful life she prizes, she reminds us that she is not claiming that it is required for freedom or moral responsibility. Wilma is not a traditional incompatibilist; rather, she holds that determinism is incompatible with the satisfaction of some of her deepest life-hopes.[41] Her satisfying those hopes requires that she have *ultimate* responsibility for some of her actions.

Some people might value the kind of agency Wilma values because they prize a kind of *credit* for their accomplishments that they regard as more weighty than compatibilist credit.[42] Wilma says that although she respects this attitude, she does not share it. Her personal concern is not with pluses and minuses in a cosmic ledger, but with the exercises of agency to which these marks are assigned. It is not credit that interests her, she says, but independence. More fully, it is independence as manifested in decision and overt action. Wilma acknowledges that she values compatibilist independence, but she reports that she values indeterministic independence more highly—provided that it brings with it no less *nonultimate* control than she would have should determinism be true. (She takes the problem of luck explored in Section II quite seriously.)

Wilma is trying, she says, to understand why some people might not share her preference for libertarian independence over a compatibilist counterpart. She reports that she is keeping an open mind, and she urges us to do the same. Wilma hopes that we can understand why, other things being equal, she would deem her life more important or meaningful if she were to discover that determinism is false than if she were to discover that it is true.

To be sure, Wilma may never know whether she has or lacks the agency she prizes, but that does not undermine her preferences. I hope that I will never know how my children's lives turned out (for then their lives would have been cut too short); but I place considerable value on their turning out well. There is nothing irrational in this. Nor need there be anything irrational in Wilma's prizing her having a kind of agency that she can never know she has.

V. A Soft Libertarian Response to the Problem of Luck

A suitable indeterminism would remove the bar that determinism constitutes for ultimate responsibility. But, as I explained in Section II, at a

---

[41] On life-hopes, see Ted Honderich, *A Theory of Determinism* (Oxford: Clarendon Press, 1988).
[42] See Kane, *The Significance of Free Will*, 98.

certain popular location in processes leading to decision, indeterminism raises a difficult problem about luck. Is there a location for indeterminism (and indeterminacy, if one wants it) that would open the door to our having the ultimacy component of ultimate moral responsibility without also letting in luck that seemingly precludes moral responsibility?

Agents' *control* is the yardstick by which the bearing of luck on their freedom and moral responsibility is measured.[43] When luck is problematic, that is because it seems significantly to impede agents' control over themselves. Now, sometimes it is claimed that agents have no control at all if determinism is true. That claim clearly is false. When I drive my car around town (under normal conditions), I am in control of the turns it makes, even if our world happens to be deterministic. I certainly am in control of my car's movements in a way in which my passengers and others are not. A distinction can be drawn between compatibilist or "non-ultimate" control and a species of control that might be available to agents in some indeterministic worlds—"ultimate" control. I certainly have the former kind of control over my car, and I might have the latter kind as well. It merits mention that ultimate control might turn out to be remarkably similar to the phenomenon that many compatibilists have in mind; the key to its being *ultimate* control might be its indeterministic setting.[44] If this last remark seems somewhat cryptic now, it will become clearer as this section progresses.

Agency of the sort that Wilma prizes is incompatible with determinism. But what, exactly, should she want to be causally undetermined, given the agency she values? Should she hope that there is an indeterministic connection between her decisions and her actions, for example—or between her judging it best to do something and her deciding to do it? Wilma reports that she has no wish for indeterminism at these locations. Being subject to weakness of will, she says, is bad enough; she has no wish for additional ways of failing to act as she decides to act or of failing to decide to do what she judges it best to do.[45] However, Wilma suggests, the capacity to make some causally undetermined practical judgments is attractive.

The basic thrust of Wilma's positive suggestion is not difficult to capture. Suppose that S, on the basis of careful, rational deliberation, judges it best, all things considered, to A. And suppose that, on the basis of that judgment, she decides to A and then acts accordingly, intentionally A-ing. Suppose further that S has not been subjected to autonomy-thwarting mind control or relevant deception, that she is perfectly sane, and so on.

---

[43] The connection between control and "moral luck" is a major theme in Thomas Nagel's "Moral Luck," in his *Mortal Questions* (Cambridge: Cambridge University Press, 1979), 24–38.

[44] Cf. my *Autonomous Agents*, 213.

[45] Cf. ibid., 203. Wilma and I regard weakness of will as compatible with determinism (see ibid., 132–33).

To make a long story short, suppose that she satisfies an attractive set of sufficient conditions for *compatibilist* freedom and moral responsibility regarding her A-ing.[46] Now add one more supposition to the set: while S was deliberating, it was not causally determined that she would come to the conclusion she did. If this further supposition can be added to the mix without entailing that S would have less control over her deliberation — and over what, if anything, she judges best — than she would have in a relevantly similar deterministic world in which she satisfies the conditions for compatibilist freedom and responsibility regarding her A-ing, then soft libertarians should be able to handle the problem that luck (good and bad) poses for them in a way that proves acceptable at least to *compatibilist* believers in freedom and moral responsibility. Again, agents' control is what measures the bearing of luck on freedom and moral responsibility. If indeterministic luck does not render S any less in control of her conduct than her deterministic counterpart is in control of the counterpart's conduct, then S is no less free and responsible than the counterpart.

In principle, an agent-internal indeterminism may provide for indeterministic agency while blocking or limiting our control over what happens only at junctures at which we would have no greater control on the hypothesis that our world is deterministic.[47] Ordinary human beings have a wealth of beliefs, desires, hypotheses, and the like, the great majority of which are not salient in consciousness during any given process of deliberation. Plainly, in those cases in which we act on the basis of careful deliberation, what we do is influenced by at least some of the considerations that "come to mind" — that is, become salient in consciousness — during deliberation and by our assessments of considerations. Now, even if determinism is true, it is false that, with respect to *every* consideration — every belief, desire, hypothesis, and so on — that comes to mind during our deliberation, we are in control of its coming to mind; and some considerations that come to mind without our being in control of their so doing may influence the outcome of our deliberation. Furthermore, a kind of internal indeterminism is imaginable that limits our control only in a way that gives us no less control than we would have on the assumption that determinism is true, while opening up alternative deliberative outcomes. (Although, in a deterministic world, it would never be a matter of genuine chance that a certain consideration came to mind during deliberation, it may still be a matter of luck relative to the agent's sphere of control.) As I put it elsewhere: "Where compatibilists have no good reason to insist on determinism in the deliberative process as a requirement for autonomy [or freedom of choice and action], where in-

---

[46] I develop sufficient conditions for compatibilist freedom in *Autonomous Agents*, chs. 9 and 10.

[47] See my *Autonomous Agents*, ch. 12; cf. Daniel Dennett, *Brainstorms* (Montgomery, VT: Bradford Books, 1978), 294–99, and Kane, *Free Will and Values*, 101–10.

ternal indeterminism is, for all we know, a reality, and where such indeterminism would not diminish the nonultimate control that real agents
exert over their deliberation even on the assumption that real agents are
internally deterministic—that is, at the *intersection* of these three locations—
libertarians may plump for ultimacy-promoting indeterminism."[48]

I develop this idea at some length in chapter 12 of my book *Autonomous
Agents*. Space constraints preclude much elaboration here, but I should at
least point out that the modest indeterminism at issue allows agents
ample control over their deliberation. Suppose a belief, hypothesis, or
desire that is relevant to a deliberator's present practical question comes
to mind during deliberation, but was not causally determined to do so
(perhaps unlike the great majority of considerations that come to mind
during this process of deliberation).[49] Presumably, a normal agent would
be able to *assess* this consideration. And upon reflection, she might rationally reject the belief as unwarranted, rationally judge that the hypothesis
does not merit investigation, or rationally decide that the desire should be
given little or no weight in her deliberation. Alternatively, reflection might
rationally lead her to retain the belief, to pursue the hypothesis, or to give
the desire significant weight. That a consideration comes to mind indeterministically does not entail that the agent has no control over how she
responds to it.

Compatibilists who hold that we act freely and morally responsibly
even when we are not in control of what happens at certain specific
junctures in the process leading to action are in no position to hold that
an indeterministic agent's lacking control at the same junctures precludes
her acting freely and morally responsibly. And, again, real human beings
are not in control of the coming to mind of everything that comes to mind
during typical processes of deliberation. If this lack of perfect control does
not preclude its being the case that free actions, and actions for which we
are morally responsible, sometimes issue from typical deliberation on the
assumption that we are deterministic agents, it also does not preclude this
on the assumption that we are *indeterministic* agents. So compatibilists
who do not insist that freedom and moral responsibility *require* the truth
of determinism—and most contemporary compatibilists do not[50]—can
lend a sympathetic ear to soft libertarians who plump for indeterminism

---

[48] Mele, *Autonomous Agents*, 235. On the relative theoretical utility of internal versus
external indeterminism, see ibid., 195–96.

[49] Regarding the parenthetical clause, bear in mind that not all causally determined
events need be part of a deterministic chain that stretches back even for several moments,
much less to the Big Bang.

[50] Around the middle of the present century, the claim that determinism is required for
these properties was relatively popular among compatibilists. See A. J. Ayer, "Freedom and
Necessity," in Ayer, *Philosophical Essays* (London: Macmillan, 1954); R. E. Hobart, "Free Will
as Involving Determinism and as Inconceivable without It," *Mind* 43, no. 169 (January 1934):
1–27; P. H. Nowell-Smith, "Free Will and Moral Responsibility," *Mind* 57, no. 225 (January
1948): 45–61; and J. J. C. Smart, "Free-Will, Praise, and Blame," *Mind* 70, no. 279 (July 1961):
291–306.

at junctures in action-producing processes at which we would have no greater control on the assumption that we are deterministic agents, provided that they can understand why these libertarians hope for such indeterminism.[51] Indeterministic luck (good or bad) at these junctures does not entail any less control than real agents have if their world is deterministic.

Is a modest indeterminism of the kind I have sketched useful to soft libertarians? I have suggested that what at least some soft libertarians might prize (that compatibilist freedom and responsibility do not offer them) is a species of agency that gives them a kind of independence and an associated kind of explanatory bearing on their conduct that they would lack in any deterministic world. The combination of the satisfaction of an attractive set of sufficient conditions for *compatibilist* freedom of choice and action, including all the agential control that involves, and a modest agent-internal indeterminism of the sort I have described would give them that. Agents of the imagined sort would make choices and perform actions that lack deterministic causes in the distant past. They would have no less control over these choices and actions than we do over ours, on the assumption that we are deterministic agents. And given that they have at least robust *compatibilist* responsibility for certain of these choices and actions, they would also have *ultimate* responsibility for them. For, in Kane's words, these choices and actions "have their ultimate sources in" the agents, in the sense that the collection of agent-internal states and events that explains these choices and actions does not itself admit of a deterministic explanation that stretches back beyond the agent.[52]

Now, even if garden-variety compatibilists can be led to see that the problem of luck is surmountable by a soft libertarian, how are theorists of other kinds likely to respond to the soft-libertarian line on luck that I have been sketching? There are, of course, philosophers who contend that moral responsibility and freedom are illusions and that we lack these properties whether our world is deterministic or indeterministic.[53] Elsewhere, I have argued that the impossible demands this position places on moral responsibility and freedom are *unwarranted* demands.[54] I will not rehearse the arguments here.

Soft libertarians can also anticipate trouble from traditional libertarians, who want more than the modest indeterminism that I have described can offer. It is incumbent upon traditional libertarians to show that what they want is coherent. And that requires showing that what they want does not

[51] Compatibilists who grant that soft libertarianism is a coherent position may have to abandon certain of their arguments against *hard* libertarianism (see my "Soft Libertarianism and Frankfurt-Style Scenarios," 136–39), but other arguments are still in the running.
[52] Kane, *The Significance of Free Will*, 98.
[53] See, e.g., Richard Double, *The Non-Reality of Free Will* (New York: Oxford University Press, 1991); and Galen Strawson, *Freedom and Belief* (Oxford: Clarendon Press, 1986).
[54] Mele, *Autonomous Agents*, chs. 12 and 13.

entail or presuppose a kind of luck that would itself undermine moral responsibility.[55] The traditional libertarian wants both indeterminism and significant control at the moment of choice or decision. This is the desire that prompts the worry about luck developed in Section II.

It should be observed in this connection that Kane's indeterministic picture has an important drawback that the indeterministic picture I have sketched lacks. Once an indeterminate effort to resist temptation has ended, there is no opportunity for the agent to exert any further control over what decision she makes. A failed effort simply is one that "terminates" in a decision to pursue the tempting course of action, whereas a successful one more happily terminates in a decision to do what one believes one ought.[56] However, considerations that indeterministically come to mind (like considerations that deterministically come to mind) are nothing more than input to deliberation. Their coming to mind has, at most, an indirect effect on what the agent decides, an effect that is mediated by the agent's own assessment of them. Unlike failed or successful Kanean efforts, they do not settle matters. Moreover, not only do agents have the opportunity to assess these considerations, they also have the opportunity to search for additional relevant considerations before they decide, thereby increasing the probability that other relevant considerations will indeterministically come to mind. *Prior to deciding*, they have the opportunity to cancel or attenuate the effects of bad luck (e.g., the undetermined coming-to-mind of a misleading consideration, or an undetermined failure to notice a relevant consideration). Regarding luck, Kanean efforts to resist temptation are quite different: again, bad luck, for example, simply *is* the effort's terminating in a decision that conflicts with what one believes one ought to do. And I know of no hard-libertarian solution to the problem of luck that is superior to Kane's attempted solution.

VI. Conclusion

Perhaps some day a traditional libertarian will find a way to lay perplexing worries about luck to rest. I have no desire to try to close the door on that possibility; the critical element of this essay is intended to challenge hard libertarians to do better than they have thus far on this score. Until then, however, we can at least understand how someone may co-

---

[55] Just as I distinguished between ultimate and nonultimate control, one may distinguish between ultimate and nonultimate *luck*. Suppose that millions of years ago, in a deterministic universe, conditions were such that today Teresa would be an exceptionally kind person whereas Tammy would be a ruthless killer. Here we have ultimate luck—good and bad. Libertarians have been much more impressed by it than by nonultimate luck.

[56] Kane, *The Significance of Free Will*, 127. This does not preclude the agent's later reconsidering the matter and coming to a different decision, in the case of decisions for the non-immediate future.

herently value ultimate responsibility and the kind of freedom and moral responsibility it makes possible more highly than she values compatibilist species of responsibility and freedom; and we can understand, as well, why the luck involved in at least one imaginable kind of indeterministic agency (the kind of agency sketched in the preceding section) can promote "ultimacy" without depriving agents of freedom and responsibility.

I have not argued that a soft-libertarian position on freedom and ultimate responsibility is *true*, but I have offered grounds for the judgment that it is *coherent*. Soft libertarians share a significant burden with other libertarians: they are committed to the view that we (or at least some of us) enjoy an incompatibilist brand of freedom and moral responsibility, a brand that requires us to function indeterministically in a way that promotes these valued properties. (Of course, hard libertarians claim that incompatibilist brands are the *only* brands of these properties.) The jury is still out on whether we in fact enjoy a suitably indeterministic agency. Even if determinism is false, it might turn out that we are indeterministic only in ways that have no important bearing on our agency. But should that be so, soft libertarians would still have compatibilist freedom and moral responsibility to fall back on.

Philosophy, Davidson College

TAKING RESPONSIBILITY FOR OUR EMOTIONS

By Nancy Sherman

I. Introduction

We often hold people morally responsible for their emotions. We praise individuals for their compassion, think less of them for their ingratitude or hatred, reproach self-righteousness and unjust anger. In the cases I have in mind, the ascriptions of responsibility are not simply for offensive behaviors or actions which may accompany the emotions, but for the emotions themselves as motives or states of mind. We praise and blame people for what they feel and not just for how they act. In cases where people may subtly mask their hatred or ingratitude through more kindly actions, we still may find fault with the attitude we see leaking through the disguise.

If there is doubt among both lay and philosophical observers about the legitimacy of our moral practice, I suspect it is because we are unsure of just how emotions involve agency and control.[1] Some emotions flood us, often unconsciously or against our will. We fall in love without wanting to; we find ourselves angry when we wish we were forgiving; we hold onto sibling rivalries long after we cease to see their point. Other emotions seem more our doing, watched over and modulated by our agency. We nurture our capacity for intimate love in the context of ongoing relationships and a will to love in certain ways; we often know how to nip unjustified anger in the bud; we can catch overweening pride and curb it. Emotions are a motley class; they include some that seem clearly to bear the labor of our will, and others that seem merely to happen to us.

Despite the different ways that we view our emotional experience, I want to argue for a limited claim of moral responsibility for emotions based on the notion of "emotional agency." Drawing on developmental literature in psychology, I shall argue that many popular and traditional views of emotions as devoid of all agency are simply misguided. From earliest infancy, we regulate and manage many of our emotions in a way that gives credence to the notion of emotional agency. This is not to say that emotions are no different from actions or that they are subject to will

---

[1] For a helpful summary of positions on moral responsibility, see John Fischer and Mark Ravizza's introduction to their anthology *Perspectives on Moral Responsibility* (Ithaca: Cornell University Press, 1993). It is important to note that the notion of reactive attitudes which Peter Strawson develops in his classic essay "Freedom and Resentment" (reprinted in the above volume) includes the notion of praise and blame for emotional attitudes as well as actions.

in the same way. The claim is, rather, that agency mediates the development of many emotions, that there are intentional bids on the part of infants for parental intervention in regulating affect, that parental responsiveness becomes a precursor to children's own intentional self-regulation. The notion of all emotions as purely passive receptivities (i.e., capacities through which we passively experience the world) is simply false. In many of our emotional experiences, from childhood onward, we are, to some degree, agents in the mediation of those experiences. Similarly, psychoanalytic theory suggests possibilities for modifying and mollifying emotions that point to a more robust conception of emotional change and agency in adult life than we often acknowledge.

Still, the notion of emotional agency may strike some as a strange one. There is, of course, a weaker position which some have supported, a position that allows the practice of praise and blame for emotions without assumptions of agency. Just as we can be proud or ashamed for things that belong to us, which we are not strictly speaking responsible for, so too our emotions can fall within that wider orbit of what it is appropriate to esteem or disesteem in a person. As Larry Blum has put it, though we are passive with regard to the emotions, they nonetheless "morally reflect" on us.[2] The idea is familiar enough in the notion of pride for one's children's accomplishments, pride or shame in one's people or nation. The idea of collective responsibility may similarly hang on this extended notion of belonging. Emotions could be like this—part of one's character in the more extended sense of things which one identifies with and "owns," but which one does not directly or indirectly will. In a provocative essay, Robert Adams has argued for a similar point: that there are involuntary sins for which we may nonetheless be blameworthy. Thus, for example, unjust anger, lack of compassion, spite and malice toward others, where these are understood not as a matter of acting in certain ways but as ways of being, may not be under one's control, though they are states for which one is ethically accountable.[3]

But I want to dispute the view that we must begin with emotions as primarily forms of passivity. The task of my essay is to construct a viable sense in which we are frequently, even if not purely or completely, agents of our emotional experiences. The point here is that there is a continuum between agency and passivity, between willing and being affected. Agency

---

[2] Lawrence Blum, *Friendship, Altruism, and Morality* (New York: Routledge, 1980), 160–207. See also Justin Oakley's valuable discussion of this position, in Oakley, *Morality and the Emotions* (New York: Routledge, 1992), 160–90.

[3] Robert Adams, "Involuntary Sins," *The Philosophical Review* 94, no. 3 (1985). Adams's account includes an important criterion of "ethical appreciation" in virtue of which we are held accountable for emotions. However, insofar as that ethical appreciation is for data we may be unconscious of (even though we should have been sensitive to it), accountability for moral perception is still not within the province of the voluntary. My view, developed in the last part of this essay, is that there are ways that we can be active and responsible even with regard to our unconscious perceptions and emotions.

comes in degrees, in the more or less. To conceive of emotional experience as fully on the side of passivity is to misconstrue what it is like to have and live with emotions. In arguing that emotions can be subject to moral ascription in virtue of a limited conception of emotional agency, I follow Aristotle's general view.

On that view, character is composed of stable and enduring states that dispose us well toward both action and emotion. To be virtuous requires that we choose well, but also that we have the right feelings. We must hit the mean with regard to both, and we are praised and blamed with regard to both aspects of our character. But this raises the question of how we can be held responsible for emotional bearing. In what sense do we choose how we feel? Aristotle's implicit answer is that we may not be able to choose how we will emotionally react to something at a given desired moment, but that we indirectly contribute, through previous actions and habits, to our emotional dispositions. Just as we become just through performing just actions and temperate through performing temperate actions, so too we develop feelings of liberality or friendliness through past patterns of behavior and affect. Moreover, on Aristotle's view, capacities for emotion and choice are not disconnected in the constitution of character. Capacities for wise choice rest on moral perception. And emotions are, among other things, epistemic capacities that allow us to track moral salience. To the extent that we are responsible for our capacities for moral discernment, we are responsible for the emotional sensitivities that help constitute it. In other writings, I have detailed how Aristotle defends his general claim that the emotional components of character are "up to us."[4] In this essay, I draw on more empirical and observational studies to give plausibility to his general position.

The plan of the essay is as follows: I begin, in Section II, by looking at the practice of holding people accountable for their emotions, especially within the context of the private sphere and the developmental framework it often provides. In Section III, I look at accountability for emotions in terms of direct avoidability and control, arguing that neither is a requirement for responsibility. In Section IV, I turn to an account of the shaping of emotional agency that emerges across developmental accounts within psychology. I continue, in Section V, with some observations about the therapeutic context of psychoanalysis, and consider some assumptions of emotional agency implicit in that context. In Section VI, I consider the connection between the therapeutic context and the Aristotelian project of character development. I conclude by arguing for the importance of developmental and clinical research in extending Aristotle's claims about emotional growth and taking responsibility for emotions.

---

[4] Aristotle, *Nicomachean Ethics*, 1103a31–b21. See Nancy Sherman, *The Fabric of Character* (New York: Oxford University Press, 1989), ch. 5; and Nancy Sherman, *Making a Necessity of Virtue* (New York: Cambridge University Press, 1997), ch. 2.

II. Holding People Accountable for Their Emotions

In thinking about whether or not we are morally responsible for emotions, we often fall under the sway of a legal model, with its tendency to paint a bright stripe between action and emotion. How a person behaves, and not her habits of mind or emotional attitudes and patterns, is what is paramount in a courtroom. That a man unleashes his anger in violence, that he stabs and rapes a woman, and not that he is an angry or brooding person, is what counts before the law. It is the acting out, not the interior life and its more subtle effects on self or others, that is socially relevant.

Outside the restricted purview of the legal sphere, however, the emotional tone of conduct morally matters. So, for example, we value the emotional dimensions of altruism—for example, expressions of sorrow and joy in others' lives, assistance conveyed to others in a way that is warm and caring—not simply as optional trim, but as partial constituents of the altruistic acts themselves. A familiar critique of traditional Kantian ethics rests on just this point—that it divorces emotional elements from the moral worth of the action, and fails to distinguish (in terms of moral worth) between those responses which rest on principle alone and those which integrate principle with a supportive and well-integrated set of emotions.[5]

In an obvious way, too, in the private sphere, the pattern and weave of emotion, and not just action, morally matter. Especially among those we know well, it is typically neither meddlesome nor presumptuous to judge emotional states and their effects on self and others. The felt hostility of a loved one conveyed in gesture, tone, or conversational tack may warrant reproach if we view those emotions as misplaced or unjustified. Parents regularly expect children not just to behave well, but to develop certain emotional resources, such as a sense of compassion for others' struggles or plight, joy in hard work and achievement, a capacity to love and form friendships without blinding jealousy or envy, an appropriate sense of anger that is neither bullying nor servile, a capacity for empathy, fear at real dangers and losses, and so on. These emotions are part and parcel of morally reasonable ways of relating to self and others.

Indeed, emotions serve specific roles in the moral life. As expressive capacities, they function as a medium by which we signal our moral interest to others, such as when we express compassion when a friend suffers, or grief at her loss; as sensitivities, they are the receptors or antennae by which we, in turn, pick up signals of moral salience or interest. They are the modes by which we track moral relevance. Thus, without a capacity for pity or compassion, we might fail to notice others' suffering, and hence fail to recognize possible moral occasions for help.

---

[5] In *Making a Necessity of Virtue*, ch. 4, I suggest passages where Kant may be able to answer this charge.

Without a sense of indignation, we might fail to appreciate violations of justice or abuses of power. Equally, an individual can be blind to her own moral concerns and conflicts, in the absence of emotions that tip him or her off to those concerns. Thus, without finely attuned emotions, we are simply insensitive to much crucial moral data and are morally bumbling in our interactions with others and our understanding of ourselves.

Moral praise and blame for emotions often have to do with these sorts of concerns. In the case of young children, the focus is primarily prospective and educative, a way of communicating approval or disapproval. In the case of older children and adults, praise and blame for certain emotional attitudes carry ascriptions of moral responsibility. We often focus on the retrospective moment, but the notion of holding people responsible for their emotions has an important prospective element as well. Typically, it means that we hold ourselves or others responsible *to take responsibility* for emotions, in the sense of trying to change things, or to undergo something of an education. In many cases, understanding constitutional differences—arising from different sensory thresholds and the like—will be important for understanding the nature of certain emotional traits and how to modify them.[6] An assessment of whether or not one has taken responsibility may hang on effort as well as results, in the very way that many of our other projects of moral self-improvement do.

There is no shortage of examples of our practice of holding people (including ourselves) responsible for their emotions. Within relationships, some emotional interactions are attuned; others are misattuned and lack empathetic sensitivity. Such interactions may be occasions warranting moral reproach, or perhaps gentle suggestions of how we would have preferred to be treated. Sometimes it is an emotional episode that calls for judgment; other times, a more long-term disposition. Thus, I can reproach myself for an unjustified outburst of hostility toward a friend, but can also reproach myself for a pattern of aggression that has a longer history and involves a series of repetitions. Similarly, I may reproach my mother-in-law for a moment in which she expressed little compassion for her grandson's travails, but can also reproach her for a more enduring character trait whereby she can be emotionally removed from others' felt losses or disappointments.

Some moments of self-reproach for experiencing certain emotions may be characterized by terrific shame and self-disappointment. But, I want to argue, my reaction in such a situation is not simply that this reflects badly on me—that I am momentarily tarnished, so to speak—but rather that I attribute responsibility to myself. In the normal case, where I am not severely mentally ill and where there are no other excusing factors, my reproach expresses the fact that I hold myself responsible for what has

---

[6] See Stanley Greenspan's work on this in young children, *The Development of the Ego* (Madison, CT: International Universities Press, 1989).

transpired, and am under a moral imperative to try to do better in the future. My responsibility is, again, retrospective and prospective. There is a sense that I have comported myself objectionably and that I could have done otherwise, but also, perhaps more strongly, a sense that I can take steps in the future that make doing otherwise more likely. Of course, this always could be just false optimism, the empty resolve of a chronic akratic (i.e., the weak-willed person the ancients describe). But certainly, holding oneself accountable for emotions (for what one has felt and, if necessary, for taking steps to modify or regulate that emotion in the future) is a common enough occurrence. And actual emotional change—however slow and subtle—is no less strange. Moreover, it could be, as I will suggest later, that many of our reports of emotions as passively experienced may themselves be unconscious ways of avoiding responsibility in the face of uncomfortable conflict.

None of this is to deny the commonplace intuition that it is reasonable to rebuke an outburst of rage more strongly when it is manifested in some physical offense toward another than when we see it, under cover, in steely eyes or gritted teeth or a shrill tone of voice. But a difference in degree does not point to a difference in kind. It may be reasonable to morally reproach a parent who takes to hitting a young child who is peevish, but it may be equally reasonable to reproach her for feelings of hatred, contempt, or indifference toward the child, whether or not they are explicitly acted out in physical violence. The language of facial expression, body language, tone of voice, availability, and comfort with physical contact is communication enough for even the youngest of children to read emotions.[7] The reproach directed toward such a parent, or that she directs toward herself, is grounded on a failure of moral responsibility, a failure to have and cultivate the emotional repertoire that goes with morally decent parenting, or what the child psychoanalyst D. W. Winnicott aptly called "ordinary, good enough mothering."[8] The moral judgment is not simply that her emotions reflect badly on her, in the way that some scandal in one's place of employment (which one had nothing to do with) may reflect badly on oneself, as a member of that institution. Rather, the moral judgment attributes responsibility and faulty agency.

Of course, some morally objectionable emotions may require a more sustained therapy than personal efforts at reform can offer; but being the subject of treatment may not be incompatible with being a proper recipient of moral judgment. And, indeed, it may be warranted moral disgust at oneself, at one's emotionally abusive attitude toward one's child, for example, that brings one into treatment and continues to motivate the

---

[7] See the compelling study of Adam and the story of maternal affective neglect: Sylvia Brody and Miriam G. Siegel, "Clinical History: Adam," in Brody and Siegel, *The Evolution of Character* (Madison, CT: International Universities Press, 1992), 299–377.

[8] He refers to this notion in D. W. Winnicott, *Playing and Reality* (New York: Penguin, 1986); see, e.g., 13n., 15, 163.

therapy. While it is unlikely that moral condemnation on the part of a therapist will be therapeutically effective, for reasons we shall discuss later, the fact that a therapist regards moral judgment as practically and morally inappropriate in the clinical context is conceptually distinct from the question of whether an individual is deserving of blame. Thus, a stance of tolerance, both in therapeutic circles and more generally, is compatible with holding people responsible for their emotions, and responsible for working on their reform.[9] The more general point is that ascriptions of moral responsibility needn't be manifest only in censorious or retributivist attitudes. And in the family, as in a therapeutic context, those other ways of approaching responsibility, through empathy and a less punishing approach, may offer more effective ways of empowering an individual to take seriously responsibility for emotions. Moreover, there is good reason to hold that someone like the above mother who then goes on to recognize her emotional deficiencies and to seek help in remediating them is less blameworthy than the person who remains oblivious to any moral failings or, perhaps worse yet, who becomes aware of them, but then does nothing to try to change.

III. STARTING AND STOPPING EMOTIONS (ON A DIME)

A standard objection to holding persons responsible for their emotions is that emotional experiences, unlike actions, cannot be started or stopped immediately, at will.[10] We can intend or desire to raise our arm or cross the street and be successful in the intention; we cannot as easily or reliably will to love someone, to stop being jealous, or to be compassionate. Similarly, in the throes of an emotional episode, such as grief for a lost love, we may try to stop feeling what we are feeling, yet the emotion can have an obsessive aspect, holding on against our will or better judgment. On the basis of this, many conclude that if moral responsibility requires immediate control, then emotions are not candidates for attribution of such responsibility. But the requirement for immediate control, even in

[9] I have heard the following told anecdotally, though I have not been able to track down the reference. Freud was once asked: "What are the three things required for analysis?" He replied: "Courage, courage, courage." It is also noteworthy that in the case of Miss Lucy R., Freud comments that the repression was, on the one hand, "a defensive measure which is at the disposal of the ego," but on the other, "an act of moral cowardice," and he says that "a greater amount of moral courage would have been of advantage to the person concerned." Though we need to bear in mind that these remarks date from the earliest days of psychoanalysis, and that they are made well outside the clinical office, still the thought expresses the expectation that a patient be responsible for working on psychological improvement. Sigmund Freud, "Studies on Hysteria," in *The Standard Edition of the Complete Psychological Works of Sigmund Freud*, vol. 2 (London: Hogarth Press, 1925), 123.

[10] For relevant discussions, see Oakley, *Morality and the Emotions*, ch. 4; Michael Stocker, "Responsibility Especially for Beliefs," *Mind* 91 (1982): 398–417; Adams, "Involuntary Sins"; and Edward Sankowski, "Responsibility of Persons for Their Emotions," *Canadian Journal of Philosophy* 7 (1977): 829–40.

the case of actions, is suspect. Some basic actions may flow from the will in an instant, but even the simple act of snapping a finger can be, for the novice, a painstaking project that builds upon incremental willings. Whistling is another example. One of the marvelous ironies of Lauren Bacall's famous message to Bogie in the film *To Have and Have Not* is that whistling isn't, as she claims it is, just a matter of putting your lips together and blowing. Like seducing her, it will require a fair bit of skill. More complex actions like playing the piano, doing philosophy, baking bread, building cabinets, painting the interior of a house, weaving a carpet, leading in battle, all cannot be done, as full-fledged activities, in an instant. They are skill-based, involve complex sequencings, and build on previous efforts. They have developmental histories. Being able to engage in them depends upon an accumulation of past efforts, as well as some humility, in the face of a world that we cannot fully control. Put differently, our will, even in the case of simple physical action, is not a wish that magically works wonders. It is subject to the limitations of materials, techniques, past trials, and the receptivity of the interpersonal world. We are simply not omnipotent when we exercise our will in this world.[11]

In this regard, being an agent of certain emotions does not seem so dissimilar. So, for example, an individual who can feel compassion for members of an ethnic group and concern for their struggles may have cultivated that concern through efforts at imaginative transport and empathy—efforts at conceiving of what it would be like to be them, standing in their shoes, facing those struggles, living those battles. Indeed, there is social-psychological research to suggest that efforts at "trading places in fancy," as Adam Smith would call it, contribute to the development of altruistic attitudes.[12] Similarly, in cases where there are morally objectionable emotions that must first be undone, such as racist hatred or contempt, a willingness to expose them to critique, to be open to conversation with those who may not always agree with one's opinions, and so on, may be part of the preparatory work of emotional reform. As we shall see in Section V, some emotions may mask other deeper-lying emotions and beliefs which must first be probed before the surface emotions can change. Appreciating the moral dimensions of a situation may require working with unconscious as well as conscious modes of responding. The more general point is that there are often ways we can indirectly control and modify emotional experience. Moreover, that we cannot start a specific sort of emotion, on a dime, so to speak, does not make it so terribly different from being able to perform certain complex actions.

[11] Stocker makes these points in "Responsibility Especially for Beliefs."

[12] J. Coke, D. Batson, and K. McDavis, "Empathic Mediation of Helping: A Two Stage Model," *Journal of Personality and Social Psychology* 36 (1978): 742–66. See also N. Eisenberg, H. McCreath, and R. Ahn, "Vicarious Emotional Responsiveness and Prosocial Behavior: Their Interrelations in Young Children," *Personality and Social Psychology Bulletin* 14 (1988): 298–311.

Again, being able to stop an action, or avoid it, on a dime, is often thought to be a condition of responsibility. It seems obvious, however, that the avoidability associated with responsibility for actions is not always a matter of immediate avoidability.[13] To stop an activity may require preparedness and a history of previous actions just as performing the activity does. I may not be able to stop my car in time to avoid hitting a pedestrian, but I am nonetheless responsible if the present unavoidability is the consequence of past acts or omissions, such as failing to have my brakes checked.[14] The point is the very familiar Aristotelian one. Things we do (or fail to do earlier on), like the stone we throw in a pool of water, have ripple effects that radiate outward, for which we are responsible.[15] We become by doing or not doing. And this is also true in the case of having emotions, of having states of character with certain emotional dispositions. The more general point is that if direct willing is not a necessary condition of responsibility for actions, then there is little reason to impose it as a requirement in the case of emotions.

To this set of remarks it may be objected that I have analogized feeling an emotion, not with performing an action, but with learning an action or skill sequence. Accordingly, we may have to learn how to snap our fingers just as we have to learn how to regulate our contempt. But once we learn a basic action, we have it in our repertoire for immediate recall in a way that we cannot as reliably call up an emotion, even one that has been cultivated. At the heart of this objection is the notion that we can never guarantee the success of our preparatory work in specific emotional displays. The relation between past efforts and present emotional outputs is too contingent to hold people responsible for their present emotions in virtue of past willings. Even for those committed to the work of emotional reform, who invest considerable effort and will to modify their emotional dispositions, there will always be moments that catch one unawares, conflicts not fully resolved, emotional expressions one regrets or condemns the very moment they slip out. The most trained psychotherapist may be provoked by the abusive patient, despite stalwart efforts at being emotionally disengaged from personal attacks and the like. Indeed, it might be argued that there is a greater practical uncertainty between the preparatory work and its effects in the emotional sphere than there is in parallel cases of developing skills and performing them.

As a matter of degree, this may well be the case, but we still should not underestimate the gap between action and success in the performance of

---

[13] For a related discussion of cognitions that cannot be stopped automatically, see the very insightful discussion of W. Gerrod Parrot and John Sabini, "On the 'Emotional' Qualities of Certain Types of Cognition: A Reply to Arguments for the Independence of Cognition and Affect," *Cognitive Therapy and Research* 13 (1989): 49–65.

[14] The example is from Oakley, *Morality and the Emotions*, 128.

[15] Aristotle, *Nicomachean Ethics*, 1114a8–22.

skills, especially when they are more complex than snapping a finger or raising a hand. Luck and other external contributory conditions go into a good performance, and though their presence may influence the outcome, this needn't preclude our being held responsible for the performance. Even though our agency may be impure, subject to passivity, luck, and uncertainty, we may still be held responsible for the performance.[16] Following a line of argument Michael Stocker has presented, the artist, scientist, philosopher, and, indeed, any creative person at work on a project, is held responsible for his or her activity, despite not knowing in advance exactly what the outcome will be—just how the glaze will turn out on this piece of pottery, precisely how the canvas will look when I declare my masterpiece finished, just what results I will publish when the experiment has run its course.[17] What we require for responsibility in these cases, as Stocker puts it, is not act-foresight ("foresight about an act or outcome of an act . . . present and clear to mind in and before acting"), but character foresight (the kind of foresight one has by having practical knowledge of a skill). For ascription of responsibility for an activity in such cases, it is sufficient that we know how to proceed, not that we know exactly what the results will be:

> For moral or practical certainty of success, given a background, is not necessary for action or activity and responsibility. This can be seen by noting that there are many physical acts which we do, and pretty much have to do without moral or practical certainty, but in regard to which we are active and responsible. We could think here once again of the explorer finding the mountain range, of an archer hitting the bull's eye at the very limit of the bow's range, finding the cure for a disease . . . creating an aesthetically satisfying sculpture, and so on. . . . In these and in so many other cases, all we can do is put ourselves in as good a position as possible to intervene successfully at an opportune moment, and make our "contribution" to the world.[18]

We might say the same about having the practical skills that lead to certain emotional consequences. We are held responsible for the physical and mental actions and omissions that prepare us to have certain mature emotional capacities constitutive of moral character traits. With certain kinds of preparations, we can reasonably expect to have certain kinds of emotional outcomes. Developing emotional skills in these ways puts us in

[16] See Thomas Nagel, "Moral Luck," in Nagel, *Mortal Questions* (New York: Cambridge University Press, 1979).

[17] See Stocker, "Responsibility Especially for Beliefs"; and Oakley's helpful discussion of Stocker's essay in terms of emotions (*Morality and the Emotions*, 136ff).

[18] Stocker, "Responsibility Especially for Beliefs," 411.

good stead to respond emotionally as we ought, but it does not guarantee that we will "hit the mean" with regard to our emotions in all the challenges we face. Exactly how criteria for responsibility for emotions are to be applied in particular contexts is not my present concern. What is my concern is to show that in a wide range of cases, attributions of moral responsibility for emotions are grounded in things we do or could have done. Though emotions are receptivities, there is an enormous amount we contribute to make those receptivities functional and morally responsive. In the section that follows, I want to elaborate upon this claim by showing how at the earliest stages of development, emotions are not purely passive sensitivities. Emotional agency becomes less alien a notion when we realize that from early infancy onward we are actively involved in organizing and managing our emotional experiences.

IV. THE DEVELOPMENT OF EMOTIONAL AGENCY

The assumption so far is that emotions are informed, more than we often acknowledge, by agency. I want to substantiate this claim by turning to developmental research on young children and their emotions. Observational studies across various disciplines in psychology indicate that infants and toddlers do not simply experience emotions as passive events, but learn various ways to control, organize, and transform their emotions as aspects of their own emerging self-agency. In some cases, self-modulation is the result of a transfer of regulation of affect from parent to child (the movement from dyadic to self-regulation); in other cases, regulation of emotions comes from the infant's own more creative construction of self-soothing methods and objects. Still other efforts at modulation involve direct bids to caretakers for assistance and co-regulation of affect within attachment relationships. At later stages, regulation involves the use of language and one's body to gain emotional mastery, as well as the use of play and fantasy to work out problems the emotions pose. In what follows, I present a picture of emotional agency drawn from convergent findings in developmental psychology, attachment theory, and psychoanalytic developmental research. Though these fields are not always linked, when they are, an unambiguous portrait of emotions as involving a clear measure of agency emerges.

I begin with the account of Alan Sroufe, a developmentalist (influenced by the study of attachment in young children) whose research has focused on the organization of emotional life during the early years.[19] On Sroufe's account, emotion emerges in a specifiable way from affect systems that begin as primarily physiologically based states of arousal and

[19] Alan Sroufe, *Emotional Development* (New York: Cambridge University Press, 1995). Attachment theory is associated with the names of John Bowlby and Mary Ainsworth.

tension.[20] With the emergence of capacities for effortful study and recognition, an infant comes to mediate an event in increasingly cognitive ways, so that the meaning of an encounter becomes constitutive of a genuine emotional response. Thus, joy, anger, and fear (emerging in the second half-year) are more cognitively differentiated responses than the precursor emotions of pleasure, wariness, and frustration reactions (three to six months), which are themselves richer in meaning than the earliest excitation and distress experiences (zero to three months).

What is important for our study is that with the incipient organization of differentiated emotions, one can see a distinct trend toward what I have called "emotional agency." Not only does emotional experience involve the effort of focused attention and cognition, but in addition, there are deliberate attempts, on the part of the infant, to manipulate the environment in order to sustain, modify, or amplify emotional experiences. We can superimpose this trend on Sroufe's stages of emotional development. Consider the three-month-old. The most vigorous smiling and cooing of the three-month-old will be in response to mobiles that she manipulates, or in response to smiles that she can herself elicit from her mother. This young infant is not merely stimulated but creates and seeks stimulation. She begins to be the initiator of a game of back-and-forth smiling where she learns how to turn on and hold on to her own pleasure. This reciprocity and positive engagement continue for the next three months with continued elicitation of pleasure and responsiveness from a caregiver, as well as frustration at failures. From seven to nine months, the social awakening continues, with the infant making more persistent and intentional bids to parents to share in emotionally positive activities. "[Infants] will vocalize, touch, cajole and initiate interactions with the caregiver (as witnessed by their persistence until they get a desired response), explore the caregiver's person . . . and with budding intentionality, produce consequences in the inanimate environment."[21] So, by eight months, a child can anticipate the joy she will find in a peek-a-boo game and make efforts to bring about that joy by grabbing the diaper that is hiding her mother's eyes.[22] During the next phase, when strong attach-

---

[20] Similarly, Stanley Greenspan speaks of this first period of life as one of global "sensory alertness" where the self is an undifferentiated consciousness absorbed primarily in physiological regulation or homeostasis. See Greenspan, *The Growth of the Mind* (Reading, MA: Addison-Wesley, 1997), 50; and Greenspan, *The Development of the Ego (supra* note 6), 6. Some classical psychoanalysts, such as Freud and Margaret Mahler following him, have viewed this early period as essentially asocial or autistic. With the influence of attachment theory as well as the object-relations school of psychoanalysis (represented by such figures as Melanie Klein and W. R. D. Fairbairn), many schools of psychoanalysis now see human social relatedness, and the emergence of emotions expressing it, as present from birth. See Daniel Stern's helpful study of this theme in *The Interpersonal World of the Infant* (New York: Basic Books, 1973).
[21] Sroufe, *Emotional Development*, 74.
[22] Ibid., 153.

ment emotions are in evidence (nine to twelve months), infants begin to regulate their separation anxiety and find ways to self-soothe, in the absence of more mature structures for internalizing and representing an absent parent. Also, by the first year, the child has the skill to regulate emotion by gaze aversion, and by other controls involving intensification and deintensification (miniaturization) of expressive behavior. So while a ten-month-old's crying is all or nothing—hard to stop once begun—by twelve months, an infant can fight to hold back tears. Pout and cry faces can appear but then evaporate.[23] Not all of these activities are intentional, though all are active ways of regulating and experiencing emotions.

The essential point is that even in the first year, infants do not experience their emotions (or emotional precursors) in a purely passive way. Through their intentional bids with adults, infants seek to elicit, intensify, and share emotional experiences; through gaze aversion and other controls of their expressive behavior, they seek ways to tolerate and manage emotions that are distressing and frustrating. Even before one year of age, the young child is figuring out how to live the emotional life, how to be more, rather than less, an agent of emotional experience.

A conception of emotional agency emerges just as vividly in the psychoanalytic developmental literature. The pioneer in this field is Margaret Mahler, with much contemporary work inspired by her broad paradigm of an observation-based account of the early development of the self and attachment relations (or "object relations" as they are called, where the focus is on the intrapsychic representation, i.e., internalization, of those relations by the child).[24] On Mahler's well-known account, the early path of emotional development moves from the phases of autism (marked by its inward rather than outward focus), symbiosis (a period of discovering others and forming attachments), to separation-individuation (the beginnings of a toddler's independence). The phases chart the "hatching out process": the "psychological birth" of the human infant that comes well after (about three years after) the biological birth of the child. For our purposes of tracking emotional agency, what is key is the cracking of the "autistic shell" during the symbiotic and separation-individuation phases. Within the latter phase, the so-called "practicing" and "rapprochement" subphases are central (I say more about these subphases below).

---

[23] The ability to mask emotions, to decouple what is being felt from its typical manifestation (for example, smiling despite intense displeasure), is a much later developmental milestone observed in preschoolers. See Carol Malatesta, Clayton Culver, Johanna Rich Tesman, and Beth Shepard, "The Development of Emotion Expression during the First Two Years of Life," *Monographs of the Society for Research in Child Development* 54 (1989): 7–8. See also Sroufe, *Emotional Development*, 107, 124–30.

[24] Margaret Mahler, Fred Pine, and Anni Bergman, *The Psychological Birth of the Human Infant* (New York: Basic Books, 1975). Leaders in contemporary, psychoanalytically based infant research are Stanley Greenspan (see *The Development of the Ego; The Growth of the Mind*) and Daniel Stern (see *The Interpersonal World of the Infant*).

Much has been written on the symbiotic phase (from roughly two to nine months), with its focus, as Sroufe has already noted, on the positive, reciprocal engagements of caregiver and infant. This is the period of intense visual dialoguing between mother and infant, of sustained facial gazing, of "mirroring" sequences in which the gleam in the mother's eyes evokes bright and shiny eyes in the child. It is the period in which attachment and merger experiences are created—often, though not exclusively, through the eyes.[25] But in addition to the development of empathetic synchronies crucial for the formation of attachment ties, the dialoguing of the symbiotic period marks the beginning of an education of the emotions. Theorists who study infants point to the psychobiologically attuned mother who does not simply mirror back the child's affective rhythms and intensities, but helps modulate them, dispensing stimulation in a way that both keeps the infant from potentially disorganizing states, and amplifies and elaborates capacities for tolerating prolonged positive stimulation.[26] These are periods of fine-tuning the synchrony, of regulating from the outside the child's capacity for experiencing the precursors of emotions in ways that are not purely passive. The parent's role, according to these theorists, is to permit the child to endure the early manifestations of the positive emotions of interest, excitement, and joy in a way that at once stretches the boundaries of tolerance without overwhelming the child.[27] Significantly, however, the child too plays a role, even in this predominantly externally driven regulation. For it is the child's cues of gaze attention and aversion that typically direct the well-synchronized parent's input:

A mother's most effective technique in maintaining an interaction seems to be a sensitivity to her infant's capacity for attention and need for withdrawal—partial or complete—after a period of attending to her. . . . Although there appears to be continuous attention to the mother on the part of the infant, stop-frame analysis uncovers the cyclical nature of the infant's looking and not looking. By looking away, infants maintain some control over the amount of stimulation they take in during such intense periods of interaction.[28]

[25] Allan Schore offers a comprehensive review of the literature across fields, on this topic and other themes in affect development; see Schore, *Affect Regulation and the Origins of Self* (Hillsdale, NJ: Lawrence Erlbaum Associates, 1994). On visual dialoguing, see especially, ibid., 71–82; and Greenspan, *The Growth of the Mind*, 50.

[26] Schore, *Affect Regulation*, 85–91; Daniel Stern, "Mother and Infant at Play: The Dyadic Interaction Involving Facial, Vocal, and Gaze Behavior," in Michael Lewis and Leonard A. Rosenblum, eds., *The Effect of the Infant on Its Caregiver* (New York: Wiley, 1974), 187–213.

[27] Malatesta, Culver, Tesman, and Shepard, "The Development of Emotion Expression"; Schore, *Affect Regulation*, 89.

[28] T. B. Brazelton and B. G. Cramer, *The Earliest Relationship* (Reading, MA: Addison-Wesley, 1990), as quoted by Schore, *Affect Regulation*, 85.

The notion of dyadic attunements (or the mutual dialoguing experiences of, typically, parent and child) has been studied extensively by Daniel Stern. In the older, nine-month-old child, affective attunements are not restricted to eye gazing, but can cover various modalities. Thus, Stern observes that in the course of interacting with her child, a parent will quite naturally respond to the child's expression or movement with an expression or movement that is similar but not restricted to the same modality, as a strict imitation or reinforcement might be. A child's irregular foot kicking may be met with hand tapping or a vocalization (bam, bam, bam, baaaam) that has the same rhythm or contour. Typically, the matched dynamic or synchrony will go on without the infant missing a beat until she experiences a misattunement by the parent, that is, an intensity, rhythm, duration, or shape of movement that is substantially out of sync with her own.

Consider the following description of an attunement, and then a "staged" misattunement:

> A nine-month-old infant is seen crawling away from his mother and over to a new toy. While on his stomach, he grabs the toy and begins to bang and flail with it happily. His play is animated, as judged by his movements, breathing, and vocalizations. Mother then approaches him from behind, out of sight, and puts her hand on his bottom and gives it an animated jiggle side to side. The speed and intensity of her jiggle appear to match well the intensity and rate of the infant's arm movements and vocalizations, qualifying this as an attunement. The infant's response to her attunement is [that] he simply continues his play without missing a beat. . . . This sequence was repeated several times.

The following misattunement was coached by the experimenter:

> The mother was instructed to do exactly the same as always, except that now she was purposely to "misjudge" her baby's level of joyful animation . . . and to jiggle accordingly. When the mother did jiggle somewhat more slowly and less intensely than she truly judged would make a good match, the baby quickly stopped playing and looked around at her, as if to say, "What's going on?" This procedure was repeated, with the same result.[29]

The child's abrupt stop and quizzical reaction to the misalignment suggests that he is not just experiencing the interaction passively, but is an attentive and active partner in the game, contributes to the stimulation, enjoys the amplification of the pattern, and then is frustrated when the

[29] Stern, *The Interpersonal World of the Infant,* 150.

shared pattern abates. In Alan Fogel's terminology, the child helps to co-construct a "consensual frame" which then becomes disrupted.[30] Similar episodes of active exchanges of affect have been described at length by Stanley Greenspan, episodes in which young children interact with parents in give-and-take games, where each partner, as Greenspan metaphorically puts it, closes the circles that the other partner opens.[31] Communicative pointing at ten to thirteen months and the capacity for joint visual attention[32] (i.e., the ability of a child to triangulate from her own eyes, to a parent's eyes, to the target object the parent is looking at) are also ways the young child begins to share objects of interest and emotional excitement with caretakers.[33]

With the onset of physical mobility and a developed musculature, the child, at about ten months of age, advances, according to the Mahlerian schema, from the symbiotic phase to the separation-individuation phase, with its central practicing and rapprochement subphases. The practicing subphase (ten to eighteen months) is just that—a period of practicing separation and the emotional self-control required as the child becomes psychologically and physically separate from parents. The rapprochement subphase (eighteen to twenty-four months) is marked by the ambivalent return to parents after discovering that independence poses challenges in terms of separations and losses, conflicts and struggles. The world is, as Mahler puts it, no longer the child's oyster;[34] the thrill of independence is marked by the toddler's realization that one's efforts sometimes fail, that there are big people out there who can often do things more skillfully than the small child can. Whatever the disagreements about the precise timing of separation and individuation, we can focus, as before, on the continued emergence of emotional self-regulation and agency during this general time period. Put generally, the problem of this period is how to regulate emotion in the face of autonomous forays into the environment. The child solves the problem, in part, as before, through deliberate, intentional bids to parents for assistance in emotional regula-

---

[30] Alan Fogel, *Developing Through Relationships* (Chicago: University of Chicago Press, 1993).

[31] Stanley Greenspan, *Infancy and Early Childhood* (Madison, CT: International Universities Press, 1992), 11–12, 70, 96.

[32] George Butterworth, "The Ontogeny and Phylogeny of Joint Visual Attention," in Andrew Whiten, ed., *Natural Theories of Mind* (Cambridge, MA: Blackwell, 1991).

[33] There are neurobiological implications of the modulation of affect in synchronized parental interactions. Numerous studies indicate that these interactions directly influence the experience-dependent growth of brain areas prospectively involved in self-regulation of emotion. In particular, Allan Schore has argued that early object relational experiences "directly influence the emergence of a frontolimbic system in the right hemisphere" responsible for autoregulation of positive and negative emotions. Thus, while initially the parent acts as a child's auxiliary cortex, through socio-emotional interactions the child develops his own capacities for emotional regulation, mediated in transformed neurological structures. See Schore, *Affect Regulation*, 89–130.

[34] Mahler et al., *The Psychological Birth of the Human Infant*, 78.

tion. Mahler refers to the phenomenon as "refueling," as regular "check-ing back" to the parent for emotional reassurance and confidence.[35]

Given the new mobility of the child, much of this information must come from distal cues (that is, cues which are at some distance from the child's own body). This is clearest in the phenomenon known as social referencing.[36] When faced with a suspicious or dangerous-appearing object, children will deliberately turn to their parents and "reference" the parents' emotional expressions in order to resolve their own uncertainty. As one researcher puts it, the child "keeps an eye" on the feelings expressed in the parents' faces.[37] Emotional signaling of this sort presupposes that children are experts at reading facial emotional cues, and that parents, in turn, regularly offer them as part of their interaction with children.[38] Indeed, studies show that children with poker-faced parents do poorly at self-regulating emotions, apparently because they lack the feedback information required to resolve questions about how to respond emotionally.[39] In a sense, the children now carry the parents' emotional expression with them, cued through voice or face, as a kind of internalized "holding framework," in T. B. Brazelton's words—a mode by which the child "contains" his own emotional responses without having to be physically held.[40] Others have referred to the checking back as "reunion transactions," moments initiated by the child that re-cement the attachment relation, with the effect of both perking up a flagging, independent infant and guiding an emotional response.[41]

Transitional objects—Winnicott's famous term for the favored blankie or stuffed animal that occupies a space between the child and attachment object (parent or caregiver)—provide another kind of holding framework that allows the child to mediate the distance between parent and external world and to regulate anxiety in venturing beyond the home base.[42] In establishing a transitional object, the child, once again, makes efforts to be "in charge" of her emotions—she invests in an object, so that when parents are not available, that object can help to take the place of parental soothing and containment.

---

[35] Ibid., 77.

[36] M. D. Kimmert, J. J. Campos, F. J. Sorce, R. N. Emde, and M. J. Svejda, "Social Referencing: Emotional Expressions as Behavior Regulators," in *Emotion: Theory, Research, and Experience*, vol. 2: *Emotions in Early Development*, ed. Robert Plutchik and Henry Kellerman (Orlando: Academic Press, 1983).

[37] K. Oatley and J. M. Jenkins, "Human Emotions: Function and Dysfunction," *Annual Review of Psychology* 43 (1992): 55–85.

[38] On face reading, see Carroll E. Izard, *The Face of Emotion* (New York: Appleton-Century-Crofts, 1971).

[39] Greenspan, *The Development of the Ego*, 36.

[40] T. B. Brazelton, B. Koslowski, and M. Main, "The Origins of Reciprocity: The Early Mother-Infant Interaction," in Lewis and Rosenblum, eds., *The Effect of the Infant on Its Caregiver* (*supra* note 26), 70.

[41] Schore, *Affect Regulation*, 99–114.

[42] D. W. Winnicott, "Transitional Objects and Transitional Phenomena," in Winnicott, *Playing and Reality*.

In the rapprochement subphase, the child's love affair with the world wanes. Independent forays into the world are tempered with the frustrations of setting out alone, and of realizing that as a toddler, one is, after all, only a small guy in a big world. The frustrations and ambivalence of going it alone pose new challenges for emotional agency.[43] The child tries to undo his actual separateness from parents and return to the early symbiosis. In Mahler's characteristically vivid terms, there is a "darting away" from the caregiver, but also a "shadowing," mirrored sometimes by a parent's own ambivalence about cutting apron strings.[44] The "rapprochement crisis," the dramatic fights of the terrible two's, come with the child's realization that the old duo unit is no longer an option, and that other paths must be tried. In place of the old pre-verbal empathy and visual dialoguing, the child turns to verbal communication to establish a new union, as well as to other symbolic forms, such as play.

What we see on the extended Mahlerian scheme is that the psychological hatching of the human child is also the hatching of a child who develops skills for dealing with emotional experiences. In symbiotic mergers as well as in independent forays and rapprochements, emotions and their precursors do not merely descend upon the young child. Rather, they are actively mediated by caregivers—but also, significantly, by the child herself, in her bids for sharing and containment, in her emotional referencing of information from trustworthy faces, in her refueling at the knee of a parent after a crawl into the big world that kindles anxiety, in her investment of love in a favorite blanket or toy that helps her to refuel without mom's help, in her turning to words and play to organize and sort out the blooming buzz of emotional experience.

Indeed, on a psychoanalytic model, one of the functions of the developing ego is precisely to organize emotional experience, so that the child is able to experience and express emotions without being so flooded by them as to be at risk of disintegration and self-dissolution. This involves capacities for various forms of internalization. Self-soothing in the older toddler requires having images of attachment objects that survive their absence. Regulating emotions, through a child saying, "No, no, no" in parental voice, similarly requires that the child can introject that parent and appeal to the introject as needed. At some point, mergers of parental and self images emerge, with more blended identifications allowing the child to provide guidance in her own voice. But this is a later development (occurring when the child is five to six years old) that, on a traditional psychoanalytic view (of superego development), requires the resolution of triadic relations (relations among the child and the two

[43] This period also corresponds to the Freudian anal period, marked by sphincter (muscular) control, and the ambivalence centered around wanting to control bowels, like an adult, and yet enjoying the old ways of being warm in one's own mess and then pampered with clean diapers in an intimate exchange.
[44] Mahler et al., *The Psychological Birth of the Human Infant*, 77–79.

parents), and the coping with emotional challenges of love, jealousy, envy, and loss that these relations introduce. Equally there are regulating mechanisms for the emotions that, on psychoanalytic theory, may be unconscious, though a part of normal as well as pathological development. Denial, splitting, isolation of affect, turning mental states into their opposites, projection, sublimation, and intellectualization are all ways we commonly cope with emotions, wishes, and thoughts that may be unwanted or in conflict with other avowed ends.[45]

Of those activities the toddler consciously engages in to regulate emotions, it is hard to overestimate the role of play and verbalization. In children who are eighteen to thirty months old, fantasy and play become ways of trying out emotions, studying solutions, safely enacting fears and wishes, modifying them, projecting them onto dolls or animals for review and manipulation. Play exploits the world of agency, of being the director of a drama and of being able to work out different scene developments. Here it becomes clear that emotional regulation comes not simply from inhibition of emotions, but from acceptance of them, from learning to own, tolerate, and express them as a part of working through them or modifying them.

For children of this age, narrating a story with emotional content is often a part of play, and an occasion that caregivers can exploit for encouraging reflection and modulation of emotion. A child's script that involves cars murderously crashing into other cars, with ambulances uninterested in rescue operations, might be a thinly veiled story about anger at a bullying playmate and feelings of retributivist revenge. The child works on the feelings in a safe place, with the very enactment and verbalization giving the child an engaged yet distanced experience that allows self-observation. There is experimentation that goes on in play, a chance to practice, but also a chance to alter how one engages in the world in non-fantasy moments. Thus, Stanley Greenspan has called pretend play "the gymnasium for the exercise of emotional ideas. The child whose own expression of anger is limited to yelling and hitting is not as advanced as one who can also have her dolls yell and hit."[46] In part, this is because play involves agency. It involves making the dolls hit each other, delaying or at least revisiting an emotional experience in a scenario in which one is now the director. Simply to be able to label and identify the emotions, as in the case (described by Greenspan) of Jason playing with his ducks in the presence of his father—"Duckie take toys away. Duckies fighting. Duckies mad"—is itself a massive form of control. For now a diffuse feeling which once could only be acted out in behavior or felt as a bodily sensation can be safely thought about, shared with his

---

[45] See Anna Freud's classic work, *The Ego and Mechanisms of Defense* (Madison, CT: International Universities Press, 1993).

[46] Stanley Greenspan, *The Essential Partnership* (New York: Viking, 1989), 156.

father in the world of thought, and conceptually connected with other representations in his world, like "mad at Mommy" because she is away, or "mad at Billy" because he "took toys" from Jason, and so on.[47] Articulating the construals that particular emotions hang on is itself a form of mediating the experience of the emotions. When put into words, the emotions can be more easily thought about, accessed, assessed, and distanced from the experience. To put emotions into words is, in some ways, to sublimate them.

Many brands of therapy of the emotions (both ancient, such as those practiced by the Stoics and those that can be reconstructed from Aristotle's work, and contemporary, such as those based on Freudian psychoanalytic theory) rest on similar assumptions—that emotions rest on conscious and/or unconscious construals of the world, and that exposure and revision of those construals can lead to emotional change. In the section that follows, I consider psychoanalysis as a context for the development of emotional agency in adults.[48] I turn to Freud's depth psychology not to distract us with issues of severe pathology, but to focus on a method for understanding emotional change and agency in cases of the so-called "good neurotic," where we can make fairly easy bridges to the relatively healthy psyche.[49]

V. Emotional Agency in the Therapeutic Context

On traditional psychoanalytic views, many of the psychological constrictions and excesses that lead to inabilities to love well or work well stem from internal conflicts whose solutions prove inadequate. The therapeutic intent of analysis is to activate self-observing capacities in ways that allow for developing more adaptive resolutions of those intrapsychic conflicts.[50] In a sense, the aim of psychoanalysis is to enable a patient to

[47] Ibid. For further discussion of verbalization as a form of emotional control, see Petra Hesse and Dante Cicchetti, "Perspectives on an Integrated Theory of Emotional Development," in Emotional Development, ed. Dante Cicchetti and Petra Hesse (San Francisco: Jossey-Bass Inc., 1982), 33–36; see also Judy Dunn and Jane Brown, "Relationships, Talk about Feelings, and the Development of Affect Regulation in Early Childhood," in Judy Garber and Kenneth Dodge, eds., The Development of Emotion Regulation and Dysregulation (New York: Cambridge University Press, 1991).

[48] There are, of course, child analyses that center around play, but I focus on the "talking therapy" of adult analysis.

[49] Indeed, it was Freud's view that psychoanalytic theory revealed the structure of the "normal" psyche, with its various agencies and stages of growth. ("Depth psychology" was Freud's term for a psychology that recognized the dynamic influence of the unconscious in mental life.)

[50] "Psychoanalysis promotes autonomy by virtue of its expansion of the analysand's ability to recognize these intrapsychic conflicts and to utilize the signal function [i.e., anxiety or depressive feeling] generated by dysphoric affect to activate self-observing capacities rather than automatically resort to regression and defense." Steven Levy and Lawrence Inderbitzin, "Neutrality, Interpretation, and Therapeutic Intent," Journal of the American Psychoanalytic Association 40 (1992): 989–1011.

gain autonomy over areas of her mental life where she has either too much or too little control.

In many cases, it is explicitly emotional difficulties that bring patients into analysis. For some, the symptoms may be an aggressive and overly jealous way of loving that leads to one botched romance after another; for others, it may be an image of self that is humiliating and shameful; for still others, it may be anger and rage that is unleashed all too easily and that causes difficulties in forming and staying in relationships; for yet others, it is simply a diffuse sense of guilt or anxiety that gets in the way and cannot be easily turned off. In each of these cases, there are patterns of emotion, thought, and action that a person decides it is time to do something about. In entering psychoanalysis, an individual takes a step toward greater mastery of her emotional life.

On the traditional approach (known as ego psychology),[51] symptoms or characterological formations are part of "compromise formations"— adaptive styles that have developed over time to deal with a conflict between different agencies (id, ego, superego) of the psyche; the compromise becomes a deal brokered to placate the different interests and pressures each agency brings to bear. A patient comes in, on this view, when the brokered deal no longer works, when painful feelings erupt—such as anxiety, shame, depression, or guilt—suggesting that some aspect of balancing the conflict is no longer effective. A key element of the patient's desire to change is that these habits no longer work, that the behavior is experienced as foreign or "ego distonic"—no longer in sync with what one approves of or who one wants to be.

A simplified clinical vignette, drawn from the writings of Arnold Rothstein, should help to explain further the approach.[52] Mr. X, a thirty-four-year-old married, successful lawyer, expresses in his analytic session enormous anxiety about being humiliated by thoughts others might have that he is gay. He reports that he became particularly anxious when he went to the police station the night before to help out an uncle who was being held by the police. Without any difficulty, he had his uncle released on bail, but was preoccupied and anxious all the time with the idea that "everyone at the precinct would think my uncle was my homosexual lover. . . . I was terrified they'd think I was gay." Based on long-term work with this patient that centered on competition with his father, Rothstein reconstructs that his fantasy of being gay was a defense against those

[51] Leading contemporary proponents of ego psychology are Charles Brenner, *Psychoanalytic Technique and Psychic Conflict* (Madison, CT: International Universities Press, 1976); and Jacob Arlow, "The Dynamics of Interpretation," *Psychoanalytic Quarterly* 56 (1987): 68–87. A classic formulation of ego psychology, from the 1930s, is that of Heinz Hartmann, *Ego Psychology and the Problem of Adaptation* (Madison, CT: International Universities Press, 1995).

[52] Arnold Rothstein, "Sadomasochism as a Compromise Formation," *Journal of the American Psychoanalytic Association* 39 (1991): 363–75.

competitive wishes to surpass his father. The anxiety was brought on by the fact that he could no longer hide from the reality that he had become successful and powerful enough to be a genuine competitor for his father. As Rothstein interpreted the situation, in a way that resonated with the patient: "Your painful fantasy helped you diminish the frightening sense [that] you were quite a man." Yet the patient's acknowledgment of that real status—that he had made it in his profession, that he had "arrived"— opened the floodgates of self-punishing thoughts and worries, of anxiety and guilt, fueled by the elements of the old conflict whose once comfortable solution now came undone.

My point in going through this example is not to assess the particular interpretation, nor the patient's own view of what is or is not humiliating. Without extensive clinical detail that tracks each session, there would be little point to such an exercise. Rather, I offer the example simply to show that the point of analysis, on this view, is to expose and work through conflict, indeed, to live through it, openly and painfully, in a way that sets in motion a developmental process. The end product of that process is a softening of the sharp edges of conflict in a way that allows for a more adaptive solution. Emotional change, on this view, involves working through conflict—with the aim, in the above case, of no longer feeling intense shame; of tolerating one's competitiveness without fear of retaliation from one's rivals or an all-consuming anger that poisons the spirit of competition; of enjoying one's achievements without having to hide from them in self-deprecating fantasies; and of loving a father at the same time that one competes with him.

(On an alternative approach—known as the self-psychology school of psychoanalysis—corrective emotional change is rooted less in an analysis of conflicts and defenses than in a rehabilitative experience whereby the self and the capacity for relationships are reconstructed.[53] Typically, this approach focuses on cases where a patient has suffered an early narcissistic injury, perhaps an emotional trauma or prolonged loss or failure of empathy in an early relationship. The analytic relationship becomes a place to repair that injury, to become whole again, to learn basic forms of relating to others and of internalizing conceptions of others and one's relationship to them in a way that helps build a more viable sense of self. Emotional change, on this view, requires something of a return to the early stages of one's development of relatedness—a return to establishing a symbiotic connectedness in dyadic relationships, and from there a move to triadic relationships and the complicated negotiations threesomes involve. For the purposes of this limited context, however, I shall restrict myself to the classical, ego psychology model.)

[53] Self-psychology is associated with Heinz Kohut and his works, *The Analysis of the Self* (Madison, CT: International Universities Press, 1971), and *The Restoration of the Self* (Madison, CT: International Universities Press, 1977).

But what is the process of "working through" conflict? How, according to psychoanalytic theory, can ingrained habits of attitude and defense be broken down and changed? Is it simply a vigilant stance toward the habits of mind, a noting of the mind's twists and turns, leaps to defense, and so on, that ultimately frees one from those overly constrictive or self-defeating modes of thought and emotion?

This is an extensive topic best pursued in the context of detailed case material and within a comparative examination of different analytic schools and clinical techniques. For present purposes, however, I shall be selective, focusing on key, shared elements of psychoanalytic technique— namely, talk, transference onto the analyst, insight, and interpretation.

Just as a child learns to identify and differentiate emotions through the talk that often accompanies play, so adults, especially those in the context of a daily hour devoted to self-examination, have a chance to capture and articulate some of the emotional flavor of recent and past events in their lives. But in addition, by lifting the censorship and editing of ordinary, non-analytic discourse (through the technique of free association or discussion of dreams), patients have a chance of acknowledging emotions that may have been only lurking on the edge of conscious experience, too threatening or conflictual to fully notice or put into words. Talk puts certain emotions on the table that otherwise would slip by undetected. With a painstaking focus on emotions, a patient can begin to analyze their appropriateness—for example: How much of one's anger is based on a warranted appraisal of another's injury to oneself? How much is a projection of a desire to injure another that one self-defensively inverts (so that *he* is now out to get *me*)? In the context of a highly trusted, ongoing, and confidential analytic relationship, a patient can talk about emotional patterns, such as passiveness, or an imperious attitude, or pervasive fears that come to be recognized as prominent themes in one's character. The patient becomes a self-observer with an understanding of the motivations and history of some of his characteristic emotions.

But analytic self-observation is not simply an intellectual and discursive process. In analytic sessions that are most productive, the enactments are in the room, the emotions not merely talked about, but experienced. In some cases, this may be a matter of affective memory, of remembering in a way that sticks one's nose right into what is recollected. In other cases, certain emotions are experienced because the grist for the mill is in the here and now of the analytic relationship itself—because an analyst was late, because he is fidgeting and not paying sufficient heed, because he has other patients who might occupy his attention or a private, family life one is reminded of by hearing footsteps on the stairway or a car pulling into the garage. Certain familiar emotional patterns get lived out against the new object of the analyst, but lived out in the presence of the patient's observing ego as well as the analyst's attentive stance. The patient is participant but also observer, as is the analyst insofar as she empathizes with the patient and experiences her own stream of consciousness in response to his story, but at the same time tries to see it all from some larger vantage point.

Grist for the mill may also come in the most subtle turn of a conversation that is again "inside" the analysis, and that a skillful analyst can pick up. While talking about a distant cousin whom a patient envies because of his earning power and elite status within his profession, the patient goes silent and then shifts to a new topic. He mentions something about the analyst's car and how it is parked in a new spot. In past sessions, the car has been the subject of the patient's envy and conflictual feelings about material and upwardly mobile ambitions. It has also been the subject of many dreams with the same theme. The analyst points out to the patient the possible connection. What ensues is a discussion of the envy that is currently in the room, hot and felt with considerable urgency.[54] Freud famously said that you cannot kill a man in effigy. The method of bringing the analysis into the room works on that dictum.

The foregoing examples are cases of what is known in psychoanalytic idiom as "transference." Experiences, emotions, and thoughts that represent familiar patterns are reenacted in the analytic relationship, but with the advantage of self-observation and minute attention to the work of defenses. In principle, the reenactment is not just one more repetition—in part, because of the analyst's nonjudgmental stance. Through a so-called "neutral" stance,[55] the analyst attempts to stand outside the drama in a way that allows the patient to see the working of his own mind rather than be embroiled in one more interpersonal conflict where the contributions from outside distract the patient from looking at the conflict within. So, for example, a punishing attitude toward a patient might simply endorse the crippling and neurotic sense of shame a patient already feels, just as an unduly permissive attitude might give the message that elements of the conflict that are causing the shame can be bypassed without analysis. In Anna Freud's famous words, the analyst "hovers evenly" over the different agencies of the mind, trying to listen for and notice the elements of conflict that the patient struggles with.[56] Interpretations that are well-timed, empathetically tuned, stated as tentative conjectures with acceptance of the ambiguity and complexity of the mental life, phrased in the language not of theory, but of the patient's own

---

[54] For the here-and-now transference, see Merton Gill, "The Analysis of the Transference," *Journal of the American Psychoanalytic Association* 27 (supplement, 1979): 263–88; and Paul Gray, "Psychoanalytic Technique and the Ego's Capacity for Viewing Intrapsychic Activity," *Journal of the American Psychoanalytic Association* 21 (1973): 474–94.

[55] For further discussion of neutrality, see my "The Moral Perspective and the Psychoanalytic Quest," in *The Journal of the Academy of Psychoanalysis* 23 (1995): 223–40; see also Levy and Inderbitzin, "Neutrality, Interpretation, and Therapeutic Intent."

[56] Freud, *The Ego and Mechanisms of Defense.*

experience and words—these are the interpretations that move the analysis along and open the path for insights.

Again, however, the insights and self-observations, the patient's own interpretations as well as resonances with those of the analyst, are typically not cool cognitive products. To have a core insight, or series of such insights over time, as to how and why certain emotions and emotional themes (such as aggressiveness, ambition, compassion, passive acquiescence, envy, an easy-going nature, difficulty with loss, and so on) organize one's life in the way they do, how they motivate or mask other emotions, how they get inverted in defense or projected outward onto others, how they lead us to idealize others and, in the extreme, to turn them into gods—all this can constitute an exhilarating achievement, the prize of long and arduous work. But the steps of the journey are themselves emotionally intense, a "living through" of those emotions of loss, ambition, aggression, etc., at the same time one realizes that some of the beliefs and fantasies on which they are based—stories, so to speak, of redemption and survival—no longer have the same purchase they once had. In many cases the stories are archaic, frozen from earlier developmental periods yet still powerful in their motivation. To expose these dramas in raw moments of regression under one's own observing eye is to have a vantage point from which to assess (and alter) those dramas, and the emotions they constitute. It is to have a vantage point for change. This is at the heart of emotional agency, on the psychoanalytic conception. In an interaction with a family member, then, one might see oneself starting to need to win this round, to be in charge, to have the final say. It is a familiar pattern, but it is seen now with a certain critical distance, and, more to the point, with far less need to win in order to feel good or to enjoy the spiritedness of the exchange. One may still be assertive, but with less blindness, less anger toward others, less shame at defeat. How one judges others when they fail to win may also be similarly altered. None of this means that progress is always forward, that there will be no regressions, no moments when one fails to catch oneself in time. The hope, though, is that the need to repeat the past has been diminished.

A shift in the language of emotions may also be a sign of enhanced emotional agency that develops through psychoanalysis. Thus, Roy Shaffer has argued that one of the goals of analysis is to analyze the disclaimers of agency couched in a patient's reports of emotional experience as passive—"I was crushed by defeat"; "The impulse overwhelmed me"; "Bad feelings about you came up suddenly." These are to be taken literally, by the clinician, as expressions of how a patient is experiencing an emotion; but at the same time, Shaffer argues, they are often fantasized and primitive ways of experiencing emotions that unconsciously resist responsibility and obscure the conflict that analytic work will, over time, expose. I quote Shaffer at length:

I have identified many of the locutions analysands use to disclaim their own actions. Examples are: "The impulse overwhelmed me" and "The thought of you slipped away." I have emphasized particularly the defensive or resistant value of disclaiming. What is being defensively disclaimed is the personal agency that would be plain if the analysand were to say instead: "I did the very thing that I consciously and urgently did not want to do" and "Unexpectedly, I stopped thinking of you." By attributing agency to impulses and thoughts rather than to oneself, the analysand disavows responsibility. . . . Through such disclaiming, one simply appears as the victim or witness of happenings whose origins and explanations lie entirely outside one's own sphere of influence—outside the "self," as some would say. . . .

It is not being advocated that action language be the enforced and exclusive or even pervasive language of the clinical dialogue. It would be fatal to clinical exploration and effectiveness to do clinical work in that way. A keen *recognition* of disclaimers is, however, technically useful, especially in analyzing resistance. And no matter what form the clinical dialogue has taken, any account of personal change and insight achieved through psychoanalysis must give a prominent place to an increase in the range and comfort of the consciously acknowledged agency and responsibility on the part of the analysand.[57]

The important point is this: We can take seriously the construction of certain emotional experiences as passive while still holding that such constructions are often unconscious ways of avoiding the discomfort of more conflictual and ambivalent states. The way one experiences emotion can change as the capacity to see one's own, albeit sometimes conflicted, role in the emotional experience is enhanced. Moreover, passive constructions may themselves be unconscious ways of avoiding responsibility for emotions.

Although psychoanalysis is often thought of as diminishing the realm of moral responsibility—through its notions of unconscious wishes, repression, and the like—the force of my remarks has been to show how it, in fact, expands the ways in which we can take responsibility for character. In so doing, it offers us a further sense of how we can be more, rather than less, agents of our emotional lives. In the brief, penultimate section that follows, I return to Aristotle and suggest that his notion of emotional development as part of character habituation can be recast through the lens of the psychoanalytic model.

---

[57] Roy Shaffer, *The Analytic Attitude* (New York: Basic Books, 1983), 241–46.

VI. Aristotelian and Psychoanalytic
Emotional Development

On the Aristotelian view, emotions are, in part, cognitively constituted affective states. They are, as cognitive psychologists have now put it, appraisal-based.[58] As I have argued at length elsewhere, emotional change, according to the account suggested in Book II of Aristotle's *Rhetoric*, is a matter of change of appraisals.[59] Feelings of anger toward another, based on an appraisal of an unwarranted injury, begin to lift when one realizes that the other was just teasing or that one was mistaken in what one heard. Envy against another may dissipate as one no longer regards another as threatening or as having something that stands in the way of one's own progress. Revising emotions is a matter of reconstruing, of seeing things in a more accurate light. The process may be slow, for certain construals may have a tenacious grip, even in the face of the conflicting judgments of a more enlightened assessment. But the goal is to bring emotions around, so that they are informed by and harmonize well with the best judgments of practical reason.

The well-known account at the end of the first book of the *Nicomachean Ethics* suggests that the process of harmonizing emotions involves a top-down chastening model. That is, appetites and emotions are to obey the judgments of reason, as a child obeys a parent's exhortations.[60] Although true virtue must involve transformation of emotion and appetite (the genuine temperance of *sôphrosunê*), and not just self-control or inhibition (*egkrateia*), an explanation of the method for a transformative rather than inhibitive process is never offered.

The psychoanalytic model can be viewed as filling in that gap, as providing the tools for effecting the deep changes that the Aristotelian model merely gestures toward.[61] Conflict, on the Freudian view, is resolved not from the top down but from the bottom up—by exposing unconscious desires and motivations that may still be deeply conflictual and disavowed, on the belief that exposure and mediation in language, reenactment and remembering within a process of transference and self-observation, are tools for substantively reshaping those desires. This may put it too baldly, however. For the process is not just one of letting out the demons in the basement—of id analysis, as it was once called and practiced in the early days of psychoanalysis. Seeing one's stances of defense—how one is poised through certain mechanisms to avoid certain painful thoughts or feelings—is itself at the heart of exposing some of those

---

[58] This is now the dominant view of emotions in cognitive psychology. See R. S. Lazarus, *Emotion and Adaptation* (New York: Oxford University Press, 1991).

[59] Sherman, *Making a Necessity of Virtue*, ch. 2.

[60] Aristotle, *Nicomachean Ethics*, Book I, ch. 13.

[61] I develop this notion of psychoanalysis as extending the ancient model of character development in "The Moral Perspective and the Psychoanalytic Quest."

demons and renegotiating the conflict. The process is meant to get at the tenacity of certain construals in a way that the Aristotelian[62] cannot begin to approach. To try to modify certain tendencies toward inappropriately directed hatred or jealousy by being persuaded (or chastened) to see things in a new light (as the Aristotelian would have us do) may simply bypass the all-important step of understanding just what is invested in seeing things in the old light. The point is not to condemn Aristotle for lacking a theory of depth psychology and unconscious motivation. It is, rather, to see Freud and his tradition as operationalizing some of Aristotle's own notions that we can change emotions so that they are less conflictual and more in sync with our best judgments of what is valuable in human living. And we do this not always by moralistic prods, but by making ourselves ready to see anew. In addition, Freud, unlike Aristotle, insists on the further point (more familiar to a Kantian moral philosophy than to an Aristotelian one) that we never fully eliminate certain conflicts, though we may revisit them with increasing mastery and more adequate resolutions.

But there is still one issue that needs to be addressed. In bringing psychoanalysis together with the ancient project of the development of character and emotion, I am claiming that psychoanalysis can itself be a context for the moral education of character. But in what sense is this so, given that the clinical hour boasts of a time and space that is morally neutral, safe from praise and blame, advice or counsel? In what sense are we held responsible for our emotions in the therapeutic setting?

This is an extensive subject, and a full exploration of the professional ethics of psychoanalysis would take us well beyond the scope of this essay. However, a number of limited points can be made. Though a psychoanalyst typically refrains from engaging in what Peter Strawson has called the "reactive attitudes" of moral judgment (e.g., emotions such as praise and blame, reproach and approval), this does not mean, contra Strawson, that the therapeutic relationship must involve a nonparticipatory and nonmoral "objective attitude," where a patient is to be "managed, handled, cured, or trained."[63] In contrast, the specific nature of analytic therapy is that it depends upon a deeply personal and engaged relationship. However constrained that relationship and however artfully timed and crafted interpretations as well as silences may be, in the ideal case, a bond is formed in which the analyst shows, on the one side, respect and patience, loving attention and deeply attuned listening, and the patient shows, on the other, a sense of attachment to the analyst and gratitude for his undivided attention and participation in the shared journey they are undertaking. Although the analyst has, in the background,

---

[62] And perhaps his modern-day counterparts in cognitive therapy.
[63] Strawson, "Freedom and Resentment," in Fischer and Ravizza, eds., *Perspectives on Moral Responsibility*.

theories of cure and treatment, the successful analytic process must follow the patient's lead and language, stories and fantasies. Flatfooted interpretations, formulaic views that miss a patient's own particular details and concerns, simply will not be part of the attunement needed for forging self-understanding and change.

But even so, if the intent of psychoanalysis is therapeutic, in what sense can the analyst react morally? Perhaps the point to stress is that the reactive attitudes of praise and blame are not the only ones characteristic of the moral stance. Empathy, support, silent encouragement, space for self-observation as well as for choice and error, are themselves attitudes that concerned persons take toward others. Indeed, they are often signs of respect for the person engaged in the serious business of taking responsibility for her emotions.

VII. CONCLUSION

I began this essay with the Aristotelian claim that we assess moral character in terms of emotions as well as actions. Moral praise and blame can extend to both. I have argued that the claim makes the most sense if we posit a notion of emotional agency. In constructing such a conception, however, we need to look beyond Aristotle's account to developmental and clinical work on emotions and their growth. These accounts extend beyond Aristotle's, but are compatible with it, in articulating the various things we do and can do to shape our emotional experience. The claim is not that emotions are actions, nor that they can be willed spontaneously, as some simple actions, once learned, can be. Rather, the idea is that we have a "say"—more of a say than we often acknowledge—in shaping our emotional capacities and sensitivities. The consequence is that, in many of our emotional moments, we are not mere passive sufferers.

This is so even from earliest infancy. Thus, despite a common belief that an infant is a helpless victim of disturbances and pleasures, contemporary research suggests this is not so at all. As I argued in Section IV, a three-month-old coos and smiles most actively when she is manipulating her environment. In the next three to six months, her pleasure increases as she becomes an active partner in mutual dialogues with her parents, talking through shared eye gazing, initiating a game of peek-a-boo, beginning to self-soothe by putting a thumb in her mouth or holding onto a "blankie" when a father's hug is not available. All these are active ways of entering and managing one's emotional life. They are ways of organizing it so that one is not overwhelmed by its intensity or fragmented by its sudden changes. Later, as the toddler ventures from mother's lap to explore the world, there is an emotional refueling at a distance, a visual checking back for comfort and security. This is an intentional bid on the part of the child for help in managing what might be unsettling emotions of fear and disappointment, and for help in knowing, from a loved one's facial expressions, just what lurks ahead. All these are ways of managing and regulating emotional experiences. They are ways, as Aristotle might put it, that we take charge, that emotions become *eph'hêmin*—within our agency. Again, at the next stage of life, through language and play, children become more artful managers of their emotional lives, labeling emotions, accessing and assessing them through words, enacting them and trying out solutions to the problems they present. What I have just described are phenomena easily recognized by observers of children. What is less easily recognized is that these are the very ways emotions come under a young child's budding dominion. They are the ways a child mixes agency with what sometimes can be an unruly and overly reactive sensitivity to the world.

The developmental story of emotional growth continues into and throughout adulthood. In Section II, I suggested ways in which we hold ourselves and others responsible for emotions and, where necessary, encourage reform in the context of familial relationships or clinical therapy. In Section V, I explored the nature of the psychoanalytic therapeutic context. In many ways, the claims of psychoanalysis can best be understood by thinking back to the newly verbal child, who learns to label and explore the buzzing world of feelings through words. This is part of the method of psychoanalysis too, with the all-important differences that many of those feelings have become hard to access, that defenses have set in to mask feelings and the conflicts they are part of, and that reason rationalizes as much as it discloses truth. What is required is a self-observation of feelings and stalemated ways of relating to others, and a "working through" of them so that one can develop more healthy and fulfilling ways of relating to others and experiencing emotions. Much needs to be said about what this "working through" process involves, and we began to explore that earlier. The primary point to reiterate is that psychoanalysis aims to enable a patient to gain control over areas of her mental life where she has either too much or too little control. This includes enhanced emotional agency. Aristotle might not agree with Freud's claim that many of the narratives and beliefs constitutive of emotions are unconscious. Nor would he support the view that letting disavowed and repressed emotions speak in "parliamentary fashion" might resolve conflict more successfully than keeping them at bay. But if the goal of character development is, as Aristotle suggests, bringing emotions in line with our best considered judgments, then a bottom-up transformation rather than a top-down chastening might promise the more stable solution. The more general point that developmentalists, Freudians, and Aristotelians can agree upon is that through certain activities, we set out with some deliberateness to be agents of our emotional lives.

Philosophy, Georgetown University

INDEX

For EU product safety concerns, contact us at Calle de José Abascal, 56–1°,
28003 Madrid, Spain or eugpsr@cambridge.org.